Reviews for *Wallis in Love*

'The best account so far of the most notorious woman – and most dangerous threat to the British royal family – of the twentieth century. Andrew Morton presents a convincing picture of Wallis Simpson's rip-roaring sexual and social adventures and her curious marriage to the Duke of Windsor…His new research adds to our knowledge of her whole career'.

Sarah Bradford, author of *America's Queen: The Life of Jacqueline Kennedy Onassis*, *Queen Elizabeth II* and *George VI*

'Remarkable. Supersedes and surpasses all previous Wallis biographies with its wealth of new detail and insight. Andrew Morton's crowning achievement.'

Christopher Wilson, author of *Dancing with the Devil: The Windsors and Jimmy Donahue*

'The best-known chronicler of the royals, Andrew Morton, provides tantalizing new details about the scandalous life of Wallis Simpson.'

Meryl Gordon, author of *Phantom of Fifth Avenue* and *Bunny Mellon: The Life of an American Style Legend*

WALLIS
IN
LOVE

The untold true passion of
the Duchess of Windsor

ANDREW MORTON

Michael O'Mara Books Limited

First published in paperback in 2021
First published in Great Britain in 2018 by
Michael O'Mara Books Limited
9 Lion Yard
Tremadoc Road
London SW4 7NQ

First published in hardback in the United States of America in
2018 by Grand Central Publishing, Hachette Book Group
1290 Avenue of the Americas, New York, NY 10104

A CIP catalogue record for this book is available from the British Library.

Papers used by Michael O'Mara Books Limited are natural, recyclable products
made from wood grown in sustainable forests. The manufacturing processes
conform to the environmental regulations of the country of origin.

ISBN: 978-1-78929-373-9 in paperback print format
ISBN: 978-1-78243-723-9 in ebook format

1 2 3 4 5 6 7 8 9 10

Front cover photograph: Mary Evans/Everett Collection
Cover Design: Claire Cater
Typeset by Ed Pickford

Printed and bound by CPI Group (UK) Ltd, Croydon, CR0 4YY

www.mombooks.com

To my mother Kathleen

Contents

Introduction

THE GRAND JAS cemetery lies to the north of the Riviera resort of Cannes, the nine-hectare site bounded by the road to the perfume-making town of Grasse.

A brief but stiffish uphill climb brings the curious and the grieving to the entrance of the Protestant portion of the 150-year-old cemetery. The stone pillars supporting the stern iron gates bear the legend 'I believe in the resurrection of the dead' in both French and English.

Inside is a roll call of the famous, the well known and the simply anonymous who were drawn from around the world to make Cannes their home – and their final resting place. The English Square, known also as the *cimetière anglais*, is dominated by a statue of Henry Brougham, who turned Cannes from a sleepy fishing village into the resort town it is today. Laid to rest among the quiet rows are sculptors, singers, pioneer pilots, dukes, soldiers – including two holders of the Victoria Cross, the United Kingdom's highest military honour – and Peter Carl Fabergé of the Russian jewellery family, whose eggs crusted with diamonds, rubies, sapphires and other gems were gobbled up by the last Russian czar. There is a Nobel Prize winner – French biochemist Jacques Monod – a rhyme of poets, including the Irish bard William Bonaparte-Wyse and writer Klaus Mann, son of *Death in Venice* author Thomas, as well as the ballerina Olga Khokhlova, Pablo Picasso's first wife.

There are lesser lights, too. Those originally from Camden Town in north London, for example, or Victoria in Australia, and, beneath a stand of cypress trees, ones from Hyde Park in upper New York State. While the Americans are well outnumbered by the British, this grave, with its badly discoloured headstone, intrigues. What an extraordinary story the marble slab covers over, of the three silent inhabitants who lie beneath. It is the grave of Herman Livingston Rogers, his first wife, Katherine Moore, and his second wife, Lucy, or Marie Lucie Catherine as she styled herself in later life. The inscriptions on the gravestone state that the first wife was 'beloved', the second 'devoted' – but what of the third woman, who also loved this wealthy Renaissance man who counted princes and presidents in his circle? She was born in a wooden shack in a mountain holiday resort and named Bessie Wallis Warfield. This woman from Baltimore married a Navy pilot, a shipping broker and a king. She deeply touched the lives of all three occupants of this particular plot in Grand Jas – and many more beyond. Though one man gave up the English throne for her, it was Herman Livingston Rogers whom she called 'the love of my life'.

Herman was Bessie's best friend, her companion, her advisor, and her surrogate husband. Just days before she married her royal suitor, a man who had prostrated himself and his kingdom in order to win her hand, it is believed that she offered to have Herman's child.

Bessie Wallis Warfield was an unlikely seductress, apparently more interested in cooking than coitus, her heart under careful control. Nor was this woman who caused so much chaos and commotion in the British constitution and in the hearts of men much to look at – raw-boned, square-jawed, outsize hands, and a rasping voice that some found irritating. Yet she enticed men into her orbit, be they single, married, gay or straight. Women, too, were fascinated by her style and her chutzpah.

Wallis was capable of love, passion and desire – but not always with the men she married. She liked to say that hers was a simple story. It was nothing of the kind. Wallis was an endlessly complex and intriguing woman, beguiling, infuriating. There is no plaque outside her Baltimore home at 212 East Biddle Street in once fashionable Mount Vernon, but there are those who believe she should be remembered with a statue on the famously unoccupied fourth plinth in Trafalgar Square in central London for saving the British from her pro-Nazi royal husband at a critical moment in their island saga as they faced Hitler's eager battalions, war-weary and alone. This is the story of a most extraordinary woman who, single-handed, changed the history of the British royal family and arguably the destiny of the British people.

CHAPTER ONE

'All is Love'

UNKEMPT, UNRULY AND UNTIDY, Miss Minerva Buckner was hardly a model teacher. She ignored school bells, bath schedules and timetables. While she had a brilliant mind and had travelled extensively around Europe, she was feared for her violent temper and mordant wit. The lazy, the slow and the stupid dreaded her classes, where she taught in French and German. 'Miss Buckner went on like a crazy person. I want to come home,' one of her pupils wrote plaintively to her mother.

There was one exception. Bessie Wallis Warfield loved Miss Buckner's classes and adored the somewhat doughy and gangling teacher with a haphazard appreciation of personal hygiene. Miss Buckner was her first love, the besotted teenage schoolgirl sitting at her feet in the wooded grounds of Oldfields girls' boarding school as she read the love poetry of Arthur Rimbaud and Rainer Maria Rilke.

> *You who never arrived*
> *in my arms, Beloved, who were lost*
> *from the start*

Indeed, the line from Rilke's 'You Who Never Arrived' could have been the theme for Wallis's hopeless juvenile enchantment.

Wallis saved her pocket money to buy Miss Buckner presents, on one occasion giving her an enormous fern from a florist in Baltimore, an hour's steam train journey away through the heavily wooded Maryland countryside.

Wallis later recalled: 'She was very appreciative. She was a very ugly woman but a very nice one. I took a great fancy to her. I had a huge crush.'

Wallis was not the only one vying for the attentions of the firmly unmarried Miss Buckner, an outsize personality with the reputation for telling 'mildly improper' anecdotes. In the polite language of the day, her 'boon companion' was fellow teacher 'Miss Alie' McMurran, the two ladies feeding birds in the woods around Glencoe and going for gentle nature rambles together where they looked for the 'earliest spring flowers'.

Wallis was fickle with her heart: she also fell madly in love with the ravishing if firm Charlotte Noland, who ran a summer camp for young girls called Burrland. Wallis spent long dreamy days and hot Virginia nights mooning over the svelte, athletic horsewoman and basketball player. In a phrase that could be culled from a modern erotic novel, she described the rangy Miss Noland as a woman with a 'mixture of gay, deft teasing and a drill sergeant's sternness'. She recalled: 'I had a terrible crush on Miss Charlotte, of course I don't know any girl who hasn't who ever came in contact with her.' She was speaking no less than the truth.

WHEN THE DIVINE Miss Noland, who later founded Foxcroft girls' school in Virginia, paid a brief visit to see her sister at Oldfields all-girls school, half the pupils swooned away. As Wallis's great friend Mary Kirk, who was more than half in love with Wallis herself, wrote to her mother: 'By the time she [Miss Noland] is ready to go back, a dozen girls will have developed a crush, Wallis is already that way and terrifically wild with excitement.' All the more so when Miss Noland, who later became co-master of the Middleburg Hunt, invited Wallis and Mary for a ride in her new car, stopping at a country store for refreshments. On another occasion in the summer of 1913, she and Wallis, now seventeen, went for a 'tiny little' ride together. Such was their intimacy that the boyish Wallis was permitted to call Miss Noland 'Lotty', the teasing sexual ambiguity of their relationship never fully expressed – nor, presumably, resolved. This friendship may have made Mary just a little jealous, and she innocently confessed to her mother, 'I cannot help thinking about Wallis all the time.'

That said, Wallis's passion for Lotty was well balanced by a crush on Lotty's brother Philip, who was more than twenty years Wallis's senior. Much to the irritation of her mother, Alice Warfield, Wallis spent days wailing and sobbing because he left her love unrequited, never responding to her ardent missives.

Her schooldays were little different from those of many pubescent young girls cloistered in the febrile hothouse atmosphere of a remote all-girls school where passion and emotion were heightened, and every tiny event treated as high drama. When Wallis sang 'Dear delightful women, how I simply love them all' at a concert, she was crooning from her heart. Older pupils exploited the mooning behaviour of juniors ruthlessly. For example, when Wallis, a school newbie, and another girl were vying for the affection of a senior girl, Wallis was told that she would be chosen only if she bought her gifts or gave her money.

In the top-floor dormitory which she shared with Mary Kirk, whom Wallis described as a 'beautiful little partridge', the two whispered confidences late into the night. However, the chatter between Wallis and the red-haired daughter of America's oldest silversmith was often interrupted by an irate teacher. Their giggly gossip centred upon other girls, their teachers and people they knew. It was not long, though, before their conversational agenda was dominated by one item: boys. Boys were the great unknown, their ways, their looks and their activities an intriguing, endless mystery. A mystery that Wallis was determined to solve as soon as possible.

She was at a distinct disadvantage. The woman who one day would be a byword for grand, reckless passion, who became infamous for her love affair with an English king, had known very few males, role models or not, in her young life. For the most part they were dead, diseased or distant figures.

Her father, Teackle Wallis Warfield, died of tuberculosis on 15 November 1896 at the age of twenty-seven, just five months after her birth on 19 June. The marriage of Teackle to her mother, Alice Montague, was strongly opposed by both their families for ruthlessly practical reasons: Teackle was in the final stages of a disease that was, at that time, highly contagious and incurable. Given the fact that certain strains of tuberculosis cause sterility, it was a miracle that he was even able to father a child.

It seems though that social proprieties trumped social disease, the couple marrying on 19 November 1895 when Alice – or Alys as she liked to call herself – was two months pregnant with her first baby. This sense of social disgrace perhaps explains why there was no fanfare or newspaper report, just a quiet ceremony in a side chamber of the Church of St Michael and All Angels in Baltimore. Again, when Wallis was born in a roughly built wooden cottage at the Monterey Inn in the resort of Blue Ridge Summit in the state of Pennsylvania, there was no announcement in the Baltimore newspapers, merely an update on Teackle's declining condition.

TEACKLE BREATHED HIS LAST at the Baltimore home of his elder brother, Solomon Davies Warfield, known as Uncle Sol, just a few weeks after his daughter's christening, which was held at Emmanuel Episcopal Church in Mount Vernon on 19 October 1896. Such was the fear surrounding tuberculosis that her sick father was not allowed to hold or touch her in case he infected his daughter. The poor man was only permitted to look at a photograph of his baby daughter three days before he died.

The TB epidemic was so severe that trainee doctors at the local Johns Hopkins medical school were instructed to sleep outside during the summer months, where the air was fresher. Even a romantic kiss could spell certain death. When Teackle Warfield was buried at Green Mount Cemetery, the family struggled to find pallbearers willing to carry his coffin.

After Teackle was laid to rest, his destitute widow found little comfort from her own family. Her father, William Latane Montague, a one-time stockbroker in New York, remained 150 miles south in Richmond, Virginia, with his second wife, Mary E. Hazlett. There were no offers of accommodation from that quarter. In the narrative of Wallis's life, her maternal grandfather plays no part – even though he stayed with her mother in her terraced house at 212 East Biddle Street during his final illness, dying in April 1909 when Wallis was twelve.

The one man who did influence her early life was her uncle Sol. In her eyes he was a grumpy curmudgeon whose grudging charity barely kept her and her mother afloat. However, he was the only family member who invited mother and baby to stay with him and his mother, Anna, in a three-storey townhouse on Preston Street in the Mount Vernon district of Baltimore.

From the beginning it was a socially and physically awkward arrangement. After all, it was Uncle Sol who had led the solemn Warfield family delegation to plead with Alice and Teackle against marriage because of his brother's terminal condition. They ignored him and other family members.

With her own family seemingly reluctant to help, Alice threw herself at his mercy. He provided shelter, food and, in time, paid for Wallis's formal education. Wallis was raised in the bosom of the Warfield family. Just as the baby's Christian names, Bessie and Wallis, represented the two sides of the family – being the names of her father and her mother's older sister, Bessie Buchanan Merryman, so she often ascribed the contradictory qualities of her character to the contrasts between the two families, the Warfields and the Montagues.

The Warfields were a reputable, somewhat stolid Baltimore family with deep-rooted business and political traditions. Prosperous and distinguished, Sol Warfield was a successful businessman in his own right and a friend to three American presidents. His financial acumen saw him appointed the youngest postmaster in the city's history. Described by the *Baltimore Sun* as a 'remarkable man sometimes approaching ruthless in his methods', he listed big-game hunting, fishing and golf as his leisure pursuits.

'Ruthless', though, was not a word that found favour in the Warfield clan. It touched a raw nerve. For they had built their various fortunes on the back of slave labour. Until slavery was abolished in 1865, the family had been slave owners and occasional slave traders, keeping their unwilling flock in order by threatening to sell them South, where conditions were more brutal and inhumane than in Maryland. While there is an 1837 agreement with regard to selling a 'Negro slave girl named Sally' in the Warfield family papers, they considered themselves benign and enlightened masters. Not that many families keep albums of pictures showing a lynching, as the Warfields did.

Wallis's third cousin, Edwin Warfield, who was elected forty-fifth governor of Maryland in 1903, gave several speeches on 'Slavery as I knew it'. Edwin himself was raised on the Oakdale plantation in Howard County, where the family's slaves were housed in a long oak cabin. His tolerance went only so far. When he stood for governor, Edwin, a Democrat, did so on a platform of white supremacy, believing that poorly educated blacks should be denied the franchise.

As governor he was involved in an attempted lynching that was as farcical as it was grotesque. In July 1906, shortly after Wallis's tenth birthday, a Negro named William Lee was due to be hanged after being found guilty of assaulting two white women. Such was the outcry that Governor Warfield had the culprit kept in Baltimore jail so as to escape a lynch mob intent on burning him alive. The condemned man was spirited away by steamboat to nearby Somerset County, followed by an angry armada of boats filled with outraged local men. The law narrowly won, and Lee was hanged on a gallows hastily erected on an island in Chesapeake Bay, before the mob were able to land. As the whole city of Baltimore was in excited tumult, Wallis would have been aware of the episode, especially as it involved cousin Edwin.

By contrast, the dramas on the maternal side of Wallis's family were entirely domestic. The Montagues were devil-may-care in this life and rarely worried about the devil in the next. The men exuded typical Southern charm, which did not, as Wallis tartly observed, 'put money in the bank'. As she would later describe, they lived a 'more hazardous, more adventurous' life, which was a polite way of saying that they were feckless. As for the women, they were noted beauties, particularly her mother, her aunt Bessie and cousin Corinne, who didn't take life or themselves too seriously. As Wallis's uncle, Major General George Barnett, observed of the Montague clan: 'They are wonderful, witty, intelligent people – and they will tell you so themselves.'

While the contrasting fortunes and characters of the Montagues and Warfields explain Wallis's background, the real emotional dynamic of her life was between Alice, her mother; Anna, her paternal grandmother; and, in later life, her mother's older sister,

Aunt Bessie. It is noticeable that in Wallis's bowdlerized memoir, *The Heart Has Its Reasons*, her grandmother takes early centre stage. Prim, proper, upright – she trained Wallis to sit with a ramrod-straight back – she always had the well-thumbed Warfield family Bible on a table next to her rosewood rocking chair. In her early sixties and still in her widow's weeds after the death of her husband twenty or so years before, she cut a striking and self-possessed figure, sitting alone in the shadows, rocking back and forth, watching and wary, her tongue as sharp as her eyes.

Though her grandmother seemed to have stepped out of one of Charles Dickens's brooding Gothic novels, Wallis had, for the most part, fond memories of her, feeling an emotional kinship with a woman of unbending principle and chilly control, aristocratic both in her demeanour and her bearing. She even named her life-size doll, Anna, after this indomitable lady.

Kind, peaceful and full of common sense was Wallis's assessment of her grandmother. Anna's advice, though, was straight out of a censorious Never-Never-Land: 'Never let a man kiss your hand. If you do, he'll never ask you to marry him. Never marry a Yankee. Never drink coffee; it will turn your skin yellow.' Her continuous stream of warnings and counsel bred in Wallis a timidity and caution about the world that lay beyond the thick oak door of 34 East Preston Street.

For all these constraints, Wallis felt that she belonged within this conservative, comfortable and socially significant milieu. The Warfields stood for stability, safety and, most importantly, status. In Baltimore, a Warfield was somebody. Wallis, prudish and particular, was much more critical of her mother. Even though she acknowledged Alice's endless sacrifices on her behalf, she disapproved of her haphazard values and rackety lifestyle. The sense of disappointment with her mother, who danced and skipped her way through life, is palpable.

Small, blonde, with striking blue eyes which Wallis inherited, Alice had a sharp tongue and a quick wit. She had a way of saying something amusing and then looking amazed that her comment made others laugh. Such was the endless flow of *bons mots* that her friends encouraged her to have her witticisms published. She followed their advice, sending her efforts to the weekly magazine *Town Talk*. Sample: 'Why do leaves turn red in the fall? Because there are so many bare limbs around.' The editor chuckled, sent her five dollars, and asked for more. It helped pay the bills.

Wallis, though, was not amused. She felt that her mother's wit was so pungent and caustic that she lost friends and soured relationships, leaving those at the receiving end of her sarcasm feeling inferior and belittled. As her sister, Bessie, acknowledged, Alice had a vindictive tongue, a quality her daughter inherited.

Wallis had cause to feel the sting of her mother's waspish barbs. 'Nobody is as ugly as Wallis when she is bored,' her mother would comment, a phrase calibrated to hurt her daughter.

As convivial and gay as she seemed, Alice clashed frequently with her daughter, the two women fundamentally differing in desire and ambition. Alice was content with her poor Southern background, her daughter never satisfied with her lot, always seeking the next rung up the social ladder. Her first words, recalled members of her family, were not 'Ma, Ma' but 'me, me'.

AS A LITTLE GIRL, Wallis named dolls after two of the wealthiest and most glamorous women in America, Mrs Astor of Virginia and Mrs Vanderbilt of New York. She would leaf through her mother's magazines looking at pictures of beautiful women dressed in jewels and furs, and point to them with a long hatpin. Then she would make up stories of balls, banquets and *billets-doux*, populating this glamorous make-believe world with princes, princesses, kings and queens.

Wallis had two other paper dolls, whom she named ABC and Gubby – two men-about-town. They were members of the exclusive men-only Maryland Club, where only the most prestigious and prosperous could enter. 'She would sit in a corner quietly having imaginary conversations and then fly into a rage if anyone interrupted her,' recalled Aunt Bessie. 'She had the greatest imagination of any child I ever saw.'

BY A STRANGE TWIST OF FATE, Wallis's neighbour, who literally lived across the street in Baltimore, was another future luminary: Gertrude Stein, an expressive dreamer who captured the zeitgeist of the Jazz Era. Stein, who would become the muse to what she called the 'Lost Generation' of American writers and artists, including Ernest Hemingway, F. Scott Fitzgerald and Ezra Pound, as well as Pablo Picasso, Henri Matisse and others, would one day write of seeing the young Wallis at play across Biddle Street, Baltimore, the street of terraced houses where they both lived.

During her days in Baltimore, Stein, who later lived in Paris with her lover, Alice B. Toklas, was a student at Johns Hopkins medical college. Even then she was a controversial character who challenged the male-dominated faculty while learning to smoke Havana cigars and how to box. In 1903, she wrote *Q.E.D.*, one of the earliest lesbian coming-out stories, based on a triangular female relationship and set at Johns Hopkins.

Once Wallis became famous, Stein was reminded of those days in Mount Vernon, penning a story called *Ida*, in which Wallis was sketched as an example of modern celebrity, of being famous for being famous. The ultimate irony of this relationship by literary association is that, while there is an official city plaque recognizing Gertrude Stein's stay in Baltimore, there is nothing to commemorate the presence of the woman who upturned a royal dynasty.

* * *

WHILE THIS IMAGINATIVE young girl dreamed of being a little princess – and was treated as one by the whole family – Wallis's mother was the model Cinderella, cleaning, cooking and sewing, wearing her fingers to the bone to make clothes for her daughter and to sell to neighbours and friends. Wallis later admitted that she happily allowed her mother to sacrifice her health and her energy in order to give her the best. 'I had great control over her because she adored me so much. Anything I did was right. I was a poor child and a spoilt child, terribly spoilt.'

Theirs was an odd kind of penury. They lived rent-free courtesy of Uncle Sol, they never went hungry – Sunday lunch was invariably roast beef and Yorkshire puddings followed by meringue and ice cream – and they had a small army of servants to care for them. In the hot summer months, when Baltimore was unbearable, Wallis had the pick of handsome working farms or country estates owned by her wealthy relatives, places where donkey rides or visits to the icehouse to pick out chilled watermelons were always on the menu.

Though Wallis and her mother never lived in poverty, their burden was living as the patronized poor relations. For longer than they cared to recall, they depended on the sporadic and casual charity of Uncle Sol, along with Alice's sewing ability, which helped pay for the little extras in life. Wallis came to hate springtime, that period of bursting buds and hedgerow bustle, as it was a chirpy reminder that while her school friends went on family excursions, Wallis was left hoping that she would be invited, knowing full well that she could never reciprocate. She remembered spring as a 'hideous' time of year.

For a girl who was all about control, her dependence on her uncle stained deep into her psyche. Half a century later, when she was reviewing this time in her life, she remembered how difficult it was for her proud mother to ask for charity – and what she described as her 'granite faced' uncle's peculiarly 'sadistic' behaviour when he handed out his largesse.

During this ritual he would pass Wallis what she called a tip, crunching up his money into a little ball before sliding it into her hand. 'You didn't know if you had five dollars or five thousand,' she recalled. 'You could hardly wait to get out of the room, you almost ran, to open your hand to see what he had tipped you.'

She insinuates that her 'ice cold' uncle had thawed towards her mother to the point where he had declared his love. Beneath the stony visage was a man with a secret appreciation for female opera singers, ballet dancers and chorus girls, whose signed portraits decorated his bachelor apartment in New York. It seems that his appreciation for his sister-in-law was not reciprocated, Alice being disdainful of his protestations of affection. Perhaps understandably, Alice found it difficult living in the same house as a man she could never love. The young Wallis caught the mood, recording in her memoir: 'A subtly disturbing situation seems to have helped precipitate the separation. She was young and attractive, living under the same roof, and she and Uncle Sol were inevitably thrown much together.'

Wallis was all for this possible marriage, feeling that her mother should have sacrificed herself so that Wallis could enjoy the lifestyle of the rich and locally famous. That she spurned his advances perhaps explains why Uncle Sol supplied only the bare financial necessities for Wallis and her mother. 'He hated to do anything for me. He did the minimum,' she complained. It is an unjust charge; Uncle Sol funded Wallis's education and social life until she married. Certainly he did more, much more, than her mother's family.

At the same time, the vivacious widow was increasingly at odds with her disapproving mother-in-law. Both were strong women who did not hesitate to speak their minds. Alice would have found living under another woman's roof – and rule – frustrating and irritating. That she wanted to make a new life for herself and began seeing suitors merely complicated matters. Eventually, Alice packed their bags and took rooms, first in the Brexton residential hotel just a few hundred yards away and then at the nearby Preston apartment house.

Alice, impetuous and careless of the consequences, swapped the relative security, comfort and compromises of the Warfield home on Preston Street for a much more precarious living, launching a paying dining club for friends and fellow lodgers. As much as Wallis subsequently opined that life was harsh and threadbare, at times her mother was able to hire two African-American maids, a cook and a butler. One butler was a master of the malapropism. When he solemnly told the assembled company, 'Dinner is pronounced', Alice burst into gales of laughter, much to the poor man's embarrassment.

The speciality of Alice's dining club was Maryland terrapin. Most days a man would come along with a burlap bag filled with terrapin, a delicacy made popular by schooner captain Albert LaVallette Jr, who started an industry selling terrapins for a dollar an inch. They were then turned into a delicate soup that cost around five dollars a bowl.

The degree of difficulty of preparing this dish added an air of luxury to the table. It required not only money, but also the skill and time to prepare it. Only the well-to-do could afford the cost of mastering the recipe.

DURING THESE DINNER PARTIES it was Alice, not her cook, who took command of the kitchen. She was the one who selected the diamondbacks and then put them in the basement to fatten up on cornmeal.

After tucking into her carefully prepared feast, washed down with expensive red Burgundy, her paying guests played poker late into the night, watched, if she was not spotted, from the top of the stairs by a wide-eyed Wallis.

'Those were great days,' she recalled. Certainly more fun than listening to the ticking of the clocks and the creak of Anna's rocking chair in the still shadows of the Warfield residence. However, in her memoir she painted this time with her mother in darker hues, as a period of privation and poverty. 'Life was such a struggle always you didn't have time to sit around and discuss family history, one was wondering where the next meal or dress was coming from,' she recalled.

She continually complained that her Warfield cousins enjoyed greater ease and certainty than she ever did. This is the heart of the matter. Wallis was brought up in a world where she wanted for nothing except stability, status and social acceptance. She felt the stigma of being an outsider, a complaint she laid at her mother's door.

In the small-minded world of Baltimore society, gossip inevitably swirled around the pretty merry widow who had abruptly walked out on the city's postmaster, a pillar of the community, and was now hosting what appeared to be nothing short of a gambling and drinking den. To those of the temperance persuasion this was only one step up from running a brothel.

Even though Uncle Sol paid for her rooms, Alice's dining club was a financial disaster. She cut her losses and lived with her sister, Bessie, for a time, before moving into her own home, a three-storey terraced house at 212 East Biddle Street. Once again, Uncle Sol may have underwritten the enterprise, allowing Alice to graduate from charging for meals to renting rooms. As Bessie commented wryly: 'Alice didn't live so much hand to mouth as room to room.' One paying guest was Johns Hopkins graduate Dr Charles F. Bove, who later recalled an 'exuberant' twelve-year-old girl with glossy black hair parted in braids like an 'Indian squaw' who helped her mother serve evening meals. He called her 'Minnehaha'; she responded with a wide grin. A few years later she was not smiling at headlines that screamed FROM BOARDING HOUSE TO BALMORAL, insinuating that Wallis enjoyed a hardscrabble upbringing. As Aunt Bessie indignantly observed: 'Did they think we were from Tobacco Road?'

At the time, though, the decision by Wallis's mother to run a boarding house was perhaps even more calamitous. The gossips had a field day, hearsay building on rumour to the point where it was whispered that Alice was living with another man. The sins of the mother also condemned the daughter.

As a young woman, Wallis was looked on with suspicion by the matrons of Maryland. Society interior designer Billy Baldwin remembered the local notoriety surrounding Alice and Wallis Warfield: 'Wallis's mother, a very striking woman, had a lover, and he slept openly in her house, which was impossible for Baltimore ladies to accept. Because of that, when Wallis came out she was almost *déclassé* and had a very hard time making the grade.'

Legend has it that Uncle Sol offered to make Wallis heir to his fortune if she returned to Preston Street and vowed not to see her 'corrupt' mother any more. Her refusal merely stoked the theory that Wallis was no better than her allegedly dissolute mother.

Actually, on 30 June 1908, after more than a decade as a respectable if down-at-heel widow, Alice remarried, this time to John Freeman Rasin, the son of the leader of the local Democratic Party who, it seemed, had lodged in Biddle Street. Once again she fell for a man who was incapacitated, Rasin suffering from heart disease as well as a chronic and painful kidney complaint, Bright's disease. While Rasin, known as 'Young Free', was remembered as an indolent fellow, his days spent sitting in his favourite chair, smoking cigarettes and reading the newspaper, it was his ill health that limited his activity. For all his failings, he did have a trust fund which, for the first time, gave mother and daughter a degree of independence from Uncle Sol.

Used to being the centre of attention, or 'centre of attraction' as she put it, and doted on not just by her mother but by her relatives, who considered her an orphan, Wallis was devastated by this turn of events. She steadfastly refused to attend the wedding, which was scheduled to take place in the drawing room at Biddle Street just a few days after her twelfth birthday.

It took all of Aunt Bessie's soothing powers of persuasion, together with the promise that she could look for a silver thimble, a dime and a ring hidden in the wedding cake, to convince the sobbing, foot-stomping girl to attend her mother's wedding. The cake paid the price. While the Reverend Francis X. Brady, President of Loyola College, performed the ceremony in front of a small group of family and guests, Wallis was in the dining room turning the cake into 'Chinese chow' in her hunt for silverware. Her behaviour provoked indulgent mirth – and from her stepfather, the placatory gifts of a fully stocked aquarium and a French bulldog she called Bully.

This episode fostered several life lessons for the young Wallis. Spoiled and self-willed, Wallis thought her mother's second marriage confirmed her belief that if she was betrayed by the woman who loved her unconditionally, then the only person she could truly trust was herself. As she matured she became her own best advisor, counsellor and friend, rarely showing the outside world any glimpse of what she was thinking and feeling. There was a core of steel to her, a toughness, that even her mother could not reach. As Wallis recalled: 'I kept greatly within myself, very self-contained. Always filled with my own ideas and plans. Looking forward never backward. Right or wrong, I made the big decisions in my life.' She always knew her own mind, whether it was choosing the fabric and style of a dress for a social event or deciding whether or not to call the doctor when she was ill. 'Don't call him, all he'll say is spinach and fresh air.'

There is no denying that little Bessie Wallis Warfield stood out from the herd, a quality greatly admired by her aunt Bessie: 'She was always an individual, always something different about her. She was the leader and knew what she wanted.'

Her self-reliance, though, was a source of frustration for her mother Alice, who resented losing authority over her growing child. On one occasion, Aunt Bessie was giving Wallis some advice when Alice burst out sarcastically: 'Why do you bother? Don't you know that Wallis knows everything?'

It was a remark that cut deep, feeding a resentment she harboured forever. 'That of course would humiliate me more than anything in the world,' she recalled. Somewhat improbably, she added: 'When I grew up and studied philosophy I wished I had been able to answer with Socrates' saying: "There is one thing I know and this is I know nothing." I only wished I could get that one back at her.'

The wedding cake saga also reinforced in her the feeling that she could get away with murder and that she was able to bend others to her will. When, for instance, she decided that mathematics, especially algebra, was beyond her, she convinced her mother to write to her teachers to say it was bad for her health. Alice did as she was bid, informing Arundel school, which she attended near to her Mount Vernon home, that the prospect of algebra brought Wallis out in hives.

Again, when the tone-deaf schoolgirl became exasperated learning the piano, she simply hid in the closet from her baffled tutor, Mrs Jackson. Sometimes her mother could bring her to heel, on one occasion using a hairbrush on her *derrière* when, in a fit of temper, Wallis flung a bottle of black ink on her white bedlinen.

Her fierce temper got the better of her at school, too – she whacked a fellow student, Jessie Webb, on the head with a pencil case because the boy answered a question in class before she could.

Not that she was a bad student. Blessed with a near-photographic memory, she was able to skim through most subjects – with somewhat biographical inevitability, her favourite topic was the study of English kings and queens – and did well in exams.

What with the simmering domestic tension between mother and daughter, combined with her stepfather's deteriorating health, it was perhaps as well that the much-maligned Uncle Sol agreed to pay Wallis's fees for Oldfields girls' boarding school, alma mater to her mother and her aunt Bessie. The school, founded in 1867 by the McCulloch family, was run on religious lines, with the Bible at the heart of its educational compass. Prayers were said every morning and girls were encouraged to learn passages from the Bible.

At first the worthy routine did not suit Wallis. Her doting friend, Mary Kirk, informed her mother that Wallis was homesick. 'She says she won't come back after Christmas,' she wrote in October 1912, shortly after Wallis had joined Mary in their rooms above the new gym. The fact that Wallis's mother and second husband had moved from Baltimore to Atlantic City, hoping that the sea air would be a tonic for the ailing John Rasin, may have contributed to her sense of isolation.

It was a blip. Wallis proved herself a star of the basketball team and popular with the other girls, except a few who were, according to Mary, 'a little bit jealous'.

Wallis had settled nicely into the Oldfields regime when, on 4 April 1913, headmistress Anna McCulloch, known as Miss Nan, broke the sad news that her stepfather had died suddenly of a heart attack. He was only forty-four.

At his funeral, Wallis was one of the few who remained dry-eyed, feeling nothing but pity for her mother, who now looked so withered and tiny in her black widow's garb. 'I don't give in to my emotions,' she observed. 'It's a Warfield characteristic, rather like the British stiff upper lip.'

At a critical time in her adolescence, Wallis was once again faced with straitened circumstances. Her mother moved back to Baltimore and took up cheap lodgings at the Earl's Court apartment building. During the holidays Wallis lived with her mother or her aunt Bessie, her mother now trying her hand as a real estate agent.

While many of her classmates, such as pharmaceutical heiress Renée du Pont, lived in splendid excess, Wallis felt awkward inviting a school friend to her mother's tiny apartment for a cup of tea. Her mother now made every stitch of her clothing, and she could not help but look enviously at the divinely fashionable and original creations her school roommate, Ellen Yuille, brought back from family visits to New York. Perhaps Wallis overstated her threadbare wardrobe. Mary Kirk recalled an occasion at a summer camp where all the girls were invited to a dance. Mary wrote to her mother and asked her to send a suitable dress, pointing out that all the girls had the same issue 'except Wallis, who has good-looking clothes for every occasion imaginable'.

Nonetheless, Wallis was at an age where she was continually measuring herself against other girls, assessing the competition in the endless race for boys. As her intense crushes on her teachers and fellow pupils began to fade, she peered more intently into the mysterious world of the opposite sex. Her first regular introduction to these strange creatures was when she took lessons at dancing school. She was utterly enchanted by dance and learned the various dance steps with eager felicity. Caught up in the thrill of movement and the excitement of performance, she dreamed of one day becoming a ballet dancer. Instead she took up roller-skating. (Her friend Mary Kirk was equally star-struck, seeing herself as the second Sarah Bernhardt.)

Before dance classes Wallis loved to dress up and then preen and parade before the shy nervy creatures at the other side of the room. She always chided her aunt Bessie for telling a story about the time she cast aside a rainbow range of sashes to decorate her dress, picking red because it stood out and would therefore act as a boy magnet. She wanted to ensure that the tremulous excitement she felt as the boys advanced towards the girls to ask them to dance would translate into being one of the first to be chosen.

For sixteen-year-old Wallis, the opportunities to meet and speak to boys were few and far between. At Oldfields, where the day began with the Lord's Prayer and a Bible story, it was against the rules to write to or receive letters from a boy. On one occasion headmistress Miss Nan tearfully announced after morning prayers that some girls had been writing to boys. For the rest of the day a line of girls sheepishly waited outside the head's study. Mary Kirk informed her mother that it was a 'gloomy and awful' day.

Imagine, then, the excitement when Mary and Wallis walked to church one Sunday and were confronted by 'a whole lot of boys' in the congregation. 'Real boys with creases in their pants and collars and ties,' wrote Mary. 'We were thrilled. Wallis and me in the choir got the best view of them and everyone else was so envious.'

When Wallis, the school's standout basketball player, and a friend were given permission to travel to Annapolis to watch an Army and Navy game, it was the talk of Oldfields. The girls were treated as minor celebrities upon their return. As one fellow pupil recalled: 'You must realize that the star basketball player would be a heroine in any school. Yet Wallis was completely unspoiled, a good person to be in school with.'

Daring, too. It is woven into the fabric of Oldfields history that Wallis would make assignations with young men who would slowly drive their cars down the single-track Glencoe Road that runs alongside the school. At a prearranged signal she would shimmy down the drainpipe from her third-floor dormitory, known as 'Heaven', and run across the lawn to meet her waiting beau. Given her keen sense of self-preservation and lifelong physical timidity, it is more likely that she climbed down the nearby iron fire escape.

A regular caller was Carter G. Osburn Jr, a young man who admitted that he was 'self-hypnotized' by Wallis's charms. Osburn, who first met Wallis at a dance at L'Hirondelle, a private social club in Ruxton, recalled: 'I don't know yet how she managed to elude the observing eyes of the school matrons, but she was never caught. We would neck, although you never called it that in those days, and then we would go for a drive.'

Racy behaviour indeed. She wasn't always so bold. Once she and several other girls did a bunk from school to go buggy riding. A guard on a nearby estate spotted them and yelled for them to scram. Wallis was so startled at the abrupt discovery and the potential for public shame that she waded into Gunpowder River and threatened to drown herself.

It is perhaps surprising that she was so daring in her pursuit of a beau. In those days, girls did not have boyfriends, only beaux, and girls went on engagements as opposed to dates. When a young lady was in the company of a suitor, she was always chaperoned, either by her mother, her sister or a trustworthy friend. The gift of Parma violets or gardenias or candy from an admirer was deemed appropriate. If the young man offered an expensive orchid, it was considered tantamount to a proposal of marriage. When Mary's beau Andrew sent her a pin adorned with garnets and opals, Miss Nan, with the agreement of her parents, made her send it back. It was deemed way too extravagant.

Holding hands was about the limit of physical contact, and any girl who allowed a beau to give her a goodnight kiss was thought fast indeed. This was a time when men were bold, girls were coy and parents perpetually nervous. A time, too, of sexual innocence, not to say ignorance. In temperament, if not demeanour, Wallis was closer to a Victorian holdout than a loose-limbed flapper. She was a talker and a tease, happy to playfully kiss her beaux and gossip about the mysteries of sex, but stopping short of anything resembling the act itself.

Later she saw herself as an exotic vamp, imitating the silent-screen queens of the day. Before she made an entrance Wallis ensured that her hair, carefully parted down the middle, was brushed a hundred times each side to keep it fashionably flat. Presentation was all.

For Wallis, Mary Kirk and her other friends, the school holidays, particularly Christmas and Easter, were the real occasions for meeting boys. According to one admirer she 'attracted men like molasses attract flies'.

At dances and other social events during school holidays, Wallis quickly gained a reputation as the belle of the ball. With her striking blue eyes, slim figure and ready, exuberant laughter, she seemed to stand out from the crowd. No matter that her clothes were homemade, potential beaux would stand three deep for the honour of the next waltz, bunny hug, turkey trot or foxtrot. She excelled at the Castle Walk, a dance popularized by ballroom dancers Vernon and Irene Castle, then at the peak of their fame and influence. 'Wallis put on quite a show,' recalled an admiring school friend, Virginia Saunders Hughes.

Invariably, the young man who was first in line to lead Wallis onto the dance floor was the diminutive if loquacious Carter Osburn. As the son of the vice president of the Farmers and Merchants Bank, Osburn's great advantage over other suitors was that he was able to borrow his father's luxury sleek black Packard automobile. Wallis turned up her nose at boys who arrived at her mother's apartment in borrowed Fords and other more proletarian vehicles. 'Not quite as exciting,' she commented drily.

Osburn was not the only one in the race for Wallis's hand. His nearest rival was the 'tall, dark, and silent' but, alas, Ford-driving Arthur Stump, a member of a prominent if controversial Maryland legal family. The other runners and riders included Fletcher Green, Harvey Rowland and Tom Shryock, later a colonel in the National Guard. Osburn tried to firmly establish his claim when he presented her with a horse. Wallis thought this ostentatious gift was not 'proper' and farmed it out to her aunt Bessie.

When she was not showing off her skills on the dance floor she was busy being Wallis, laughing, gay and arch. 'At all these parties Wallis was the centre of everything and I was her adoring swain,' recalled the love-struck Osburn. 'She could tell a story with verve and charm, a gift she had inherited from her mother.'

Not everyone was impressed. Wallis, as she would do throughout her life, had the knack of polarizing opinion. While she and her loyal friend Mary Kirk were thick as thieves, constantly on the telephone, the Kirk family viewed her as a malign influence and were somewhat shocked when she announced during dinner that the man she would one day marry would have to have lots of money. It was, as Mary's elder sister Buckie later recalled, the kind of thing a 'nice girl' never said out loud.

Nor did nice girls deliberately set out to snare beaux who were wooing their school friends. Precocious in the ways of the world, Wallis instinctively practised the basic techniques of seduction, methods that served her well for the rest of her life. First she found out about a boy's interests and then was raptly attentive as he talked about his plans and passions, her mesmerizing blue eyes never wavering as she gazed adoringly at her prey. In short order his interests became her interests, Wallis collecting admirers as acquisitively as, in later life, she would also collect jewellery. If they were another girl's beau, so much the better, that evening's conquest confirming her desirability.

Her cousin, the writer Upton Sinclair, knew her well enough to give voice to her seduction techniques in a one-act play titled *Wally for Queen!*, which he penned at the time of the abdication.

'Don't forget,' Wallis tells the king, 'I'm a Baltimore girl and we are terrors. We practice impertinence – it's supposed to be cute. We vamp our dancing partners at the age of four. Men have no chance at all in our town.'

Dr Parnell Hagerman, the former head of school at Oldfields, who has spoken to the families of Wallis's contemporaries, concludes that Wallis alienated many other girls in her relentless attempts to date boys, available or not and regardless of whether she wanted them. Hagerman observes: 'She became very adept at breaking up relationships, at getting what she wanted. The way she did it seems very normal to our eyes but at her age and time it was very sophisticated.'

With the tunnel vision of the lovesick, Wallis's beau, Carter Osburn, sensed the hostility towards his girl but blamed her rivals: 'She was a real man's girl and other girls envied her with all their catty little hearts.' Wallis's pithy phrase, 'All is love', which she wrote in the girls' yearbook when she finished school in the spring of 1914, is greeted with a cynical grimace by Dr Hagerman. 'Yeah, right,' growls the former Bostonian head of school.

Not that Wallis would have cared one jot. From the moment she kissed and hugged her flower-bedecked classmates at the farewell May Day parade, Wallis had only one thing on her mind: to secure a place as one of the forty-nine young ladies of that season chosen to make their formal social debut at the famous Bachelors' Cotillion. She had seen the excitement of her older cousin Anita Warfield when she came out a couple of years before. Now it was her turn.

That her mother was hardly of the first social rank mattered little. It would have taken a brave member of the Cotillion committee, who chose that year's debutantes, to omit Solomon

Warfield's niece from the list of the premier families in Baltimore. By now Solomon Warfield was viewed as Mr Baltimore, the forceful and magnetic banker and railroad director credited with regenerating the city after the calamitous fire of 1904, which left the downtown, including his own bank, the Continental Trust, a smouldering ruin.

What is more, Uncle Sol had promised Wallis that he would throw a similar party for her as he had for her cousin Anita, when he had taken over a theatre and entertained the great and the good of Baltimore in some style. Wallis could hardly wait, mentally counting down until the big day in early December.

With school rapidly receding in the rear-view mirror of her life, she focused on important matters – organizing herself and her wardrobe for her next social engagement. Dances, dinners and day trips with a laughing group of guys and gals were her daily diet. There would be lunches at the Baltimore Country Club or the Stafford hotel oyster roasts and steak at Green Spring Valley, dances at Lehman's Hall, or drives out to the rolling country.

Carter Osburn was always available to squire her around town, his father's Packard a familiar sight outside her mother's Mount Vernon apartment. Not only did he take her to dances; the deep-pocketed young beau even hired a box at the Lyric Theatre, where they saw the Russian prima ballerina Anna Pavlova. When he was not by Wallis's side, he was on the telephone, playing songs by Al Jolson down the crackly line. Her favourite was 'My Yellow Jacket Girl'. It was, as she recalled, so romantic.

Every twist and turn of their romance she reported to her confidante and foil, Mary Kirk, either on the telephone or racing breathlessly into her house to tell her the latest. Mary's parents were distinctly unamused by this giddy behaviour, the two girls egging each other on. When Wallis accepted a dare to dress as a man and enter the hallowed portals of the all-male Maryland

Club, they could be forgiven for thinking that she was leading their daughter astray.

The fact that they usually went out as a pair meant they could convince their parents they had no need of a chaperone. They pushed their luck; one evening they were chatting late into the night with their beaux on the veranda of Wakefield Manor, the plantation home of Wallis's aunt, Lelia Gordon. Eventually, a bedroom window slid open and an angry maid cried: 'Wallis, send those boys home and come to bed.' On another occasion, she and Mary were ensconced in the drawing room at the Kirk household chatting with two suitors. Suddenly there was a loud bang on the ceiling as Mary's father hurled his shoes on the floor to signal that the young men should leave.

In the dizzy social whirl, Wallis and Mary barely noticed the outbreak of the First World War at the end of July 1914. They were having too much fun. Europe was a faraway land of which Wallis knew little. In any case, everyone said it would all be over by Christmas. She and her beau would never have imagined that within three years Carter Osburn would find himself waving a giant Stars and Stripes flag and heading a spontaneous march of thousands in downtown Baltimore to demand that America enter the war.

At the time, she had her own D-Day, waiting for the arrival of the coveted invitation to the Cotillion. That October her relief was unconfined when a stiff envelope arrived announcing that she was one of the chosen ones. 'If you don't go to the Cotillion, you're nothing, and if you do it's so boring,' she said later.

So boring that it consumed the next two months as she agonized over her dress. While white was *de rigueur*, Wallis went for drama, copying a dress worn by her idol, actress and dancer Irene Castle, who was then starring in Irving Berlin's first Broadway show, *Watch Your Step*. She posed for fittings, practised her dance steps in her bedroom mirror, and took tea with fellow debutantes as the big day at the Lyric Theatre approached.

Escorted by her handsome cousin, Henry Warfield, and her uncle, Major General George Barnett, she arrived in style, her uncle Sol lending her the Warfield Pierce-Arrow, then the luxury motor car of choice for Hollywood stars and business moguls. Her nagging fear that no one would ask her to dance never for a moment materialized, Wallis tripping the light fantastic until dawn. The round of dances, teas and parties continued unabated through Christmas and into spring, Wallis eagerly anticipating her crowning moment of glory when Uncle Sol threw a coming-out party in her honour.

One day he called her into 'Solomon's Temple', the nickname for the Continental Trust bank where he presided, and announced that, because of the slaughter in Europe, he considered it far too frivolous to host a party in these sombre times. Much against Wallis's will, he insisted on making a public announcement to that effect, taking an advert in the local newspaper to explain why her debutante ball had been cancelled.

Wallis was devastated, feeling that she had been made to look foolish in the eyes of Baltimore society. After all, she had accepted numerous invitations from other debutantes on the understanding that her family would reciprocate. 'Naturally it was a fine gesture on his part,' she recalled, 'but for a young girl it was a crushing blow.'

Though her uncle Sol cancelled her debutante party, her aunt Lelia felt no such reservations, in April 1915 generously hosting a tea dance for her in the Marine Barracks in Washington, DC, which was attended by scores of her friends who travelled from Baltimore especially for the grand affair.

Whatever the disappointments she felt because of Uncle Sol's decision, she could console herself with the fact that she was still being ardently pursued by Osburn and Stump, young men from eminently suitable and established Baltimore families. In the race to the altar, the determined Mr Osburn reckoned he could already hear the distant sound of wedding bells, the banker's son believing that he was all but engaged to the belle of Baltimore. Wallis's family, though, had other ideas.

CHAPTER TWO

I Married a Sadist

CAPTAIN HENRY MUSTIN looked over the chaotic scene confronting him and shook his head in despair. 'Scandalous,' he muttered to himself as he reviewed the piles of driftwood choking the wide beach and the abandoned Navy buildings, some damaged during the Civil War, others wrecked by the great tidal wave and hurricane of 1906. Mustin, now forty but still trim and lean as befitting a one-time world record-holding athlete, had been given the unenviable task of turning this ramshackle spot outside Pensacola on the Florida coast into the US Navy's first air station.

'The whole place is in a scandalous condition, I surely have a job on my hands,' he wrote to his wife and Wallis's cousin, Corinne Montague, on 21 January 1914, a couple of days after landing in the teeth of a raging storm. 'It looks as if it had been abandoned for fifty years and since then had been used as a dump.'

But Naval Aviator No. 11 was made of the right stuff. Only a few days later, Mustin, who first flew in 1911, and his command of nine aviators and twenty-three enlisted men had cleared the beach sufficiently to house their allocation of seven aircraft. By 2 February 1914, the runway was built and graded so that the inaugural flight could take place.

Within two weeks of the Navy's first aeronautical school opening, the deadly perils daily facing those magnificent men in their flying machines became tragically evident when Mustin's friend Lieutenant James Murray, Naval Aviator No. 10, drowned after his Burgess D-1 flying boat crashed into the sea from a height of 200 feet. There would be many more tragedies as men tried to master these fickle and frail machines. Mustin led from the front in this perpetually risky business, in November 1915 becoming the first pilot to be successfully launched from a ship by a catapult. For this feat of daring he was awarded the Legion of Merit.

Once the air school was on a firm footing, Mustin sent for Corinne and their two sons and installed them in Quarter A, a historic military building said to be haunted by the ghosts of a previous commandant and his mistress, who perished during a yellow fever epidemic. For a time the Mustins took their meals at the Old Mill Inn for $25 a month.

With her famous Montague charm and gaiety, coupled with a deserved reputation as a Baltimore beauty, Wallis's older cousin soon established a warm and welcoming atmosphere for base personnel. While her adoring if taciturn husband ensured the new Navy aviation school was run in a shipshape fashion, she gave it the feminine touch, regularly hosting dinners for the men who put their lives on the line every day – the sound of the crash gong signifying that a pilot had crash-landed was a regular and chilling occurrence. Wallis knew nothing of these daily dangers when she received a letter from Corinne inviting 'Skinny', Corinne's nickname for her, to spend a few weeks with the Mustin family on the base.

The invitation came at an opportune time. It had been a hard winter – her beloved grandmother Anna Warfield died in December following a fall, and she had been wearing the black of mourning ever since. During this time she had declined every party, turned down every dinner invitation. Her mother had taken the opportunity to write to Wallis's love-struck beau Carter Osburn, asking him to give her daughter time and space in his headlong pursuit of her hand in marriage. It was the prelude to their eventual parting. Alice was not the only family member who felt that Wallis, still only nineteen, was racing to the altar in order to beat her rivals rather than because she was with a suitable man.

Years later, Wallis put a brave face on this teenage romance. 'There was no question of deciding anything. I was too young to be thinking of getting married. It was all for the fun of the thing. In those days girls were really very moral.' At a time when only three women in a hundred went to college, and marriage was the only sure-fire route for a woman to win power, status and stability, Wallis was skirting around the limited choices facing women.

Following a family conference in April 1916, it was agreed, albeit reluctantly, that Wallis could break her mourning, pack her party dresses and take the train south. She would be accompanied by a family friend who would be her chaperone for the journey. The family thought that a few weeks spent in quiet seclusion under the improving wing of Corinne and Henry Mustin, away from the romantic distractions of Carter Osburn and other Baltimore beaux, would bring her down to earth.

She would be in the Florida sunshine on a military base in the company of dozens of daring young men in crisp dress uniforms. What could possibly go wrong? Alice realized the moment she received Wallis's first letter that her strategy had badly backfired. Letters from Wallis, who hated putting pen to paper, were perfunctory and peppered with a list of gripes. This time it was different, Wallis telling her mother that she had met 'the most fascinating aviator' in the world at a lunch in the Mustins' home. At a time when First World War air aces like the Red Baron, Albert Ball and William Bishop were household names, military aviators were the astronauts of their day.

In Wallis's eyes they were 'godlike creatures who had descended to earth from a strange and adventurous realm'. Her Adonis was

Aviator No. 20 (though he was the eighteenth qualified Navy air pilot), a slim yet rugged young man with flashing eyes and wit to match. Wallis was instantly beguiled by Lieutenant Earl Winfield Spencer Jr, who, despite holding only the lowly rank of lieutenant, was the base's senior instructor. 'Every generation has its own set of heroes and mine were fliers,' she recalled.

From a family of seven, with an English mother and an American stockbroker father, 'Win' was raised in leafy Highland Park, then a tiny community north of Chicago. He enrolled in the Naval Academy in July 1906 when he was seventeen. His records indicate he was a decent student, though he certainly seems to have played the class clown, accumulating numerous demerits for 'talking in the section', 'sky larking in the college corridor', and 'smiling in the ranks'. He had such a good singing voice that he earned the nickname Carus, after the Italian tenor Enrico Caruso.

When he graduated in June 1910, the student yearbook, *The Lucky Bag*, described him as 'brimming with high spirits, a merry devil and a good comrade. There could not be a better shipmate.' He first served on board the USS *Nebraska* before trying his hand at the newfangled art of flying, much to the consternation of his superior officers.

In Wallis's eyes he was a real man, a 'strong, assured, sophisticated' fellow who was in a different league to the teenage boys back home. Impatient in love as she was in life, it took Wallis a mere forty-eight hours to be hopelessly smitten. 'I knew I was in love – in love at first sight, yes, but nonetheless completely, totally and helplessly.'

She didn't even care that he only drove a Ford. For the next eight delirious weeks Lieutenant Spencer squired her to the movies, to Saturday-night dances at the San Carlos Hotel, and even, unsuccessfully, attempted to teach her to play golf. All the while, her aunt Corinne was their chaperone, discreetly making herself scarce when they went shell hunting along the beach so they could have time alone.

In true Hollywood style, Win proposed as the lights came up at the end of a silent movie. His real-life screen queen was flattered but asked for time so that she could break the news to her mother, her aunt Bessie and the rest of the clan. When her mother gingerly mentioned the time-honoured difficulties of marriage to a military man – poor pay, long absences and frequent moves – starry-eyed Wallis saw the hardships as part of a great adventure. Usually when she ignored her mother, Wallis was prepared to listen to her aunt Bessie. Not this time. Wallis's mind was made up. She was determined to snare a trophy husband who would impress her friends – and enemies. As Mrs Merryman recalled: 'I told her to stop and think but she wouldn't. There was no thinking done. She was beguiled by the moonlight, the white uniform, Florida and flying.'

Her aunt Lelia was equally pithy. 'You just married him out of curiosity.'

That fateful summer, when Win arrived in Baltimore for a formal family 'viewing', he charmed the ladies and impressed the menfolk. Even Uncle Sol acknowledged the flier's down-to-earth manner. The engagement was announced on 19 September, Wallis showing off her diamond ring to as many of her school friends as she could find. Not only was she the first of her year to announce her engagement, but the fellow in question was one of the most glamorous and exotic members of the male species. Later, the competitive Miss Warfield recognized that her forthcoming nuptials had more to do with the chase than the capture. 'To be the first was not only a great honour, it was also regarded as very smart and chic. With my ring on my finger I went all over Baltimore, waving my hand at every opportunity.' She had little time to consider the character of the man she was going to marry, his occasional brooding silences, his flashes of jealousy and unpredictable moods. She was too busy organizing her big day.

FOR AN ANXIOUS FEW DAYS, though, it looked like the Montague curse would blight Wallis's moment of triumph. The wedding, arranged for 8 November 1916, in Christ Episcopal Church, where Wallis had been confirmed, looked certain to be cancelled. Just a few days before Win was due to head north to Baltimore, his Pensacola naval base was devastated by a hurricane, which flattened hangars and beach workshops, wrecked planes and battered the control tower. It was such a ferocious storm that offshore a ship sank, drowning twenty passengers and crew. In total the 18 October hurricane caused more than a million dollars' worth of damage, crippling the base. With the prospect of America entering the First World War growing closer every day, all hands, including Win's, were needed in the clean-up operation.

In spite of the turmoil in Florida, Lieutenant Spencer and several fellow officers who were ushers were given leave. It helped that Wallis's cousin Henry Mustin was the base commandant. The *Baltimore Sun* described the evening wedding as 'one of the most important of the season'. Win's best man was his brother Dumaresque, a Yale graduate, while Wallis was given away by Uncle Sol, watched by her maid of honour, Ellen Yuille, and chief bridesmaid, Mary Kirk, who, to Wallis's delight, caught her bridal bouquet. It would be another eighteen months before Mary Kirk walked down the aisle. Like her best friend, she fell for a military man, Captain Jacques Raffray, a French liaison officer who was assigned to Washington when America entered the war in 1917.

After all the excitement of her big day, Wallis now found herself alone with her military man. She and Win sat in the back seat of Aunt Bessie's car as they were driven to the Shoreham Hotel in Washington, DC, where they spent the first night of their honeymoon. As Bessie prepared to make her farewells, Wallis whispered plaintively: 'Are you going to leave me with this strange man?' Her aunt replied: 'Yes, my dear. The rest is up to you.'

SHE FACED HER FIRST NIGHT as a married woman, traditionally a moment of nervous trepidation, knowing little about 'the facts of life'. It is ironic that a woman who would become the swirling centre of conjecture about her sexual orientation, exotic bedtime techniques and numerous lovers was at the time utterly ignorant of the mechanics of sexual congress. In that, she was no different from the majority of her contemporaries. For all her fascination with the opposite sex, she recoiled in a fluster when Win kissed her on the mouth shortly after asking her to marry him, and looked on in disapproval when he pulled out a bottle of gin from his suitcase when they arrived in their hotel room in the dry state of West Virginia during their two-week honeymoon.

Wallis, who was teetotal for the first years of her marriage, pinpointed his heavy drinking as the root cause of the eventual collapse of their union. Yet she admits that she was unduly intolerant of drinking – following in the censorious footsteps of her grandmother. Even her mother found her too rigid, telling guests to hide their drinks when she entered the room unexpectedly. 'Here comes Carrie Nation,' she would whisper, comparing her daughter to a radical member of the temperance movement.

Nonetheless, the first few months at the Pensacola base were a happy time, Wallis fitting easily into the life of a Navy wife. For a girl who had never boiled an egg it was helpful that Win's salary enabled them to pay for a maid and a cook. She learned to play poker, he played the fool, entertaining fellow officers and their wives with his impersonations of vaudeville stars. What amused other midshipmen during his days at naval college did not find favour with his wife, who somewhat prissily frowned on his remorselessly extrovert behaviour, his pranks and practical jokes.

As her aunt Bessie later recalled: 'He was a showman, an exhibitionist. He would put on a funny hat and expect you to laugh at him. Well, you could laugh one evening but you couldn't for life.'

The laughter died in April 1917 with America's entry into the war. In short order Win was ordered to Squantum, Massachusetts, just outside Boston, to set up a new naval air station to train pilots. While he worked around the clock, Wallis, friendless and with time to kill, wandered the streets, visiting exhibitions and museums. She even watched the unfolding drama of real-life court cases; the juicier the better. Her mother's warning that military life was punctuated with frequent absences and constant upheaval was rapidly coming true. No sooner had Win got the pilot production line underway in Boston than he was sent to Canada to report on pilot education programmes. Then, in the autumn of 1917, he was ordered to California to set up a huge new airbase on North Island near San Diego. Though it was a signal acknowledgement of his organizational ability and leadership, Win was bitterly disappointed. All the time he was on the East Coast he had lobbied for a berth on the front line in Europe – he envied his younger brother Dumaresque, who sailed to France in June and was now combat flying as part of the Lafayette Escadrille squadron.

In spite of his pleading, his superiors consistently declined his requests, informing him that they needed his experience on the home front. As a result the newlyweds spent their first wedding anniversary shuttling across country to their new berth. They stopped first in Washington, then saw his family in Chicago before spending a night at the Grand Canyon on their way west. On their first wedding anniversary, as they stood on the rim of this magnificent natural wonder, Win earnestly reaffirmed his love and devotion to Wallis, his simple words affecting her deeply. She later recalled: 'He was neither a poet or philosopher but there was something touching about the simplicity of his promise that nothing would come between us.'

There was little time for fine words. From the moment they took possession of a sweet, two-bedroom apartment in Coronado, Win was working eighteen-hour days, as he and a skeleton crew raced to turn a barren slice of land into an operating Navy airbase. In just seventy-two hours he and the men under his command built barracks, washrooms and five classrooms, and installed a water and sewage system. Whatever else Wallis may have complained about, there was no faulting Win's absolute commitment to the war effort.

No sooner was he seeing solid progress in the construction and organization of the base than he was devastated by news from the front line. In January 1918, his adored younger brother Dumaresque was killed. Early reports indicated that Dumaresque, who had already been awarded the Croix de Guerre and Medalle Militaire for his bravery, had been shot down while returning from patrol over German lines. Later it was revealed that he had been practising aerobatics and had pulled out of a turn too late. Win mourned his brother's death long and hard, the bottle helping to dull the pain.

With drink came a barrage of insults and a volley of innuendo about his wife's failings, mainly focusing on her inadequacies in the kitchen. In public he was jaunty and jovial, in private brooding, introspective and morose. It was something of a relief that he left her to her own devices for much of the time, setting off for the base at dawn and not arriving home until long after nightfall.

His frustration at being prevented from serving abroad like his brother was palpable, Win writing pleading letters to his Navy friends as well as making a formal transfer request to his line commander, Captain Edward Irwin. 'I came to San Diego under protest,' he wrote. 'I wanted foreign service . . . and have always hoped for an opportunity to fight.' Referring to the 'heartbreaking' jobs he had been given, Win pointed out that the results of his labours were only apparent when the next fellow came along. Even though Captain Irwin was sympathetic and appreciative of his 'hard work', sadly there was no suitable replacement available.

While Win stewed, Wallis enjoyed the perks that came with marriage to a commanding officer. He had his own Navy barge to ferry him from the mainland to North Island, as well as a chauffeur-driven Packard car. This was more like it. As befitting their station, they were invited to numerous prestigious social events, notably dinner with President and First Lady Wilson at the US Grant Hotel and a ball in honour of Secretary of the Navy Josephus Daniels and his wife Addie at the Hotel del Coronado.

Wallis made a coterie of new friends who would stay with her for the rest of her life. They included Marianna and Rhoda Fullam, the daughters of Rear Admiral Fullam; Rita Chase, the wife of New Jersey businessman Ralph; and later Katherine Moore Bigelow, a Red Cross nurse who served in France and was widowed just after the end of the war. Though at that time Katherine was walking out with William Thaw, the brother of diplomat Ben Thaw, she would go on to play a central role in Wallis's life.

As her social life became more varied and sophisticated, Wallis would attend dances at the Cuyamaca Club, bridge or poker nights and barbecues at the dirigible hangar on North Island. Sometimes Win was with her, sometimes not, in which case she would join a party of fellow officers and their wives.

When they appeared together as a couple, Win and Wallis were showstoppers. Socialite Mrs E. Clarence Moore was part of a small convivial group sitting in the Hotel del Coronado when Wallis and Win walked into the lobby. 'Our gay conversation was suddenly silenced by the arrival of an unusually good-looking couple who were passing through the casino,' she recalled. It was the new base commandant and his wife. 'After that evening Wallis and Win were frequently in our group, sometimes playing golf, sometimes enjoying informal parties.'

Even her mother, who came to visit, was impressed with the social life led by the commanding officer's wife. Instinctively, Wallis always put on the smiling mask, the impervious façade that revealed nothing of her inner turmoil and hurt. Though there were opportunities, she said nothing to her mother about her issues with Win. As a young girl she had learned to keep her own counsel. Nothing in her adult life would change that.

FOR A CHANGE OF SCENE, Wallis would occasionally range north with a girlfriend, staying at friends' homes in Santa Barbara and Pebble Beach. Whatever her private concerns, in public Wallis was the life and soul, her friend Marianna Fullam describing her as the one person she would love to spend a year with on a desert island because of her 'vitality and gaiety'. Others complimented her on her poise, style, candour and sparkle, her wit engaging the attention of silent-screen comedian Charlie Chaplin and actor John Barrymore when they stayed at the Hotel del Coronado. Harvard graduate Henry Flood Robert remembered Wallis as 'darned attractive though I wouldn't call her a beauty. I found her vivacious and fun loving. When she entered a room the focus was on her.'

Her fabled poise deserted her, however, when she took on the nerve-jangling challenge of organizing her first-ever dinner party at home. Armed with her 'bible' – Fannie Farmer's cookbook – she invited a young naval couple who lived nearby to act as guinea pigs. The menu seemed straightforward – tomato soup, roast beef and artichoke. It was the hollandaise sauce that was to prove tricky.

As the dinner hour approached, Wallis got herself into such a state that for the first time in three years of marriage she allowed

Win to mix her a cocktail. It was, she believes, a double martini. While it hit the spot, Wallis was so relaxed that the meal suffered, with most of the sauce splattered on the kitchen wall. Their guests duly arrived, Win poured them a cocktail, and Wallis asked them to be seated. Then she opened her bible and read out the menu she had tried to prepare. She recalled telling her guests: 'This is what you were *going* to have for dinner. Everyone agreed that I had read a beautiful dinner – in fact it sounded so delicious that we all got up and proceeded to the Hotel Coronado and ordered it.'

An amusing story, but also revealing of Wallis's elusive character. She told this tale of culinary failure to her ghost writer Cleveland Amory when she was preparing her 1957 memoir, *The Heart Has Its Reasons*. He later quit, accusing Wallis of wanting a biography that was more make-believe than real life. Amory's place was taken by Colonel Charles Murphy. In his version, which was eventually published, the evening was a culinary triumph, a night which set her off on her eventual career as an eminent hostess.

If this trivial story was deliberately changed to place Wallis in a flattering light, what then of more significant stories relating to her lovers, husbands and friends? As Foxcroft headmistress Charlotte Noland, whom Wallis considered the model of an ideal woman, told Amory during his research: 'I knew her from the time she was a child and I have never known anyone who could all her life so conveniently avoid the truth.' In the world of Wallis Spencer, much was lost in translation.

SHE IS NOT THE ONLY ONE. In the royal world of the House of Windsor, truth, image and invention are an uneasy linguistic Esperanto. For instance, when the then Prince of Wales first visited Canada in 1919, he met with a crowd in a village outside Toronto. Nine months or so later, the village teacher gave birth to a baby boy. She subsequently claimed the father was the Prince of

Wales, with whom she had enjoyed a brief but amorous encounter. It was a story she told everyone until the day she died. On her gravestone it states clearly that she was the wife of the Prince of Wales. This was a potentially enticing story, except that the same teacher was equally emphatic that she had been awarded the Nobel Prize for literature.

For when royalty comes to town, even the clearest memory becomes clouded. A year later, in April 1920, the Prince of Wales visited San Diego en route to a tour of New Zealand, Australia and all points Far East. The golden-haired prince, radiating charm and charisma, held a clamorous reception on board HMS *Renown* to thank the locals for their overwhelming welcome and their stalwart support during the First World War.

It was subsequently reported that Lieutenant Commander Win Spencer and his wife had been part of the receiving line who shook the hand of the future king. Years later Win even speculated that Wallis may have spoken to the prince. 'She was with me most of the evening but as I recall she slipped away for a few moments and may have been received by the prince,' he informed reporters in 1936. Not to be outdone, the flamboyant Lord Louis Mountbatten, who joined the prince on his journey, told author Charles Murphy that not only did Wallis meet the prince but she subsequently chided him for failing to recall their encounter, especially as she was 'dressed to kill'.

In fact neither Wallis nor Win were within a hundred miles of the Prince of Wales when his battleship dropped anchor in San Diego harbour. Win was at March Field airbase in Riverside, California, flying land planes and learning bombing techniques. His wife was busy being the life and soul at a polo dinner near San Francisco. On 31 March 1920, according to the local newspaper, she had boarded the Lark Southern Pacific Pullman train for Monterey, where she stayed at Del Monte Lodge as the house guest of Mrs Jane Selby

Hayne, an outstanding polo player, who had recently divorced golf champion Robin Hayne. When not out riding or playing polo, Wallis and Jane Selby Hayne attended numerous dinners and other social events to mark the end of the polo season.

Wallis was in her element, captivating a fascinating variety of rich and occasionally available men. She and Jane socialized with Samuel Finley Brown Morse, owner of the Del Monte properties, Australian painter Francis McComas, mining heir George Maurice Heckscher, as well as a pair of dashing English majors who formed the backbone of the national polo team. Historian Benjamin Sacks suggests: 'Perhaps the coquetry of Wallis with the several poloists at the Morse dinner-dance held in Pebble Beach might have discomfited Isabella [her hostess, Mrs Luther Martin Kennett], who preferred to close the book on the trip north as a topic of conversation.'

The suggestion was that with Win out of sight, Wallis was at her most teasing. Wallis had always prided herself on her 'gay and flirtatious' nature, admitting that she 'was brought up to be as entertaining as one can be at a party'. She also acknowledged that her husband became an ugly drunk when he watched her behaviour at social events. He would lapse into moody silence or become loud and aggressive. Other times he would simply go off on his own into the night. While Wallis attributed the breakdown of her marriage to Win's morose personality and the frustration he felt regarding his career, which stalled after the war ended, others suggest her own seductive behaviour played a not insignificant part. Even staunch friend Marianna Fullam, later Emory Sands, strongly believed her flirtations drove her emotionally inarticulate husband to 'exasperation' – and to reach for the bottle to drown his sorrows.

IT WAS NOT ALL TEARS and tantrums. In November 1920, the couple celebrated their fourth wedding anniversary with Henry and Corinne Mustin, Wallis's mother and assorted friends. The Mustins were now back on the West Coast, which was, as far as Wallis was concerned, a blessing. Each time Win went away on a variety of temporary new assignments, Wallis nursed the hope that when he returned to their Coronado home he would be a changed man. Those hopes were usually dashed by day two of his homecoming.

She tried to see the sunny side when, in August 1921, he was permanently reassigned to Washington to take up a desk job at the Bureau of Aeronautics. His achievements at North Island had been considerable, overseeing the men under his command – at one time there were 2,000 men and officers on the base – who flew 35,000 hours without a single fatality. Not that his Navy superiors appreciated his efforts.

When he failed his navigation exam during his bid for promotion to lieutenant commander, the examining board did not take into consideration that for the previous four years he had been an active naval aviator and hadn't been near a ship. Fortunately, Rear Admiral William Fullam, whose daughters were Wallis's great friends, personally intervened. Lieutenant Spencer's war work in San Diego, he averred, had been of the greatest importance of any officer in the Navy. Moreover, his position as a junior officer had needed great tact in dealing with fellow commanding officers. 'He is reserved, taciturn and abrupt but this is entirely from embarrassment and diffidence,' wrote Fullam. The recently retired commander in chief of the Pacific fleet went on to state that of all the officers he had met during his career, Spencer was among the first rank because of his 'cool head, nerve and high sense of duty. I should not hesitate to assign him to command a cruiser under war conditions. It is my observation that he puts duty before pleasure at all times.'

With that ringing endorsement the board had little option but to allow Lieutenant Spencer a second chance at the navigation exam, which he duly passed. He arrived in Washington with a promotion but little appetite for the political stew that was the postwar Navy

Bureau of Aeronautics, as the Army and Navy vied for control. In his heart he wanted to be back at sea or in the air.

Unhappy and demoralized, Win, according to Wallis's account, took out his frustrations on her, becoming increasingly sadistic and bullying. On one notorious occasion he locked her in the bathroom at the Brighton Hotel on California Street, where they were staying. Ignoring her frenzied knocking, he went out, leaving her in solitary confinement for hours. She was afraid to shout for help, as the hotel management had already warned them about their noisy behaviour. Frantically she tried to pick the lock with a nail file. Taking Wallis's story at face value – most bathrooms lock from the inside not the outside – it was an emotionally exhausting and frightening evening.

AS SHE PONDERED her future she realized that her marriage was beyond repair. She wanted out. In those days divorce was unthinkable – the financial consequences unpalatable, the social stigma often unbearable. Divorce was only for the very rich or the very foolish. She was neither, but her dire circumstances forced her to think the inconceivable.

In Wallis's settled view, Win's bombastic personality and his drinking had driven her five-year marriage to the brink of collapse. Her own restless, impatient personality, her flirtatiousness and her fierce temper, did little to help keep the domestic peace. Wallis recognized that unlike her mother, who had found the secret of inner peace, she was never really content with anything – or anyone – in life. Whatever Win did was a disappointment, his subdued, introspective personality merely encouraging him to go into his shell in the face of her complaints.

It irritated her that he was not blessed with her facility for being able to read others. Within minutes she could see through people, divine their hidden motives and personal qualities. Irascible and impatient, it drove Wallis wild when Win could not see or understand that some people did not like him or wished him no good. All he would do was laugh off her warnings or say she was exaggerating.

This, though, was nibbling around the edges. At the heart of their marital difficulties was their sex life, or rather lack thereof. Wallis would later confess that throughout her marriage, through the good times and the bad, they had never consummated their union. In an age of sexual ignorance and primitive birth control, her reluctance to engage in sexual congress was not unusual but still created considerable barriers to marital happiness. Coming from a large family, it was only natural that Win wanted to become a father himself. The frustrations felt on both sides can only be imagined. Watching Wallis flirt with other men and knowing he was going home to a stone-cold bed was hardly a recipe for marital accord.

It has been suggested by, among others, biographers Anne Sebba and Michael Bloch, that her reluctance to engage in sexual activity was the result of her being born, if not a man, then with ambiguous genitalia, a condition now known as a 'disorder of sex development' (DSD). An early sign is a girl with strong muscles, athletic prowess, long legs and large hands. Certainly Wallis conformed to this template. Queen Mary's official biographer, James Pope-Hennessy, suggested that with her flat, angular body she was 'not a woman at all'. Over the years it became commonplace to suggest that she was in fact hermaphrodite, her sexuality as ambiguous as the conundrum of her eventual appeal to the king of England. She had a hysterectomy for ovarian cancer in 1951, which suggests that she was wholly female. What remains enigmatic is the secret of her sexual allure. In short, what did men see in her?

IT SEEMS, FROM THE TESTIMONY of Herman Rogers, the central male figure in her life, that with her first husband Win she enjoyed an occasionally sado-masochistic but ultimately unfulfilling marital ritual. 'He beat her – and she loved it,' Rogers later told Wallis's erstwhile biographer Cleveland Amory. Though Wallis has subsequently been described as a dominatrix, with Win Spencer she adopted a different role, that of a provocative submissive. Her flirting would be the starting gun for their sexually charged dance. Matters would then escalate, Wallis goading him, a leery Win lashing out, his gin-fuelled violence perversely viewed by Wallis as a sign that he desired and felt some kind of aberrant passion for the sharp-tongued woman standing before him. 'Wallis had a temper of her own and they had frequent yelling matches, and sometimes he would hit her and she would throw things', her biographer Ralph G. Martin wrote.

But when he left her alone, when he chose not to speak to her for sometimes a day at a time, this she could not tolerate. At least violence was an acknowledgement of her existence. This, though, was a dance without consummation, frenzy without resolve. It was the last sick, hopeless dance of a doomed romance. She was learning the hard way that she had fallen in love with the glamorous image, not the man, and that for a long time their union had been shored up by their brisk social life and her supportive circle of mainly female friends, and padded out with his frequent deployment on Navy business. Much as Wallis would have hated to admit it, her mother was right: there was no romance in marrying a Navy officer. She had fooled herself that she was in love. Ruefully, she realized that her real motivation had been to beat her Baltimore contemporaries to the altar. In her immaturity, Wallis had made a cataclysmic mistake.

Eventually she sought out her mother, then working as a hostess at the Chevy Chase country club in Maryland, and explained that she wanted a divorce. Even though she never mentioned the embarrassingly intimate details, her mother was as horrified as if she had confessed to murder. She was not appalled at her son-in-law but at her daughter for even contemplating such a step. Neither a Montague nor a Warfield had divorced in three hundred years. The very idea was preposterous. 'Unthinkable' was the *mot juste*. Practical as ever, she also pointed out very firmly that as a divorced woman Wallis would face social disgrace and financial ruin. Not to mention the shame she would bring upon the family. Separation possibly, divorce never.

Wallis faced the same mortified refrain when she called upon her beloved Aunt Bessie, now living near her sister as a paid companion to a well-to-do spinster. While Bessie would later concede that Win was a 'sadist who she could not live with', at the time she was in lockstep with her sister.

As Wallis, shaken and subdued, contemplated their reaction, she realized that they were from a generation where women had no status or rights, their lives utterly governed by the whims of men. The war, especially the introduction of millions of women to the workforce, was splintering those moral absolutes and placing a generation of mothers and daughters into conflict.

In the nineteenth century virtually every campaign, from temperance to female emancipation, was cast as a mother–daughter alliance. In the 1920s, after the war had left the world, as cartoonists frequently depicted it, 'in crutches and its arm in a sling', that alliance crumbled before a consumer-driven revolt of young women against prudish Victorian matriarchs. Life was, according to feminist writer Susan Faludi, 'a celebration of a motherless girl culture of flapper dance-a-thons, petting parties and gin fests. The powerful new forces of Hollywood, national advertising, automobiles and urban jobs enlisted young women into a commercial version of emancipation.' While the Jazz Age presented an image of 'beautiful people buoyed up on bootlegged champagne bubbles', the new decade promised young women like Wallis in the 'Ain't We Got Fun' generation the freedom to shop, display their bodies and to smoke, to drink and drive with the boys – and throw it in the face of their mothers. Postwar America was a jittery, restless nation, a sink-or-swim democracy bobbing about in an ocean of insurrection and revolution. Living for the moment, morning, noon and night, was the mantra of the Bright Young (wealthy) Things who could afford to buy those special candles that burned at both ends. This reckless, devil-may-care attitude was exemplified by the novelist F. Scott Fitzgerald and his beautiful wife, Zelda, who were notorious not only for their prose but also for their propensity for leaping into fountains at Union Square and in front of the Plaza Hotel in New York. While the Big Apple had taken over from exhausted London as the premier city for conspicuous consumption and excess, the noise and values of the blaring Jazz Age had not spread far beyond Manhattan.

Arguments about changing social mores and the independence of modern women still cut little ice in Uncle Sol's Baltimore bank, where Wallis was forced to swallow her moralizing medicine from the man whose good name meant everything. He railed against the very idea of divorce. 'I won't let you bring this disgrace upon us,' he thundered, before ending his peroration with a request that she give her marriage one more try.

She did as she was bid, hoping against hope that Win would be jolted to his senses. It was but a brief reprieve. After spending yet another night wondering what Win was doing when he failed to return home – drink or another woman or both – Wallis had had enough. She asked her mother if she could move into her apartment at 2301 Connecticut Avenue. Reluctantly, her mother agreed.

Win was resigned to his fate. When she told him her plans, he said: 'Wallis, I've had it coming to me. If you ever change your mind I will still be around.' The die was cast. For Wallis, hers was a brave and bold move, eschewing safety, status and security for a very uncertain future.

Comfort came from an unexpected quarter. On 18 October 1921, she received an anguished and 'heartsick' four-page letter from her mother-in-law, Agnes Spencer. While Agnes acknowledged that her son's disposition did not make him the easiest person in the world to get along with, she recalled her visit to see them in Pensacola, where 'your wishes and happiness were his first consideration'. She finished sadly: 'I wish I could do something to mend matters but I fear that there is little to be said or done.'

Wallis's husband, a gentleman to the last, added his own postscript to their marriage when he was tackled by reporters during the abdication crisis in 1936. Nursing a broken leg from a fall on ice, he told the assembled throng: 'She is one of the finest women I have ever known. My work did not allow me to partake of the social life which Wallis loved so dearly. Gradually we drifted apart. I suppose that is the price we pay for a career. She was the leader of the social life at Coronado but became lonely during the times I was at sea with the fleet.'

Shortly after Wallis walked out, Win finally got his wish to return to general Navy service. Just before Christmas 1921 he was ordered to join the USS *Chaumont* and take this slow boat to China and join the American fleet. If Wallis was all at sea regarding her future, Win was returning to his first and perhaps only love: a life on the ocean waves.

CHAPTER THREE

'He was Simply Irresistible'

COURTNEY LETTS' FIRST MEMORY of Washington was of when she was just six and she joined the other children of the wealthy and influential at the traditional Easter Egg Roll on the White House lawns, her activities watched by the benign moustachioed figure of President Theodore Roosevelt.

As the granddaughter of a US senator and daughter of Frank C. Letts, president of the National Grocery Company, who supplied foodstuffs to the masses, privilege and status were Courtney's birthright.

As a teenager she taught the nervously dapper F. Scott Fitzgerald how to ice-skate and later invited him to join her family at their country estate at Lake Forest in rural Illinois. He arrived complete with his own electric curling iron to wave his hair, and when he was, eventually, dressed and ready she took him to several parties.

The loquacious aspiring writer was, according to her friends, a 'terrific success'. It was Courtney who introduced the novelist to her beautiful friend Ginevra King. He promptly fell head over heels in love, his golden girl becoming for a time his romantic interest and his muse. She was the template for the flirtatious yet distant Daisy Buchanan, the anti-heroine of *The Great Gatsby*, the classic American novel that captured the spirit of hardness and hedonism of the Jazz Age.

When Fitzgerald so brilliantly described a postwar world where the social elite lived with the 'insouciance of grand ducs and the casualness of chorus girls', he was thinking of Courtney, Ginevra and the other gilded youth who comprised their social circle.

Years later he sent Courtney a first edition of his first masterpiece, *This Side of Paradise*, complete with a long dedication. 'You will probably find yourself and your mother in it,' he wrote. 'I hope you will not mind what I wrote.'

Courtney, Ginevra and two other beautiful Chicago friends, Margaret 'Peg' Carry and Edith Cummings – a brilliant golfer dubbed the 'Fairway Flapper' – were known as the Big Four, a quartet blessed with beauty and social brilliance. Their daily doings were lovingly celebrated by the mass circulation media.

As Fitzgerald described, they had class and certainty, that effortless sense of privilege born out of wealth and what the English aristocracy like to call 'breeding'. They didn't need to try as hard, floating through life as if to the manor born. As the man himself observed about the very rich: 'They are different from you and me.'

When Courtney Letts drifted languidly through the social whirl of Chicago, Washington and later Paris, it was remarkable how often her life intersected with the less rarefied world of Wallis Spencer. Though the two women did not formally meet for a quarter-century, they were the fiercest of love rivals, for a time Courtney becoming Wallis's romantic doppelgänger.

Not only were they wooed by the same men, they were often mistaken for one another, though Courtney was more conventionally feminine and rounded whereas Wallis's features were hard, masculine and angular. And it was Courtney who was chosen by the *Chicago Tribune* as one of the twelve most beautiful women in America. Wallis was not on the list.

Before Wallis moved to Washington, both women had married impetuously to handsome and handsomely attired Navy officers;

both were now separated and looking for a way out. Unlike Wallis, Courtney was a mother to two children. For a time they lived a short walk from one another. Courtney and her children stayed with her mother at 2342 Massachusetts Avenue, a substantial 5,800-square-foot brownstone on what was known as Diplomats' Row. Wallis shared rooms with Alice at the eight-storey Carthage apartment building on Connecticut Avenue.

They were both cast from the feminine mould of the prewar-era woman who didn't or couldn't work and subsumed her own ambition in her pursuit of finding a wealthy husband or benefactor. Wallis and Courtney had married young, trying to impress their peers rather than make a sensible choice. Wounded by their folly, they were not about to make the same mistake again. As Courtney's granddaughter, Courtney Hagner, observes: 'Nana was so like Wallis in many ways. Always able to put on a perfect front and if there was any issue, to disguise it.'

They may have lived near to each other, but socially they were worlds apart. Where Courtney effortlessly glided into the best parties, the fanciest dinners and the ritziest receptions, Wallis had her nose pressed firmly against the window, desperately looking for a way in. When Courtney went to the Chevy Chase country club to improve her tennis backhand or meet friends, it was Wallis's mother, as one of the hostesses, who was there to greet her. By the time Wallis was noticed by Courtney she was no longer living with her mother.

In a diary written by Courtney and revealed for the first time in this volume, she tartly describes the reputation Wallis enjoyed during her Washington sojourn.

In those days she hardly had a smart dress in which to go about. She was little known in Washington except among the young set, where she lived as the separated wife of a poor naval officer. For three years she lived in a small flat on Connecticut Avenue with a divorcee who worked in a shop to support her son. Between them they enjoyed all the small jealousies of women, the clamoring for invitations to the most important balls and important dinners they would never reach. Wally Spencer she was then. Small, slender, vivacious and witty. Witty with the hard-boiled slapstick wit which always amuses.

Unsurprisingly, her cutting caricature focuses on cash, class and background, the fact that Wallis lived with a woman who actually worked for a living. And in a shop of all places. It is all so reminiscent of Tom Buchanan's sneering dismissal of Gatsby in the climactic confrontation in the Plaza Hotel in *The Great Gatsby*: 'Mr Nobody from Nowhere.'

WHILE THE 1920S are invariably defined as the Jazz Age, that brief cacophonous period of casual sex, cocaine, screeching trombones, drunken cocktail parties, women smoking in public, and the outrageous behaviour of the Bright Young Things, life in Washington was barely touched by this spinning social vortex. It was a place where federal bureaucrats were heavily outnumbered by the military and diplomatic corps, a fact that pleased the incoming president, Calvin Coolidge, a small-government conservative who took office in 1923 after the sudden death of Warren Harding.

For all the talk of jelly-bean boyfriends and flapper girls, when Wallis arrived in Washington in the summer of 1921 she discovered that the nation's capital was in fact a quaintly provincial town dominated by a handful of old, established Southern families known as the 'Cave Dwellers'. This tight-knit group, Wallis noted with the bitterness of one frequently rejected, 'operated their social slide rule as they saw fit'. As a separated woman, her name did not appear in the *Social Register*, the careful list of all the prominent families and diplomats in town.

During her first few weeks in Washington, Wallis lived with her mother, though Wallis moved when it became clear that Alice did not approve of her daughter going out without a chaperone and returning home in the very early hours of the morning. 'I was trying to make a new life, and yet every night my mother would sit up as if I was a child,' she later complained.

Fortunately, her friends the Neilsons were going to New York for a time, so they agreed for her to stay in their apartment until their return. It was an exhilarating period. For the first time in her life she was living on her own, her everyday needs covered by the $225 Win sent each month.

When the Neilsons returned in the summer of 1922, Wallis, now twenty-six, moved in with talented portrait artist Dorothy McNamee, the daughter of Admiral William T. Swinburne, the former commander of the Pacific fleet, while McNamee's husband, Luke, the director of the Office of Naval Intelligence, was on overseas assignment.

As Dorothy, introspective and shy by nature, spent much of her time in her Georgetown studio, Wallis's circle increasingly revolved around that postwar phenomenon: single, separated, widowed and divorced women making their way in the world. The right to vote, grudgingly passed into legislation in 1920, symbolized that new-found independence. Her 'desert island' companion from Coronado, Marianna Sands, who was also separated from her husband, and her sister Rhoda were now living in Washington. It helped, too, that wealthy socialite Alice Vandergrift Garrett took her under her wing, loaning or giving her clothes so that she always looked stylish at the various lunches, tea dances and white-tie dinners she was now attending.

During this time Wallis became firm friends with the sassy Ethel Noyes, whose father headed the *Washington Star* and whose brother Newbold was married to her cousin Lelia Barnett. They made a merry group and while, as Courtney indicated, Wallis was never invited to the best parties, where the *Social Register* prevailed, she had the supreme advantage of being a woman in a town where eligible, well-educated bachelors were in a distinct surplus.

For a time Wallis and Ethel shared the same beau – the rumbling bass-voiced Welsh journalist Willmott Lewis. Not only was he the London *Times* correspondent in Washington, he acted as the urbane unofficial ambassador incognito, enlivening many a reporter's copy with *bons mots* and insights into the thinking of the British government.

A commanding presence, he was eventually knighted for his services to the Crown. At the time Ethel, who married Lewis in 1926, quipped: 'Well, it took King George to make a lady of me.'

Willmott, who later boasted that he could have earned $100,000 for kissing and telling of his numerous trysts with Wallis, was the conversational star of a weekly lunch group known as the Soixante Gourmets.

This was a witty and eclectic gathering of diplomats and journalists who met at the Hamilton Hotel to poke holes in foreign policy and fun at one another. The only stipulation was that each member had to bring a lady guest. Step forward Wallis, Ethel, Marianna and their ilk. Wallis had never been in company quite like this. At any time one of six languages could be heard, while insider political and diplomatic gossip flowed like the wine that accompanied these leisurely affairs. The men were urbane, knowledgeable, attentive and witty. It was at these gatherings where she met her first prince, Gelasio Caetani, the first Fascist Italian ambassador to Washington, a man of impeccable manners and effortless courtesy, as befitting the descendant of two popes.

This was a long way from the days of Pensacola and Coronado – and the taciturn silences of Win.

She graduated from being seduced by the sky-high glamour of the first aviators to the high-flying conversations of the diplomatic and journalist cadres. It was so exciting, an exhilarated and animated Wallis enjoying being squired around by a small army of ardent beaux. 'The surplus of agreeable, attractive, unattached men made the diplomatic set a green pasture for women on their own,' she recalled. It also meant that she was raised up several rungs in precedence in the studiously hierarchical world of Washington society. No longer was her nose pressed so firmly against the glass.

WHILE FOR WALLIS this period in her life was 'a special paradise', it was a paradise where the serpent of temptation lurked in rumble seats and sofas. Her sexual code was not to fall for light affairs of the moment and, as she later confided, never to allow a man to journey below her intimate 'Mason-Dixon Line'.

One man did manage to cross the line into the inner sanctum of her heart.

Even at a distance of thirty years and two marriages later, Wallis became lyrical and rheumy-eyed as she spoke of the smoothly charismatic Latin Casanova who stole – and broke – her heart.

Cautious to the last, she scratched 'No' when her ghost writer revealed the name of the man she fell for, striking through emotional passages that revealed too much of her heart. 'His name is of no consequence,' she averred, her coyness indicating that he was very much of consequence.

She described him as 'suave and handsome', with jet-black hair, dark deep-set eyes, and a rare combination of urbanity and effervescence. 'To talk with him was an experience. He seemed to be playing with life as he played with words but underneath he had stern principles and a burning ambition, which was supported by broad scholarship and wide experience.'

He was the embodiment of the Renaissance man, a competition golfer, skilful bridge player, accomplished horseman, a connoisseur of wine and a practised heartbreaker. Wallis was putty in the knowing hands of the saturnine, monocle-wearing Felipe Aja Espil, the highly regarded and hugely ambitious Argentinian counsellor at the Washington embassy.

SHE WAS NOT THE ONLY ONE. From the moment Espil, a lawyer by training, arrived in 1916 from Buenos Aires, he cut an urbane swathe through Washington society. It was not an entirely smooth passage. The devout Catholic was disconcerted to find at his first hotel, the Willard, that the men's bathrooms had no doors and the men had no shame. Now safely ensconced at 1806 Corcoran Street near fashionable Dupont Circle, Espil quickly gained a reputation among men of affairs as a serious man with a strict mission to represent his country ably and effectively.

When Wallis came into his orbit, he was seen as a rising star earmarked as a future ambassador. One magazine profile would later describe him as 'the Mona Lisa of the Andes, a handsome Beau Brummell who orders his clothes from tailors in London's Savile Row'.

He could speak four languages fluently, read widely – not just American newspapers but the *Congressional Record*, too – and had little time for those who were not as *au courant* as himself.

Wallis knew she had to up her game if she wanted to earn and keep her Latin-American paramour. She was in the major leagues now, and though he delighted in her wit and gaiety, she instinctively knew he wanted something more in a wife.

Every day she read newspapers from cover to cover and occasionally even opened a book. Not that she read the whole work. Wallis developed a technique where she read the first couple of pages and the ending and then picked out a relevant quote from somewhere inside the tome. In a social situation she would use the quote as an opening conversational gambit before going on to talk with insight and intelligence about the book of the moment. It left many a dinner-table partner duly impressed. Wallis used this technique for the rest of her life, always to striking effect.

In Felipe's book, however, Wallis would never be the heroine of his life, merely one character among many. Though he regularly squired her to various social events and enjoyed her home cooking – Southern fried chicken was then her speciality – unfortunately for Wallis, she was not the only girl on his arm. As his granddaughter Courtney Hagner recalls: 'Felipe was charismatic and knew it. He was the star of many of these parties and Wallis was just one of the girls he dated.'

Wallis was his Becky Sharp, witty and socially striving, good for a fun night out but not a long-term companion or, heaven forbid, his wife. After all, she was a Protestant and still married. As Courtney Hagner observes: 'He was a typical Latin man in that he wanted lovers but also a woman who would be by his side who was ambitious, well-dressed, and from a good established family.' A family fortune would also help.

Wallis, though, was smitten. The woman who exulted in self-control totally lost her head and heart. Felipe, some nine years older than Wallis, became, if not the love of her life – that would come later – her grand passion. As Wallis later confessed: 'My head spun first and then my heart. Even in my mind there was no question I was becoming involved. The man was irresistible and my resistance was at a dangerous low.'

She was prepared to do anything to keep him. Wallis, then twenty-seven, considered converting to Catholicism and moving to Buenos Aires if needs be. She gave herself completely to Felipe in a way that she never did with Win. For once the flighty, careless Montague side of her personality dominated, Wallis sharing Felipe's bed while still married. 'Wallis was mad about him,' recalled a friend. 'She would have done anything. I have never seen a woman so in love.'

However, the brooding handmaidens of her passion were jealousy, possessiveness and rage, Wallis succumbing to temper tantrums when she learned that her lover was squiring other women. The more jealous she became, the more she drove him away, her hot Latin lover cooled by the climate of reproach and argument. As Felipe's granddaughter recalls: 'Wallis was very needy and bitchy. Vindictive, too.'

Felipe had his eye on the prize – and it wasn't Wallis but rather the position of Argentinian ambassador to the United States. Before that goal all personal considerations took second place. Though she flung herself at him, he drew away. Some thirteen years later, one of his diplomatic colleagues pithily remarked: 'Felipe had a higher regard for his career than Edward the Eighth had.'

Wallis should have seen the writing on the wall when he failed to invite her as his partner to the party of the year, a ball given by wealthy former diplomat and company director Lawrence Townsend and his wife at their fashionable Twentieth Street mansion, close to Espil's home. When Wallis raised the subject with her lover, Espil was nonplussed. 'I cannot,' he told her, 'ask Mrs Townsend to invite my mistress. *Ça ne se fait pas*. It is not the done thing.' In a fury Wallis flew at him and scratched his face. Within days all of social Washington was buzzing with this story, the phrase '*Ça ne se fait pas*' quickly becoming an oft-used social put-down.

Unknown to Wallis, Espil was quietly romancing his ideal woman in the shape of Courtney Letts, now Stillwell. They met at an intimate dinner at the British Embassy. 'You look like an old friend of mine,' he said. 'Who?' asked Courtney. 'Wallis Spencer,' he said before moving on to other topics. Courtney, who was formally separated from her husband, Wellesley H. Stillwell, found Espil charming, gracious and serious. Like Wallis and many others, she fell for him. In turn he was enchanted by her beauty and civilized conversation – not to mention her social standing and her wealthy background.

There was one big stumbling block – her Midwestern father, who was terrified that any of his daughters would ever marry a 'foreigner, especially a Latin'. He warned her: 'They make difficult husbands for American girls. They are usually unfaithful.' When Espil asked her to marry him she was flattered, but mindful of her father's admonition, she declined. Unspoken was the fact that she wanted a man with money to support her and her children. Espil's mid-level diplomatic position as counsellor would not provide for her needs . . . just yet.

The following morning a box of long-stemmed American Beauty roses arrived. A little white card was nestled deep inside. 'Goodbye, *Chiquita*, I understand your problems but I will never forget you. With my most sincere respect and admiration, Felipe Espil.'

When Wallis discovered that Espil was two-timing her she flew into a jealous rage and furiously stormed into his apartment. Armed with a pair of sharp scissors, she went into the bedroom wardrobe and cut all his dress trousers at the knee.

Their relationship continued to limp along. Needy, jealous and controlling, Wallis would not leave Espil alone, every social event becoming an ordeal. Finally, he had had enough. He decided he couldn't deal with her temper and tantrums any more. With perhaps more than a touch of Latin hyperbole, he later claimed that he escaped from her one morning by catching a boat back to Buenos Aires and sailing out of her life. They met again in Virginia three years later. By then the flame of passion that fuelled their affair was extinguished. Wallis and Espil were just old friends.

As he recalled of their tempestuous relationship: 'She is a very dominating creature, *the* most dominating woman I have met in my life. She has a quick temper. She demands a great deal. When a man finds himself under the spell of a woman like that it can take years of his life to get away. I decided I couldn't live that way any longer. I was tired of it.'

As he sailed south, he left behind two women whose hearts had been touched by his presence. Both independently decided to travel to Paris, the City of Light, to seek a discreet divorce – and to make a fresh start. In the autumn of 1923, Wallis received a surprising letter from her cousin Corinne inviting her to travel to France for a couple of months.

Corinne's husband, Captain Henry Mustin, had died in August, following a long illness caused by his heroic efforts to save a fellow seaman swept overboard at sea. As she was still in her widow's weeds and was leaving her three young boys behind, Corinne's decision to travel to Europe in the midwinter may have raised a few eyebrows among her family and friends. Paris also had the benefit of being out of sight of prying eyes, a place where she could make a start in the hunt for a prospective husband.

She thought 'Skinny' would be the ideal travelling companion and doubtless sensed that the best cure for Wallis's man trouble was to leave Washington for a time.

Wallis, still licking her wounds following her emotionally bruising love affair with Felipe, was enthusiastic, especially as she had heard that divorce in France was relatively cheap and straightforward. With only Win's allowance to support her, she realized that she could afford to pay for the trip only if Uncle Sol helped. During yet another uncomfortable interview in his New

York apartment – this time his customary rant focused on French morality – he palmed her five $100 notes to facilitate the journey.

Meanwhile, Courtney, her life running on parallel lines, had an easier time. Some months later her father, Frank, who doted on his eldest daughter, generously offered to send Courtney and her children, Homer and Louise, to Paris for a year, where she could divorce quietly, 'away from the publicity in the States'. She took an apartment at 8 rue Georges Ville near the Bois de Boulogne, hired a maid, enrolled for a correspondence course at the Sorbonne, and took art classes at the Louvre. The glorious year she spent in Paris was a 'cure for any continuing heartaches'. It would be some months before her path once more crossed with Wallis's.

For Wallis's part, Uncle Sol's largesse now made it possible for her to join her cousin on her great adventure. They booked a passage on board a former troop ship, the *President Garfield*, she and Corinne sharing a cabin on the rough crossing to France.

Their passports are something of a curiosity. Both women, who were vouched for by diplomat Stanley Hawk of the State Department, wore hats for their official photographs, Wallis confirming that she was indeed born on 19 June 1896 – contrary to various dates published after she became notorious – and gave her address as 2908 N St. NW, Washington, a pretty townhouse in Georgetown.

She listed her height as five feet four inches, her eyes blue, her nose straight, hair brown, chin square and her face oval, with a mole on the right side of her cheek as the only distinguishing mark. It seems they planned a more extensive visit to Europe, besides France listing Italy and Britain as other ports of call. On 9 January 1924, they embarked, arriving in Paris a week or so later in the middle of the night without a plan or – more importantly– a hotel room booking. It was not a good start.

They found themselves cheap lodgings and within a couple of days Corinne, rather conveniently, 'suddenly remembered a friend in Paris, a bachelor officer who had been a close friend of her husband'. In short order, Commander William 'Imp' Eberle, the assistant naval attaché to the American Embassy, had arranged to take the two castaways for dinner. With him was the tall, handsome, imposingly patrician figure of Harvard-educated Elbridge Gerry Greene, a member of a prominent and radical Boston family whose grandfather advocated interest-free banking. He had been at the American Embassy for nearly two years, arriving from a previous posting in Sofia, Bulgaria. 'That dinner proved the happiest kind of beginning,' Wallis recalled. 'We became a foursome.'

Greene and Eberle showed the girls a good time, taking them for motor rides outside Paris at weekends and wining and dining them in town. The memory of Espil began to fade just a little as Wallis enjoyed an uncomplicated, amusing relationship with a man two years her junior. That Gerry Greene was away from his desk so much entertaining Wallis did little to alter his reputation as a frivolous practitioner of the art of diplomacy. 'Indolent' was how a colleague described the lanky, bespectacled Bostonian.

Wallis rather than the embassy benefited from his attentions. 'We became quite fond of each other,' Wallis recalled. As the weeks turned to months, she remained confused about her feelings: whether to obtain a divorce and pursue Gerry or remain married to Spencer. 'I had not been able to make any definite plans for divorce and yet the present status of my marriage was of a past without a future.'

Fate now took control. When Corinne returned to America to see her family, Wallis decided to stay on in Paris, a decision made all the easier after the arrival of her boon companion Ethel Noyes, who needed to finalize her own divorce in order to marry Willmott Lewis. Spurred to review her own situation, Wallis was shocked to discover it would cost $5,000 if she wanted to finally free herself from Win.

While they had been separated for nearly three years, he had continued to write regularly, reminding her of the good times and suggesting a reconciliation. Now in command of a river patrol craft, USS *Pampanga*, in China, he invited her to join him in Hong Kong, where he was stationed. If she agreed, he could secure her a berth on board the USS *Chaumont*, which was sailing from Virginia in July at the start of a six-week voyage to the Philippines. Once there she would change ships for the final leg of the journey to Hong Kong.

At the same time, she learned from her lover Gerry Greene that he, too, was shortly to be transferred from Paris to Peking (Beijing) with a promotion to first secretary. Like Wallis, he would be sailing to the Orient sometime in July.

As she pondered her options, she knew that if the reconciliation with her husband didn't work out, Gerry was waiting in the wings. He had even promised to pay all her travel and accommodation if she made the journey from Hong Kong to Peking.

While she considered her future, her friend Ethel Noyes informed her that she was returning to America and offered to share the cost of her return trip. The fates were working overtime to send her sailing to the Far East.

While she was running with the Navy hares and diplomatic hounds, what Wallis did not realize was that her romantic rival, Courtney Letts, was also hovering. Before Wallis left Paris, Courtney Letts came for tea at the small Parisian apartment Gerry shared with fellow diplomat Harold Tittman, later ambassador to Peru. In pride of place on his polished wooden table was a framed photograph of the woman Courtney now knew as 'Wally Spencer'.

'You two look alike,' said Gerry, a refrain Courtney was becoming familiar with. Even with Wallis around, Greene began wooing Courtney, who was going through the expensive rigmarole of divorce.

In her secret diary she described her relationship with Gerry Greene: 'We became friends. I was in Paris divorcing. Six months later he asked me to marry him. He came to America where we met again. He sailed for China for his post in Peking. I refused to follow him. He went off, I thought sadly.' It seems that Greene was juggling two romances, courting both women that spring. He may have been lazy at work, but he was a busy young man romantically.

While the diplomat and the Navy wife sailed for China, Courtney headed back to her hometown of Chicago following the death of her father, Frank C. Letts, in May 1924. Here, in what subsequently proved to be an extraordinary and somehow prophetic encounter, Courtney, who had already enjoyed romantic liaisons with two men in Wallis's life, met her doppelgänger's future royal husband.

On the evening of 13 October 1924, Courtney found herself engrossed in conversation with the Prince of Wales, listening intently as he unburdened his soul. When they were not sharing intimate secrets, he was whisking her around the dance floor at the Saddle and Cycle Club on Chicago's fashionable Lake Shore Drive. Of all the women in the Windy City, it was Courtney who had been chosen to occupy the seat next to the son of King George V at a dinner held in his honour. Though his hostess, socialite and fashion maven Lucy Blair Linn, sat on the other side, the prince devoted most of his attention to Courtney, who was dressed to impress in a white Chanel chiffon gown she had bought just before leaving Paris.

That a newly divorced woman was seated next to the Prince of Wales was a sign of changing social mores.

Courtney, who brought a diarist's eye to her royal encounter, recalled that he 'had the charm of a restless, observant, appealing boy. He told me he had just turned thirty and was feeling old.' She continued: 'We talked and talked and talked about his life in England, about the deadly "boringnessy" of such endless ceremonials as laying corner stones and attending services.'

It was a familiar refrain, his 'woe is me' attitude quickly becoming his conversational shtick. He was not the first, nor the last, royal prince to complain about the special, excruciating boredom and predictability of the royal round, which was – and still is – an integral part of the job.

Besides his strangely appealing charm, her main impression, even on a brief acquaintance, coincided with the concerned opinions of his courtiers, his family and his close friends, who worried about the calibre of the character behind the smiling, effortlessly appealing public image.

Astutely, she described him as 'an unhappy man, perplexed, of a restless nature seeking madly for amusement, for pleasure snatched here and there between the official exigencies of his responsible state and the ever-present thought of the future, which as long as he might live he knew he could not try to escape. He even appeared to want forgetfulness in his moments of frivolity and escape.'

What she found the most shocking was his determination to drown his princely sorrows in alcohol, not eating a morsel of food throughout the evening. Instead he frequently asked the two footmen standing behind his chair to refill his glass with either champagne or wine. 'He dismayed and depressed me,' she recalled, noting that she had never seen a man consume so much alcohol.

'I cannot say truthfully that he was intoxicated. He knew better. But the spirits within him added to his strange, feverish, restless ways.'

While Courtney was the chosen one for the evening, she was not sufficiently engaged or starry-eyed to go beyond conversation and dancing. Others were. He did find a sexual conquest for the night, a woman who pursued him and won him in the garden. Courtney recorded the sequence of events in her private diary:

They danced most of the evening together. He ordered his train to New York delayed and when the time came he barely caught it. Photographers snapped him – with her – in the garden, but someone broke the [photographic] plate. The husband of the woman in red, who had openly bragged that afternoon that she would 'get him' and get him she did . . . appeared to be pleased. It was small wonder that others were heard to say, that night and for days and weeks afterwards, 'I always knew he had cheap taste. Imagine carrying on as he did with . . . her.'

It was indeed an amazing and undignified performance, and it is well known that he behaved in a similar manner in every American city he visited. Is it any wonder that Great Britain has not wanted its heir to the throne to return again to these shores because, so the excuse is given, of the way in which the press had treated him.

Her memory of that evening was accurate, the *Chicago Tribune* reporting that his train, which was due to depart from Polk Street station at 12:30 a.m., waited for a further three hours before steaming into what remained of the night.

The newspaper noted that the woman 'most favored' by the prince throughout the evening was Josephine Ordway, the wife of financier Lucius P. Ordway. She was 'a tall and sinuous beauty' with whom he danced many times.

It was the start of a fascinating long-distance relationship, Lucius and Josephine keeping in contact with the prince. 'Do let me know the next time you are in London,' he told them before he caught his train. And they did.

Two years later, when they were in Paris on holiday, it was reported that the prince had called Josephine several times from Biarritz, the fashionable French beach resort on the west coast, where he was on holiday. It was noted that the Ordways, who were visiting Britain for May and June, enjoyed a full diary in smart society circles because of her friendship with the prince.

A restless prince with his eyes trained on the western horizon, a vivacious married American, a compliant husband proud of his association with the future king. A pattern was emerging, his stopover in Chicago but a dress rehearsal for a captivating and dramatic performance that would astonish the world.

CHAPTER FOUR

'The World's Biggest Tease'

WALLIS'S ESTRANGED NAVY husband never really stood a chance. When he stood on the quayside in Hong Kong waiting for her liner, the white-hulled *Empress of Canada*, to dock in Hong Kong harbour in early September 1924, Lieutenant Commander Win Spencer represented the flotsam and jetsam of her past.

Within a matter of weeks he was – metaphorically speaking – washed overboard; Wallis sailing off to a brighter future, a convoy of suitors in her wake. In the three years since they had separated, Wallis was a changed woman. No longer the giddy ingénue, she had known passionate love and tasted the bitter tang of rejection, as well as the thrill of the chase and the conquest. Now twenty-eight, she was a fully paid-up woman of the world.

That Win was 'tanned, clear-eyed and charming' and assured her that he hadn't touched a drop of alcohol since she had agreed to see him again, mattered little. In her heart, her feelings towards him were stone dead.

As she later confessed:

Almost from the first minute I knew I was not going to find in China a new way of life – at least not with Win. He met me at the dock and we discovered that we were as far apart as we had ever been. Actually since each separation had left new scars and made each new start more difficult, we were farther apart. Time had taken too much of a toll on what feelings we still had left for each other, and although we did our artificial best it was no use.

In her memoir, however, she falsely describes their first few days together as an 'utterly satisfying second honeymoon'. She was being too kind to his memory. Within two weeks they were back in the old routine; he was drinking heavily, opening her mail and accusing her of carrying on with fellow officers and local men. In a further act of degradation, he forced her to accompany him to a local sing-song house or brothel, where he boasted he had spent some time. The consequences of her subsequent description of this visit would last a lifetime.

As she recalled: 'To his already formidable repertory of taunts and humiliations he now added some oriental variations. I gathered that during our long absence he had spent a considerable amount of his time ashore in the local sing-song houses. In any event, he now insisted on my accompanying him to his favorite haunts, where he would ostentatiously make a fuss over the girls.'

This mutated into the legend that Wallis worked in an oriental brothel and, under the sexual supervision of an American madam called Gracie Hale, studied the techniques that would pleasure even the most recalcitrant of men. Her skills, such as the 'Cleopatra clip', where it was said that she picked up a sovereign using this ancient sexual art, found their way into what became known as the China dossier. Supposedly the compendium of rumour and hearsay was eventually placed in front of Prime Minister Stanley Baldwin and King George V for their delectation and disapproval. Suffice to say, no such document has ever been discovered. Like so many stories of unbridled carnality that surround royal personages, it remains a deliciously unprovable urban legend. That Wallis had, by her own admission, men swarming around her, taking her out, giving her presents and paying for her stay, does rather imply that she had not the slightest need for any training in Hong Kong's sing-song houses.

What remains a continuing mystery is why on earth Wallis chose to describe her involuntary visit to a place where prostitutes operated, where opium was on offer, and where gambling and drinking were the norm. For a habitually discreet woman, who hid behind an impervious mask, it was a remarkably rash confession, one that came to haunt her.

For all Win's faults, Wallis stayed in his Navy-supplied apartment in Kowloon on the Chinese mainland for three months. She even followed his gunship, USS *Pampanga*, on patrol along the Pearl River from Hong Kong to Canton (Guangzhou). Since the collapse of the Qing imperial dynasty in 1911, China had been in the grip of sporadic conflicts between various warlords who were backed by Russian, Japanese and Anglo-American interests. As a reminder of the fighting, travellers would occasionally see the bloated bodies of Chinese soldiers floating down the Pearl River.

While on patrol, the *Pampanga*'s one six-pounder and three three-pound guns were constantly primed for action. Pirates were a constant threat, the gunboat's modified engine room was the heart of the ship and protected by heavy-gauge metal bars. As American ships did not allow women to sail with the crew, Wallis travelled on board a British vessel, eventually arriving at Shamian Island close by mainland Canton, a multinational domain administered by the British and French. A sign of the general unrest were the strategically placed machine gun emplacements and the rolls of barbed wire that surrounded the island.

Her own defences were raised when she discovered that Win was now drinking before breakfast. It was clear that she was married to an incorrigible alcoholic, and she felt that divorce was the only sensible option. She heard that in Shanghai, a thousand miles north, there was an international court where she could obtain a cheap divorce. Left unsaid was the fact that Shanghai was a thousand miles nearer to her paramour Gerry Greene and the American Legation in Peking. It was time to bid a final farewell to her husband.

He paid for her berth on a steamer bound for Shanghai, reluctantly accepting of her decision. As he bid her a friendly adieu on the gangway, he told her: 'Pensacola, Boston, Coronado, Washington, and now Hong Kong – we've come a long way, only to lose what we began with.'

She and her travelling companion, Mary Sadler, the wife of Rear Admiral Frank H. Sadler, arrived in the jostling cosmopolitan city of Shanghai in November 1924 and promptly took rooms in the Palace Hotel in Shanghai's International Settlement. The International Settlement, comprising some fifty thousand bankers, soldiers, diplomats and others from around the world, was a self-contained town within the sprawling city. It was not a place for the unwary; in the myriad streets, white slavery, brothels and street prostitution proliferated. According to an official census, in 1922 there were 124 registered courtesan houses and 401 courtesans.

The influx of White Russians who had fled their home country following the 1917 revolution merely added to the tumult and air of chaotic exile in a city where strikes, riots, boycotts and radical anti-foreignism were on the rise. Even the most self-absorbed visitor could not fail to sense the ugly underbelly of violence and lawlessness lurking in the crowded city streets. It was not a place to venture out alone, especially for an American woman. In a city that was an exotic panoply of sights, sounds and smells, the most striking and mysterious creatures of all were American women travelling without male escorts. Female emancipation during the Roaring Twenties had its limits.

As historian Craig Robertson observes: 'In those days it was not done. Travelling separately from your husband was very unusual. She would have attracted attention to herself as something of a curiosity.' Invested with an air of mystery and spice, Wallis very quickly realized that among the burgeoning male populations she was indeed a prized acquisition. As she recalled, somewhat lasciviously: 'I had now learned what to all women would be a most fascinating fact about China: the proportion of men to women, which must have been at least twenty to one. It is no exaggeration to say that an American girl could have had an engagement every hour if she had wished. Accordingly I decided to avail myself of such favorable odds.'

She had arrived in Shanghai with a letter of introduction to a man she called 'Robbie', probably the north London-born architect Harold Robinson. She sent him a note and he responded with a basket of exotic fruit. For the next few weeks he squired her around the enclave, taking her to cocktail parties, the Shanghai Race Club, and dancing at the sunken courtyard of the Majestic Hotel on Bubbling Well Road.

Her visit coincided with the opening of various new cabaret venues, which were a welcome alternative to the stuffy men-only Shanghai Club and sedate tea dances at the Astor House Hotel. Wallis was not slow in availing herself of these exciting new places, her escorts being invariably British businessmen who, she came to realize, played as hard as they worked. Though always in demand, she discovered, too, the attentions paid her were not always honourable. As she recalled: 'Men were hungry for unattached women there, and that made you think a lot how attractive it was to be alone, though all these men's intentions were not so attractive.'

Her own marital business had run into another financial cul-de-sac. As in Paris, divorce in Shanghai was wildly expensive, way beyond her means. Though life in Shanghai was 'good, very good', she needed to explore her options with Gerry Greene, who was pining for her nine hundred miles north in the American Legation in Peking.

Somewhat preposterously and improbably, she stated in her memoir that she agreed to a friend's suggestion to go on a shopping trip to Peking. At first, second and third glance, the very idea was foolhardy. At that time, two factions were duking it out for control of Chinese Peking in what became known as the Second Zhili–Fengtian War.

Travel to and from the capital city was fraught with danger, trains regularly stopped and ransacked or fired on or both. In the autumn of 1924, when Wallis proposed to undertake this shopping trip, the US State Department was concerned about the safety of these trains.

It has been suggested, primarily by biographer Charles Higham, that the real reason why Wallis, a nervous and superstitious traveller at the best of times, embarked on such a dangerous journey was that she was a courier secretly recruited in Washington and charged with delivering highly classified documents to the American Legation in Peking. Given that it took a leisurely six months or so for Wallis to reach Peking from Washington, this was, by any standards, a remarkably amateurish way of conducting diplomacy. This theory was first inspired by Wallis's decision to renew her passport in July 1924, only six months after it was first issued. Her official sponsor was Harry W. Smith, a senior figure in Naval Intelligence. Armed with this new special document she now had official clearance to act as a courier for the American government.

Like many stories surrounding Wallis, it is a myth. As American passport historian Craig Robertson explains, in those days, passports were regularly issued for single trips, and a special passport was usually supplied to someone associated with government business, such as a diplomat's wife or a member of a delegation.

Of course, the real reason for her decision to embark on such a perilous journey had nothing to do with shopping or spying; it was men. After all, the besotted Gerry Greene, described by Courtney Letts as being like 'clay' in the hands of a woman like Wallis, had gallantly offered to pay for her expenses to come to Peking.

The trip was as dangerous and nerve-racking as predicted. First she and her friend took a ferry to Tientsin (Tianjin), barely surviving a storm that threatened to capsize the ship. They were then scheduled to board a train for the perilous overland journey to Peking. Before they left, the American consul in Tientsin officially placed them on notice that the train was likely to be attacked because of the war and that they could be taken hostage. If so, they would be outside the protection of the American government.

At this, Wallis's companion blanched and decided to stay put. Her husband would not have approved. Wallis took a chance. For a woman whose superstitions ranged from fear of peacock feathers and aeroplane flight to thunderstorms, it was a remarkably bold and uncharacteristic decision, inspired by the prospect of seeing Gerry Greene again.

On the journey she found herself sitting opposite an overweight American who introduced himself as Eddie Mills. He worked for the Salt Gabell, a historically important government-run commodity and taxation operation, and became, in Wallis's parlance, one of her 'intimate friends', a favourite among her many beaux. On the journey his unflappable demeanour helped calm her misgivings, especially during the frequent impromptu halts when bandits swarmed through the carriages. She arrived in one piece, though she was met at the station by Colonel Louis Little, the head of the Legation Guards, who gave her a personal dressing-down for her folly.

Once ensconced in the Grand Hôtel de Pékin in the Legation Quarter, Wallis was able to soak up the myriad sights and sounds of the Chinese capital, a walled city where the gates were closed at dusk, giving a sense of separation from the outside world.

Like Shanghai, Peking was a lively international city with a large diplomatic and business community as well as wealthy tourists, particularly Americans, who bought houses in the city to enjoy the exotic cosmopolitan society. For the first year in the city, a foreigner was called a 'griffin', named after races involving Mongolian ponies. Wallis duly became a griffin.

The social life of Peking in the 1920s has probably never been bettered, with lavish parties, duck and goose hunting in the autumn, spring race meetings held at Pao Ma Chang, or polo played on the protective Legation Quarter glacis – an esplanade surrounding the legation. The hub of the community was undoubtedly the Peking Club, which boasted tennis and badminton courts, a swimming pool, an ice-skating rink and two golf courses, as well as a ballroom and restaurants.

Many foreigners, including Americans, flocked to China because the moral code was looser and less disapproving than in their homeland. Unlike in Prohibition America, they could eat, drink and be merry. Add into the mix hundreds of available single men and married men on their own, and here was a ready-made recipe for sexual shenanigans and freewheeling behaviour. A version of the Jazz Age with an oriental twist – and a splash of soda.

Typical of the carefree frivolity of Peking was Lady Bredon, the seventy-year-old widow of the former inspector general of Chinese customs. She lived in regal style in the palace of a former Manchurian prince. One day she arrived at a reception with her arm in a sling. Solicitously, American diplomat Lewis Clark asked how she had hurt herself. Gaily she replied: 'Colonel Love swore to me that his wife was in Tientsin, but she came back unexpectedly and I broke my arm jumping out of the window!'

Her sexual exploits paled by comparison with the outlandish lifestyle of Constance Crowninshield Coolidge, the wife of American diplomat Ray Atherton, a man whose stellar career began in Peking during the early 1920s and resulted in him becoming the first American ambassador to Canada. Known by one of her many lovers, Harry Crosby, as the 'Queen of Peking', she was a thrill-seeker who loved gambling, sex and horse-racing. Tall, graceful, slim and charismatic, she was an exotic and very wealthy thoroughbred raised from generations of upstanding Boston Brahmins. The writer Speed Lamkin later described this early trustafarian as being 'touched by a divine fire'.

Others named her 'The Lady of the Golden Horse with the Diamond Eyes', a woman with an inexhaustible appetite for new thrills, new places and new relationships. She lived in a temple, rode cross-country on horseback, inadvertently went into battle, and was a passenger in a plane that performed one of the first loop-the-loops ever seen on mainland China. Her Chinese ponies, named 'Why Not' and 'If Not', represented this approach to life.

By the time she was forty she'd had at least twenty marriage proposals, several dozen lovers and four husbands, leaving behind a trail of broken hearts, including that of novelist H. G. Wells. During her time in Peking she enjoyed a very public liaison with English diplomat Eric Brenan, who wrote her endless poetry and then threatened suicide when her ardour cooled.

In such a tight-knit community it was inevitable that Wallis would eventually pay homage to the 'Queen of Peking'. Constance dates their first encounter to her time in the walled city, Constance becoming one of Wallis's closest friends, an outsize character who stayed by her side before, during and after the abdication.

They were very different personalities: Constance inquisitive, curious and adventurous, grabbing life by the lapels; Wallis cautious and somewhat conventional. Both, though, shared the ability to command a room and captivate a dinner table. Like Constance, Wallis had her fair share of men professing undying love and devotion. Typically, her first response to the bewildering sights and sounds of Peking was not about the language, the culture, the temples or the vibrant street scenes but the availability of men. She noted: 'There are no extra women in Peking and must be a thousand extra men. So of course it didn't make any difference if you had a harelip, you were a belle in Peking. So I had a marvellous time.' For her, Peking was a place where every woman was a Cinderella and midnight never struck.

First on the scene was Gerry Greene, who appeared with two Tibetan terriers, one for Wallis, which she named Gaga, the other for himself, which was christened Whiskey. The American first secretary took her to dances, cocktail parties and all the other social events in the crowded diplomatic calendar.

She was quite the character, as diplomat Lynn Winterdale Franklin, the newly appointed consul for Hong Kong, described when he encountered her at a luncheon at the American Legation. Just as Lynn and his wife, Butler, were arriving, another rickshaw pulled up behind them and out stepped a 'charming' American girl, 'very simply dressed, just a little shirtwaist and skirt, and holding a lovely piece of silk'. She waved in acknowledgement to Lynn, who said: 'Oh, how do you do, Mrs Spencer.' After they met their host, Gerry Greene, Lynn took his wife aside and whispered: 'Dear, I don't want you to have anything to do with that woman.'

In the days when separation and divorce were not taken at all lightly, Franklin, who was raised in Virginia, took a dim view of Wallis. She was a woman with a reputation, his attitude only confirmed by his harrowing encounter in Hong Kong several weeks earlier with the man he described as 'that poor fellow', Lieutenant Commander Spencer.

Clearly heartbroken, Win had sought an interview with the new consul, during which he confessed: 'I couldn't bring Wally here to stay in these dreadful little hotels. They love her in Peking, she's fun and she's doing the embassy good, so I won't ask her to come back.' Then he burst into tears before going off to drink himself into a stupor. Franklin told his wife: 'It was the most pathetic thing I'd ever seen.'

As far as Wallis was concerned, Win was well out of sight and mind. She was the life and soul at that lunch, regaling the assembled throng with a story about how one of the American diplomats, presumably Greene, had tried to teach her to drive and she had managed to hit a wall. As Butler later recalled: 'She kept everyone laughing.'

She was amusing herself with more suitors than the infatuated Mr Greene. Wallis vigorously played the field, dating eligible bachelors ranging from dashing Army officers to diplomats from the Norwegian and Italian Embassies. A special favourite was Alberto da Zara, a handsome blond naval attaché to the Italian Embassy.

Descended from a line of cavalry officers, he was a poet, linguist and horseman who seemed, understandably, to have little enthusiasm for the role of naval attaché in a nation without a recognizable navy. Though he was eventually promoted to admiral, his true passion was horses, and he described in his memoir how one of the most frequent spectators at the Peking horse shows of 1925 was Wallis Spencer. 'In those days she wore a classical hairdo which fitted the beauty of her forehead and eyes,' he recalled. Da Zara, who never married, always carried a signed black-and-white photograph of Wallis wherever he was posted, a reflection of what his aide in China, Lieutenant Giuseppe Pighini, described as a 'very close relationship from which love developed into a lasting friendship'.

Probably through da Zara, Wallis was introduced to the dashing and glamorous Italian aristocrat Count Galeazzo Ciano, the playboy son of a First World War hero. Although seven years younger than her, the young diplomat became very attached to the separated American, even though their encounter was brief. Long after Wallis had returned to America, Ciano, who later became Mussolini's son-in-law and foreign minister, served for a time as Italian consul in Shanghai. In popular mythology, however, her casual relationship with Ciano morphed into an affair while she, too, was in Shanghai, and she became pregnant. Wallis, fearful for her reputation and her prospects of ever remarrying, procured an abortion which, according to legend, was so badly mishandled that she was never able to have children. That neither party was in Shanghai at the same time is rather lost in the shuffle. Myth trumps reality every time.

There was also, according to journalism professor Parry D. Sorensen, a mysterious unnamed Chinese official who had an affair with Wallis and then subsequently tried to blackmail her when her romance with Edward VIII went public. Given the fact that during her 'Lotus Year', Wallis made little or no effort to meet any Chinese people – men or women – and exhibited a distinct lack of interest in Chinese customs, conversation or culture, this tale seems unlikely.

For the most part, her male friends were American, notably Gerry Greene, Colonel Louis Little, and her train companion, businessman Eddie Miles. When she added up her various beaux, she reckoned that half a dozen men paid court during her stay. For all the excited and often implausible chatter about her many lovers, her abortion and her training in exotic sexual techniques, what is true is that during her stay in China Wallis met the most significant man in her life.

As in all the best romances, their eyes met across a crowded room. Or rather, she saw her old friend Katherine Moore Bigelow from her days at Coronado as she was dancing with her partner, Gerry Greene, in the ballroom of the Grand Hôtel de Pékin, where Wallis had been staying for the previous three months. As Wallis described the moment: 'We recognized each other instantaneously. In that telegraphic manner peculiar to women, we succeeded in communicating to each other, in the instant of mutual rediscovery, the essential facts about each other: that Win and I were separated and that she had remarried. A moment later her husband, Herman Rogers, came up, an unusually attractive man, with a lean, handsome face, brown wavy hair, and the bearing and look of an athlete.'

Which indeed he was. Herman was a keen swimmer and diver, an excellent polo player, and also an outstanding oarsman who in 1919 captained the American Army rowing team in the Inter-Allied Games in Paris and at the Henley Royal Regatta.

By birth, bearing and behaviour he was to all intents and purposes an American aristocrat, a cultured and sophisticated man who pursued beauty and spiritual enlightenment as vigorously as he played polo. He was five years older than Wallis, and his father, Archibald, was a wealthy railroad director who owned a mansion, Crumwold, on the Hudson River in Dutchess County, New York. Their immediate neighbours were the Roosevelt family. Sara Delano Roosevelt was Herman's godmother and Franklin Delano Roosevelt a childhood playmate and school friend of Herman's older brother, Edmund. He attended Groton School and then Yale, graduating in 1914 as a member of Phi Beta Kappa.

During his time there he was tapped to join the Skull and Bones secret society, the nesting place for future politicians, judges, diplomats and media barons. He briefly studied civil engineering at the Massachusetts Institute of Technology before signing up for service when America entered the war in April 1917. Commissioned as a captain, he was promoted to major and commanded the Second Battalion, 10th Field Artillery, seeing action on the Meuse-Argonne line in France.

It was while he was on his way to the front on board a troop train that he first set eyes on his future wife. At that time Katherine, the daughter of a doctor from Colorado Springs, was working as a Red Cross nurse, doling out coffee and cookies to soldiers on the platform of Amiens railway station in northern France. He was smitten by the sight of the tall blonde with an easy grin and dimples to match. 'That's the girl I am going to marry if I survive the war,' he told a fellow officer.

At the time, though, she was married to Ernest Bigelow, the son of a commercial lawyer. It was a curious union, the couple marrying in January 1916 and then six months later Katherine, her sister Constance, and her mother, Alma, sailing to Paris, where her stepfather, Commander William Randall Sayles, had been appointed naval attaché to the American Embassy. She and her sister promptly enrolled in the Red Cross and Katherine never saw unhappy Ernest, who died of tuberculosis in May 1919, ever again.

Fate was indeed taking a hand in shaping the future of the newly widowed Katherine. In the summer of 1920 she was invited to a cocktail party in Manhattan, which was also attended by Herman, now the manager of a New York engineering company. They got to talking, and during their conversation she brightly identified herself as the nurse whom he had vowed to marry one day. It did not take long for Herman to pop the question: their engagement was announced on 14 September 1920, followed ten weeks later by their wedding at the chapel of St Bartholomew's Church in New York on 27 November. They travelled to Honolulu in Hawaii for a lengthy honeymoon.

Once married, Herman gave up tinkering with civil engineering, he and Katherine packing their bags to explore the world. First they stayed in Florence before travelling to the East. 'I don't know who they are but they are very good looking and attractive,' Constance Coolidge wrote to her grandmother when they first arrived. They eventually met and, as with Wallis, became the fastest of friends.

During their early days in Peking, Herman believed that their globetrotting experiences could be distilled into the great American novel or a work of philosophy. These literary ambitions remained unfulfilled, though he did write a detective story set in New York, which has yet to be published. When Wallis met them in Peking they were enjoying their second visit to the capital, the couple living in a house in Tartar City, near the Hatamen Gate, one of the many gates in the city. They had carved out a very civilized, aesthetic life, taking daily lessons in Mandarin from their teacher, the goatee-bearded Mr Wu Wen Ming, reading out loud from an improving work or practising the techniques of Herman's newfangled toy, a cine camera. Then of course there was swimming, and the games of poker and polo, to break up the many and varied intellectual pursuits Herman dabbled in.

After the Rogers had further sized up Wallis over luncheon, somewhat impulsively Katherine asked her to join them as their house guest. At first she politely refused but after three months of living in a small hotel room and with the prospect of servants and space, she was soon persuaded. Given Wallis's penchant for flirting with other men and taking what was someone else's, Katherine's invitation was rather brave and potentially risky. As Wallis's biographer Charles Murphy observed: 'After all, he [Herman] was exactly the kind of man for whom her Baltimore breeding had prepared her; patrician, well-to-do, handsome, cultivated, generous, and at ease in whatever milieu chance placed him.'

During her six-month stay she proved herself an amiable and amusing companion and friend. For her it was 'the most delightful, the most carefree and the most lyric interval of my youth'. Their lives were a study in genteel idleness and self-indulgence. As Wallis admitted: 'The life I led was one of complete uselessness.' Every morning before breakfast the trio went horseback riding on the glacis. After a leisurely breakfast they often swam in the American Legation pool, played tennis, watched polo or went sightseeing.

Wallis loved to shop, and she and Katherine would go to the various artificer streets, such as Silver Street, Flower Street, Furniture Street, Jade Street and others, where Wallis would have clothes made to measure or would add to her growing collection of jade. A favourite store was the Clock Shop, which did not sell clocks but was where she bought silks, linens and other materials, often borrowing dresses and other clothes from newly arrived visitors so that their up-to-date style could be copied. She also loved to wander through the travelling weekly fairs. On one occasion she was thrilled to buy a coral necklace for thirty cents, bartering the stallholder down from his opening price of thirty dollars. When she arrived home she discovered that the coral was red-painted dough and the thread made from human hair. Undaunted, when the trio went to an amateur camel race, Wallis was so enamoured by these bad-tempered but hardy creatures that she wanted to buy one and race it herself.

For the first few weeks, out of politeness, Wallis joined her hosts at their Chinese lessons but soon dropped out. 'Wallis would come but wouldn't stick at it as she never does with anything,' noted Herman, who realized that for all her bright banter and beguiling personality she was a lazy woman, never truly wanting to test herself, happy to remain within her own comfort zone. She was as impatient with Chinese language and culture as she had been with golf when Win had tried to teach her.

While they worked on their language skills, she would take an afternoon nap before dressing for dinner. Then her rickshaw boy would transport her to the homes of friends, parties at the various legations, or for dinner at a Chinese restaurant.

Or the trio would stay at home and entertain, usually rounding the evening off with a card game. Gerry Greene was a regular visitor, as too was the Belgian ambassador, who had reason to regret his first encounter with Wallis. In a late-night poker game he lost $225 – the equivalent of Win's monthly allowance.

At weekends the threesome and a gaggle of friends travelled to the Black Dragon Temple in the Western Hills, which Herman had rented. There they enjoyed cooking in the open air, meditating, and exploring the many deserted temples and other religious ruins.

As part of this sybaritic lifestyle, Wallis was a very welcome addition to the household – witty, amusing and gay. Her personality perhaps reminded Katherine, who was friendly yet somewhat reticent, of her young sister Constance, a bubbly extrovert who harboured ambitions to go on the stage. Her mother, Alma, who joined them for an extended stay in early 1925, may have agreed. Whereas Katherine was 'very ladylike' and quiet, 'Wally' would play the fool, dressing in a kimono and adopting the pose of popular American comedian Fanny Brice for Herman's camera or chatting gaily into the lens when she returned from a polo match.

Wallis was a character. No doubt about that. Complex, contradictory and coquettish – 'the world's biggest tease' was Herman's settled judgement – whose saucy, knowing wisecracks left many a beau wanting more. 'Chase me, I'll run slowly' was a familiar phrase, as was 'You come too close, you go too far.'

By degrees, Wallis subtly altered the marital dynamic between Herman and Katherine. This was not a sexual *ménage à trois* – none of the threesome seemed to be especially sexual animals – more of an exchange of power. When Wallis arrived at their home she was virtually penniless and was dependent on their largesse, Katherine taking her on shopping trips to have clothes made or altered. By the end of her stay Wallis was sending Herman off to buy her stockings and underwear. It was an exercise in control. As Felipe Espil had discovered, Wallis was a dominating personality, with a temper to match.

'She could make me do anything,' Herman later admitted, somewhat ruefully. Perhaps his attraction to strong women lay in his family background. His older brothers were like Herman, quiet, civilized and reticent. His sisters were formidable characters, strong-willed and authoritative. Even though Herman's sister Nellie Schley was confined to a wheelchair, she was still able to run a thousand-acre New Jersey farm, barking out orders to the men from the veranda of her house.

Wallis managed to get under Herman's skin in a way that this quiet, serious-minded man found surprising. She added the spice to Katherine's steady, dependable character. For all her faults, he found himself somewhat enamoured, their relationship that of the teacher and his precocious student, or brother and rambunctious younger sister. At sunset Herman and Wallis would walk together along the parapet wall overlooking the city, perhaps watching a camel train hastening to enter the city before dusk. During their walks, Herman tried to educate his pupil, pointing out features of historic interest. As far as Wallis was concerned, Herman was accessible but unobtainable; she recognized that the couple lived by the 'highest ideals' and that they were very happy together. Too bad. In Herman she had found her ideal man.

She carefully alluded to the sexual tension between them in her memoir, her autobiography notable for what she doesn't say and for obscuring the truth of her life.

Wallis described how Herman would often read to the two women in his life, one book in particular posing a moral dilemma that the threesome thoughtfully discussed. The quandary, as Wallis described it, was 'whether a wife who had been momentarily and bewilderingly unfaithful should tell her husband of her slip from grace. Katherine and Herman prided themselves on being modern and sophisticated; they held that relations between the sexes should be based on forthrightness and candour; that the old conventions had become hopelessly outmoded; and that any intelligent relationship must take into account the human drives and foibles.'

Given that, at the time, it was gossiped abroad that they were involved in a curious *ménage à trois*, it is as if she is trying to tell us something, confessing, obliquely, to an affair with Herman. As with her visit to the sing-song house, she had no need to raise the questions posed by a long-forgotten novel. Herman himself asserted that Wallis much preferred to talk about sex than perform the act. 'It never occurred to him that Wallis may have fallen in love with him,' observed Charles Murphy.

THIS IDYLLIC LIFESTYLE was rudely shattered on 30 May 1925, when the Shanghai police, who were led by British officers, fired on a peaceful pro-nationalist march, killing and wounding dozens of demonstrators. What became known as the Nanjing Road Incident in turn inspired the May Thirtieth Movement, an anti-imperialist, pro-nationalist uprising that made life very uncomfortable for the expat community throughout China, including Peking. Many Chinese servants walked out on their overseas masters, Chinese shopkeepers refused to cater for foreigners, especially the British, while gangs of students and others roamed the streets harassing and beating the hated *laowai*.

The American ambassador tasked First Secretary Greene with the role of leading a fact-finding mission on behalf of American interests, to investigate the causes underlying the bloody incident.

He and his fellow diplomats spent time in Shanghai, his subsequent report earning him 'high commendation' for its intelligence and thoroughness. It marked the end of any dalliance he enjoyed with Wallis, and four years later, in 1929, Greene returned to his Boston family roots, marrying a 'sharp-tongued' Back Bay girl, Ruth Thayer. He left the diplomatic service in 1935 before trying stockbroking with mixed success.

The unrest throughout the country matched the tumult in Wallis's heart. She had been away from America for a year, had had a marvellous few months in Peking and Shanghai but was no nearer making sense of her future and no closer to divorcing Win.

With a thousand kisses and promises to see each other soon, Wallis said goodbye to Herman and Katherine in early September 1925, not realizing until she had gone how much she would miss them, particularly Herman. His was a friendship that would endure. In her coy way she observed: 'From my experience with Herman Rogers alone, there is truth in the saying that friends made in China always remain friends.'

With fewer regrets she also left her Tibetan terrier, Gaga, in the care of the Rogers, before heading to Japan on the first leg of her journey back to Washington. Typically, the incorrigible Mrs Spencer disembarked in Yokohama, Japan, because of a man. Or rather men. 'I had a beau,' she recalled. She took a train to Tokyo when she was reunited with her male friend, whose name is lost in the mists of address books. 'We went sightseeing. In fact there were two or three men I knew there. That's why I stopped off.' As she sailed on to the United States on board the *President McKinley* she became seriously ill with an 'internal ailment' that left the shipboard doctor puzzled and Wallis needing an operation when the ship docked in Seattle. This mystery operation has often been connected with her ambiguous gynaecological condition. She was well enough to travel east from Seattle, Win waiting for her in

Chicago, where he took her to see his family in Highland Park. Wallis spent a few days there recuperating.

Win, sober and courteous, then accompanied his wife on the final leg of her journey to her mother's apartment in Washington. It was the last act of a man of simple needs and standards who, try as he might, loved the bottle rather more than he ever loved his wife.

She arrived back in Washington to discover that her mother had at last found happiness at the third attempt: she was going to marry a distinguished-looking widower, Charles Gordon Allen, who had a son named Bounce and his own home. With characteristic wit her mother announced that she was firmly on her last lap.

As for Wallis, now in her thirtieth year, she had yet to begin the race.

CHAPTER FIVE

Wallis Stole My Man

W ALLIS'S WANDERING DAYS were over. At least for the time being. After sailing around the globe in the vain search for a divorce, the Baltimore girl discovered to her 'astonishment' that she could obtain one in the neighbouring state of Virginia, ancestral home to the Montague side of her family, for the princely sum of $300.

Though naturally there were hoops to jump through. She had to produce a letter from Win stating that he no longer wished to live with her, be separated from him for three years, and live in Virginia for two years. In order to fast-track the proceedings so that she would be free by late 1927, Win would have to backdate his letter of separation. He went along with the scheme, which was clearly collusive, dating his letter to June 1924, when he was first assigned to the Far East. His letter ticked all the relevant boxes: *'I have come to the definite conclusion that I can never live with you again. During the past two years since I have been away from you I have been happier than ever before. Please be kind enough not to annoy me with any more letters. Yours, Win.'*

That settled, she now had to establish residency, choosing to stay in the Warren Green Hotel in the leafy town of Warrenton, just twenty-four miles from her cousin Corinne at Wakefield Manor and a short train journey to Washington. Before moving into her new abode, she visited her mother to pack up her belongings. Alice was now finally reconciled to Wallis proceeding with her divorce. 'If you and Win can't get on, there's no sense in your trying to pretend that you can,' she commented.

Not that she was especially keen on her daughter spending a year living alone in a country hotel. She offered to travel with her and spend a few days helping to get her settled. Wallis declined, saying: 'Nothing could possibly happen to me in Warrenton. From what I hear about the Warren Green Hotel, it would be a proper place for a bishop's daughter.'

Her mother, who usually had the last word, replied: 'Perhaps so, but you are no bishop's daughter.'

'I shall conduct myself as if I were one,' Wallis said. 'Besides, like Moses I am going into the wilderness to reflect.'

She was certainly travelling to a social wilderness, swapping the bright lights of Paris and the delights of Peking, the dinners, the dances and the beaux, for room number 212, a miserly fifteen-by-twelve-foot chamber, and a shared bathroom. Her temporary home was decorated with 'faded flowered wallpaper, a high brass bed, battered night table, imitation mahogany bureau . . . a classic example of what my mother used to call "inferior decorating"'. Hardly the suite of rooms and servants she enjoyed with the Rogers.

The days of chatting with ambassadors, antiquarians and military attachés were now distant memories. Instead she was on nodding acquaintance over breakfast with harassed men carrying attaché cases, travelling salesmen who formed the bulk of the hotel's weekly trade. As she recalled: 'For a woman seeking a divorce, the price also included the prospect of being voluntarily buried alive for two years.'

She did, though, make new friends and renew acquaintances, her circle including former school friends from Arundel and Oldfields; a one-time crush called Lloyd Tabb, her first boyfriend from the Burrlands summer camp; fashion designer Jane Derby; and – remarkably – Dr Miles Lewis Allen, the physician who delivered her.

'On the whole, my first year at Warrenton was the most tranquil I have ever known,' recalled the party girl who had spent her twenties obeying the rallying cry of poet Edna St Vincent Millay and had burned the candle at both ends. 'I simply rusticated, and when I wasn't rusticating, I vegetated with equal satisfaction.'

Short of transport, she was taken in tow by an old beau, Hugh Spilman, who squired her around in his old three-pedal rattling flivver. Then working as a lowly $125-a-week teller at the Fauquier National Bank, he introduced her to the horsey set, played golf with her on a nine-hole course, and played poker late into the night. She was, he duly reported, a bad-tempered loser.

Young Spilman, though, was besotted. 'I was pretty crazy about her even though she was an awful little flirt,' he recalled. Of course, Spilman was simply not in her league, so when he finally screwed up the courage to ask her to marry him, her refusal reflected realism rather than romance. 'You're poor, I'm poor, and we both need money,' she told him.

Later she told her friends that she would have married Hugh 'if he knew how to read anything besides the *Daily Racing Form*'. While Spilman was devoted to racing guides, the intellectual runners and riders in Wallis's world, so she claimed, were novels by F. Scott Fitzgerald, Sinclair Lewis, Somerset Maugham and Ford Madox Ford. For someone who boasted that she never read a book all the way through, Wallis was also, according to her account, busily declaiming poetry and wrestling with the history of philosophy. One book particularly captured her attention. Unusually for her, Wallis read it from beginning to end.

This was *The Passing of the Great Race*, a bestseller written by lawyer and eugenicist Madison Grant, who argued for scientific racism, asserting the superiority of the Nordic, or what the Nazis would call the Aryan, race. Jews, the Chinese, people of colour, Roman Catholics, even the French all failed the eugenic test of racial superiority. As part of his overarching argument, Grant supported the sterilization of 'undesirables' and 'worthless race types' in order to reinvigorate the dominant Nordic ethnic group. Such was the impact of Grant's thinking on the then-unknown German political rabble-rouser Adolf Hitler that he wrote to the author saying that his book had become his 'Bible'.

Like thousands of her fellow white Protestant Americans, Wallis subscribed to Grant's thesis. She was from a class, an age and a region where, quite unselfconsciously, Wallis and her friends, including Mary Kirk, were nonchalantly racist. Unsurprising given that her family were one-time slave owners who considered the local black population to be at the bottom of the social pyramid, unworthy of the franchise. In letters and table talk she casually referred to people of colour as 'niggers', 'coons' or 'darkies'. Indeed, it was not until the Second World War, when Wallis was based in the Bahamas, that she first shook the hand of a person of colour.

In correspondence, Wallis and her friends would refer to someone as 'a Jew', in a way that was not so much personally disdainful as indicating their place in the social pecking order as someone not of the first rank. On one occasion, for instance, she wrote to her aunt Bessie, describing how her friend, diplomat Martin 'Mike' Scanlon, had married a woman who could not bring herself to 'marry the rich Jew' and so had accepted Scanlon's offer instead.

During the 1920s what was known as 'polite discrimination' towards Jewish people was a growing feature of American life. At that time Jews were barred from numerous social clubs and societies, such as golf clubs and the Freemasons, discriminated against in employment, particularly for white-collar jobs, prevented from visiting some resorts, and subject to a quota system at Ivy League and other colleges. Like others of her class, Wallis's automatic social reflex was anti-Semitic, a mindset that played an important part in the next phase of her life.

From time to time Wallis left her books, newspapers and magazines behind and travelled to Washington to see her mother or to New York to stay with Mary Kirk and her husband, Jacques Raffray, at their charming apartment in Washington Square.

Like many of Wallis's girlfriends, Mary was keen to see her friend happy, settled and married once again. She had visited Wallis in Warrenton and appreciated Wallis's need to get out of Dodge. The matchmaker in her believed that once her divorce was finalized, Wallis should marry again as soon as possible. She was now thirty, and the clock was ticking – for her looks, her chance of starting a family and of achieving financial security. Whenever Wallis arrived to stay, Mary would always ensure that a possible suitor was lined up to be given the once-over. Mary was, as her younger sister, Anne, remarked, a 'useful friend'.

In the winter of 1925, Mary and her husband were guests of Ernest Simpson and his wife, Dorothea, at the opera. For some reason, Jacques had to drop out. Mary contacted the Simpsons and asked if a friend of hers who had recently returned from China could take his place. Enter Wallis. Her first impressions of her host were of a man who seemed too serious, but upon second glance she noticed his twinkling blue eyes and mischievous smile. That he was of Jewish descent did not feature in the description of that first fateful encounter in a chain of events that was to rock an empire.

At Christmas that year, the Simpsons were invited to a party at the Raffrays' apartment. Wallis was there, too, and clearly made a favourable impression on Dorothea, who later recalled: 'She was witty and clever, far cleverer than I. She made any party something special.' Wallis and Dorothea, though, were like night and day:

Dorothea was diffident, withdrawn and prone to illness, Wallis the life and soul of any gathering.

At first Dorothea didn't see her as a threat, even though Wallis had clearly caught the eye of her husband. Ernest, a year older than Wallis, was always happy to come over to the Raffrays' to make up a fourth for an evening of bridge. From time to time he would partner with Mrs Spencer, and slowly but surely the Wallis magic, her ability to mesmerize a man by focusing her burning blue eyes on what he was saying, seemed to be working. In their conversations she appreciated his wonderful mind, which was 'playful and good humoured', but he also exhibited a curiosity about the world which she found stimulating and rather sexy. Ernest, who won a poetry prize at school, was always ready to declaim a stanza or two and had the knack of making up rhyming couplets for any social occasion. 'Well read and very sure of himself,' was the verdict of Clare Boothe Brokaw (later Clare Boothe Luce), then an editor of *Vanity Fair*, who attended one of the Raffrays' parties.

The sly, unstated chemistry that existed between the married man and the eager, unattached woman exploded that Easter of 1926. After attending the traditional Sunday parade, Ernest and a fellow Guards officer arrived at the Raffrays', bursting with bonhomie and bright smiles after enjoying the hospitality of various New York hostesses. They were, according to Mary's sister Anne, 'the souls of amiability and glamour, and they brought the odors of fresh spring flowers with them'.

Wallis was ready to pick the bloom. Anne continued: 'There, all ready with her open arms, was Wallis, with her heart on her sleeve, and seemingly saying to Ernest: "You are a gallant Knight on a White Charger, coming to rescue me from the wicked world of poverty and oblivion where most of my friends go, never to return to the bright life of fame!" I can see her beautiful blue eyes now and her square hands clawing the air in ecstasy.'

She certainly had her talons directed at Ernest, a man who was, to all intents and purposes, Herman Rogers Lite. Like Herman, he had gone to an Ivy League college – Harvard rather than Yale – was a competent linguist, was interested in foreign cultures and was widely travelled; during his school summer holidays his father took him to Britain and Continental Europe. Unlike Herman, Ernest had a full-time job, working at his father's shipping company, Simpson, Spence & Young, which had offices in London and New York.

His nationality was similarly split; his father, also Ernest, was from a Jewish family, the Solomons, originating from Warsaw in Poland. Ernest Sr became a naturalized American citizen shortly after he arrived in New York in 1873. An Anglophile to his fingertips, he was thrilled when his daughter Maud, twenty years older than Ernest Jr, married a prominent British Member of Parliament, Peter Kerr-Smiley.

By contrast, Ernest's mother, Charlotte, the daughter of a well-connected New York lawyer, was hostile to the Old World, found the French dishonest and the English dull. If Wallis had the conflicting characteristics of the Montagues and Warfields in her make-up, so Ernest enjoyed – and endured – the push and pull of his joint American and British heritage.

In the midst of the First World War, Ernest finally decided where his true loyalties lay. He abandoned his studies at Harvard and sailed for England, believing that it was his patriotic duty to fight for king and the country of his father's birth. He enlisted in the Officer Cadet Battalion of the Household Brigade, and in June 1918 was gazetted second lieutenant in the Coldstream Guards. He remained in training until the armistice, never seeing action.

At the end of the war, he decided to become a naturalized British subject even though he was back in New York and worked for his father. When he walked down Madison Avenue dressed in his pinstriped suit and Guards tie, carrying a rolled umbrella, his moustache neatly trimmed, he had the air of a classic English gentleman heading for his office in the City of London.

Like his sister, Ernest had made a good match, in February 1923 marrying lawyer's daughter Dorothea 'Dodie' Parsons Dechert. Her great-grandfathers were respectively a US senator and a chief justice of the Massachusetts Supreme Court. They lived on the fashionable Upper East Side where, a year later, Dorothea gave birth to her second daughter, Audrey. She already had one daughter, Cynthia, from her marriage to former Princeton student and sometime businessman, James Flanagan Dechert.

So while Wallis found Ernest attractive, sensible and cosmopolitan, he shared another, unwelcome, characteristic with Herman – an inconvenient wife and, additionally, a highly inconvenient daughter and stepdaughter. The useful Mary assured her friend that though Ernest had not been married long, he was unhappy.

Mary and her sister Anne had taken tea with the fragile, prematurely greying Mrs Simpson at their Upper East Side apartment, and duly reported to Wallis that she was ill and 'neurotic'. Shortly afterwards, Dorothea sailed for France and the American Hospital of Paris, where it seems she had treatment for a nervous condition. Ernest was left behind, lonely and vulnerable. As he and Wallis began seeing one another on a more regular basis, it wasn't long before Wallis's mother got wind of developments in New York. It was not hard to imagine her horrified response. An impetuous marriage to a drunken sailor aviator was one thing; the deliberate seduction of another woman's husband who was the father to two young daughters was quite another.

Alice discussed her concerns with her sister, Bessie, who had a solution, suggesting Wallis accompany her on a Mediterranean cruise that summer and autumn. A change of scene from Warrenton would do her good, and maybe the company on board the cruise would take her mind off her latest enchantment. 'Your mother tells me that you think you may be falling in love again,' Aunt Bessie queried.

They sailed from New York and into the Mediterranean, steaming by the whitewashed villages along the Amalfi coast before landing at Trieste in northeast Italy. From there they motored along the French Riviera and travelled to Paris.

As Aunt Bessie predicted, there were several shipboard beaux who took her dancing after dinner and generally paid court to her. They included a Pennsylvanian lawyer and later a 'tempestuous and gallant' Irishman who learned to take no for an answer.

Her stay in Paris brought back bitter memories of her past rather than thoughts of her bright future. After dinner one evening in late October 1927 she saw on the front page of the American edition of the *Paris Herald Tribune* a story about the death of her uncle Sol. While versions vary, Wallis, 'upset and scared', hurried back to the Hotel Lotti to tell her aunt. Bessie had herself just received a cable from Wallis's mother, informing her of Sol's death. Aunt Bessie sighed: 'Sol Warfield may not have been the most tolerant man on this earth but he was good to you, Wallis.'

Wallis searched her heart for something to say but struggled, reflecting only on his coldness and how he saw her as the black sheep of the family.

Even though they sailed for New York as soon as they were able, they missed Uncle Sol's funeral – and the reading of the will. It was widely expected that Wallis, whom Sol had legally made his ward, would be left the bulk of his estimated $5 million fortune. Instead she learned that he had bequeathed his money and his country estate, Manor Glen, to be used as a home for distressed gentlewomen in memory of Anna, his mother and Wallis's grandmother. For her part, Wallis received the interest every quarter on $15,000, which was held in a trust fund. Even this meagre amount – interest rates were around two per cent in 1928 – ceased upon her remarriage. Wallis learned to her horror that two months before his death, Uncle Sol, enraged that Wallis had gone ahead with her divorce against his wishes, had changed his will.

Wallis was not just *angry* about Uncle Sol and his will; she was, according to Mary Raffray, *furious*. She fumed at the injustice and raged at the hypocrisy of her uncle who, as she had concluded from the many photographs of female singers and actresses in his New York apartment, was not averse to a pretty woman. In her eyes he had shirked his chance to ensure her financial independence, forcing her continued reliance on men. His mean-spirited gesture was another example of him 'tipping' her – this time from beyond the grave.

After talking it over, she and another relative contested the will, the legal back-and-forth taking another three years to resolve. (On appeal she received a larger pay-out, approximately $47,500 worth of US stocks, the money not paid until January 1930. By then the stock market had crashed and Uncle Sol's stocks were worth a fraction of their previous value. Once again Montague luck snatched defeat from the jaws of victory.)

In the midst of the drama over Uncle Sol's will, Wallis finally got her divorce. On 6 December 1927, just a few days after her return from Paris following her three-month European trip, her divorce petition was submitted to Fauquier County Circuit Court, where it was heard by Judge George Latham Fletcher. During the various dispositions made by her mother, Win and others, Wallis swore on oath that she had not seen Win for three years. Their encounters in Hong Kong and more recently in Chicago, where she had stayed with his family for a few days, were conveniently forgotten. The judge may have raised his eyebrows at the inconsistencies but turned a blind eye, granting a divorce decree on 10 December.

'It was just a matter of incompatibility,' observed Wallis's lawyer, Aubrey Weaver.

There seemed to be no hard feelings, Win Spencer coming to the courthouse before the divorce was granted and chatting with his soon-to-be ex-wife. 'Wallis and he shook hands and departed friends,' Weaver recalled.

She was now free to remarry, the primary candidate for her hand being the pinstriped figure of Ernest Simpson, who had also, somewhat conveniently, recently secured his own divorce. While Wallis saw herself as a passive observer in this marital drama, Ernest's now ex-wife Dorothea, frail and with little energy, saw things differently. Her early favourable impressions of Wallis had understandably soured, and she accused her now of infiltrating her life while she was ill and snatching her husband away. 'Wallis was a very helpful woman. First she helped herself to my apartment, then she helped herself to my clothes, and finally she helped herself to my husband.'

He was not the only contender for Wallis's hand. With jaunty exaggeration, her Warrenton beau Hugh Spilman liked to boast that he proposed to her every day. He claimed that during her stay in Virginia she had had at least thirty different proposals, many from young men who attended the regular parties hosted by her cousins, the Barnetts, in the horsey town of Front Royal.

As a gambling man, though, Spilman would have put his money on Ernest Simpson. He was a racing certainty to win the prize. During her visits to New York he took Wallis to the theatre, out dancing, and had shown her the sights. He was down-to-earth, sensible, sober and kind – the exact opposite of her first husband. Indeed, when she had initially met him, he and Dorothea were part of the Temperance movement.

Ernest was thoughtful, too, taking at face value Wallis's boast that she had read widely while biding her time in Warrenton.

He gave her armfuls of books to read, notably Lytton Strachey's 500-page biography of Queen Victoria. As he would later discover, her real literary diet was fashion magazines leavened with the odd work of light fiction. His choices were indigestible.

More palatable was his serious talk of marriage. He had already told her that when they were free he would like her to be his bride and partner in life. She had hesitated. Having pursued him and wrested him from the arms of another, she now had second thoughts. There was much to consider.

Freeing herself from Win had taken the best part of a decade, during which time she had led a rootless, somewhat self-indulgent life. She didn't want to make another mistake.

Then there was Ernest's ambition to live in London, learning the details of the shipping business away from his father's constant interference. While Ernest loved England and the English, Wallis knew nothing about the country, its customs or its climate. She would be saying goodbye to her mother, her aunt, the Montagues and her loyal circle of friends for an uncertain future.

Moreover, she would not just be taking on another husband and a new country but becoming stepmother to a little girl, Ernest's daughter Audrey. Wallis as a mother, even at one remove, is not an image that readily springs to mind. Then there was the fact that Ernest was part Jewish. While she was never explicit in referring to his ethnicity, in her memoir she made oblique allusions to his race, writing that Ernest had always yearned 'to follow the ways of his father's people'. In a knowing jab, she suggested that Ernest never seemed to be an 'altogether typical Englishman'.

Perhaps most significantly, she also nursed the belief, based on her lawyer's advice, that she was odds-on to become a wealthy woman. The signs were that the court case involving Uncle Sol's will would go in her favour. The winter of 1928 was a time of uncertainty but also of hope that she could hit the jackpot. If Lady

Luck smiled on her she would never need to rely on men again. Stick or twist. She decided to hedge her bets. First she said yes to his proposal, then no, and finally asked for more time to consider. In the meantime, the newly divorced Ernest sailed for London and a new life.

She had only the modest settlement from Win to rely on, and Wallis's friends encouraged her to take a job. Her friend from Warrenton, Jane Derby, ran a dress shop in New York, and Mary Raffray worked in a fashion store run by a Mrs John Betz on 57th Street. Ernest's ex-wife Dorothea had worked in the same store for a time. When she was in New York, Wallis visited the store every day, invariably going out for lunch with Mary.

As shop owner Mrs Betz recalled: 'She was always chic, she loved clothes and knew how to wear them with an air.' It seemed the commercial world of fashion was calling but, even though she had contacts, she never pursued a career working in an up-market dress store where her fashion and sales sense would have been put to use. Instead she dipped her toe into the waters of fashion by entering a writing competition where the prize was an editorial job at *Vogue* magazine. For a woman who considered writing letters to be one of her pet hates, it was hardly surprising that her essay on spring hats was rejected.

Somewhat curiously, she spent three weeks in Pittsburgh with her friends Morgan and Elisabeth Schiller, learning how to be a saleswoman for their tubular steel scaffolding company. Even though Morgan was keen on the prospect of employing a sassy young woman to convince hard-boiled construction engineers about the benefits of his product, Wallis was not persuaded. She walked away from his job offer, citing her poor mathematical ability.

Now living in a top-floor garret hotel room in a freezing New York winter, her savings diminishing daily and with no work on the horizon, it seemed that her options were rapidly running out. As she pondered marriage to Ernest and life in a strange country, out of the blue she received an invitation from Herman and Katherine Rogers to join them at their new villa, Lou Viei, in the coastal town of Cannes on the French Riviera. It was to be something of a China reunion as Constance Coolidge was also joining them.

There was an ulterior motive behind her acceptance of their invitation. Ostensibly she wanted their advice on whether she should remarry so soon. As the Rogers had never met Ernest Simpson, this seemed an odd proposition. In truth her hesitation spoke volumes about her feelings for Ernest. She simply didn't love him the way she had Win Spencer in the early days of their marriage, or Felipe Espil during their torrid affair in Washington, nor did it appear that she felt the same easy companionship she enjoyed with Herman Rogers. She didn't need to sail more than three thousand miles to ask a question when the answer lay much closer to home – in her heart.

Before committing herself to solid, dependable Ernest, she wanted to see for herself the state of the marital union between the man she would have married in a heartbeat and her friend Katherine Rogers. She had pried one man away from his wife. Why not another? When she arrived in Cannes, she was disappointed to discover that Herman and Katherine were still happy and close, neither of them suffering the seven-year itch.

As Herman's stepdaughter-in-law Katharine 'Kitty' Blair observes: 'Knowing Wallis's personality, when she went to the South of France it was probably to see my stepfather and sound out if he would make a move regarding divorcing Katherine. At the very least she needed Herman's approval to go ahead with the wedding.'

It was the arrival of the Queen of Peking herself, Constance Crowninshield Coolidge, that really drove Wallis into the arms of Ernest Simpson. As Constance relayed the story of her disastrous second marriage, Ernest became more and more appealing.

Since they had last seen Constance, she had divorced American diplomat Ray Atherton and then in October 1924 married an impecunious French count, Pierre Chapelle de Jumilhac. Though she became Comtesse de Jumilhac, the marriage itself was a disaster. The first months – when she was beguiled by this 'charming cad', in thrall to his physicality and wild ways – were a sexual adventure. He was, she confessed, a most affectionate and exciting lover. As Constance told her diary: 'The first years with Pierre were worth a whole life. I was a slave of love and he passionately loved me.'

She paid a high price, her husband squandering much of her fortune on buying horses, gambling and drugs. When he was high on cocaine he got angry and beat her cruelly, on one occasion bursting her eardrum.

By the time the Comtesse de Jumilhac blew into Lou Viei, the bloom was off the rose. Her husband's behaviour, particularly his drug use, was now so outlandish that Constance was also actively considering divorce – she finally won her freedom a year later. She may have been a rich adventurer with a healthy appetite for men and sex, but at that time of crisis in her own life, someone like safe, kind and gentle Ernest may have been very appealing.

The same thought occurred to Wallis as she, Herman and Katherine listened to Constance's lurid account of her failing second marriage and then discussed her own future with the dependable and mature Englishman.

Wallis loved men – but not in the same way as the Queen of Peking. Her vision was much more traditional, of a woman as a steady helpmate rather than a wild romantic. 'I was a product of my upbringing – a Southern girl brought up to believe that a woman's role is to marry, bring refreshment, variety, amusement and if possible love into a man's life.'

With Constance's experience firmly in mind, Wallis wrote to Ernest in June accepting his offer of marriage. Ernest wrote back at once and said he had already begun making arrangements. 'I put all my wistful thoughts behind me,' she wrote. 'I was happy.'

She said goodbye to the Rogers and the countess on 23 June 1928 – only four weeks before her wedding day. She took the train to Paris, where she bought a yellow wedding dress with a matching blue coat before catching the Golden Arrow boat train.

She arrived in England just three days before her wedding, Ernest meeting her at Victoria Station with a brand-new yellow Lagonda touring car and a chauffeur called Hughes, who was wearing a uniform of a rather more subdued colour. After installing her in a service flat in central London they headed off to ritzy Bond Street to buy her a wedding ring. Amid the excitement, her first impressions of London were 'gray, shapeless, and blurred'.

'I felt like I was entering a man's club,' she recalled.

The couple spent the first night alone, catching up on the last few months. On the second they were joined by Ernest's father, a 'tiny dwarf-like figure, with piercing eyes and snowy white hair' – a caricature description of an elderly Jewish businessman – who left Wallis in no doubt that though he was retired he kept an iron grip on his shipping company.

Before her wedding day she took the trouble to send a telegram to her Warrenton beau Hugh Spilman: UNEXPECTEDLY I FIND MYSELF MARRYING ERNEST TOMORROW MUCH LOVE. The wording suggested, as ever, that she was backing reluctantly into the marriage contract.

THEY MARRIED ON A SUNNY and warm summer's day at Chelsea Registry Office at eleven in the morning of 21 July 1928. While she was taken to the venue by their new chauffeur, the brief ceremony was a far cry from the romantic church service she enjoyed the first time around in Baltimore. She was hurried through gloomy corridors to a tatty room where a bored official gabbled through the requisite legal vows before pronouncing them man and wife. Even Ernest remarked it was a 'cold little job'. After several glasses of 'good champagne' at the sooty Great Western hotel near Paddington Station, they headed for Paris and a honeymoon visiting the châteaux and vineyards of the Loire valley and beyond into northern Spain.

Wallis was happy. Or so she told herself.

CHAPTER SIX

This Weird Royal Obsession

I T WAS UNDOUBTEDLY the worst year of her life. Wallis Simpson hated England and loathed the English. She detested their quaint customs, their ridiculously tiny counties and especially their crumbling castles, which Ernest loved to visit, spending hours poring over inscriptions on tombstones, inspecting wall hangings and flags, admiring the stone masonry. Newlywed Wallis would sit shivering in the car, bored, irritated, wondering what on earth she was doing. 'I'm sick of seeing old things. I want to see something young,' she wailed.

She had no time for English people, didn't get to the pitch of their humour, their strange adoration for the monarchy, their militaristic history, their quiet pride for the flag, and their ludicrous love of dogs and horses. They were a continuing mystery. Long before royalty entered her life, she had decided that the English were not worth a dime. Or a threepenny bit. Or a half crown. Or a ten-bob note. Or whatever name these people called their ridiculously complicated currency.

Not that she understood more than one word in five. Half the time she had no idea what these odd people with their blank faces and mouthfuls of bad teeth were saying. With all the pointing and gesticulating, she could have been back in Peking. They certainly didn't understand her.

And London. What on earth did Ernest see in the place? Drab, grey, depressing, like the weather. When it was not cloudy it was raining and when it was not raining it was foggy. Gloomy Mondays, Tuesdays, Wednesdays. Not that she could see the sky from the basement kitchen of her rented house. It was like a prison, dark, tiny and damp.

And then there was her sister-in-law, Maud Kerr-Smiley. Nothing smiley about a woman twenty years older – and light years away in attitude. She was all careful condescension and snooty superiority. 'Who on earth does she think she is, telling me what Ernest wants for his supper, calling me every day with her "suggestions" about where I should buy the meat, the fish, even my underwear.'

All that 'little brother' this and 'little brother' that. 'There developed between us a subtle struggle over who would manage Ernest's life,' Wallis tactfully recalled. It was like trying to join a secret society where she didn't know the rules. So hard to know what these people were thinking as they sipped their cups of tea and nibbled their tiny cucumber sandwiches.

When she said the word 'okay' Maud gave her a freezing look. It was as though she had just goosed the Archbishop of Canterbury. So if 'okay' is not okay, what was? She realized that this was not a club she wanted to join.

As she later recalled: 'I began by not liking London at all . . . the most unfriendly community I had ever known. All cold, gray stone and dingy brick, ancient dampness and drabness and a purposeful hurry and push in the streets. It evoked in me a bone-deep dislike. There was about the city a pervading indifference, a remoteness and withdrawal that seemed alien to the human spirit.'

She felt that English women, too, were an alien race, especially Maud's social circle. Wallis considered them suppressed and inhibited, their opinions safely submerged in a sea of small talk. She was determined to be a Yankee, standing up for the Stars and

Stripes whatever the social consequences. Accustomed to saying what was on her mind, she seemed to startle or amuse Maud's circle with her outspokenness. 'I was by no means prepared to accept the British advertisement that British goods were best.' Nor was she prepared to repudiate her own country as she had seen other Americans do – not least her husband.

When Maud gave luncheon parties to introduce Wallis into her circle and teach her the niceties of English etiquette, she discovered to her horror that this young lady wasn't for learning. Romantic novelist Barbara Cartland was a young society hostess invited to meet Maud's American sister-in-law. She remembered her as 'badly dressed and aggressively American'. The queen of romantic fiction sniffed: 'She also told us rather vulgar stories and I was shocked to the core.' She hadn't changed much, if at all, when Cecil Beaton saw her for the first time. 'Her voice had a high nasal twang. She was loud and brash, terribly so – and rowdy and raucous. Her squawks of laughter were like a parrot's.'

Reflecting on Wallis's early days in London, Ernest Simpson recalled her 'loathing' of his adopted country. She made the error of over-protesting her Americanism. 'I had to quiet her down and persuade her that not everything American was best,' he recalled. 'It was the old adage: when in Rome . . .'

Alienated from her social world, Wallis withdrew into herself, her brashness replaced by silence. Her response to questions was monosyllabic, her demeanour subdued. Even her sister-in-law was concerned, telephoning her brother to see if there was something amiss between the newly married couple. Over supper one evening Ernest asked her what was going on. Wallis haltingly explained that she felt like she was treated as an anthropological curiosity by Maud's circle of friends.

As her impulsive American ways were embarrassing his sister and their friends, she was trying to be more like the English, quiet and reserved. Ernest told her that he had married her for her American naturalness and ordered her to end the experiment in trying to be British. That evening he took her dancing to the Savoy. 'We had a lovely time,' she recalled.

Yet her sense of isolation gnawed at her spirit. With Ernest spending long days in the office, Wallis spent her days wandering the shivering streets or visiting the sooty sights. 'I had many a miserable hour wondering what would become of me.' She had no intimate friend, no one to chat with or take to lunch. Above all she had no one to share gossip with.

She discovered in those early months that the one topic of gossip that united all classes of society, from duke to doorman, was the British royal family. Initially she found the fascination with the royal family baffling. 'That a whole nation should preoccupy itself with a single family's comings and goings – and not too exciting ones at that – seemed to me incomprehensible,' she observed.

In time, though, she became intrigued by the ornate and stately language employed in the Court Circular, the official record of royal events, which stood in stark contrast to the scurrilous chatter about the royal family that passed across dinner and bridge tables.

The focus of most of the table talk was on the Prince of Wales. He was Town Topic number one, and in the autumn of 1928 constantly in the news, what with his planned safari in Africa with his brother, the Duke of Gloucester, his visit to Egypt, and a trip to Ypres to join war veterans remembering their fallen comrades. There would soon be wild gossip about the Duke of Gloucester and his open affair with the married aviatrix Beryl Markham, whom he met in Nairobi. It amused his elder brother that for once he was not the focus of wagging tongues.

Yet everyone had a story about the Prince of Wales, even Maud Kerr-Smiley. She never tired of telling of the day at the end of the First World War when she hosted a ball at her house in Belgrave

Square, where the Prince of Wales, who was on leave from his Army unit, met his first long-term lover, Freda Dudley Ward. The lacemaker's daughter, who was married to a Liberal member of Parliament, was the prince's wife in all but name, encouraging, consoling and supporting the future king. Given future events, Mrs Kerr-Smiley may have regretted stimulating Wallis's interest in the royal family.

Soon Wallis would have a story of her own to tell friends over cups of tea – or something stronger. In fact she would have several tales about her encounters with the future king, real or imagined. The little girl who pointed at pictures of glamorous models in magazines and then made up stories about them now focused her vivid imagination on the Prince of Wales.

DURING WALLIS'S FIRST bitterly cold winter in London in 1928, the capital and the rest of the country were on tenterhooks about the health of King George V, who had succumbed to a serious lung infection. Such was the concern that the Prince of Wales, on safari in Africa, was summoned home to undertake his father's duties. Like everyone else, Wallis read and discussed the daily bulletins about the king's medical progress.

In her memoir she tells of the day she was being driven past St James's Palace in central London on her way to pick up Ernest from his office in the City. She saw the scarlet-coated sentries stiffen as a black Daimler limousine raced into the street from inside the palace walls. Craning her head, Wallis caught a 'glimpse' of a 'delicate, boyish face staring straight ahead'. Her chauffeur turned and said in awed tones: 'Madam, that was the Prince of Wales.'

Besides the somewhat pedantic fact that the direct route from Upper Berkeley Street, where the Simpsons had a rented house, to Ernest's office at St Mary Axe in the City does not go anywhere near St James's Palace, Wallis conjured up a second version of the story. She told her ghost writer Cleveland Amory that she was out walking one day when she saw the prince pass by in a coach adorned with what looked like the royal coat of arms and drawn by two black horses. It seems that he was making the short journey from Buckingham Palace to St James's Palace. As it was a closed coach, she did not get a good look at the prince. If the incident did occur, it may have been when the prince stood in for his sick father and represented him at a levee, a ceremony involving the presentation of male dignitaries and held at St James's Palace.

So two stories. One or the other may be true. Or they both may be figments of her fevered imagination. Long before she had even met the prince, it is clear that she was fascinated by him, if not infatuated. She enjoyed a much more memorable, albeit long-distance, encounter in June 1929 when she and Ernest attended the Trooping of the Colour, the time-honoured exercise in pomp and pageantry to celebrate the king's official birthday. She observed him carefully as he rode on horseback from Buckingham Palace behind his father, George V.

During the various military drills on Horse Guards Parade, she focused her attention exclusively on the Prince of Wales. She dreamily described the event: 'He sat on his horse with perfect military bearing and what seemed like the complacent calm of the whole British Empire. I found myself wondering about him not as a future king but as a human being. I thought he had a wistful face.'

As the ceremony came to a close and the royal party made their way back to Buckingham Palace, Wallis thought that there must be something more, that fate would take a hand in pushing them together. She had even told Aunt Bessie that she intended to meet the Prince of Wales.

Her behaviour was not unlike that of other women who projected themselves into the life of the prince, some becoming so obsessed that they came to the attention of the Metropolitan Police and its plain-clothed detective division, the Special Branch.

In those first months, when Wallis was lonely, friendless and had time on her hands, daydreaming about the Prince of Wales was but a pleasant diversion in a dull, cheerless round. She filled out her days with household chores and shopping, she and Ernest setting aside an evening a week to go over the accounts, carefully examining the paper ledgers supplied by the greengrocer, butcher or fishmonger.

'Ernest was extremely meticulous,' she recalled. 'He would run down the list, asking if I had had the weight of apples listed, the amount of spinach. I was seldom over budget. We lived frugally but well.'

For his part, Ernest remembers that Wallis, who was in his words 'scarred by poverty', would fly into a violent rage if a bill had not been paid on time. He was used to paying quarterly or biannually; she wanted accounts paid weekly. Wallis lived in terror of inheriting her mother's spendthrift reputation.

Weekends were usually well-planned outings organized by Ernest to visit a castle, a cathedral or some other ancient monument. His choices tested her patience and her short temper. Her indifference tested his. As a result, rather than being enjoyable excursions, they became exercises in mutual incomprehension and irritation. Their mood was hardly lightened by the country inns they often stayed in. For the most part the clientele was elderly, dinners served promptly and silence the watchword in the communal sitting rooms. Any sound above a whisper attracted a sharp look and a harrumph.

Ernest, who loved history and was a fund of abstruse knowledge, could not understand why Wallis was so bored. As Wallis had little interest in Britain, particularly its 'glorious' past, she wanted to get these visits over as soon as possible. On one occasion, after Wallis had hurried through Warwick Castle and was waiting impatiently for Ernest outside, he caught up with her and said rather petulantly: 'I don't see what's the use of doing this unless you stop to look at things. You can't do a castle like that.'

When Wallis told him that she had seen everything, her marital didact proceeded to test her on what she should have noticed. After passing the test, she casually mentioned that she thought the interior clock was unusual. Ernest looked surprised. 'What clock?' he asked. They went back inside and there indeed was the clock, as Wallis had described it. For once Ernest was impressed. 'You certainly have a photographic mind,' he said. 'And,' Wallis replied, 'a twenty-four-hour memory.'

A welcome interregnum in these outings came courtesy of Herman and Katherine Rogers, who invited the bickering newlyweds to join them for Christmas and New Year at their Riviera home. For Wallis it was a welcome respite from the 'brown fog' that greeted every winter dawn in London. More important, it gave her the chance to spend time with the *other* man in her life. For Yale-alumni Herman, it was the first opportunity he had had to run the rule over Harvard-educated Ernest, for whom it was finally a chance to meet the man Wallis never seemed to stop talking about.

Wallis was summoned to a less welcome reunion a few weeks later when she received a cable saying that her mother had been taken seriously ill. She had suffered a thrombosis which had affected her sight and left her bed-bound. Wallis and Ernest sailed in May for Washington, where Wallis was shocked by the sight of the worn and helpless woman she had always considered indestructible. But the old Alice was not far from the surface. She asked if Wallis was wearing a brown dress. Wallis told her mother that she was and that she had bought it in London. 'Thought so,' she commented drily. 'What made you choose such an unbecoming colour?' It was easy to see where the Wallis bite came from.

For Alice it was her first encounter with her son-in-law. She made an extra effort to be cordial and charming, reminding him that her only daughter was like a box of explosives that needed careful handling. 'There are times when I was afraid of having put too much of myself into her – too much heart and not enough head.' As most observers were struck by Wallis's hard exterior, this was an odd comment, an example of her mother's wry humour perhaps.

Ernest returned to England, Wallis remaining on for a few days until the doctor and Aunt Bessie suggested that as there had been no change in Alice's condition, Wallis should go back to London. A few months later she was summoned across the Atlantic again. This time she went alone as a passenger on board the *Olympic*, sister ship to the ill-fated *Titanic*. When she disembarked in New York in late October, Mary Raffray was there to meet her. Her mother was in a coma. Within hours of Wallis reaching her bedside, Alice died, on 2 November 1929.

At this time of grief and loss, Wallis lashed out at her husband, four thousand miles away. A day after Alice died, Ernest, who was staying at the Guards Club as the lease on their furnished house had ended, wrote a tender note to his wife.

SWEETHEART, I have been thinking all day of my poor darling, and grieving for her in her sorrow hourly. I wish I were beside you. How I miss you and long for you ... the days without you are a weary succession of emptiness. This MUST be the last time that we are parted.

Her response was to accuse him of cheating on her or at the very least flirting with other women. In hurt but placatory tones he replied:

DARLING LITTLE Sweetheart, you make me very sad when you say I have bruised our love . . . I am decent and loyal to the core. I have not looked sideways at anyone nor felt the slightest desire to do so. At all times I have felt proud to belong to you and wanted to be wholly yours . . .

Surely we can have faith in each other, you and I. One in body, one in love, one in sorrow, one in joy.

It may have been the first but it would not be the last time that Wallis, insecure and jittery, would accuse her husband of betraying her trust. Years later, Ernest, who loved writing amusing verses and declaiming Latin in the original, reflected on the letters Wallis wrote to him. Wallis's ghost writer Cleveland Amory asked him: 'Were they witty?' His choked response spoke volumes.

Amory noted: 'There was a long pause as Ernest chose his words with care. "No, they weren't, they were never fond. They were never the letters of a really happy person."'

Then Amory asked if she was happy when she was with him. There was a slight shake of the head, a fleeting sad smile, and Ernest looked quickly away.

At this unhappy time, Wallis was not only mourning her mother, but like the rest of the world, the Simpsons were licking their wounds after the Great Crash of 1929, which wiped billions off the value of stocks and heralded the beginning of the Depression. While Ernest's shipping business rode out the storms for a time, it was not long before the couple were scrimping and saving.

The one shaft of light in a gloomy winter was her discovery of an apartment where she could at last put down her roots. Even though money was tight, there was enough to spare so that she could redecorate and modernize 5 Bryanston Court, a three-bedroom apartment in Marylebone in central London. It became the love of her life. Wallis enthused about making a home for herself and her husband. It marked a genuine turning point in her life, her marriage and her time in London.

At last she felt able to give free rein to her nascent creativity. This time she and Ernest spent their leisure time scouring London for antiques, old things they *both* liked. 'For the first time in my life I had the means and the opportunity to create the kind of setting I had always wanted, a place where good things out of the past would intermingle gracefully with good things of the present.'

With a little help from a young Dutchman called Schreiver and interior designer Syrie Maugham, the wife of novelist Somerset, she created a comfortable and welcoming apartment. While her own bedroom was a very feminine pink, suggesting that Ernest slept elsewhere, she didn't entirely neglect Ernest's interests. In the sitting room one wall was lined with shelves to house his treasured first editions and original manuscripts written by, among others, Charles Dickens. Taking pride of place was his favourite book, A. A. Milne's *Winnie-the-Pooh*. On the occasional tables in the sitting room Wallis placed jade, porcelain and her own small collection of lacquer boxes which she had picked up during her travels in the Orient.

She imported the American tradition of the cocktail hour, where her growing circle of mainly American friends dropped in for drinks and conversation for an hour or so in the early evening. Unlike Ernest, she recalled, she had the knack of fixing a decent cocktail for their guests. And, in a prod at the British, she made sure that her drinks were ice cold.

Word got around, and her salon attracted businessmen, journalists, politicians, lawyers and diplomats as well as a smattering of pretty girls. For the first time since she arrived, Wallis was beginning to find her feet, her skill as a hostess gradually blossoming. Her married life developed a convivial rhythm of theatre and maybe dancing, occasional suppers at the Savoy, dinner parties, and drinks interspersed with bridge or poker.

In this Wodehousian social world, she had also managed to find a gem more valuable than rubies, namely a fine Scottish cook named Mrs Ralph, who had learned her sauces and soufflés under the watchful eye of the French chef to Lady Curzon, one of London's most notable hostesses. Jeeves would have been satisfied.

Ernest certainly was. 'Brilliant', he called her and had nothing but praise for her ability as well as Wallis's penchant for Southern, Chinese and French recipes. They were unusual but highly effective in drawing sincere compliments from their dinner guests.

Just as he applauded her skill as a hostess, he marvelled at her ability to remember the names, backgrounds and foibles of her guests or those they met at social events. She had, he realized, a photographic memory for recalling who was seeing whom, who was divorcing whom, who was cheating on whom, who was on the up, and who was on the way down. It was an essential skill for any social climber, Wallis displaying an unerring instinct for focusing exclusively on those who were important or useful.

In time, minor aristocrats and even royalty walked through her front door. The Simpsons became friendly with the 2nd Marquess and Marchioness of Milford Haven; the marquess was the brother of Lord Mountbatten who, as Wallis knew, was close to the Prince of Wales.

If these guests were important acquaintances, then Major 'Mike' Scanlon, at that time still a dashing bachelor who was the air attaché at the American Embassy, came under the 'useful' heading. He was known for giving smart parties at his small flat in Chelsea, and it was at one such gathering that Wallis and Ernest met Benjamin Thaw, who was then secretary to the embassy, and his wife, the former Consuelo Morgan.

All those hours leafing through issues of *Tatler* and *Harper's Bazaar* had not gone to waste. She knew exactly who Morgan was: the older sister of twins Thelma Furness and Gloria Vanderbilt, one of whom was married to a shipping tycoon, the other briefly married to a scion of the legendary New York family.

Most important, Lady Furness was apparently the new squeeze of the Prince of Wales. Wallis did the only thing she could do. 'Connie and I became close friends as quickly as possible,' she recalled.

While not as pretty as the twins, at least from what she had seen of them in magazines, Consuelo was vivacious, funny and chic. Wallis was sure that it was only a matter of time before she was introduced to Thelma. And then who knows?

She now knew a girl who knew a girl who danced – and more – with the Prince of Wales. It would soon be her turn to cut in.

CHAPTER SEVEN

'Mission Accomplished'

THEY WERE BRED for sex, rich men and marriage. From the day they were born in 1904, twins Gloria and Thelma Morgan were treated like prize cattle or thoroughbred racehorses, cosseted, cradled and carefully groomed.

Their nanny applied white cream to their hands and arms every night before putting on white gloves in order to keep their flesh plump and alluring. They were forbidden to climb or run, lest exercise develop their muscles and make them unfeminine.

In the first week of every new moon in the American Legation in Barcelona, where their father, Harry Hays Morgan, was consul, their domineering half-Irish, half-Chilean mother, Laura Delphine Kilpatrick Morgan, would make them stand still while she cut their eyelashes.

This way, according to ancient Latin superstition, they would grow up to be beautiful women with long, lustrous eyelashes. If they ever disobeyed their watchful mother she would scream: 'Twins, in the name of all that is holy, do you want to be old maids?' Her constant admonition was for them to be beautiful, charming, entertaining but above all to 'marry rich men'. A rich man provided the only ladder to the social stars. In another age they would have been bred as courtesans, in another country they would have been trained in the arts of the geisha.

Their domineering mother taught them to stay their tongues, to be decorous and to present a pleasant face to the world, no matter how they felt inside. Her favourite saying was: 'Never confide in anybody, never tell even your pillow.'

As a result, Thelma grew up watchful, calculating and hard, Gloria reckless and foolhardy. Both were skilled at seduction, be it in conversation or in the bedroom. With such a ruthlessly ambitious mother, how could they have been anything else?

During the First World War the family moved to London, a visit remembered because Thelma had a couple of teeth knocked out during a tennis game, much to her mother's anguish, and they spotted a young man darting out of St James's Palace and climbing into a black Daimler sedan. 'That's the Prince of Wales,' their chaperone whispered reverentially to her flock. On a subsequent stay in New York, their mother carefully pointed out where all the rich families lived. Her obsession was with the Vanderbilts, 'the royal family of America', as she called them.

By the time they were sixteen, the girls, known as the 'Magnificent Morgans', were living in their own townhouse in New York and winning bit parts in silent movies. Unfortunately, Thelma couldn't act. Nor, for that matter, could she boil water, make her breakfast, press a dress, or mend a glove. She left those chores to others.

Striking-looking, if rather artificial and mannered, Thelma was brimming with the chutzpah of youth. When she was seventeen, she set up her own movie company, starring in its first and only film, *Aphrodite*. During this experience she got to know producer Sam Goldwyn and then later dated the silent-screen comedian Charlie Chaplin. He was the first man Wallis Simpson and Thelma Morgan had in common. The difference was that while Wallis enjoyed a jolly luncheon with the comedian, Chaplin wanted to marry Thelma. Her mother thought Thelma was mad to even consider the notion, ordering her to return to New York.

She duly married a wealthy man from a wealthy family, telephone heir James Vail Converse, known as Junior. Even though he was nearly twice her age, with a reputation as a roué, her mother considered him, or rather his bank balance, quite a catch. But he was not in the same league as the man her sister Gloria snagged. She landed a member of America's royal family. That Reggie Vanderbilt, too, was twice her age, a hopeless alcoholic and invariably impotent mattered not. He was a Vanderbilt with a $7.5 million fortune, which compensated for his other failings.

Predictably, neither marriage lasted long. Soon the girls were on the prowl, looking for other big game. They were fascinating creatures, mysterious, seductive and alluring. 'And believe me they knew it,' recalled their dressmaker and business partner Sonia Rosenberg. 'They were big-time operators and the world was theirs.'

During her brief, boozy marriage to Reggie, Gloria Vanderbilt would use Sonia's dress store dressing room or her house for other assignations. She was pathetically needy, having one-night – or one-afternoon – stands for no physical or financial reward.

'It was drink, drink, drink, carouse, carouse, carouse,' recalled Sonia. 'Drugs, dope, men, women. Finally I kicked her out.' The older woman, though, always felt sorry for the twins, realizing that their lives had been twisted by their 'wicked, cruel' mother. Their older sister, Consuelo, was an entirely different creature, charming, sensible and mature. For a time Sonia employed her as a saleswoman in her store.

It was through Gloria that Sonia, a Jewish fashion designer from New York's Lower East Side, first met the Prince of Wales. She recalls that it was Gloria, not Thelma, who was the first sister to seduce the future king. He joined Gloria one summer in Biarritz, the fashionable French resort, where she had rented a villa. When Sonia, who was touring the fashion houses of Paris on business, came to visit, she was introduced to the prince. He subsequently named her his 'Little Disraeli', a reference to Britain's first Jewish-born prime minister. At the time, she had no idea who Disraeli was or what his racial origins were.

While Gloria enjoyed a brief liaison with the Prince of Wales, her twin had captured big game in the form of Lord Marmaduke Furness, the owner of the Furness Withy shipping line and reputedly the second-richest man in England. Like an accountant running the rule over a company, Thelma was advised about his social status and finances by her friend, socialite Beth Leary, a lover of Prince George and a walking encyclopaedia of *Debrett's*, the blue-bloods' bible. She was still only twenty-one when she married the rough-hewn widower, whose language was as colourful as his love life.

Her hunting days were not over yet. Like her eventual love rival, Wallis Simpson, Thelma had a fascination with the Prince of Wales. She read the newspapers each day principally to see where the prince was and what he was doing. On one occasion Thelma, forthright and impulsive, bought a rail ticket to Paris when she heard that he was travelling to France. The first meeting was simple. She walked up to him in his carriage and said: 'Sir, I am Lady Furness, Gloria Vanderbilt's twin sister.' Another version has it that the prince sent his equerry to her railway carriage and asked her to join him for the journey. That she was on the train in the first place is testament to her resourcefulness. As Sonia Rosenberg recalled: 'Those girls read the papers as a Wall Street broker might stock quotations. They followed every move of rich and important men.'

It is noticeable that at their first 'official' meeting, at a ball hosted by Lord and Lady Londonderry, the prince made a beeline for Lady Furness, suggesting a previous acquaintance. As they waltzed and talked together she noticed his slightly guttural German accent.

Given her forthright behaviour and her enduring interest in the prince, it is likely that the meeting, which was a prelude to their affair, was not quite as fortuitous as Lady Furness made out. In her version, they met by chance in the bucolic surroundings of the Leicester Agricultural Show in June 1929, where a bored Prince of Wales was pinning rosettes onto prize cattle. Their encounter seemingly involved more planning and cunning than she has suggested. After all, she was still smarting from her husband's decision to go to the South of France with the international gold-digger and sometime actress Peggy Hopkins Joyce. What better way to humble her husband than to seduce the Prince of Wales? During their conversation at the agricultural show, he asked her to dine with him the following week at York House, the London home he shared with his younger brother, Prince George. She accepted with alacrity. It marked the beginning of the end of her marriage and the start of a five-year affair with the prince.

She was not the only one on the prowl. The prince's twelve-year affair with his mothering married lover, Freda Dudley Ward, was stuttering to a close. At the height of their love affair he had written to her four, sometimes five, times a day, but now he realized that Freda, who was cultured and well read, was drifting into the arms of a rival, Lord Pembroke's cousin, Michael Herbert. A year later she divorced her husband for him.

By then the prince had wandered into pastures new, remaining friendly with Freda but spending his days and nights in the arms of Lady Furness. She remembers that love was in the air on that first royal date. The moment Thelma set eyes on the prince in the 'enchanted world' that was York House, her heart quickened. After a cocktail, they went for dinner at the Hotel Splendide on Piccadilly and then danced to Viennese waltzes.

She later told her erstwhile ghost writer, Helen Worden Erskine:

Just he and I was all that mattered. It seemed so natural, so right. We talked of many things, surface talk, yet beneath it I knew and he knew that this was it. For the next five years he came first in my life.

I dined every night with him. Whatever we did we did together. We shared all our experiences. It was as if there had never been Duke [her husband] or any other man in my life. I was his wife in all but name.

Just as the prince's gracious character contrasted with her husband's bluster, so Thelma was a soothing, somewhat bland counterpoint to the intelligent but endlessly challenging Freda. 'Thelma was gay and friendly and chattering, always chattering,' observed dressmaker Elsa Schiaparelli. 'But she had no sense of wit or repartee.' Both women, though, were beautiful and discreet, the prerequisite for a royal mistress.

As for Thelma's husband, he was so thrilled that his wife had merited such attention from the Prince of Wales that he organized a party in his honour at the prince's favourite nightclub, the Embassy on Old Bond Street. In the world of the Prince of Wales, Thelma's husband did not exist, the future king taking it for granted that he came first. 'In our class in England, extramarital romances are the rule rather than the exception,' recalled Thelma. 'Half the wives I knew were in love with men not their husbands.' During an East African safari in 1930, Thelma split her time between the prince and her husband, both men having organized these wildlife excursions independently. When Thelma was with her husband, the prince would write or cable every day, penning love letters to her, which she read by the flickering light of the camp fire. When she eventually managed to join the prince's safari, their tents were placed next to each other.

'This was our Eden and we were alone in it,' she wrote. 'His arms about me were the only reality, his words of love my only bridge to life. Every night I felt more completely possessed by our love, carried ever more swiftly into the uncharted seas of feeling, content to let the prince chart the course, heedless of where the voyage would end.'

At the end of the safari, she decided to formally separate from Duke. Even though her royal affair was by now an open secret – she was spoken of as the Princess of Wales – Thelma insists that they never discussed marriage and she never considered becoming queen. She thought it unrealistic. Not only was she a divorcee, she was a Roman Catholic, an even worse sin. Under British law, Catholics are specifically excluded from the line of succession. This did not stop society gossips suggesting that Thelma's baby boy, Tony, was fathered by the prince; a story that followed the boy for the rest of his life.

Watching this developing royal romance from afar was Wallis Simpson, her blossoming friendship with Consuelo Thaw eventually giving her an entrée into the social circle of Consuelo's titled and quietly infamous sister.

The two women have very different recollections of their first meeting and of Wallis's subsequent encounter with the Prince of Wales. In Wallis's famous version, in early January 1931 she and Ernest Simpson were asked as guests to Burrough Court, the Furness hunting lodge in Leicestershire, as Thelma's sister Consuelo had to drop out at the last minute.

They travelled to Melton Mowbray on the 3:20 afternoon train. Wallis, who was nursing a heavy cold, described how, in between sneezes and sniffles, she learned to dip a curtsey. Meanwhile, Consuelo's husband, Benny Thaw, gave etiquette advice, a suggestion that Consuelo found 'hilarious'. As it was foggy, the royal party, consisting of the Prince of Wales, his younger brother, Prince George, and Lady Furness, were delayed, leaving the Simpsons nervously killing time by drinking copious cups of tea in the drawing room of Burrough Court.

When they finally arrived, the Simpsons were quickly introduced, the sickly Wallis rallying sufficiently to chide the Prince of Wales for his opening conversational gambit about how American visitors feel about the lack of central heating in English country houses. She retorted: 'I'm sorry, sir, but you have disappointed me.'

'In what way?' he asked. Wallis responded feistily: 'The same question is always asked of every American woman who comes to your country. I had hoped for something more original from the Prince of Wales.'

Lady Furness finds the conversation not just preposterous but swears Wallis never even met the prince at Burrough Court. She argues, convincingly, that she would never have invited two strangers to spend the weekend with the Prince of Wales at her home. Not only was the prince averse to meeting people he didn't know, she had enough mutual friends to call on to make up a party.

As for the conversation about radiators, Wallis's memory is so much hot air. 'Poppycock,' Thelma said. 'Had this retort of Wallis's been true, it would have been in bad taste, no matter to whom addressed. To be so rude to the Prince of Wales would have been the height of bad manners.'

Instead Lady Furness pinpoints an afternoon tea party at her home at 21 Grosvenor Square in central London around Christmas 1930 as the first time she and the prince met Wallis Simpson. According to her version, her sister Consuelo had telephoned ahead and asked if she could bring Wallis along.

After she arrived, Wallis and Thelma made small talk about mutual friends and the London season. Thelma was struck by her blue eyes, which 'sparkled like sapphires', her large hands and her flat toneless voice. Yet there was a charm in the attentive way she listened and humour in her comments. Consuelo was right, thought Thelma, Mrs Simpson was fun. 'I did like her,' she recalled.

As they were chatting, the butler announced the unexpected arrival of the Prince of Wales. When he walked into the drawing room, accompanied by Thelma, he saw the chattering throng and said, 'Oh, a party', in anticipation of an evening of fun and laughter. Thelma damped down his expectations. 'No, darling, just a few friends. You've met all of them except an American, Mrs Simpson, who seems to be fun. Consuelo brought her.'

She was introduced and, like any woman meeting the Prince of Wales for the first time, was nervously impressed and rather tongue-tied. As she later recounted: 'In our first meetings I did not say more than five or ten words to David. Most of the time I was too awed to say anything and instead spent my time watching him and seeing how he looked and acted and did things. I was fascinated by this.'

Though she may have said little, in January 1931 she was able to write to her aunt Bessie, 'Mission accomplished', a jokey reference to her previously stated ambition to meet the Prince of Wales one day.

In the early spring of 1931, while the Prince of Wales and his younger brother George were on a three-month visit to Argentina, Thelma saw her new friend frequently, sometimes more often than she wished. Thelma recalled: 'She would call me up practically every day, asking "What are you doing? Where did you go last night? Will you lunch with me tomorrow?"'

Wallis's excitement was evident in a letter to her aunt Bessie saying that she hoped Thelma would ask them to join her at some social event involving the prince. While he had been away in Argentina she had followed his royal progress carefully, studying photographs of him in newspapers and magazines. She concluded that he was a withdrawn and lonely spirit and felt herself increasingly drawn to this man of mystery.

Though Wallis was the social supplicant in relation to Thelma, from time to time she enjoyed a brief moment of one-upmanship.

In April 1931, she invited her one-time lover Felipe Espil, who was shortly to be made the Argentinian ambassador to Washington, to a KT – or cocktail party – at Bryanston Court. While Ernest was not thrilled to entertain his wife's former paramour, Thelma was deeply impressed, especially as she was hosting a reception the next day at her Grosvenor Square home to celebrate the prince's return from his successful visit to South America. For Thelma it was a nice coup to be able to invite the future ambassador along. Wallis was proving to be a useful friend.

As she gradually insinuated her way into the outer royal circle, little by little Wallis was building up a picture of the Prince of Wales that fell somewhere between the august language of the Court Circular and the chatter of the salon. She learned that the man who was born two years before her, on 23 June 1894, and was christened Edward Albert Christian George Andrew Patrick David, was known as David by his family and closest friends. Thelma called him PW, a name she devised based on the first letter of 'Prince' and 'Wales'.

She discovered that his childhood was deeply unhappy – he'd been beaten by his nannies, bullied by his schoolmates at the Royal Naval College in Dartmouth, and his tutors had been invariably cruel and manipulative. The prince once regaled a party about the time he and his brothers caught frogspawn in the pond at Windsor Castle and his mother, Queen Mary, who wanted to sack their vile French tutor, asked the cook to serve the spawn on toast and present it to him. He promptly fled the castle.

Wallis discovered, too, that the prince's relationship with his father was chilly and distant, the prince and his brothers living in fear of the man ironically dubbed 'Grandpa England' by his doting granddaughter Princess Elizabeth. Yet in time it was clear that they agreed on more things than they disagreed on – both men, for instance, had a healthy regard for Germany's coming man, Adolf Hitler.

The common belief that his mother was so cold and distant that he sought a series of mother–son relationships among his paramours was, as Wallis discovered, contradicted by their clearly warm, affectionate bond. Queen Mary had a particular soft spot for her eldest son, which meant that, in her eyes, he could do no wrong. As far as she was concerned, it was those who surrounded him who led him astray. (Little wonder, then, that during the abdication and its aftermath the elderly queen considered that her beloved son had been beguiled by an American sorceress.)

When Thelma taught him how to do petit point to stop his continual fidgeting and give him something to do with his hands, the first piece he worked on was an embroidered paperweight, which he duly presented to his mother. Queen Mary presided over the annual Christmas party for servants, and every year she opened the waltzing with her eldest son. 'Those watching always felt that here was a gentle and sweet relationship, a real mother-and-son love,' recalled Thelma. 'The prince worshipped her and talked about her quite often, his father little.'

Besides his mother, he was perhaps closest to his younger brother Prince George, who shared the royal apartments at York House. Rosy-cheeked and so tall that he stooped when he spoke to others, Prince George was the most artistic of the royal children – and the wildest. His piano playing was delicate and delightful, his private life complicated and of concern to his parents, his family and senior courtiers.

The handsome royal bachelor squired any number of unsuitable women around town. They included boogie-woogie pianist Edythe Baker, socialite Betty Lawson-Johnston, glamour girl Sandra Rambeau, and aristocrat Mary Montagu Douglas Scott, later the Duchess of Buccleuch. However, it was his grand passion for socialite Kiki Preston, dubbed 'the girl with the silver syringe', that set alarm bells ringing. Not only did she encourage him to take drugs, but she and Jorge Ferrara, the bisexual son of the Argentinian ambassador, were reputedly in a drug-fuelled *ménage* with the young prince. As Thelma recalled: 'PW hated Kiki. Hated her. Like all dope fiends she tried to get others to take it, and that's what she did to Prince George.' For once, the Prince of Wales took charge, effectively exiling Kiki to Switzerland and placing his brother in a nursing home, where he was weaned off his dependence on morphine and cocaine.

Drugs were one thing. Drink quite another. The two brothers matched each other cocktail for cocktail – the Prince of Wales's favourite during Thelma's reign was orange blossom, a mixture of gin, orange juice and Cointreau. A normal princely night out would begin with cocktails at York House at seven-thirty, dinner at a restaurant, and then on to a nightclub – the Kit-Cat, Quaglino's, the Embassy, and Café de Paris were favourites – the evening ending as milk bottles were landing on the capital's doorsteps.

Often the party went back to York House for drinks and dancing to the gramophone. On one occasion the Hollywood stars Fred and Adele Astaire delighted the assembled throng with some fancy footwork. For much of his adult life the prince was a sucker for Hollywood actors and entertainers – as well as American women. Another time, the prince invited the American bandleader Paul Whiteman and his band for an impromptu late-night performance. As York House was too small to accommodate the group, they all headed for Lord Curzon's commodious but mothballed London home, where his daughter Baba Curzon, future wife of the prince's equerry, Fruity Metcalfe, was part of the party, and convinced the staff to take the covers off the furniture. The only mishap was when the rather weighty Prince Henry, the Duke of Gloucester, sat on an antique table and promptly broke it.

At another supper party, given by Lady Juliet Duff, the guest of honour was the giant Italian boxer and world heavyweight champion Primo Carnera. Known as the Ambling Alp, Carnera had won a bout with the American pugilist Young Stribling, who was disqualified in the fourth round. The prince, who watched the fight at the Royal Albert Hall in November 1929, was so impressed by Carnera's physique and height – he was six feet seven inches tall – that he asked him to carry his rather portly friend Lord Birkenhead around the drawing room. Even though he was a big man, in Carnera's arms Lord Birkenhead looked like a child.

The results of burning the candle at both ends were obvious. Often the prince was so hungover that he would either arrive late for a public engagement or not at all, his stuttering but steadfast brother, the Duke of York, regularly stepping in for him.

He was, though, keenly aware that the older generation were keeping a beady eye on his behaviour – and his wardrobe. One morning the king greeted him with the admonition: 'I hear you were not wearing gloves at the ball last night. Please see that this does not occur again.'

That he found the Court boring and many royal duties mind-numbing did not help his standing with his father. He made no attempt to disguise his loathing of what he called 'princing' – the daily round of public engagements where the prince was paraded before his public. It was the theme of many of his letters to Freda Dudley Ward, expressions of undying love meshed with a forlorn sense of desolation. As early as Christmas 1919 he told Freda that he was 'so so sick of this bloody job', a theme he returned to time and again. 'What I wouldn't give to chuck this P of W job,' he told her in August 1927, adding: 'I'm so fed up with it you know and don't fit in.' Long before the abdication, his continual griping about his role meant that he would often blurt out his disaffection to complete strangers, as on that night in Chicago with Courtney Letts. In 1927, the American society gossip writer Elsa Maxwell was equally astonished when she happened on the prince when

From the beginning, the life of Bessie Wallis Warfield was touched by tragedy. Her father, Teackle Wallis Warfield, died of tuberculosis when she was four months old. Just before his death, he was shown this picture of his daughter. As he gazed at the picture he told Wallis's mother, Alice: 'I hope she will be like you and I hope she will be happy.'

Even though she was brought up by her mother, Wallis, aged two, wanted for nothing and admits that she was spoiled as a child, indulged by both branches of her family, the maternal Montagues and paternal Warfields.

Wallis and her beloved aunt, Bessie: Mrs D. Buchanan Merryman, her mother's sister. She considered Wallis the most imaginative little girl she had ever known. Aunt Bessie was a constant in her life, by her side before, during, and after the abdication.

Highly competitive and used to getting her own way, Wallis, then a ten-year-old schoolgirl, wanted to be the first at everything. When she was a pupil at Arundel school she once hit a classmate on the head for daring to answer a question before she did.

Wallis's favourite teacher was the untidy and sharp-tongued Minerva Buckner (right), who taught French and German at Oldfields boarding school in Maryland. Wallis developed something of a crush, using her allowance to buy her presents.

A unique picture of Wallis, then aged around eleven, with her hair down and wearing the uniform of Arundel school, which she attended for six years. 'I enjoyed nearly every minute,' she later recalled.

A confident young woman, Wallis couldn't wait to leave school

Knowing and artful, Wallis wrote: 'All is Love' in the final yearbook at her senior school.

Clearly apprehensive, Wallis prepares to walk down the aisle at Christ Church in Baltimore on November 8, 1916.

Her groom, Lieutenant Commander Win Spencer, was one of the first-ever navy pilots, who were then deemed as glamorous as astronauts. In the early days Wallis thought so, too.

Lieut. Comdr. E.W. SPENCER, JR.
U.S. Navy

Wallis's mother warned her daughter that life with a naval officer would not be easy. After bouncing around the country, the newlyweds found themselves in Coronado, Southern California, where Lieutenant Commander Spencer was put in charge of running a new airbase. The desk job soon noticeably affected his waistline.

As the wife of the new commanding officer, Wallis was quite the local celebrity, here captured by photographer Lou Goodale Bigelow.

Stylish and vivacious, Wallis cut quite a dash in Southern California. Here she is, arm-in-arm with silent film star Charlie Chaplin and her friends Marianna Sands (left) and Rhoda Fullam.

A group of Coronado socialites, looking rather bored and cold, watch a game of polo. Wallis is second left. Typically she is on her own, her husband being occupied with navy business.

Wallis (back centre) rather glumly faces up to an evening of fancy dress with a Chinese theme at the Hotel del Coronado. Little did she know she wou shortly find herself bound for the Orient.

Dreaming of royalty. Legend has it that when the Prince of Wales briefly stayed in San Diego on his way to Australia he met the then Wallis Spencer and her husband. Both later confirmed the story, even though in reality they were hundreds of miles away.

Wallis split from her first husband and lived in Washington, where she met and fell madly in love with the suave Argentinian diplomat, Felipe Espil. Unfortunately her feelings were not reciprocated.

She sailed for Paris, where she met American diplomat Elbridge Gerry Greene. When he was posted to China, he invited her to join him, offering to pay her passage and other costs.

During this period, Wallis was shadowed by her doppelgänger, Chicago-born beauty Courtney Letts. Not only did she bear a remarkable resemblance to Wallis, she was also romanced by the Prince of Wales and courted by both Espil and Greene at the same time as Wallis. Letts later married Espil.

After a torrid but failed romance with diplomat Felipe Espil, Wallis packed her bags and headed for Paris, in the hope of securing a cheap divorce from her husband Win Spencer. Her passport picture, taken just before Christmas 1923, shows a rather mournful, badly dressed Wallis.

Wallis's estranged husband asked her to sail to Hong Kong, where he was now stationed, to try and salvage their seven-year marriage. She also had an invite to stay in Peking (Beijing) from besotted American diplomat, Gerry Greene. As a result she secured a second passport, leading to the false assertion that she was a courier spy for the United States.

Wallis models a kimono for her friend Herman Rogers. She loved her time in the Orient, especially as unattached men outnumbered women ten to one. She did, though, have a special place in her heart for Herman.

A courtly couple, Wallis and her second husband, Ernest Simpson, who is seen here in the uniform of the Coldstream Guards, pose before her presentation at Buckingham Palace in the presence of King George V and Queen Mary. Wallis borrowed her tiara and headpiece from Lady Thelma Furness, then mistress of the Prince of Wales.

Freda Dudley Ward, the wife of a Conservative member of Parliament, was mistress to the Prince of Wales for most of the 1920s. Ironically they first met during an air raid at the home of Ernest Simpson's sister. At the height of their affair he would write or call her a dozen times a day. Here she is in 1918, with her daughters, Penelope and Angela.

Thelma Furness – pictured with her son Tony – who became mistress to the Prince of Wales after her husband, shipping magnate Duke Furness, cheated on her with an actress. She found the prince's constant need for entertainment a strain, drafting in her friends, including Wallis and Ernest Simpson, to help shoulder the burden. The prince, however, doted on Tony, even buying him a set of miniature golf clubs.

Wallis prepares for a quiet dip in a secluded rocky cove during the infamous voyage of the *Nahlin* steam yacht where the international media made merry discussing the relationship between the twice-married Mrs Simpson and the new king, Edward VIII. The British media remained silent on the issue.

There was much discussion among the party on board the *Nahlin* about whether the new king should appear in public bare chested or visit local cafés in shorts. He chose to do both.

Locals on the holiday island of Rab, off the Croatian coast, commemorated their 1936 royal visit with an engraved stone monument, Wallis's surname is spelt incorrectly.

Wallis and her 'rock' Herman Rogers, stroll round the gardens of Balmoral in Scotland. It was the only time Edward VIII entertained a house party at the royal Highland home. Wallis agreed to come only if Herman and Katherine Rogers accompanied her.

he was sitting alone at the bar during a party at Lady Millbank's London home. He told the garrulous American: 'I don't want to be king. I wouldn't be a good one.' For once, even she was lost for words. It was not just the job he hated but the system; he referred to royal engagements as 'stunts' or 'camouflage' and a successful event as 'good propaganda'. His well-worn complaint and cynicism about the institution he was destined to helm was critical during the abdication.

In the time-honoured tradition, royal officials, as with his mother, did not blame the prince; they complained about the malign influence of those who surrounded him. Lady Furness was firmly in the line of fire. Her American ways, her hedonism and her indifference to any consideration that did not bear directly on her own pleasure were seen as encouraging the prince's own selfishness and self-indulgence. If Wallis ever heard these criticisms, they will have cut little ice as she listened wide-eyed to stories, past and present, of the prince's exploits. It stirred the Montague in her soul and it made her own life seem rather dull and insipid. For a girl who loved parties and dancing, the quiet evenings spent with Ernest going through the household accounts or weekends traipsing around ancient piles had little appeal. She was achingly jealous of Thelma's life of laughter, quick wit and quicksteps. Once again she felt, as in Washington, on the outside looking in.

So when Consuelo suggested that Wallis be presented at Court she realized instantly that it was her admission ticket to the world's most exclusive club: English Society. As was her pattern, she gave the impression that she was extremely reluctant to go through the rigmarole and treated the whole palace palaver as a rather silly joke, agreeing to take part only at the insistence of her friends. She was not being entirely honest. The reality was that in order to make her debut before the king and queen at Buckingham Palace she was prepared to jump through all manner of time-consuming administrative hoops.

In her day, divorced women could be presented only if they could show that they were the innocent party. Wallis had to be keen enough to obtain the necessary notarized legal documents from Virginia and then present the papers to the palace authorities. That was before she could even think about the dress and all the finery needed. Fortunately, Consuelo's white satin dress fitted perfectly, while Thelma let her borrow her embroidered train, the traditional three-white-feathers head ornamentation, and a fan. The finishing touch was an outsize costume-jewellery cross to give the outfit a touch of individuality. By early June 1931, she was ready for her curtain call – along with several hundred other ladies.

Like the others, she was a knot of nerves, worrying about her train, her curtsey, her headdress and vividly aware of the stories – oh, the horror – of women fainting before the sovereign. There was even the apocryphal tale of the Prince of Wales catching a woman who had fainted and carrying her out of the ballroom in his strong arms. She remembers the presentation itself as a nerve-racking blur, and yet in her later account she had the wit to remember a conversation between the Prince of Wales and his great uncle the Duke of Connaught in which the prince commented on the 'terrible' lighting. The prince added: 'It certainly doesn't do much for the women.'

That night Thelma gave a supper party and invited the Simpsons to drop in. When the Prince of Wales arrived he congratulated Wallis and asked if she had enjoyed herself. 'Yes, indeed, sir,' she is said to have replied, 'but the lighting in there is terrible. It certainly doesn't do much for the royal males.' Once again, as at Burrough Court, accounts diverge significantly. Wallis was seemingly all witty insouciance in the presence of the prince. Thelma has an entirely different recollection. She remembers Wallis as a woman who viewed her presentation as a 'matter of life and death', and when the prince arrived was still in misty-eyed raptures about the Court and the pageantry.

The crowning glory of a dreamy day came at the end of the evening as Ernest and Wallis were waiting for a taxi home. The prince had left before them, but when they walked outside he was still talking to his aide, George Trotter. To their astonishment he offered them a lift home, which they accepted with trembling alacrity. 'I have never forgotten the excitement of climbing into that car,' Wallis recalled, adding: 'I think Ernest if possible was even more thrilled.' The prince refused their offer of a nightcap, but it did raise Wallis's hopes that one day he would honour their humble abode by joining them for a KT. As she explained to Aunt Bessie: 'You have to work up to those things gradually and of course through Thelma.'

It would be six months before they saw the prince again.

EVEN THOUGH SHE was slowly climbing the social ladder, the view did not especially intrigue her. She still found the English for the most part 'dull and uninteresting' and tended to socialize with Americans living in London. When her friend from school, Mary Raffray, came to stay for a few weeks that summer, the contrast between her guileless enthusiasm for all things British and Wallis's jaundiced opinion was vivid. Wallis warned her, for instance, that a cocktail party in Kensington would be a dreary affair, stating authoritatively that this area of London was infested with ageing aunts. Actually, Wallis was misstating Edward VII's comment about Kensington Palace, that it was an 'aunt heap' as all his mother's female relations lived there. In fact Mary found the occasion delightful and cordial. As she told her family: 'I am completely fascinated by London. I love the look of it.' She enjoyed wandering around the streets, the squares, and poking into the hidden nooks and crannies of the charismatic metropolis.

When she visited Westminster Abbey in the company of Ernest Simpson, she had met a fellow Anglophile. In time their enthusiasm for the sights of London would translate into eagerness for one another.

During that sunny summer visit, Mary was not only enchanted by the city but somewhat in awe of her friend's circle of friends, briefly meeting the Prince of Wales during her stay. By now Wallis had conjured up something of a fashionable salon at her Bryanston Court apartment. 'Her dinner parties have so much pep that no one wants to leave,' observed Mary. She was suitably impressed by Wallis's interior decorating skills – save for her pink plush bedroom, which she found rather too much.

During Mary's visit Wallis was preparing for a girls-only holiday in Cannes in the South of France with boon companion Ethel Noyes – now Lady Lewis – Consuelo and her sister Gloria Vanderbilt, and a new friend, Nada, Marchioness of Milford Haven, the daughter of Russian Grand Duke Michael. Mary Raffray came with Wallis as far as Paris, where she was hit by a taxi, the accident leaving her badly bruised and shaken but not critically injured, though she stayed in hospital as a precaution.

Suitably reassured by her friend's improved condition, in August Wallis went on to the South of France to be reunited with Herman and Katherine Rogers. She and Lady Lewis stayed at their villa, Lou Viei, while the others stayed in a hotel. It was a belated Fourth of July reunion for a crowd of Americans that included Sarah Elkin and former model 'Foxy' Gwynne. Herman added a touch of culture to KT hour by inviting local French composer Amédée Joseph Gabriel de Vallombrosa to the party.

Usually the lazy routine involved sailing out to an island on Herman's yacht, swimming in a hidden cove and then enjoying a picnic on the beach. For Wallis it was a welcome respite from business worries, the depressing London weather and juggling the household budget. Ernest, alone and miserable, was left behind to watch the pennies and try to keep the shipping business afloat.

In her memoir she says briefly and incorrectly that Ernest was with her on the holiday. The reason became clear afterwards. Three years later her Riviera vacation made headlines for all the wrong reasons when the sexual shenanigans during the holiday were revealed during a truly sensational custody battle between Wallis's friend Gloria Vanderbilt and her sister-in-law Gertrude Whitney over her daughter, also named Gloria.

Gloria's maid, Maria Caillot, gave evidence stating that while Nada and Gloria were staying at the Cannes hotel in August 1931 she saw them openly kissing 'like lovers'. Gloria's lesbian affair was proof positive that she was morally unfit to have custody of her own daughter. The sharp-eyed maid further revealed that Gloria pursued a merry-go-round of parties, was often drunk before breakfast, and was a devotee of erotic literature.

At the time, the fact that Wallis had gone on holiday with Gloria and Nada, the latter by then well known for her lesbian lifestyle, merely added to the lurid speculation about Wallis's own sexuality. As her biographer Michael Bloch noted: 'There can be no doubt that, all her life, Wallis – with her rather masculine appearance, her brittle and self-possessed manner – exercised a great fascination on lesbians.' Whether, apart from her female school crushes, that attraction was ever reciprocated has never been conclusively resolved.

Whatever the subsequent sexual rumours that swirled around Wallis, that summer she was well on her way to becoming a fully paid-up member of the Prince of Wales's set. She met him again just before Christmas at a drinks party hosted by Thelma. After consulting with Thelma beforehand, she tremulously asked him if he would like to join them for supper at Bryanston Court. Thanks to Thelma's behind-the-scenes work, the prince graciously accepted.

As this was to be her sternest test as a hostess, she decided on a typical Southern dinner of black bean soup, grilled lobster and fried chicken Maryland. The whole affair went swimmingly, and the prince paid her the compliment of asking for her recipe for raspberry soufflé. Her kitchen goddess, Fannie Farmer, would have been proud. The stressful evening did, though, expose the tensions in the Simpson marriage. 'She was snappy at Ernest,' recalls Thelma, a snob to her polished fingertips. 'It was all: "Stand up, sit down, empty ashtrays." Ernest seemed servile, not quite out of the top drawer. Not to the manor born.'

After their successful dinner party, the Simpsons received a note from the prince in late January 1932 inviting them to spend the weekend at Fort Belvedere, his beloved weekend retreat. Once again Thelma was the hidden hand in wrangling the invitation. Even before the words 'Yes, please' were out of her mouth, Wallis was worrying about her wardrobe for the most important weekend of her life.

CHAPTER EIGHT

A Shortlist of One

I N THE END it was the one-eyed Admiral Lord Nelson, the hero of the Battle of Trafalgar, who saw to it that Wallis Simpson secured a berth at the table of the Prince of Wales.

The prince, raised and educated in a naval family, always had a love for Britain's naval heritage. He found a fellow enthusiast in Ernest Simpson, the two amateur historians batting dates back and forth when he was a guest at Bryanston Court. When Thelma suggested that they invite the Simpsons to the Fort for the weekend, initially the prince demurred. His conversations with Wallis, such as they were, felt awkward and stiff. He also found that her voice, a mixture of Southern drawl and attempted received English pronunciation, grated on him. He agreed to Thelma's request with the proviso that she did not sit him next to Mrs Simpson. 'I can't stand her voice,' he told her.

Of course, Wallis was unaware of this social juggling. As an artful social climber, she felt only the extreme elation of reaching the royal summit. Fort Belvedere, a dilapidated castellated folly on the edge of Windsor Park, was not a Buckingham Palace or a Balmoral, but the prince was proud to call it home. It was where he was at his most casual and at ease, the future sovereign, a wicked billhook in one hand, doing weekend battle with the weeds advancing on his garden kingdom.

Excited but also 'scared to death' by the prospect of spending a weekend in the prince's company, Wallis, who guzzled newspaper and magazine gossip about the prince as well as the morsels that Thelma and others fed her, was expecting several evenings of dancing and drinking until dawn. She was not alone in that mistaken view of the prince's nocturnal behaviour.

Edward's father viewed Fort Belvedere on a similar moral level to Sodom and Gomorrah. In 1929, when the prince had asked his father, George V, for permission to make the royal 'grace and favour' property his country retreat, the monarch had expostulated: 'What could you possibly want that queer old place for? Those damn weekends, I suppose.'

His censorious father would have been as perplexed as Wallis when she first walked into the drawing room to see the future king engaged in what he called his 'secret vice' – sewing a needlepoint backgammon cover. The surprises did not end there. Every evening at 6:30 prompt he went for an invigorating steam bath; he would also stand on his head at the drop of a hat, and regularly came down for dinner dressed in a kilt. Late at night he liked to march around the battlements playing the bagpipes, often accompanied by a Guards piper.

During a simple dinner of Duchy of Cornwall oysters, roast beef, salad and savoury, Wallis noticed that Thelma and the prince's aide, George Trotter, worked hard to keep the conversation flowing and the prince amused. There was a little light card playing, a jigsaw puzzle to attack and a brief interlude of dancing to the gramophone. When the prince coached Wallis at a card game called Red Dog, Wallis eagerly noticed that it was their first interaction in which he had treated her as a woman rather than a guest to whom the host is just being polite. Thelma snobbishly noted that Wallis played cards like a 'little embassy secretary'.

This, though, was hardly the louche royal world of popular imagination – the prince headed for bed well before midnight, to be ready for his next sortie in the garden. Thelma would follow soon afterwards, the unspoken ritual being that he would join her in her bedroom and leave at 8:30 in the morning. When George V telephoned early one morning, the prince's butler, Finch, was flustered when he could not find him in his bachelor quarters. Finally he located him in Lady Furness's bedroom.

At first Wallis may have been disappointed to discover that the heart of royal darkness was a jigsaw puzzle, a needle and thread, and a gardening billhook, but she soon realized that the prince loved his time at his country retreat. Fort Belvedere was the first place in his life that he had been able to call home, the prince enlisting the help of his then lover Freda Dudley Ward, who had a flair for interior design, to remodel the place. He put in extra rooms, a swimming pool and a tennis court. Unusually for a member of the royal family, he didn't even keep a horse for riding out. As a younger man he was a fearless steeplechaser, but after a few spills his father and Prime Minister Stanley Baldwin had famously asked him to stop this risky sport. It never worried him. The prince's twin passions were flying and golf, a game at the nearby Sunningdale course being part of his weekend ritual.

While Freda began the remodelling of the Fort, Thelma took the credit for redecorating his bedroom in the maroon-and-blue colours of his Guards regiment. As Queen Mary had refused to let him borrow pictures from the Royal Collection, Edwina Mountbatten loaned him four oils of hunting scenes to give the place a homely feel. The royal retreat was comfortable – even including radiators in every bedroom – but Wallis left thinking that it was very much a home for a bachelor. Even his terrier dogs, Cora and Jaggs, were unfriendly to female visitors, yapping and snapping when she came into the room. Not that she liked dogs – though she worked hard to be friendly, eager to be a good guest.

As Thelma later remarked: 'My father always said, "It's more difficult to be a good guest than a good host." Wallis was a good guest trying to make a niche for herself, trying to please.' It was clear that she wanted a return ticket.

During that first weekend, Wallis, who was a quick study in human relationships, caught a flavour of the dynamic between her host and hostess. Though Thelma, rather suggestively, liked to light his after-dinner cigar, a knack she had learned in Cuba, there was no question that she was the dominant figure in their relationship. It was clear that the prince, an inherently nervy man, idolized her, allowing her to, as Wallis observed, 'lead him around like a lap dog'.

She realized, too, that Thelma's dominance at the prince's Court came at a price – she had to work hard to keep him amused and entertained and needed other lively guests to shoulder the burden. As Thelma later recalled: 'It was difficult with the prince. Very difficult. All the time you were on the *qui vive* [on the lookout]. You had to be gay and full of *joie de vivre* to keep him entertained. He was extremely nervous. He must always be doing something.'

As Ernest and Wallis drove back to central London on a wintry afternoon in late January 1932, Mrs Simpson had much to ponder about that weekend. Her 'man of mystery' had become even more mysterious, the king of nightclubs and needlepoint.

Divining his complex character would have to wait; the Simpsons had problems of their own. Such was the state of Ernest's shipping business that they tried to move out of Bryanston Court in order to save money. They gave up their car and made economies elsewhere. A trip to Tunis was paid for by their host, while their summer holiday with Aunt Bessie travelling round France and Austria was cut short by the recurrence of Wallis's perforated ulcer, which required days of bed rest.

By contrast, the prince and Thelma enjoyed a rather more playful summer, as guests of his good friend Eric, Lord Ednam, now the newly minted 3rd Earl of Dudley, who had rented a villa in the hills above Biarritz. As well as the prince and Thelma, he had invited Prince George and a number of wealthy American heiresses and socialites, including Barbara Hutton, Chicago socialite Julie Shipman, and Prince George's lover, Beth Leary.

Two years earlier, in July 1930, Eric's wife, Rosemary, had been tragically killed in a plane crash. Thelma remembers that it was the only time she ever saw the prince cry. They were staying at the Fort when George Trotter broke the news. He was devastated, tears rolling down his cheeks. Thelma recalled: 'It was a terrible shock for him. He crumpled at the news. I've never seen a man more genuinely unhappy. He was very, very sad for a long time.'

The prince explained to Thelma that he had met the then Lady Rosemary Leveson-Gower, the daughter of the Duke of Sutherland, in 1917 when she was working as a Red Cross nurse in France. Then aged twenty-three, the prince fell in love and promptly asked her to marry him. When he broached the subject with his parents, they would not hear of it. Even though the king had proclaimed that his children could now marry English commoners, it was felt that there was a 'taint in the blood', that is to say a streak of madness, in Lady Rosemary's mother's family, the St Clair-Erskines. Lady Victor Paget, one of Rosemary's closest friends, recalls that the prince was 'bitter and furious' about the king's decision. 'I don't think he ever forgave his father. I also felt that from that time on, he had made up his mind that he would never make what might be called a suitable marriage to please his family.'

All his later relationships were with married women or women he met for casual liaisons. The only exception was Princess Marina of Greece and Denmark, who was wooed by the prince throughout 1926 but, according to diarist Chips Channon, Freda Dudley Ward 'at the last moment, interfered and stopped it'.

As for Lady Rosemary, in 1919 she married the prince's close friend Eric, then Lord Ednam, his host that summer. After they married, the prince was a frequent visitor at Himley Hall, the Dudley family seat, and it was subsequently rumoured that their eldest son, William, was sired by his godfather, the Prince of Wales. He had often visited the family home when Rosemary was alone. As with Thelma's son, Tony, this gossip pursued William till the day he died – though he bore the rumours with good humour.

During their holiday in Biarritz, the prince was an indulgent father figure to Thelma's son. Though only five years old, Tony was a proficient reader, the prince encouraging him to read articles from *The Times* out loud. He bought the boy a miniature set of golf clubs, teaching him the rudiments of the game at the local Chiberta golf course, which was designed in 1927 by Tom Simpson with the prince in mind.

More adult entertainment was provided by Thelma's one-time beau, silent-screen star Charlie Chaplin, and the famed Russian opera singer Feodor Chaliapin. Both performed for the delighted prince at a restaurant in the nearby resort of Saint-Jean-de-Luz. (Chaliapin made the Prince of Wales's love life seem positively prosaic; he managed to have two separate families by two different women in Moscow and St Petersburg while he dwelt in Paris.)

The holiday is best remembered, though, for an incident that began the slow uncoupling between the prince and his paramour. On impulse Thelma suggested that she would like to go to Lourdes, the Roman Catholic shrine in southern France where the waters were famous for curing the sick and the lame. As the hundred-mile journey along narrow roads would take all day, the prince suggested he fly her there. Within hours the prince and Thelma found themselves kneeling in a muddy field in supplication as a priest went by carrying the Blessed Sacrament.

Though it was a private and supposedly anonymous visit, word got out, and when the prince returned to York House he found a deluge of letters asking why the future head of the Protestant Church of England was praying at a Catholic shrine. The consensus, inside and outside the palace, was that a certain Lady Furness was leading the Prince of Wales astray.

The end of the Biarritz holiday marked another more significant turning point. Once back in London, Thelma decided to formally go ahead and divorce her husband, Duke. After all, she reasoned, they had been separated for three years and there was no chance of a reconciliation. Her friends pleaded with her to reconsider, seeing the consequences, social and financial, of her folly. What she failed to realize was that she was unknowingly signing her own death warrant, her decision unsettling the status quo between her and the Prince of Wales. As a married but separated woman, and a Roman Catholic, she was the ideal foil for the prince. There was no chance of her ever marrying the prince or of her marrying another. He had a wife in all but name, available but not free. It was a trade-off. In turn she enjoyed the status of proximity to the throne. As she later observed, somewhat ruefully: 'The biggest mistake I made was in divorcing Duke. But after all the Prince of Wales was very glamorous. I thought it would last forever. I was wrong.'

As the weekends at the Fort should have taught Thelma, the prince was a creature of habit. He liked the familiarity of routine. Though he was now turning forty and still a bachelor, for all his adult life he'd had a woman by his side. And that woman was married.

Thelma should have learned from her own experience. In 1929, when Freda Dudley Ward decided to divorce her husband, William, it was no coincidence that the prince's gaze just happened to fall on Thelma Furness. Their 'chance' encounters on a train to Paris and at a cattle show in Leicester were orchestrated by two social predators looking for new mates. Their union worked smoothly because both knew the rules. Now Thelma was breaking the compact that existed between them.

In January 1933, when a judge granted Thelma a divorce on the grounds of her husband's adultery, she was skating on very thin ice. Her husband was not slow in remarrying, a few months later taking the plunge for the third time with strapping six-foot Australian adventuress Enid Cavendish, the widow of Brigadier General Frederick Cavendish, known as 'Caviar'. Duke showered her with jewels and bought her a tame cheetah. But there was no doubt as to who was the bigger cat.

From the moment Thelma told her royal lover that she was now divorced, consciously or unconsciously the prince was on the prowl, hunting fresh meat. This was one leopard who did not change his spots. In the back of his mind, he knew that at some point in the not-too-distant future, the newly single Thelma would announce that she had found another rich man and that she intended to remarry. It was all so predictable. It might happen in days or weeks or it could take months. But it would happen, of that there was no doubt. Signs of waning adoration were easy to spot. Thelma booked herself into a hotel in Wales for two weeks for a rest cure, as she found life with the prince rather 'strenuous'. She came to rely more and more on her friends to keep the prince entertained. For his part, whether or not he would ever admit it, the prince was casually on the lookout for a married woman who would dance attendance on him and a husband who would do a Nelson – that is to say, turn a blind eye.

Thelma's divorce in January 1933 coincided with more frequent invitations for the Simpsons to spend weekends of scything, singing and dancing at the Fort. A regular absentee was Ernest, who was often abroad on business trips as he endeavoured to save his company. Wallis became, in her words, 'a merry widow', flitting from the Fort to parties and dinners in London and the Home Counties. On one occasion she went skating on the nearby lake in Windsor Great Park with the Duke and Duchess of York.

It was not all high jinks. During one sedate weekend, an exasperated Wallis complained that Thelma's father was reading out loud from Dickens' *David Copperfield* as his daughter and the prince worked silently on their needlework. When Prince George was a guest, evenings were much more lively. After dinner he would play the piano, usually beginning with 'Love's Old Sweet Song', which is more popularly known as 'Just a Song at Twilight', before segueing into tunes the party could dance to. His elder brother loved to sing along to the drinking song from Sigmund Romberg's hit Broadway musical *The Student Prince*.

Not only were invitations to the Fort more frequent, but the prince took to calling on the Simpsons at Bryanston Court for dinner or a KT. Wallis and Ernest were accepted as part of the prince's inner circle, and from around this time, invitations to grand social events began to plop through the letter-box.

Her burgeoning British social life was put on hold for a couple of months when, at the end of March 1933, Wallis boarded the *Mauretania* for a much-anticipated voyage to Washington and Baltimore to visit family and friends. As the Isle of Wight dropped below the horizon, a messenger dashed over with a cable wishing her a safe crossing and a speedy return. It was signed Edward P., the prince's name garnering her respectful treatment for the journey. As she commented: 'Let me be candid: The attention was flattering. I enjoyed every minute of it.'

In her memoir she stated that she and Ernest sailed together and that the princely 'Bon Voyage' telegram was addressed to them both. In fact, Ernest stayed in London, Wallis sailing alone, her ticket paid for by Aunt Bessie.

Her assertion was Wallis's way of disguising the prince's growing interest in her; she was always eager in her memoirs and elsewhere to suggest that she was the innocent at large, buffeted by forces beyond her control. 'If the Prince was in any way drawn to me,' she wrote, 'I was unaware of his interest.' She was being deliberately insincere, her false inclusion of Ernest on her solo Atlantic voyage proof that she was well aware of the implication behind the prince's message. In her airbrushed narrative, decorum always trumped ambition and desire. In fact, now that Lady Furness was single, if still attached to the prince, the future king was gently testing the water elsewhere – without getting into hot water. He was not the only one. Unknown to Ernest, the prince or Thelma, Wallis was about to embark on a little hunting of her own. They were not the only big cats in the social jungle.

DARK-HAIRED COURTNEY LETTS, a renowned social beauty, celebrated Arctic explorer and best selling travel writer, carefully opened a silver photo frame displayed on a side table in the library of the Argentinian embassy in Washington, where her fiancé Felipe Espil was ambassador. There were tears in her eyes but anger in her heart as she took out a glossy black-and-white photograph of an angular-faced woman, gazing unblinking into the camera lens.

She struck a match and watched, with a mixture of glee and regret, as the picture of Wallis Simpson flared into flames, disintegrating before her eyes. While she felt shame at having given in to her deep if irrational feelings of jealousy, she felt a sense of release, too. In some way, burning Wallis had broken the spell cast over her by her love rival, who had recently returned to Washington for a two-month visit.

This behaviour was provoked by an earlier conversation with the embassy's Spanish butler. The night before, he had watched in horror as Wallis made her way to the second-floor bedroom suite occupied by Felipe.

She and Lady Lewis had spent what seemed like an eternity looking over his collection of photographs, pausing for some time over the pictures of Courtney, the two women sizing her up. Eventually the butler, who was appalled that women had entered these bachelor quarters, interrupted their snooping. 'I went in and asked if there was anything they needed,' the butler later told Courtney, adding with scarcely disguised disdain: 'They laughed and went downstairs.'

The news of Wallis's late-night incursion provoked mixed feelings in Courtney's heart. She knew all about Wallis's torrid dalliance with her future husband during the 1920s when Wallis was still married to Navy aviator Win Spencer. Questions, though, remained. What was she doing in Washington? Why had she visited the Argentinian Embassy? And what was she doing in Felipe's bedroom? Though she trusted her fiancé, she remembered her father's warning about dating Latin men. The worm of doubt entered her soul.

There was already talk in diplomatic circles that Wallis's second marriage, to Ernest Simpson, was in trouble. Could it be that the ambitious Mrs Simpson was testing the romantic waters with her former flame? That, at least, was how Courtney Letts interpreted Wallis's behaviour.

She found it suspicious that Wallis had wangled an invitation to dinner at the Argentinian Embassy, a dinner, moreover, which Courtney was unable to attend and which was hosted by Felipe. Nor was this the first time they had met since their grand affair. When Felipe had been in London a couple of years earlier, they had seen each other at several cocktail parties, notably at her home at Bryanston Court and a reception for the Prince of Wales hosted by Lady Furness.

If she had been present at the embassy dinner, Courtney would have been even more apprehensive. She would have noticed that Wallis had dressed to impress, wearing a black chiffon dress with a white gardenia, her hair brushed so finely that, as society photographer Cecil Beaton would later describe it, 'a fly would slip on it'. At the same time, she would have been consoled by the studiously upright behaviour of Felipe, who kept his distance from her, only speaking with Wallis towards the end of the evening.

The next day, still recovering from the butler's horrified observations, Courtney was astonished to come across Wallis sitting nearby having lunch with two other women in a Washington hotel. Even though their paths had crossed romantically, with both Felipe and Gerry Greene, they had never met, and so they ignored one another.

Courtney was dining with an out-of-town friend who was not aware of her engagement to Felipe, and it was her friend who spotted Wallis in the restaurant. 'Do you know Wallis Simpson?' she asked. In order to see what she would say, Courtney answered in the negative.

'I wonder why she is here,' her friend continued. 'I hear she and her husband don't hit it off any too well. She was Espil's mistress for several years.'

Courtney later recorded in her diary: 'Said just like that. I felt a horrible shock run through me. We continued eating. I fled soon after with a "Sorry, I have an engagement immediately after."'

As concerned as Courtney was, she need not have worried. What she didn't realize was that the girl from Baltimore had attracted the attention of a man of far grander title than a mere plenipotentiary, namely His Royal Highness the Prince of Wales. Several months later, on 28 July 1933, Courtney and Ambassador Espil married, the first ambassador for fifty years to marry in post in Washington. Though Courtney was now safely hitched, she kept a beady eye on Wallis from afar, quizzing passing diplomats and politicians about developments in Britain. Her husband, too, would continue to play an unexpected role in romantic affairs of the royal House of Windsor.

Unaware of the suspicion she had aroused inside the Argentinian Embassy, for the next two months the girl known as Wally had a gay old time, catching up with her friends and squired around Washington by any number of admirers. A particular favourite was American diplomat and wine connoisseur John C. Wiley, who was soon to marry the artist and writer Irena Baruch. She had such fun that the prospect of returning to dull domestic routine back in London in May held little appeal. Wallis had enjoyed the spotlight of attention from her 'boys'.

Once back in London, Wallis yearned to be with her compatriots. Even invitations to the Fort or out to nightclubs with the prince and Thelma failed to excite her enthusiasm.

Her spirits were lifted when in June an influx of American diplomats, including her Washington beau John Wiley, arrived in the capital for the London Economic Conference, where sixty-six nations gathered to discuss the global crisis.

Wiley treated her to a birthday lunch on 19 June, and that evening the prince and Thelma hosted a birthday dinner for her at the cavernous Quaglino's restaurant on Bury Street. The prince gave her a present of an orchid plant for her thirty-seventh birthday, promising that with careful tending it would bloom in a year. So it did.

The modest present, the kind that the prince might give to his housekeeper, hardly suggested a budding affair. Nor, six months later, did his Christmas gift of a framed photograph – a standard royal present for senior servants – anticipate the deluge of gems to come.

While the departure in July of the American diplomats had left a hole in her social calendar, it was soon filled by the much-anticipated arrival of Lelia, the daughter of her cousin Lelia Montague Barnett. The younger Lelia was at the centre of a marital merry-go-round that had turned the Montague clan upside down. Lelia's married sister Anne had fallen in love with Newbold Noyes, the married journalist brother of Wallis's great friend Lady Lewis. Unfortunately for Anne, Newbold Noyes was madly in love with her sister Lelia, who was also married. When Lelia and her friend Madge Larrabee arrived in London, Wallis was eager to catch up with the twists and turns in this unfolding family drama, a drama that eventually left all three marriages in ruins.

For their part, Lelia and Madge were given a sense of cousin Wallis's proximity to the Crown. When they visited her at Bryanston Court after a night out at the theatre, they were thrilled to meet the Prince of Wales and Lady Furness. He played the bagpipes for them, stood on his head, and presented Madge with a book of war photographs that he had intended for Ernest. They all had such a jolly time that the prince didn't leave until three in the morning.

When Lelia and Madge returned home, Wallis couldn't help but feel homesick. London seemed somehow even emptier and less gay without the American diplomats and her cousin. She envied Thelma when she told her that she, too, was sailing to New York in January to see her sister Gloria. 'I am going to miss Thelma terribly,' she told her aunt. Days before Thelma sailed, Wallis met her for lunch at the Ritz hotel. During their meeting, Wallis recalled, Thelma said: 'I'm afraid the prince is going to be lonely. Wallis, won't you look after him?' Thelma's memory is rather different. It was Wallis who blurted out: 'Oh, Thelma, the little man is going to be so lonely.' To which Thelma responded: 'Well, dear, you look after him for me while I'm away. See that he does not get into any mischief and for heaven's sake stop calling him "the little man".'

'It was later evident,' said Thelma ruefully, 'that Wallis took my advice all too literally. I trusted Wallis. It never entered my head that she was making a play for the prince.'

Given subsequent events, the implication of Thelma's account is that Wallis was waiting in the wings and swooped down on her man once she was safely out of the way. Thelma was betrayed by a trusted friend.

The reality was that Wallis was a bystander in an emotional untangling involving the prince and Thelma. The prince was Thelma's to lose, not Wallis's to win.

In Thelma's account, she said her fond farewells to the prince at the Fort. As she drove away, the forlorn figure of the future king standing in the driveway made her regret her decision to leave. After all, there was no particular reason for her visit to America. It was, in her words, to 'recharge my batteries', to see her sister and take a trip to California. The prince sent her long and frequent cables, all carefully coded to conceal their intimate nature.

When she and her sister Gloria arrived in Hollywood, they were the talk of the United Artists studio, especially after Thelma received a long-distance telephone call from the prince. It was a brief and inconclusive chat, the prince desperately wanting to know when she was coming home. Then a storm in the Atlantic ended the conversation prematurely.

A storm was indeed brewing. Shortly before leaving for England, Thelma attended a dinner party in New York, where she was seated next to Aly Khan, one of the richest bachelors in Europe. He was the playboy son of the Aga Khan, who was regarded by Ismaili Muslims as the divine descendant of the Prophet. Aly, who was only twenty-two, already had an international reputation as a sportsman, driving his sports cars as hard as he rode his horses. Dark, handsome, attentive and effortlessly charming, he wooed women easily. Thelma was no exception.

The morning after the dinner party, he sent five dozen, long-stemmed American Beauty roses to her apartment, and he dined with her that evening at the fashionable Colony restaurant. The next day there were more roses, followed by cocktails at the Ritz-Carlton. He asked her to join him for lunch the following day but she refused, saying that her ship was due to sail.

When she entered her stateroom on board ship she found the cabin crowded with roses and a note from Aly that read: 'You left too soon.' As the *Bremen* slipped out of New York, her phone rang. 'Hello, darling, it's Aly. Will you have lunch with me today?'

Thinking it was a ship-to-shore call, she answered gaily: 'Where will it be, Aly? Palm Beach or New York?'

Aly laughed: 'Right here. I'm on board.' He entertained and flattered her all the way back to England, asking her to marry him during the six-day voyage. 'The road with the prince leads nowhere,' he shot, an arrow that hit an emotional bullseye in Thelma's heart. When they docked at Southampton, Thelma offered to give Aly a ride back to London in her car. As they waited to disembark, the prince called her on the ship's telephone and asked her to join him at the Fort for supper. She said she couldn't as she was giving a friend a ride to London. She and the prince arranged to meet at her London home for supper instead.

It was a stiff, awkward and somewhat forlorn reunion. The prince talked about the rotten weather, the state of the garden at the Fort, and his golf, until finally, as they sat sipping coffee by the fireplace, he spoke about what was really on his mind. 'I hear Aly Khan has been very attentive to you,' he said, his blue eyes burning into her. 'Are you jealous, darling?' she asked. A heavy silence hung between them. The damage had been done. He informed her that people were gossiping and it would be better if they just saw each other now and again and let the relationship end naturally. 'I thought that was very nice of him,' she recalled. He asked her to the Fort that weekend, and she – 'like a nitwit' – asked him if the Simpsons could come, too, as they were gay and it would make matters easier.

The next day, Thelma called Wallis and asked if she could visit her at Bryanston Court. When she arrived, she was surprised to see Wallis looking more chic and groomed, her clothes more expensive and her voice more English. Thelma told her story about Aly and how she was amazed that the prince did not want to make a new start. Or at least offer to make a new start.

Wallis reassured her that the prince was 'simply lost' without her, answering in the negative the inevitable question about whether the prince had transferred his love to another American. 'Thelma,' she said, 'I think he likes me. He may be fond of me. But if you mean is he in love with me, the answer is definitely no.'

While Thelma had showed her hand, the poker-faced Mrs Simpson was playing her cards close to her chest. There had indeed been an emotional step change in her royal relationship. While Thelma was away, Wallis joined the prince and his friends, NBC radio executive Fred Bate and his wife, 'Gebe', at the Dorchester hotel. During dinner, the prince and Wallis made a soul connection over the unlikely subject of working practices in Britain and America. The prince had just returned from the industrial north of England and, encouraged by Wallis's unwavering eye contact and focus, he let down his guard, chatting enthusiastically about the limitations of his job and the role he believed royalty could play in shaping Britain's future. Amid talk about American labour unions, industrial output, steel scaffolding and radiators, a bond was forged. From the moment he said: 'Wallis, you're the only woman who's ever been interested in my job', she knew the prince was also interested in her. When she asked him directly if he was lonely and he replied, 'Yes', she knew that she had made a bond. The prince looked at her with new eyes, something clicking deep in his soul. She was no longer the house guest or hostess *manqué*, but a woman of interest.

Novelist Upton Sinclair, who was Wallis's cousin, sketched out her seduction technique in his short play *Wally for Queen!* It was remarkably like her encounter at the Dorchester. Wallis coyly explains to Edward her skills at making herself 'helpful' to a man:

> *A woman notes that men like to talk about themselves. She learns to listen and be interested. Every man, no matter how much he blusters, is really lonely and uneasy – a child to the woman. It's her task to make him wonderful to himself – and not let him know she is doing it.*

From that evening, the 'helpful' Mrs Simpson increasingly became the focus of his attention. He would call her on the telephone two or three times a day, arrive at the Simpson home early and stay late, regularly sitting down with the couple for pot-luck suppers. It soon became clear to Wallis, as it had been to Thelma and Freda, that the future king was a profoundly lonely man who needed constant attention and coddling. As the weeks passed, the dinners with the Simpsons as a trio became dinners *à deux*, Ernest happy for his wife to dine alone with the prince. Not only did he consider it an honour, it gave him time to focus on trying to save his ailing shipping business. While Thelma was away, the prince asked Wallis to organize his weekends at the Fort, and her friends – who included Kitty and George Hunter and Gladys and Patrick Anderson – joined the Simpsons in entertaining him. It was noticeable that Wallis was always the first to be asked to join the prince for after-dinner dancing. The most obvious sign of their growing friendship and convivial intimacy was the fact that the prince now affectionately teased her accent, much to her smiling irritation. It was not long before the rumour mill began churning, Wallis throwing her hands up in mock exasperation. 'I'm not in the habit of taking my girlfriends' beaux. I think I do amuse him. I'm the comedy relief and we like to dance together.' For all her complaints that the prince was 'exhausting', secretly she was loving it all.

Not that Wallis gave a hint to Thelma of her true feelings or the cordial familiarity she now shared with the future king during their awkward *tête-à-tête* at her London apartment. Then the telephone rang. It was the Prince of Wales. Wallis answered the call but when she returned made no mention of the content. She did, though, agree that she and Ernest would travel down to the Fort together for the weekend.

At dinner the first night, Thelma, nursing a heavy cold, sat opposite the prince while Wallis sat next to him. He picked at the salad with his fingers and Wallis patted his hand, as if saying, 'Naughty boy, you must not eat with your fingers.'

Thelma recalled that moment: 'I was so surprised that I caught her eye and shook my head at her. She looked straight at me and I knew what had happened. Wallis of all people. Wallis to whom I had given my clothes, loaned my court train, staged parties, coaxed the prince to invite to the Fort and even gone to for advice.'

After dinner she retired to bed early, blaming her cold. For once, she was not on hand to light the prince's after-dinner cigar. A little later the prince came into her room and sat on the edge of the bed. She looked him in the eye and said: 'Is it Wallis, darling?'

He said, 'Don't be silly', and got up and walked out. The next morning, she left the Fort and went to Paris where (surprise, surprise) Aly was waiting. They then drove down to Spain for a riotous pell-mell week of champagne, caviar and fornication, cold forgotten.

What infuriated Thelma was that, even though she had been open and honest about Aly, Wallis had never given a hint that matters had changed between her and the prince. 'Why didn't she tell me before we went down to the Fort? I gave her such an opening. She could have said: "Oh, darling, I am so happy you have told me because since you've been away this is what's happened. We couldn't help it, it just happened." After all, I couldn't have been a dog in a manger.'

The reason why she couldn't have been a dog in a manger was because she wasn't being entirely honest herself. According to her friend and business partner Sonia Rosenberg, her passionate romance with Aly began much earlier than she suggested and was the justification for sailing to New York in the first place. During their time in New York, Aly gave her jewellery and clothes, buying her every style of dress from Sonia's store. 'Thelma was Aly's lover long before she and the prince broke up,' recalled Sonia.

As with Duke Furness and the Prince of Wales, Thelma tried to have it all, wanting both Aly and the prince in her life. 'Thelma didn't leave the prince, he left her. It was over Aly,' Sonia remembered. 'She came to America for him. I know, I was there. The prince heard about it and he cabled her to come back. She was a little frightened. Here she is stupid. She let Aly come back on the same ship with her. Even though he was not the jealous type, it was just too much for the prince. She could have stayed with the prince. He was crazy about her. Again, she was a fool. She went to the well too often.'

From the moment she drove out of the Fort on her way to Paris, her life went downhill. Aly soon cheated on her. (He eventually married Joan Barbara Guinness in May 1936 after she fell pregnant.) A few days after her royal departure she called the prince from Paris about a charity event she was organizing for him. The prince coldly told her that he had decided to cancel it. She replied: 'I suppose it's said that the king can do no wrong. I don't like to hang up on anybody, but goodbye.' With that, she banged down the receiver.

In a last jab, she wrote: 'I wish to God he had found somebody who could make him happy and not a figure of fun.'

Her abrupt departure from Fort Belvedere meant that there was now a job vacancy for the post of the Prince of Wales's mistress. In the spring of 1934, there was a shortlist of one.

CHAPTER NINE

A Bounder, a Libertine and a Spy

WALLIS AND ERNEST celebrated their sixth wedding anniversary in July 1934 by going their separate ways; he sailed for New York on business, she travelled to Biarritz. The departure signalled the beginning of the end of their marriage, the period when Wallis fell in love with another man.

For the next two months, she spent every day as guest, companion and confidante of the Prince of Wales, sunbathing, eating, talking, getting to know one another. He had taken a spacious villa in the hills above Biarritz, the resort where he had entertained various mistresses, including Lady Furness and her twin, Gloria Vanderbilt. None, though, ever spent quite as long with the future king as Mrs Simpson. Since Thelma's dramatic exit, Wallis had slipped seamlessly into her role as hostess and entertainer in chief of the Prince of Wales. She had kept the prince at bay sexually by ensuring that she never was with him in a situation that would encourage greater intimacy. Their holiday would test that resolve to the limit – and beyond. It seems she succeeded in remaining chaste, both Wallis and the prince declaring that they never had carnal relations before they eventually married.

Ostensibly her aunt Bessie was her chaperone, although she left the small royal party to go on a motoring tour when the prince and his guests joined Lord Moyne on his yacht *Rosaura*, a converted channel steamer, for a cruise along the Portuguese and Spanish coast.

After weathering a fierce storm, they eventually reached Formentor on the island of Majorca, where they spent the days swimming and daydreaming on the beach, and the evenings watching flamenco dancers or dancing themselves on the beautiful lantern-lit terraces overlooking the sea. For both of them it was a special five days, the time when, as Wallis described it, they 'crossed the line that marks the indefinable boundary between friendship and love'. They had reached a point of no return in their relationship.

As she later confessed: 'I had indeed met a man. David and I were falling in love. There was nothing either of us could do about it – like all true love stories it had to be. It took us a while to realize what was happening, and we did not quite know what to do. There was no long-range or short-range plan. I was still married and that was that.'

The prince marked this romantic interlude by composing a slow melody for the bagpipes, which he called 'Majorca', and quietly handing her a diamond-and-emerald charm for her bracelet, purchased when they reached the seaside town of Cannes in the South of France.

Within hours of their docking, Wallis was reunited with the *other* man in her life, Herman Rogers. He and Katherine had only just returned from a month-long cruise on their yacht, the *Angélique*, when Wallis and the prince came a-calling. That night they entertained the couple and the other two in the party – Posy Guinness, the beautiful cousin of Lord Moyne, and the prince's equerry, Major Jack Aird – at their villa. After Herman showed them his films of Peking and Bali, the six of them went out on the town until five in the morning. The next day they sailed to Saint-Tropez, the prince having such a good time that he invited Herman and Katherine to join them on a trip to Lake Como in Italy.

In a breathless and hitherto unpublished six-page letter to his sister, Anne, Herman described the events of the holiday. Typically, the ever-discreet friend never once hinted at a relationship between the prince and the woman he and Katherine hosted for four months in Peking. Of the trip he wrote: 'Wallis is quicker on the trigger than anyone I know, and we always had something to laugh at. It couldn't have been more informal or more fun.' They swam, played golf, hired sculling boats, dined late and woke at noon. Herman got on famously with the prince, something of a shipboard 'bromance' developing between the two men. 'He couldn't be more generous, or simple or more fun to be with. I have never met anyone with so much charm. All the stories you hear of his drinking and foolishness are wrong. No one could be more thoughtful of others.'

The Rogers returned to their Cannes home to find themselves the centre of gossip and a 'terrible jealousy' among the local community. Herman wrote to his sister Anne telling her that one so called 'friend' had remarked: 'Of course the Rogers would never see anything of the prince normally – he's just slumming now.' That was but a fraction of the rumour and hearsay that began to erupt around Wallis. When Aunt Bessie, who had been reunited with the party at Villa d'Este by Lake Como, managed to see her alone before she sailed for New York, she voiced her concern to a resolutely unconcerned niece.

Tentatively she broached the subject of the Prince of Wales's fondness for Wallis, but Wallis airily brushed her observations aside. For once, Aunt Bessie continued her questioning. 'Isn't this all very dangerous for you? If you let yourself enjoy this kind of life, it will make you very restless and dissatisfied with everything you have known before.'

Wallis wouldn't hear of it. 'It's all great fun. You don't have to worry about me – I know what I am doing.' Grimly, her aunt told her that she could see 'no happy outcome' to this situation.

Her concern was entirely for Wallis who had, following her failed marriage to Win Spencer, seemingly found stability and contentment with Ernest. Bessie had been sure that her niece was at last enjoying married life and that her husband, an educated, witty fellow, clearly adored her. 'He had a marvellous mind for history and dates,' she recalled. Wallis could do worse, much worse. Now Wallis was risking being left high and dry because of a summer infatuation with the Prince of Wales. It was bound to end in tears once the prince's attention was captured by another bright, shiny object.

Never for a moment did Aunt Bessie imagine that it would be Ernest who was left maritally marooned. As she recalled: 'She [Wallis] would have stayed with Ernest, but she was hit by this avalanche. On the other hand, I suppose it is quite a compliment to be picked out.'

As far as Wallis was concerned she was a woman of the world enjoying her time in the royal sun, knowing that soon enough the sun would set. She was now thirty-eight and surmised that she had only a few years left before she was firmly placed on the shelf. As she recalled: 'I had on my return no illusions about my future or rather the future of David and myself. No girl in her right mind would have ever thought that a king would abdicate over her.'

Her Montague side enjoyed living the dream, her Warfield half realized it would come to an end soon enough. All the evidence from the prince's life pointed in that direction. As she later recalled: 'There were at least a dozen girls who had lasted one summer with David, but when the next year rolled around they were forgotten.' For the moment, she was happy being Wallis in Wonderland, and her husband seemed content to indulge her as she lived this enchanted lifestyle.

In her mind she was simply playing the prince's game like those who had come before her. When the prince gave Wallis a dog, a cairn terrier he called Slipper, for Christmas, she smiled inwardly, knowing that he had also given a dog to Thelma, a Pekinese called Puff, at a similar stage in their relationship.

Then there was the diamond-and-emerald charm he had handed her in Cannes. It was not too personal and would not raise too many questions from an inquisitive husband – rather like the black-and-white pearl earrings and cabochon emerald ring he had given Thelma. As Thelma remarked: 'How can you give a married woman a lot of expensive presents without her husband knowing about it?'

Ernest knew all about what the prince was giving his wife – before Christmas 1934 she had added two bracelets and a diamond hairpin to the charm. Typically, he complained about the cost of insurance rather than what it said about his wife's relationship with the future king. As Thelma described him: 'Ernest was the dog tray type – faithful come what may. Royalty could do no wrong.'

From what Wallis had gleaned from her earlier conversations with Thelma, she would not have expected much more from the prince. Thelma had discovered that, what with paying for receptions and dinners at her Grosvenor Square home, it was an expensive business being the Prince of Wales's mistress. In the early months of her attachment, Wallis had the same complaint, albeit on a lesser scale. As royalty never carries money, she was the one dipping into her handbag to tip waiters, hatcheck girls and the like.

Once back in London after her two-month holiday with the prince, there was no stopping the very merry go-round for Wallis. She and Ernest were weekend fixtures at the Fort, and the prince became such a regular at Bryanston Court that it was he, rather than Ernest, who fixed the drinks and handed around the canapés.

'Keeping up with two men is making me move all the time,' she wrote to her aunt, emphasizing that everything was 'just grand' between the threesome. She returned to Burrough Court in Melton Mowbray, the place where she had apparently first met the prince, for several weekends, though Thelma was now no longer in residence. Staff recall that after one late-night party, the prince was pushed around the grounds in a baby's pram by Wallis. It was perhaps symbolic.

Edward was so very different from the other men in her life. They were sensible and centred, placing career above affairs of the heart. There was an emotional flywheel that modulated the behaviour of Felipe, Herman and Ernest. They were mature men of proportion, quiet calm and imperturbability. The prince was such a contrast to this that Wallis found him hard to read. He was childlike in the way his feelings lurched from undying devotion to cold indifference, brooding on suicide one moment, savouring ecstasy the next. His love letters reflected his all-or-nothing behaviour, the prince falling in love hard and fast. 'I love you so so madly & desparately [sic]. I worship and adore you my sweetheart and cannot bear being away from you.' The note could be to one of any number of his lovers, though this was written to Freda Dudley Ward.

Simpering, self-pitying and spoiled, he is revealed in his correspondence as a man whose character was in complete contrast to the traditional royal stiff upper lip and the informal royal motto: 'Never complain, never explain.' Years later his mistress of more than six years, Freda Dudley Ward, was asked if she ever loved the man who signed himself her 'little slave' or 'little parpee' (puppy). 'Oh no,' she replied crisply, 'he was much too abject.'

Little wonder that Wallis initially struggled to divine the real man behind the public image. Few could, as he did not fit the template of what the public expected from royalty. Though he exuded an air of quiet authority and endearing natural charm, the prince was the least tranquil of men – lonely, restless and somehow empty. Socially ambitious, Wallis was drawn to him as much for his image as his personality; for what he could conjure as much as what he had to say for himself. As to what attraction she held for him, she ticked off her humour, sense of fun and independent American spirit. That, though, got her only so far. Perhaps her curiosity about his world and her appreciation of his isolated life and position counted for more than she knew. Then she was stumped. After all, as she acknowledged, there were many others who were prettier and better dressed than she.

These deeper considerations were laid aside in the affairs of the moment. Much of that fall of 1934 was spent 'babysitting' another royal, ensuring that Prince George kept out of mischief before his glamorous November wedding to Princess Marina of Greece and Denmark at Westminster Abbey. Before the big day there were numerous receptions and dinners, culminating in a state reception hosted by the king and queen at Buckingham Palace. First he introduced Wallis to Prince Paul of Yugoslavia, who realized from his demeanour that the prince was in love again, with yet another American. Then he took her and Ernest to meet the king and queen. As she made her way through the throng she was watched, as she later recalled, by 'all those cold, jealous English eyes'. Though the meeting was brief and the conversation merely banal platitudes, the Simpsons had at last planted the Stars and Stripes on the social equivalent of Mount Everest – meeting the King and Queen of England at Buckingham Palace.

After joining the prince to greet the New Year at a London nightclub, Wallis had real mountains to climb a few weeks later when, much to Ernest's irritation, she joined the prince's skiing party in Kitzbühel, Austria. For a woman whose life had been geared towards control, the idea of flying down a slope with two pieces of wood strapped to her ankles was her idea of hell. She described the two-week vacation in the winter of 1935 as 'one long horror'.

Even when she was relegated to what the Austrians call 'slopes for idiots', she fell constantly, finishing the day frozen and bad tempered. The only respite was when the prince decided to return via Vienna, allowing for three days of shopping and dancing to the tunes of the 'waltz king', Johann Strauss.

Socially she was now dancing with the stars of the aristocracy. Once news had seeped through London society that Wally was the new squeeze of the Prince of Wales, her life took a decidedly upward turn. Doors opened, invitations landed and gifts showered, so much so that she installed a second phone line and considered hiring a social secretary to deal with all the stiff white cards. When she entered a restaurant, heads would turn, knowing looks would be exchanged, and voices would be lowered as whispered confidences were shared.

Wallis was not only a social celebrity but also a perplexing conundrum. What did the Prince of Wales see in the angular wife of a struggling shipping agent as opposed to the younger and decidedly more beautiful Lady Furness? Or the pick of European royalty and nobility for that matter?

It was a question that would exercise powerful minds for many years to come. Social London wanted to know more about the lady from Baltimore. Theories abounded. She was a low-born sorceress who used her sexual abilities to seduce the prince, the future king being in thrall to an obsession rather than love. Queen Mary, like many others, believed that her son was under some kind of malign spell that would, in time, be broken.

The result was that while she and Ernest were invited to as many smart dinners as they could digest, Wallis was well aware that she was the main course, the social equivalent of the bearded lady. 'I know that many people only invited me out of curiosity and looked forward to criticizing me as soon as I had left the room.'

Occasionally she enjoyed wielding the knife. Out of the blue, a so-called friend from Baltimore, who had been in London for many months, called her on the telephone. 'It never occurred to me that you were *the* Mrs Simpson everyone is talking about,' she said. Wallis replied:'But it never occurred to you to call me as Mrs Simpson', and promptly put the phone down.

For the brilliant but intensely competitive society hostesses who stalked the ballrooms and dining rooms of Knightsbridge, Mayfair and Belgravia, Wallis was fresh meat to throw before the social lions who dined at their tables. At that time the quirky queen of social London was Lady Emerald Cunard, a tiny, twittering canary of a woman who cheeped and chirruped around her guests, encouraging them to preen and parade. She soon swooped on Wallis, just as she had on Thelma Furness a few years before, when Thelma was the latest attractive addition to the prince's aviary.

On that occasion, Lady Cunard linked arms with Thelma as they were leaving the dining table. She told her much younger companion: 'Now Thelma, you are new here. You must let me sponsor you and show you the ropes.'

She offered to give Thelma a party and encouraged her to start a salon on the lines of Madame de Maintenon, the influential second wife of French king Louis XIV. The goal would be to bring Queen Mary into her orbit and give Lady Cunard further influence. A somewhat bewildered Thelma responded: 'I wouldn't know what to do with Queen Mary even if I had her here.'

Four years later Thelma was sardonically amused to learn that Lady Cunard had used the same bait in an attempt to lure Wallis Simpson into her lair. 'Now, my dear, I will launch you,' Emerald told her. 'Remember our goal is the queen.' As Wallis came to appreciate, it was Lady Cunard's lifelong ambition to bring Queen

Mary under her artistic influence, a testament to her relentless drive and unquenchable spirit. In order to do so, she publicly professed to adore the sparky American. Of the woman who never willingly read a book, she said, without irony: 'Little Mrs Simpson is a woman of character and reads Balzac.'

Born Maud Alice Burke in San Francisco, Emerald was raised in modest circumstances, but marriage to a shipping heir, Sir Bache Cunard, changed her fortune and gave her the opportunity to indulge her passion for the arts, sponsoring operas and other orchestral works conducted by her lover, the conductor Sir Thomas Beecham.

She made her name, though, as a hostess, literary tyros, political heavyweights and beautiful women being the staple of her legendary parties. Lady Cunard was careless of the conventional dinner party pairings, saying that she brought people together for conversation and not mating.

The table talk was often sparkling, eclectic and provocative, former prime minister Lloyd George considering her the most dangerous woman in London because she encouraged indiscretions from even the most strait-laced of politicians. She was challenging, mischievous and whimsical; her speciality was throwaway lines such as 'Christ had a very unpleasant face, and John the Baptist's was little better.' Early on in their friendship, she disconcerted Wallis when she informed her that, unlike her new friend, she no longer liked her home country. 'You see, dear, I don't play golf, bridge, and I don't drink.'

The prince would often arrive unexpectedly at her Grosvenor Square home, at first with both Ernest and Wallis in tow, later just with Wallis. While others would be nonplussed, Lady Cunard, who thought nothing of organizing a lunch for twenty-four, a dinner for fifty and a supper party for sixty on the same day, simply joined them for another supper at the Kit-Cat club.

*

LADY CUNARD WAS not the only society hostess inviting Wallis to her parties. Her great rival, Lady Sibyl Colefax – tall, distinguished and dark-haired – sat her next to Winston Churchill during one luncheon, at which the future world leader engaged in a running battle with the American journalist H. R. Knickerbocker, who had just returned from a visit to the Soviet Union with favourable views of the Communist system.

Though Wallis was entertained by such society luminaries as Lady Portarlington, Helen Fitz-Gerald and the razor-sharp Lady Oxford, who counselled her to be careful, as her views would be construed as the prince's thinking, her undoubted favourite was the irrepressible interior designer Elsie de Wolfe, Lady Mendl.

Born in 1858 to a New York doctor, Elsie de Wolfe became a well-known actress who was celebrated more for her fashion flair than her ability as a thespian. In the 1880s she became intimate with theatrical producer and literary agent Elisabeth 'Bessie' Marbury, the lesbian couple being coyly nicknamed 'the Bachelors'. They travelled frequently to Paris, where the climate was more tolerant for gay and lesbian lifestyles. Here Elsie made a name for herself as a talented interior designer, in 1913 publishing a bestselling book on the subject. By the mid-1920s she was a self-made millionaire, her name a brand on everything from cars to cigarettes, an international personality celebrated in song by the likes of Noël Coward and Cole Porter.

She shocked everyone, but especially her long-time lover, Bessie, when in 1926 she married the British diplomat Sir Charles Mendl. Though they lived separately, this unusual arrangement allowed the acquisitive interior designer, now a diplomat's wife, to live in Paris tax-free and to sport an aristocratic title.

It was her close friend John 'Johnnie' McMullin, social columnist for *Vogue* magazine and confirmed bachelor, who first introduced her to Wallis, and Wallis soon became her eager protégée in all matters of interior decoration, entertainment, health fads and fashion. She was responsible for Wallis's signature Windsor style, a look that could be characterized as neat elegance. She lived by the genteel credo: 'Be pretty if you can, witty if you must, and be gracious if it kills you.'

More practically, Elsie and John helped Wallis purchase *haute couture* at a discount, Wallis making frequent shopping forays to Paris for the latest offerings of Elsa Schiaparelli and the American designer Mainbocher. For the Simpsons, who had long lived beyond their means, it was crucial to have such social backers as they climbed ever higher up London's social ladder.

Shortly after their first meeting in London, Lady Mendl invited Wallis to stay at her home in Paris. It was a memorable and also uncomfortable visit. When she arrived at the apartment on the avenue d'Iéna, Wallis was received, as was Elsie's custom, in her bathroom, where she was lying on a sofa surrounded by soft leopard-skin pillows. It was not until later that Wallis met Sir Charles Mendl, who immediately disconcerted her by saying: 'My dear, you must change your hair. You look as if you are going out riding.' At that time she was sporting her signature look, hair parted down the middle with a large chignon at the back. Dinner did little for her confidence. She later recalled: 'Sir Charles was obviously unable to understand for the life of him why the Prince of Wales should be attracted to me.'

Though Wallis cultivated and was cultivated by titled hostesses, unlike the previous mistresses of the Prince of Wales, her elevation divided London society. While there were many who tried to bask in the royal glow, there was perhaps a majority, particularly among those closer in age and social proximity to the king and queen, who found Wallis and her husband simply below the salt. Her fellow American, Nancy Astor, Virginia born and the first woman member of Parliament, was horrified by the prince's latest obsession.

It was Nancy's firm conviction that only well-born Virginian families should have access to the royal family, and Wallis was neither. She was appalled when fellow spectators lined up to pay court to Wallis when she accompanied the prince into the show ring during Ascot race week. 'I don't see how they could. I would swim home rather than queue to shake hands with the king's mistress.' She pointed the finger of blame at her rival hostess, accusing Lady Cunard of being a 'disintegrating influence' for promoting Mrs Simpson and encouraging her in her belief that she and her husband were accepted in such exalted society.

Nor did Lady Astor, who had occasion to play golf with the Prince of Wales, approve of the moral behaviour of the future king. She accused him of acting like a 'libertine', a stinging remark that infuriated him. His private secretary, Alan Lascelles, recalled that the Prince of Wales resolved to have nothing more to do with Lady Astor. 'Kind friends repeated this, as kind friends so often do, and he never forgave her.' The feeling was mutual. Years later, the Windsors and Lady Astor were sailing to New York on the same liner and the prince proffered an olive branch, inviting Nancy to meet his wife. She refused.

At first those in royal circles had welcomed Mrs Simpson's sobering presence in the prince's life. Unlike Thelma Furness, she was not a heavy drinker and had managed to curb the prince's excesses. She had also improved his notorious timekeeping, scolding him for bad manners if he kept people waiting. Her predecessor had been taught from birth that little people didn't matter, so her puppy-dog prince followed her lead. However, as the months passed and the prince became more rather than less smitten with the lady from Baltimore, consternation mounted at Court.

It was Wallis's ill luck to have entered his life when the marital clock was officially ticking. In June 1934 the prince turned forty. That same month Wallis celebrated her thirty-eighth birthday.

Everyone from Queen Mary down wanted to see a dynastic marriage of some kind to someone in the rapidly evaporating pool of suitable candidates. 'Oh, Mama, don't bother me with that now,' he would tell the queen when she raised the subject. Even Hitler was concerned, ordering his diplomatic envoy, Joachim von Ribbentrop, to find a suitable German princess for the royal bachelor. The royal houses of Sweden, Greece and Italy all strived to offer a candidate as a bride for the Prince of Wales. And there were, of course, the well-born mothers who tried to push their entirely suitable offspring into the prince's path. He ignored them all.

Wallis came to realize that, through no fault of hers, the prince had developed a complex about single women, however eligible and pretty. She concluded that her biggest weakness – that she was married – was also her greatest strength. Wallis intended to keep it that way. Years of knocking around the globe and dealing with the amorous male had taught her the value of being occasionally elusive and mysterious.

On one occasion when the prince was on an official visit to the Channel Islands, he called her at Bryanston Court and asked the maid to tell Wallis to call him back urgently. She never returned the call, even though he delayed his return from the islands in the hope of hearing her voice. Once back in London, he raced over to Bryanston Court in a state of great agitation, as he wondered if she had been taken ill. She recalled: 'I took his hand. "It's nothing," I said. "Nothing at all except, you see, I have a rule. I never call men."'

Wallis's hold over the future king was not only inspiring intrigued tittle-tattle among London society; it soon came to alarm the British Establishment. Within days of returning from her skiing trip to Austria in the early spring of 1935, Wallis and Ernest found themselves under the gimlet gaze of Scotland Yard, home to London's top detectives.

It seemed that the whiff of blackmail was in the air, or at least the suspicion of blackmail. In a society defined by class, rank and snobbery, why else would the future sovereign spend so much time with a struggling shipping agent who, somewhat oddly, spent a lot of time in Europe, particularly Norway and the port of Hamburg in northern Nazi Germany? As for the compelling allure of his rather plain wife, her abilities excited the darkest sexual speculation.

The Yard's best detective, Special Branch superintendent Albert Canning, who focused on monitoring Communists and trade unionists, was put on the case. On 25 March 1935, a brief report landed on the desk of the commissioner of the Metropolitan Police, Sir Philip Game, and was doubtless discussed with the home secretary, Sir John Simon.

It was the first of a number of reports that continued up to the abdication. At first, Canning put a spotlight on the personality and business interests of Ernest Simpson, describing the sophisticated businessman with a penchant for poetry as a man of the 'bounder type', who hoped to make capital out of his wife's association with the Prince of Wales. Later reports suggested that when the prince became king, Simpson was hoping for high honours such as a baronetcy or even a diplomatic post, possibly in China. Canning's reports, laced with racism, snobbery and rumour, accused the Simpsons of being Jews who hosted any number of undesirables, including drug addicts, at their supper parties.

As if this were not enough to whet the appetites of the powers that be, Canning, who was promoted for his efforts, suggested that besides her affair with the Prince of Wales, Wallis had another secret lover. It took him some weeks to find out his name, but by July 1935 he felt able to report that Wallis was seeing a Ford used car salesman, Guy Marcus Trundle. According to Canning he was 'a very charming adventurer, very good-looking, well bred and an excellent dancer. He is said to boast that every woman falls for him.'

It seems that most of this information was supplied by the garrulous Mr Trundle himself, the Mayfair-based salesman telling Canning that he received expensive presents and money from the besotted American. He met her at social gatherings but intimate relations took place at secret rendezvous. For a woman who complained about keeping two men happy, a third would have left her exhausted.

There was more. At the same time that the home secretary was hearing about Guy Trundle, London society was abuzz with gossip about Wallis and no less a personage than Adolf Hitler's diplomatic envoy, Joachim von Ribbentrop. The couple, who first met at Lady Cunard's Grosvenor Square home, were said to be enjoying a torrid affair, von Ribbentrop regularly sending to her London home bouquets of seventeen carnations, some say roses, the number signifying the number of times they had slept together. In this febrile climate, the wildfire rumours soon circulated in Downing Street, Buckingham Palace and the German Embassy in London. The story even reached the ears of the Nazi leader, who quizzed the former sparkling-wine salesman turned diplomat about his fizzy private life.

Naturally her former friend Thelma Furness helpfully fanned the flames of speculation by cattily – and falsely – suggesting that Wallis was earning pin money as an informal sales agent for von Ribbentrop's sparkling-wine company. In her languidly dismissive way, Thelma recalled her own encounters with the German diplomat. 'Ribbentrop was stocky, stout, and genial. He could easily have been a head waiter. That type. Rather shiny. Wallis didn't particularly care about the Germans but was great friends with Ribbentrop, and she had a good excuse because she was selling champagne.'

She was not the only one to comment. At the time, Courtney Espil, now the wife of Wallis's diplomat ex-lover, noted in her diary: 'We all know she was a great friend of Ribbentrop when he was the ambassador in England.' In short order the story reached the ears of President Roosevelt's intimates. Mathilde Welles, wife of Under-Secretary of State Sumner Welles, told Courtney that the real reason why Queen Mary refused to receive Wallis was not because of her divorce or being a low-born American but because she was an intimate of von Ribbentrop.

It was but a small step from selling champagne on behalf of a leading Nazi to passing on high-level gossip during pillow talk. Though few ever considered her a spy, there was concern that the American's lack of understanding of what was and was not a secret could have led her to being unwittingly indiscreet around unfriendly ears. Though Wallis resolutely denied any impropriety, saying that she had met von Ribbentrop only twice, her ghost writer Cleveland Amory is not so sure. In the six months that he spent with her, Amory teased out the fact that she had met von Ribbentrop frequently. On one occasion, she was surprised when someone came upon her and the pompous diplomat in the German Embassy in London. They were both on their knees, looking over a map of Europe. So was Wallis a German spy? Helpful as ever, Lady Furness shrugged and said: 'One couldn't possibly say yes or no, because she wouldn't tell her pillow.'

Though Wallis was oblivious to the official police and palace interest in her behaviour, she got a sense that she was under the microscope at the state ball in May 1935 to celebrate King George V's Silver Jubilee, which was held at Buckingham Palace. After the king and queen had taken their seats on the dais, the dancing began. 'As David and I danced past, I thought I felt the King's eyes rest searchingly on me. Something in his look made me feel that all this graciousness and pageantry were but the glittering tip of an iceberg . . . filled with an icy menace for such as me.'

Perils lay much closer to home. Ernest's tolerance of the prince's behaviour and his wife's compliance was wearing thin. He had taken a dim view of his wife's decision to go skiing with the prince in Austria and had abruptly declined the invitation to join the prince in Biarritz. At times, he considered her behaviour as simply humiliating. Harvard-educated Henry Flood Robert, whose family had known Wallis from her Coronado days, remembers a lunch party at Bryanston Court where the most memorable moment came when the butler entered the room at about four o'clock to announce that the prince's automobile was at the door to take Wallis to Fort Belvedere. She duly excused herself, leaving Ernest Simpson to entertain their guests. 'Wallis's departure for Fort Belvedere was like a command performance,' recalled Mr Robert. 'I felt sorry for the deserted host, Ernest.'

There were, though, compensations. The prince appeased him with the gift of a bolt of brown-and-beige hound's-tooth tweed made up by the prince's tailor into an overcoat exactly the same as one owned by the Prince of Wales. More importantly, the prince agreed to sponsor him for admittance into his own lodge of the secretive Freemasons organization. Though Sir Maurice Jenks, who presided over the lodge, agreed to the prince's request, fellow Freemasons bridled, arguing that they could not accept the admission of a candidate on the word of his wife's lover. Before Ernest was finally admitted, Sir Maurice had the ticklish task of quizzing the future king about his sexual relationship with Mrs Simpson, the prince angrily denying any impropriety, a position he would doggedly adhere to both before and after his marriage.

His behaviour suggested otherwise. He was a lovesick, middle-aged man who could not bear to be apart from Wallis, or, his 'eanum' – the prince's word for 'tiny, poor or pathetic' – for a moment. Their relationship had graduated from frequent telephone calls to love letters, most sent by the prince to Wallis. A love note dated July 1935 set the tone for a cascade of correspondence penned by the prince, Edward using the acronym 'WE' to signify Wallis and Edward.

A boy is holding a girl so very tight in his arms tonight. He will miss her more tomorrow because he will have been away from her some hours longer and cannot see her till Wed-y night. A girl knows that not anybody or anything can separate WE – not even the stars – and that WE belong to each other for ever. WE love each other more than life so God bless WE.

As he had with his previous amour, Freda Dudley Ward, the prince would bombard Wallis with phone calls day and night, pace the Fort restlessly into the early morning before sitting down to write yet another love letter. Though he knew that Wallis and her husband were sleeping in separate bedrooms, it drove him wild with jealousy to know that she was spending time with Ernest when she could be with him. At times the prince overstepped the bounds of propriety, on at least one occasion staying on too long at Bryanston Court and then calling her late at night on the telephone. Wallis, exhausted from juggling her home and love life, then had to placate her irritated husband. Practical and matter-of-fact, Wallis could be forgiven for believing that she was being swept away on an avalanche of unbridled emotion. It was disconcerting. She affectionately chided the childish prince over his behaviour: 'Sometimes I think you haven't grown up where love is concerned and perhaps it's only a boyish passion, for surely it lacks the thought of me that a man's love is capable of.'

Ever down-to-earth, however, Wallis took his heartfelt missives with a pinch of salt, enjoying her time with the prince for as long as it might last. 'I might as well finish up any youth that is left to me with a flourish,' she wrote, dismissing reports in the American press that she and Ernest were on the brink of divorce and describing Edward as 'the man of my dreams'. By July 1935, it was clear that the prince, infatuated, in love, obsessed, or a mélange of all these emotions, was tentatively hinting at marriage. It consumed his waking hours, in the middle of the night Edward writing to her from his ship, HMS *Faulknor*, during the naval review:

> *Oh! A boy does miss and want a girl here so terribly tonight*
> *. . . Please, please Wallis don't get scared or loose [sic] faith*
> *when you are away from me. I love you more every minute*
> *and no difficulties or complication can possibly prevent our*
> *ultimate happiness.*

At that time those complications were, as far as the prince was concerned, awkward but reasonably straightforward. He needed to muster the courage to speak to his father, retire from the succession and give his brother, the Duke of York, a number of years to become used to the position as the king's successor. There were numerous historical precedents for the second son becoming king, though this was normally triggered by the death of the first in line to the throne. The most recent example was when his own father became Prince of Wales following the death in 1892 of his elder brother, the Duke of Clarence.

After all, reasoned the prince, the sky had not fallen in when, in 1917, the king had changed the family's name from Saxe-Coburg and Gotha to Windsor and allowed his offspring to wed English commoners rather than German royalty. Similarly, if Edward had moved aside to allow his younger brother to take his place while his father was still living, there would have been little public dismay.

As his friend and supporter Lord Mountbatten argued: 'Look how easy it would have been: the old king would still be on the throne, with the Duke of York warming up on the sidelines. Then, when the time came there'd have been no violent dislocation, only a smooth painless transition. The prince would have remained in England to help his brother, if need be, and Mrs Simpson would have become a royal duchess.'

The prince, who had held his counsel so as not to disrupt the Silver Jubilee celebrations in May, decided to speak to his father when he returned from a continental holiday that summer. From August to October, he and his party travelled through the South of France, Austria, Switzerland and Bavaria in southern Germany. Wallis ensured that Herman and Katherine Rogers were included in the party. Not only were they familiar faces, they were guests who pulled their weight, always aware of their social obligation to keep the future king entertained.

During the long holiday the prince did his best to smooth his eventual approach to his father, in Paris taking the trouble to see the French president, Albert Lebrun, and Prime Minister Pierre Laval. Herman sat next to Wallis and acted as her translator during lunch, Wallis enjoying an animated discussion with communications minister François Piétri. Once George V heard of his eldest son's diplomatic behaviour he sent him a note expressing his delight. Now was the time to strike. Fatally, the Prince of Wales delayed.

MEANWHILE, FOUR THOUSAND miles away, as the prince was loading dresses from Wallis's shopping trip to Mainbocher onto his private plane, Ernest was in Washington reassuring Aunt Bessie that all was well in their marriage. He told her that he was sufficiently confident in their marital togetherness to ask his first wife, Dorothea, if their ten-year-old daughter, Audrey, could live with them in London.

It was not a plan that found favour with the singularly unmaternal second Mrs Simpson. She complained that it would create extra expense and discomfort having to accommodate the growing girl and a governess in their small apartment. It was *most* inconvenient, and Wallis breathed a sigh of relief when Dorothea eventually vetoed the plan.

During his heart-to-heart conversation with Aunt Bessie, Ernest emphasized that he still adored Wallis and that her relationship with the prince had hit them both 'like an avalanche'. While he was not alarmed about their future together, Mrs Merryman was, leaving Ernest with a dire warning: 'No woman can resist for long the attention the prince is paying Wallis. I've watched her. There is no possible outcome but unhappiness for the three of you.' Ernest's response took her aback. 'Perhaps,' he replied, 'but both Wallis and I have profited from his friendship.'

Ernest was not being entirely candid. Wallis's school friend Mary Raffray had separated from her French husband, Jacques, the previous year. During his time in New York, Ernest and Mary began an affair, the couple falling head over heels in love. Theirs was a union of hearts and minds, soul mates who loved antiques, historic buildings, London's architecture and the British countryside. They even planned to write a book together chronicling the out-of-the-way squares, statues and relics of old London.

When he returned to London, Wallis not unnaturally noticed subtle and not-so-subtle changes in their relationship. He was now indifferent as to her whereabouts and the time she spent with the prince. Like Thelma before her, she was Edward's wife in all but name, hosting his dinner parties and organizing his life. At Christmas she bought and wrapped the 165 presents for his staff – as Thelma had done before her. The price she paid was her marriage. As she noted in her memoirs: 'We were going our separate ways, the core of our marriage had dissolved; only the shell remained – a façade to show the outer world.' It was to be their last Christmas together as a married couple.

That Christmas, Edward spent a 'terrible' few days at Sandringham with his family, the only light relief coming when he was able to call Wallis on the telephone. Hearing her voice gave him the strength to go on. With all the family present, now was as good a time as any to raise the subject of marriage to Mrs Simpson. Once again he stayed his hand – this time because of the king's fading health. He waited, hoping that in time something would turn up.

On New Year's Day he sent Wallis a brief note saying: 'I know we'll have *Viel Glück* [good luck] to make us *one* this year.'

His *Glück* was about to run out.

CHAPTER TEN

Wally for Queen!

T HE TWO WOMEN in the life of the Prince of Wales behaved
very differently the moment the life of his father, King George
V, drew peacefully to a close on 20 January 1936.

The prince was with his family standing by the king's bedside
at Sandringham House in Norfolk as he passed. When the royal
doctors bowed to him and called him 'Your Majesty', he realized
that he was now king, and his first instinct was to kiss his mother,
who was at the head of the bed. He was somewhat taken aback
when she rose and walked towards him and proceeded to drop a
very, very low curtsey. Then she kissed his hand and said: 'Your
Majesty.' Her ingrained sense of monarchy was such that she
instinctively put aside her own sense of loss to pay obeisance to
the new king.

Meanwhile, Wallis was at the cinema with a friend, American
hostess Betty Lawson-Johnston. At the end of the presentation
the audience, knowing that the king was gravely ill, stood for an
emotional rendering of the national anthem. Afterwards, Wallis
went to her friend's home for a nightcap. The butler interrupted their
conversation to inform her that she was wanted on the telephone.
It was the new king, clearly in a state of great distress. In between
sobs he announced, 'It's over', and said he would return to London
in the morning. She murmured her sympathy before putting down

the phone. It was only afterwards that she realized she had been talking to the new king and was one of the first people outside the immediate royal family to learn the historic news.

The episode marked the difference between the two women, Queen Mary responding to the symbol, Wallis to the man. This conflict between duty and desire, stiff upper lip and trembling beating heart, would characterize the brief reign of King Edward VIII, a reign defined by his forlorn and ultimately hopeless attempt to square this circle. As Edward was to discover, there was no constitutional alchemy that could fuse the public and private elements of his life. As his friend and lawyer Walter Monckton later recalled: 'From the start he was torn between his genuine desire to exercise the influence and prerogatives of kingship and an equally strong desire to live as he pleased.'

In the early days of the new reign, the presence of the married American who, with only a handful of others, watched the historic moment at St James's Palace when Edward was proclaimed king, remained largely unnoticed. However, this medieval ceremony had the effect of making Wallis realize that the future would be very different for them both.

As far as the man and woman in the street were concerned, the transition of hereditary authority from one generation to another was as seamless as it was timeless. Newspapers in Britain and the empire welcomed the new sovereign as modern, democratic and pragmatic, a monarch for whom, as the *Times* stated, 'men, not books, are his library'. Which was just as well as he never willingly read a book in his life.

Those in the know, in Parliament and at Court, assumed, wrongly, that he would untangle himself from any improper emotional attachments. Days after the king's funeral, Ronald Tree, a friend of Winston Churchill and a Conservative member of Parliament, wrote to his wife, Nancy, saying: 'He will have to amend his ways in those respects and he does not really appear to have any real friends.'

It was a sentiment shared by the majority. As the chancellor of the exchequer and future prime minister, Neville Chamberlain, noted in his diary: 'I do hope [the king] pulls up his socks and behaves himself now he has such heavy responsibilities, for unless he does he will soon pull down the throne.'

The new king thought his relationship was a closely guarded secret and would have been furious had he realized that Scotland Yard had been tailing the Simpsons for the previous eighteen months. Moreover, his late father and his closest courtiers had for some time been acutely aware of his stated intention to marry Wallis, a fact that, according to the Archbishop of Canterbury, clouded the king's closing days with anxiety, not for his son but for the future of the monarchy.

This rather begs the question that if George V was aware of and was concerned about his son's relationship with Mrs Simpson, why did he not instruct his private secretary, Lord Wigram, or another trusted confidant, to raise the matter? Just as the Prince of Wales was guilty of prevarication, so too was the late king. It proved fatal. This concern spilled into the political arena, Prime Minister Stanley Baldwin acknowledging that he was aware of 'trouble brewing'. He doubted that the king would 'stay the course'. Not that Baldwin, with or without Scotland Yard's assistance, had ever had much faith in the future king, once agreeing with a Buckingham Palace courtier that it would have been better had the prince broken his neck during his steeplechasing days than occupy the throne.

The first hint of foreboding came at the procession for George V's lying-in-state at Westminster Hall, when the Maltese Cross on top of the Imperial State Crown fell off the coffin and rolled into the gutter. King Edward VIII spotted the incident and later wondered if it was indeed an omen for his own short reign. The second sign came during an emotional confrontation with Ernest Simpson over dinner at York House, when his reign was barely twenty days old. Bluntly, the king told Ernest that he was in love with his wife and wanted to marry her. At first Ernest was so taken aback that the businessman, who signed himself the king's 'loyal and devoted servant', dared to call him 'mad' for even contemplating such a course of action.

He then pointed out that even if Wallis and he divorced, Edward would never be permitted to marry her and remain king. Ernest argued, correctly, that the king had to consider both the weight of ecclesiastical tradition and the royal family's moral position as the apex of family life and values. At this the king became very emotional and broke down.

A witness to this historic drama, Ernest's friend Bernard Rickatson-Hatt, the chief editor of Reuters news agency, who was present at the dinner, gave a rather different account. It was, he said, his friend who opened the conversation, asking the king point-blank about his intentions towards his wife. 'Are you sincere? Do you intend to marry her?' he asked. The king rose from his chair and said: 'Do you really think I would be crowned without Wallis at my side?'

Suitably assured, Ernest promised to stand aside if Wallis wanted a divorce, with the proviso that the king would look after her financially whether or not they eventually married. Given Ernest Simpson's budding relationship with Mary Raffray and his constant business worries, money was a prime consideration. He was clearly unwilling to pay alimony for his second wife, though secretly shaping a potential future with his third. Nonetheless, Rickatson-Hatt described Ernest as being 'profoundly unhappy' with this arrangement. Their plan was clearly collusive and thus illegal in the eyes of any divorce court. However, as a loyal subject he was willing to lay down his wife for the king of England.

For such an extraordinary meeting to take place so early in the reign suggests that marriage was uppermost in the mind of the new king. He realized that the clock was ticking if he wanted Wallis by his side as queen consort for the coronation in Westminster Abbey, which was due to take place in May 1937. As he later admitted: 'The trouble was, I didn't know just how the job could be brought off. It was because of this uncertainty that nineteen thirty-six was such a prolonged agony for me.'

It did not take long for Downing Street and Buckingham Palace to hear of this worrying development. Baldwin's trusted advisor Maurice Jenks, the former lord mayor of London who helped Ernest Simpson join the Freemasons, informed the prime minister that Simpson had seen him and told him the scarcely believable news that Edward VIII was in love with his wife and intended to marry her.

Other senior officials suggested that the stench of blackmail was in the air, Simpson leveraging his position for financial gain. Baldwin sucked on his pipe and sat on his hands, arguing that whatever the king might feel, the prospect of the Defender of the Faith marrying a twice-divorced American with two husbands still living was simply unbelievable and therefore unworthy of serious consideration. Other advisors took the practical course and suggested that, short of deportation, Simpson should be reminded of his own marriage vows and encouraged to take his wife back to America where she belonged.

The settled view among men and women of the world was that the king should marry a suitable candidate and keep a mistress. This was an arrangement that had worked for kings, princes, dukes and lords for centuries. After all, the king's grandfather, Edward VII, was devoted to both his mistress, Alice Keppel, and his wife, Queen Alexandra. It was an arrangement which, conducted with discretion and diplomacy, had been perfectly acceptable to the public and the parties concerned. Even Wallis, with her scant knowledge of English history, understood that this was the king's best option. She observed: 'It's a very lonely job – and it's a tragedy that he can't bring himself to marry without loving. The English would prefer that he marry a Duke's daughter to one of the mangy foreign princesses left.'

Obstinate as ever, Edward VIII begged to differ. He wanted nothing less than a public marriage to the woman he loved. Wallis soon realized what that meant. As the new king felt the strain of his lonely and onerous position, he invested all his emotional energy in her. She was his lightning rod and back stop, grounding him during the storms that assailed him. It was exhausting work. Now she knew how Lady Thelma Furness had felt, the king being continually on the telephone, writing love notes, demanding her presence at the Fort or visiting her at Bryanston Court for supper. 'Of course I am very fond of him and proud and want him to do his job well and he is so lonely and needs companionship and affection, otherwise he goes wrong,' she told her aunt in January. She was pleased that she was considered a 'good influence' on the new king.

There were glittering compensations, in both her growing jewellery collection and the shower of gilt-edged invitations for dinners, galas and balls. That she had the ear and heart of the king gave her tremendous prestige and position, queen in all but name. Her desk was awash with notes and cards sent by the great and the good eager to curry favour.

The indomitable Lady Oxford wrote that she was 'natural and kind', Chips Channon thought her a woman of 'charm, sense and balance and great wit with dignity and taste'. Society beauty Diana Cooper described her as 'good and kind and lovable', diplomat and politician Harold Nicolson thought her 'virtuous and wise', while Sibyl Colefax arranged to have a key scene from a West End drama about divorce and remarriage called *Storm in a Teacup* staged in her drawing room so that the king and Mrs Simpson could watch it together in privacy.

Wallis was so firmly established as the king's paramour that when she casually met Lady Furness at various social occasions, she considered asking her to dine at Bryanston Court – just like the old days. Watching the passing parade from Washington, Courtney Espil could not help reminding herself of Wally's former station. 'What a good joke Wally must be thinking it all. Remembering her former snubs by Washington's most exclusive, remembering her struggle to keep up and get ahead and now loaded with the famous jewels of the crown of England.'

Her observations were spot on; Wallis treated the first months of the king's reign as something of a hoot. In March, when she and her friend Foxy Gwynne went to stay at the Hôtel Le Meurice in Paris so that she could stock up with the spring fashions, she brazenly paraded her closeness to the king to all and sundry. When the king telephoned her, which he did four or five times a day, she deliberately left open the booth door so that her friends – as well as guests in the hotel lobby – could listen in as she coolly responded to his passionate utterances of love and devotion.

At the end of one conversation, an open-mouthed Loelia, Duchess of Westminster, had heard enough to appreciate that the king was very serious indeed about Mrs Simpson. 'What are you going to do about it?' she asked. Wallis emphasized that *nothing* would *ever* come between her and Ernest. The duchess remembered that conversation when she heard that Wallis had served divorce papers on her second husband.

Wallis was coy, cool and calculating, a complete contrast to her besotted monarch. He thought of her constantly, called her endlessly and fretted when they were apart. It was flattering, but it was also wearing for a matter-of-fact woman of the world like

Wallis. In matters of amour she was much more contained – even regal – than her royal suitor. Where he wore his heart on his sleeve, Wallis presented a mask to the world, rarely giving in to emotion, always in control. Her long-time friend from Peking, Constance Coolidge, the Comtesse de Jumilhac, was emphatic – Wallis did not love the king nor for that matter had she *ever* been in love with anyone. 'From the moment they first met, he wanted her to divorce Ernest,' she said. 'It was not the other way around.'

Even in their private letters, the wild passion, excitement and desire that characterize the early phase of a love affair were entirely absent in Wallis's scribbles. Her voice was that of a prissy housekeeper or an admonishing hostess, encouraging David to do better in either his manners or his social arrangements. 'I didn't see a green vegetable on the menu. Sorry to bother you but I like everyone to think you do things well,' she gently scolded when he was due to entertain during their holiday in the South of France.

She had in spades what writer Janet Flanner described as the 'American woman's tendency to reform men in small ways'. (*Full disclosure: My wife is from California.*) Her letters to friends and family are chatty but focused on the practical and particular: the purchase of corsets, face cloths, jigsaw puzzles and kitchenware. As her second husband wryly admitted, Wallis felt little in the way of romance even if she had had the imagination to lose herself in a love affair. Her life was about being in control – of herself, her staff, her kitchen, her table and her husband. If Edward ever pined for a passionate response to one of his clingy, childish but clearly love-struck missives, he was kept waiting. As a candidate for the greatest royal love affair of the century, even Wallis would agree she would not pass the audition. For a woman who listed going to the dentist and writing letters as her pet hates, it is evident that wringing an adoring response to the prince's *billets-doux* was truly like pulling teeth.

She was fond rather than fanatical, loving rather than love-struck, a woman groomed in the school of hard knocks. The words 'hard' and 'brittle' were adjectives frequently linked to Wallis. Unbeknown to one another, the American ambassadors to Spain and Great Britain, Alexander W. Weddell and Robert W. Bingham, respectively, came to remarkably similar conclusions after their separate meetings with Wallis.

Weddell described her exterior as suggestive of 'armour plate or some substance slightly harder than diamond. But very pleasant, very genial, very witty', while Bingham remembered a woman who was 'beautifully dressed and wore beautiful jewels, is quite intelligent but brittle and hard'.

She exposed her emotional toughness when she explained to her aunt why she had chosen the king above her husband. 'I am forty and I feel I must follow my own instincts as regards my life and am quite prepared to pay for my mistakes. I know I can only control the financial side of the future and that I can't insure against heartache, loneliness etc. but if the worst happens I shall have to be like the Arabs and fold my tent and steal silently away.'

By coincidence, Constance Coolidge, Comtesse de Jumilhac, had embarked on what turned into a frisky ten-year romance with the English novelist H. G. Wells. Though their love affair began at the same time as Wallis's, it could not have been more different from what was later universally billed as the 'royal romance of the century'. Their steamy sensual correspondence revolved around the themes of sex and desire, love, dreams and food.

'I wish I was in bed with you now,' Wells wrote in February 1935, shortly after they met in the South of France. It was a frequent refrain, Wells declaring that 'the dear close sweetness of love is my incessant need'. Constance would tease him by saying that she was still in bed and would love for him to be able to 'creep' beneath her warm sheets. The old time-traveller described Constance as a sexual animal. 'With so many of us sex, having served its purpose, becomes an incurable habit, and that I think is the case with her.' Another note was explicit: 'I want to be firmly between your legs deep inside you my lovely mistress to touch your soft breasts.' While Wallis would have been aware of her friend's amour when she saw her during her visits to Paris, she recoiled from these expressions of sexual intimacy.

Wallis was more concerned about kitchen sinks than romantic dramas. Yet it was she who was at the swirling centre of speculation about her erotic techniques, her jewellery collection and her ambition to become queen. While British newspapers remained silent about the presence of Mrs Simpson at Court, European and American newspapers had undertaken no such collective *omertà*. According to the febrile American press, Queen Mary had been kicked out of Buckingham Palace to make room for Wallis and her entourage, Edward had shouted down Prime Minister Baldwin for daring to question his choice of bride, while Wallis had been given an extravagantly sumptuous gift in the form of Queen Alexandra's emeralds by her besotted royal beau. When she was asked about these stories twenty years later she expressed her bafflement, describing the rumours as 'venom, venom, venom'.

The woman who admitted to Herman Rogers that she had not slept with her first two husbands was not about to break that habit during her courtship with the king. When Wallis's journalist cousin Newbold Noyes, himself no stranger to sexual shenanigans, spent the weekend with the king and his paramour at Fort Belvedere, he came away with a real appreciation of the emotional dynamic between the couple.

He recalled that when the king entered the drawing room where they were all waiting, he 'fairly ran across the length of the room, obviously anxious to be near Wallis and to see her again without a glance to either side. She rose, curtsied, and said, "Good evening, sir."'

As Noyes later told Courtney Espil: 'Wallis was not his mistress, I'm willing to bet my money on that and we are speaking in a strictly adult manner. I know now, looking back, that he meant to make her his wife more than a year before the abdication crisis. I think he expected to abdicate from the time his father died.' The newspaperman's conclusion was based on watching the interaction between the couple, noticing the small gestures, or absence thereof, which suggested a deeper intimacy. His instincts were confirmed by the king's decision to sue for libel an otherwise oleaginous tome called *Coronation Commentary*, which suggested that Edward and Mrs Simpson were intimate before they eventually married.

Those who knew the king well shared Noyes's view. Winston Churchill, who indulgently treated him like a second son, believed that their association was 'psychical rather than sexual, and certainly not sensual except incidentally. Although branded with the stigma of guilty love, no companionship could have appeared more natural, more free from impropriety or grossness.' It was a theme taken up by the king's lawyer, Walter Monckton, who had known him since his Oxford days. As far as he was concerned, it was a 'mistake to assume that he was merely in love with her in the ordinary physical sense of the term. There was an intellectual companionship, and there is no doubt that his lonely nature found in her a spiritual companionship.'

Practical as ever, Wallis, who admitted that she was baffled by his adoration for her, had a more prosaic explanation for their attraction. As she later explained: 'I liked the city and he liked the country but both of us liked flowers and gardening and preferred having a house and home life to apartment or hotel living and a life of travel. For our vacations I liked swimming and he liked golf but both of us preferred sea to the mountains.'

She liked bridge and plays, Edward poker and musical comedies, but both liked dancing. 'All in all we thought alike and agreed on most subjects, our standards and values of life were the same.'

Though she was still married to another man, it was not for much longer. By the spring of 1936 there were four people involved in the Simpsons' marriage: Wallis, Ernest, the king and her old school friend Mary Raffray. It was getting a little crowded – and complicated. For strict legal reasons and afterwards for the historical record, all four combatants played their cards very close to their chests. At the time, Edward was in love with Wallis, Wallis was in love with King Edward VIII – if not with the man, certainly with the fringe benefits of dating a king – while Ernest and Mary were now lovers. The simplest solution to the predicament the quartet found themselves in was to agree to divorce and then remarry. They were, though, treading on dangerous ground.

As Wallis had discovered to her cost, divorce was in those days a complex process with many legal traps for the unwary lover. One of the most common was the allegation of collusion. If it could be shown that the Simpson divorce had been agreed upon by the various parties involved, the divorce court judge would rightly conclude that there had been an illegal conspiracy to deceive.

The York House dinner was highly suspect, especially as the king had promised that if Ernest divorced Wallis he would secure her financial future for her lifetime. She confirmed in a confidential letter to Aunt Bessie that this transaction had indeed taken place. The issue of collusion was so sensitive that when the king ultimately wrote his memoir, titled *A King's Story*, in 1951, his lawyers George Allen and Walter Monckton suggested that a passage dealing with the Simpson divorce be deleted lest it raise potentially embarrassing questions about the role of the king in breaking up the marriage. Allen wrote to publisher Daniel Longwell: 'I suggest that readers ought not to be given smallest hint when author admitted to himself his love for lady still less his wish for marriage. Such information invites criticism that either he was ready to break a home or divorce was collusive. It would also draw criticism on lady.'

The arrival of Mary Raffray as a guest of the Simpsons in March 1936 further complicated matters. Wallis was left in no doubt that her friend was much more eager to spend time with Ernest than with her. When Wallis spent a weekend alone at the Fort with the king, Ernest and Mary set off on a three-day excursion to sites of historic interest around London, the couple spending at least one night together at a hotel in Dover.

When they arrived back in London, Wallis announced that they were entertaining the king at Bryanston Court. He arrived early and Mary was sent to entertain him while Ernest and Wallis were finishing dressing. As Mary rose from her curtsey, he asked: 'How were the chalk cliffs?' – an obvious reference to her tryst with Mr Simpson at the port town. Long afterwards she complained to a friend that 'That nasty little king had put detectives on us.' Right conclusion, wrong person. It was her friend Wallis who had hired her shadows.

It was a *very* civilized state of affairs, the quartet spending the first weekend in April together at a house party hosted by Lord Dudley at Himley Hall. During their sojourn, the king scribbled endless love notes to Wallis. 'A boy loves a girl more and more and more' was typical. It had become an incessant and exhausting refrain, Wallis complaining that 'the job of amusing kings in mourning isn't easy'.

What with keeping the king entertained, dealing with her own marital issues and acting as unofficial royal hostess, Wallis, like Thelma before her, was so worn out that her nervous indigestion, which plagued her throughout her life, forced her to take prolonged bed rest.

Presumably the exquisite diamond bracelet from the Paris jewellers Van Cleef & Arpels, which he gave her that weekend, helped to keep her smiling. Sometime afterwards, Queen Mary visited Lord Dudley and insisted on a tour of the house, during which she reviewed that fateful weekend. She duly noted the proximity of the bedrooms and shared bathrooms of Wallis, the king, Ernest and Mary with the pithy phrase, 'I see, very convenient.'

Not that Ernest was overly concerned. The following weekend he organized another weekend away with Mary, driving to the remote Two Bridges Hotel on Dartmoor in the holiday county of Devon. Unfortunately for the lovebirds, it was not as remote as they thought. They had the ill fortune to be spotted by the king's lawyers, Walter Monckton and George Allen, who were themselves enjoying a weekend away from the capital.

Just to tie the whole affair with a pink bow, in early April Mary flew to Cannes, where she wrote two letters on Carlton Hotel stationery and sent them to her hosts in London. To Ernest she wrote an affectionate love letter thanking him for his flowers, to Wallis a bread-and-butter thank-you note. Fatally, she put them in the wrong envelopes, so that Ernest received the letter meant for his wife and vice versa. Realizing her mistake, Mary sent a frantic telegram to Wallis saying: DO NOT OPEN LETTER ADDRESSED TO YOU AS IT IS NOT FOR YOU. Of course, Wallis could not resist such an entreaty and duly opened the letter she should have left sealed.

She wasted no time in telling her friends about the contents, presenting herself as the innocent victim of her husband's duplicity. As her social circle were well aware of her place in the king's affections, few were convinced that this was human error rather than part of an elaborate plot. When Constance Coolidge was told by Katherine Rogers of the mix-up she, like others, viewed the incident with a sceptical eye. In a letter to her father she observed caustically: 'She told this story to Katherine but it sounds rather fishy to me. I wonder if the whole divorce wasn't agreed on together.'

By contrast, Herman, who was as close to Wallis as any man, sincerely believed that she was the innocent party in this affair, indignantly writing to his godmother, Sara Delano Roosevelt, mother of the sitting president: 'As to Mrs S Divorce I realize that many people believe it was based on collusion. I can only tell you that I KNOW there was no collusion – that king or no king she would have fought her action and that she had complete justice on her side. Time will undoubtedly prove the truth of this.'

Maybe he was being too much of a gentleman. For a woman with a fierce temper, Wallis's response to Ernest's infidelity was surprisingly muted. Where was the jealous fury who raged through the wardrobe of her Argentinian diplomat lover? Where, too, the sharp-tongued harridan who drove her first husband, Win Spencer, to drink and violence and also terrified her present husband? As the deceived wife, she could be excused for uncorking her volcanic temper, especially as one of the culprits in this marital merry-go-round was her best friend from childhood.

Instead her reaction was bloodless, almost indifferent, suggesting a carefully orchestrated break-up. Wallis gave the impression of being resigned to her fate, accepting even of Ernest's wish that Mary still join them for meals and that she accompany them to social gatherings. 'If it makes him happy I suppose it's only fair for me to do it,' she told her aunt, limiting herself to caustic comments about Mary's 'naked' wardrobe, calling her 'Buttercup' after a black hat trimmed with that flower, which she brought from New York.

As fishy as all this was, Mary's misplaced love letter and Ernest's hotel hopping helpfully removed the king from playing any public part in the collapse of the Simpson marriage. Just so the watching world got the message, the names of Ernest and Wallis Simpson appeared together in the Court Circular on 28 May, the couple attending a dinner at York House in the presence of Prime Minister Stanley Baldwin, the Mountbattens, politician Duff Cooper and his radiant wife Lady Diana as well as the American aviator Charles Lindbergh and his wife, Anne. As the guests mingled, the king told Wallis, who had organized the table decorations, that this was his opportunity to introduce the prime minister to 'my future wife', a suggestion that earned an immediate rebuke from her.

A few days later, on 5 June, the king summoned Ernest to the Fort for a man-to-man talk about the provisional timetable for the Simpson divorce. Far from being an impartial observer, the king, obstinate, jealous and needy, was making the running, eager to see Wallis set free. As Wallis's biographer Michael Bloch observed: 'Nothing matters to him except their eventual union. He is therefore determined to break up the marriage of Wallis and Ernest. To that end he is forever pressing, pleading, conspiring, cajoling.'

Edward's lawyer George Allen had advised him that the timetable was tight. It would take six months from the granting of a divorce to securing a decree absolute to enable Wallis to marry again. The coronation was scheduled for May 1937, and the king wanted Wallis by his side as his wife and queen. He duly reported to Wallis: 'My talk with Ernest was difficult this evening but I must get after him now or he won't move. It's so unsatisfactory until it's all settled and WE really are one.'

Once Ernest agreed to the king's plan the atmosphere between the four grew frostier. Wallis refused to speak to Mary, and Ernest found himself excluded from most social gatherings involving the king. Mary wrote to her sister Anne: 'On the outs with Wallis, but for God's sake keep that under your hat. So do not move in royal circles any more.' At the next York House dinner, Wallis appeared in the Court Circular as present on her own. She sat at one end of the table while Lady Willingdon and the Duchess of York sat either side of the king. Lady Willingdon recalled his bizarre behaviour, saying that for fifteen minutes or so the king was entertaining, but then his attention wandered and all he could do was look at Mrs Simpson.

After a pause he said, 'Isn't she looking wonderful tonight?' Lady Willingdon agreed but then the king continued: 'She is the most wonderful-looking person and the most wonderful person in the world.' At this royal gush, Lady Willingdon touched her forehead, suggesting that he was not right in the head.

The Simpsons' last public outing as a married couple was a weekend together at Blenheim Palace in June. The curtain, though, was falling on this act of the royal drama. On 21 July, the arrangements necessary for a smooth divorce were in place. Ernest and a woman called Buttercup Kennedy – clearly Mary Raffray – were witnessed eating breakfast in bed together at a hotel in Bray where they were guests. On 23 July, Ernest received a standard legal letter accusing him of adultery. He promptly moved into the Guards' Club.

The divorce wheels firmly in motion, in August Wallis joined the king on board the steam yacht *Nahlin* for a planned cruise along the Dalmatian coast. It was a cosy guest list of old friends, including Lord and Lady Brownlow, the Duff Coopers, and Mr and Mrs Reliable, Herman and Katherine Rogers. If ever there was a time in her life when Wallis needed trusted friends around her, this was it.

Not only were Herman and the king enthusiastic oarsmen and swimmers, they enjoyed discussing naval history. With Herman around, Wallis could relax a little. He was the one man who had never, ever let her down. If only things had been different. She would have been Mrs Rogers, an appellation she would have coveted at one time. No matter, Herman remained her confidant and her sounding board. As much as she liked Katherine, she was a tad too quiet and retiring for Wallis's tastes. Wallis was at heart a man's woman, and Herman was the man of her daydreams. Her feelings for him were proprietorial: she saw Herman as her prime ally and confidant, rather resenting Katherine's dominance in his life. Hers was a dog-in-a-manger affection, wanting Herman for herself alone. He was, she later confessed, the only man she had ever truly loved.

Almost from the first day, Wallis needed Herman's steady reassurance. She feared that the cruise was cursed by Montague 'luck', that unfortunate ability to snatch misery from the jaws of happiness. The whole party were shocked when Commander Jessel, captain of one of the accompanying duo of naval destroyers, was critically injured after being hit by a motor launch as he was taking an evening swim. Then the lifeboats on the starboard side of the *Nahlin* were crushed to matchsticks when the yacht lurched into the rock wall of the narrow Corinth Canal that links the Gulf of Corinth to the Saronic Gulf in the Aegean Sea. Wallis needed a stiff drink from the ship's well-stocked temporary bar, which had been installed after removing the library.

Socially the group, particularly Wallis, had to navigate equally narrow waters. There was much debate on board about the decorum of the king going out bare-chested in public. A sovereign clothed only in a pair of loose-fitting shorts was not, his advisors believed, consistent with the image the king emperor should project. They threw up their hands in horror when he insisted on sitting outside at a café table on one of the many Greek islands they visited. They may not have appreciated his informality but the residents did.

Wallis and the king managed to create a bubble where all was love and adoration. When the peasant folk from the impoverished island of Korcula staged a torchlight procession in their honour, the king whispered to Wallis that they had done this because 'they believe a king is in love with you'.

From time to time slivers of the outside world managed to pierce their protective carapace. When the party stopped briefly at Brdo in Yugoslavia on the outgoing journey, Princess Olga, the wife of Prince Paul of Yugoslavia, made a deliberate point of not receiving Wallis as the king's lady. Later, when the group arrived in Turkey, Queen Mary made it known that she did not approve of the king taking his mistress to the First World War battleground of Gallipoli, where so many British and Dominion soldiers had died.

After the four-week cruise Wallis spent a few days in Paris, nursing a cold and catching up on the gossip with her friends Foxy Gwynne and Gilbert Miller. As she leafed through the shoal of newspaper cuttings which had been sent by her American friends and family, she realized that *she* was now the epicentre of gossip across two continents.

'The Yankee at King Edward's Court', yelled one headline as the American press lasciviously charted life on board the royal 'love boat'. London society was equally inquisitive, Wallis's shipmate Lady Diana Cooper endlessly if decorously answering the question on everyone's lips: were Wallis and the king sleeping together?

'I haven't the least idea,' she told her interlocutors irritably. 'How should I know? Though I'm perfectly sure they did.'

As she lay on her fevered bed of pain in her Paris hotel room, Wallis had the first chance in months to review her options without interruption. She didn't like what she saw. In the next few weeks she planned to divorce a man who, for all his faults, had proved a steadfast if unexciting companion. She was swapping steadiness and certainty for an unclear future. Pondering the possible scenarios, she could hear her mother's voice in her ear: 'You are never satisfied with what you have or what you are or have become. Never. Never. Never.'

She realized that for the past few years the unrealistically romantic Montague side of her had been chasing a dream, a fantasy of one day becoming the Queen of England, empress over the biggest empire the world had ever seen. That dream was now tantalizingly close. But what price personal happiness, what price Wallis? Was she in love with the man – or the position? Or both? She feared that she was selling her soul for a rainbow of promises from a man who had made similar vows to others. It was time to give her sensible Warfield personality a chance.

She needed to play for time, telling the king that she was too sick to travel to Balmoral, where he was due to be in residence.

In between sniffles she sat down with pen and paper, writing and posting the royal equivalent of an 'It's not you, it's me' letter, thus ending their relationship. She told him that she was 'amazed and shocked' by the publicity that her impending divorce and friendship with the king had attracted and wrote of her 'deepening misgivings' regarding their future. It was her duty to go back to Ernest – if he would have her.

'I am sure you and I would only create disaster together. I want you to be happy. I feel sure I can't make you so, and I honestly don't think you can me.'

She foresaw trouble with the prime minister and the government and felt that she could not put Edward in a position where he was forced to relinquish his throne. To end the lie that she was a gold-digger, she promised to liaise with his lawyer George Allen and return the money he had settled on her.

It was all too little, too late. The king would not accept her leaving for a solitary second. In between threats to shoot himself if she did not join him at Balmoral he prostrated himself before her, a man worshipping at the shrine of love. 'You see I do love you so entirely and in every way, Wallis. Madly tenderly adoringly and with admiration and such confidence,' he wrote.

In the end she surrendered to his entreaties, waving her fragrant white handkerchief. Before agreeing to join him at Balmoral she insisted that Herman and Katherine accompany her on the journey north. She needed friends by her side before she entered the lions' den.

As ever, nothing went quite to script. Gallantly the king drove to Aberdeen station to pick up his beloved and her friends. In order to do so, he cancelled his presence at the opening of a local hospital, citing Court mourning. He asked his brother the Duke of York and his wife to do the honours in his stead.

When he was photographed in his jaunty goggles, kilt and tam o'shanter standing by his open-topped tourer outside Aberdeen station, the waves of disapproval were felt far beyond the Scottish border. Inevitably, Wallis was in the firing line. 'Down with the American whore', said a slogan chalked on one wall. Inside the Highland pile, she was deliberately snubbed by the Duchess of York when she and her husband visited the king. 'I have come to dine with the king,' she announced as she brushed past Wallis.

Not that Wallis gave the duchess or any others at the Highland gathering any hint of her inner turmoil. During the weekend, she seemed gay and carefree, laughing and joking with Prince George and Mountbatten, giving the impression of having a high old time. Her mood was captured by Herman Rogers who, as he had on the *Nahlin* cruise, brought along his trusty cine camera.

He filmed the king out stalking, standing on a cliff looking out over the lonely misty moor at the White Mounth, and shot the party playing an Austrian game called arrow golf, which Mountbatten, Prince George and the king all tried.

What is striking about Herman's eleven-minute silent movie is how the moving image captures the many moods that scud across Wallis's face. In still photographs she usually looks rather grave and subdued, the camera catching her masculine angularity. By contrast, she could be another person when the movie camera films her – her face animated, eyes alight and often amused, gestures quick and darting. She chats easily with the guests, often the centre of light-hearted banter, her expression bubbling over with mirth. Photographer Cecil Beaton was struck by her staccato conversation, which was 'punctuated by explosive bursts of firework laughter that lit up her face with great gaiety and made her eyebrows look attractively surprised'.

The other enduring feature of the black-and-white reel is the easy intimacy existing between Herman and Wallis. As they walk around the Balmoral gardens they exude a comfortable familiarity, rather like husband and wife. An outsider watching the reel who did not know the story of Edward and Mrs Simpson would be hard pressed to say with certainty who was Wallis's partner, Herman or the king.

As Herman's second wife, Lucy, later recalled: 'Wallis was the great love of his life. But it was a purely platonic relationship. He was such a straightforward man that he would not have had it any other way – and he would never have divorced Katherine, who knew how he felt about Wallis but put up with it. But if Herman had become a widower earlier, before Wallis met the duke, I'm sure he would have married her. In fact he told me so.' In the next few months Herman's resolve would be sorely tested.

When she left Balmoral, Wallis had a date with destiny. On 27 October 1936, her divorce was scheduled for hearing in the Suffolk town of Ipswich, seventy miles northeast of London. Known as the birthplace of King Henry VIII's right-hand man, Cardinal Wolsey, home of naval hero Lord Nelson, and a setting for Charles Dickens's *Pickwick Papers*, the market town was soon to earn worldwide recognition as the location for a divorce which would ultimately change the course of royal history.

Not that the British public were going to hear about this dramatic turn of events anytime soon. Thanks to a compact between the bullet-headed press baron Lord Beaverbrook and the king, the British press kept a gentlemanly silence. Edward argued successfully that it was unfair to publicize Wallis's private affairs simply because she was a friend of the king. Her unwanted notoriety was making her ill and distressed.

The American and European press would have none of it, charting every moment of Wallis's life. Whenever she left her new home on Cumberland Terrace in Regent's Park – the king paid the £32-a-week rent (£2000 today) for eight months and installed a private telephone line to Buckingham Palace – she was photographed and followed. When the king was spotted waiting patiently for Wallis when she went to the hairdresser's, it made scandalous headlines everywhere except Britain. Wallis found the attention wearing. It became such a strain that the king asked the Metropolitan police commissioner if patrols around her rented home could be beefed up. He duly obliged.

With such day-to-day scrutiny it was something of a relief when in early October she travelled to Felixstowe, an unremarkable coastal town near Ipswich, where she stayed for several weeks before the hearing in order to establish residency. She travelled in the king's Buick driven by George Ladbrook, the king's chauffeur, and was represented by the king's lawyer. Naturally all expenses and fees were paid by the king.

On 27 October, after a nineteen-minute court hearing, Justice Hawke duly granted the decree nisi with costs after hearing of Ernest's adultery with a certain Buttercup Kennedy. When she arrived back at her rented house in Regent's Park, Wallis, punch-drunk and brooding about her future, received a welcome letter from the man who had been her knight in shining armour, a man who solved problems rather than generated them. Their relationship, already close and steadfast, would become even more intimate in the coming weeks.

Herman Rogers, who was not prone to hyperbole in his correspondence, was, for him, recklessly affectionate towards her. He wrote:

I can't tell you how sorry we are that you should have to go through this dismal time, I wish you had asked us to stay around – or to come back, if we could have been of any help to you. You know we'd have been only too glad to. That goes for the future as well – and please remember it if you ever need us. You are still my one living example of a perfectly wise and complete person. We are with you always. Come to us if and when you can – or call us if you want to.

Her call for help was not long coming.

CHAPTER ELEVEN

'You God-damned Fool'

THE PLOT WAS simple but audacious, to blow up King James I and his Protestant Parliament and strike a blow for the Roman Catholic faith. Fortunately, the king got wind of the conspiracy and, after a search of the Houses of Parliament on 5 November 1605, barrels of gunpowder were discovered along with a man named Guy Fawkes, who was holding a slow fuse. He and his fellow conspirators were arrested, tortured and then hanged, their bodies cut into quarters and dragged through the streets of London. Every 5 November, in celebration of the thwarting of the Gunpowder Plot, bonfires are lit, effigies of Guy Fawkes are burned and fireworks launched.

On Bonfire Night 1936, the king's friend Charles Winn, a member of the Yorkshire family who own Nostell Priory, attended a friend's firework party with a number of fellow aristocrats. High on the bonfire a straw effigy was well alight. 'I see you have Guy Fawkes up there,' he remarked to his host.

'Oh no,' said his friend, 'that's Wallis Simpson.' He continued, laughing: 'Now, an unmarried man needs a girl now and again, but *marrying* her? Can you believe it?' While the British public remained in the dark about the existence of the now twice-divorced American, Winn's experience that night demonstrated that the flames of publicity were crackling ever nearer.

Among the widening circle of those in the know, events were moving apace. The ashes from the nation's bonfires were still smouldering as members of Parliament were gripped by open talk of either an abdication or Wallis's replacement by an eligible European princess. Guests at a dinner party hosted by Lady Colefax were consumed by rumours that the king intended to make Wallis the Duchess of Edinburgh and marry her. Diarist and MP Harold Nicolson observed: 'The point is whether he is so infatuated as to insist on her becoming queen or whether the marriage will be purely morganatic.'

A gaggle of aristocrats cornered the American ambassador at one soirée and warned him that the situation was 'grave' and the monarchy 'in danger'. Amid this hysterical speculation, Emerald Cunard nursed the delicious possibility of being the power behind the throne after a rather tipsy Leslie Hore-Belisha, minister for transport, told her that Edward was to marry Wallis in the chapel at Windsor Castle and that a new pro-king government would be in power within weeks.

The gathering conflagration centred on exactly whom the king could marry. Under the Royal Marriages Act he could choose anyone he wished – apart from a Roman Catholic. As Wallis was Presbyterian, she passed that test. The subject of conflict was not her nationality – wealthy American girls had been keeping the British aristocracy financially afloat for a century – but that she was twice divorced with two husbands still living. This directly contradicted the teachings of the Church of England, which the king, as Defender of the Faith, was vowed to maintain. Archbishop Cosmo Lang wrestled with the 'heavy burden' he felt at possibly consecrating Edward as king. If the latter then went ahead and married Mrs Simpson it would 'shake the foundations of the Church's influence and teaching'.

Not only did Edward have to hurdle objections from the Church, he faced opposition from the Dominions, Parliament and the Cabinet. Early on, Stanley Bruce, the Australian High Commissioner and former prime minister, laid down the gauntlet, saying that his country would leave the empire should Wallis marry the king.

A clash between king and Parliament would create an explosion that even Guy Fawkes would have been proud of. King versus country. It was a recipe for a constitutional crisis.

From the beginning the king seemed to have no conception of the forces ranged against him, and even if he did, stubborn as he was, he was sure he could find a loophole. After all, didn't his charm, his popularity among the people and his lifelong service to the empire count for anything? On this occasion, the answer was no. He believed, wrongly, that his popularity as king translated into personal popularity. On such an intimate matter as his choice of bride, he felt that John Bull would rally behind him. Wallis, knowing little if anything of the British constitution, believed it, too, arguing that a radio broadcast to his loyal subjects would swing the tide in his favour. Baldwin shut that door pretty sharpish, informing the king that he could not make a broadcast without the consent of his ministers, and consent would not be forthcoming.

Feeling trapped and helpless, Wallis even consulted her own advisor, former American actress now celebrity astrologer Nella Webb, at her London home. Her prophecy was not too wide of the mark, the seer telling Wallis: 'The opposition to you cannot be sidestepped. It will have to be faced or managed. You may be able to rise above it. The bonds of love will be made secure and fast . . . a marriage could occur sometime next year. In August or September.' Besides consulting her astrologer, Wallis's other contribution was to suggest that Edward hire a New York public relations whizz kid to present the king's case to the world.

Within days she needed no crystal ball or PR handout to tell her that the opposition was already at hand. On 13 November, the 'phoney war' ended when the king's private secretary, Alex Hardinge, sent a letter alerting him to the fact that within the next few days the press were likely to go public regarding his friendship with Mrs Simpson. Furthermore, should he insist on marriage to the American divorcee, the government would resign and a general election would be called. His advice was that Mrs Simpson should go abroad without delay.

As obstinate as he was foolhardy, the king was adamant that she should stay and told her during a tense evening conversation at the Fort that if the country would not approve of them marrying, he would go. On 16 November, he repeated this threat to Baldwin. That same day he went to Marlborough House for dinner with his mother, Queen Mary, and sister, Mary. They were shocked and disbelieving when he said he was prepared to give up the throne for Wallis. While his mother retained her dignity and composure, she later gave vent to the sense of betrayal she and the royal family felt regarding his utterly selfish behaviour.

'I do not think you have ever realized the shock which the attitude you took up caused your family and the whole nation. It seemed inconceivable to those who had made sacrifices during the war that you, as their King, refused a lesser sacrifice.' It was not long before he had similar audiences with his three brothers, who took the news with varying degrees of shock and anger. Bertie, the stuttering, somewhat slow Duke of York and now king-in-waiting, was utterly devastated while, according to Lady Furness, the Duke of Gloucester slapped his elder brother across the face.

All the while, the king undertook his duties impeccably, opening Parliament, inspecting the Home Fleet, and, more contentiously, visiting the impoverished mining towns of South Wales, where he uttered the phrase that would define his brief reign – 'Something must be done' – in relation to the near starvation and unemployment suffered by so many families.

As the king walked past the hollow-eyed, hopeless parents and their ragged urchins, Wallis was dining at Claridge's with newspaper proprietor Esmond Harmsworth, who suggested morganatic marriage as a way out of the impasse. Unheard of in Britain but common on the Continent, especially in German royal houses, it was a form of marriage where the commoner, in this case Wallis, did not take the royal husband's rank or title upon marriage. It would, though, require special legislation. The king was distinctly cool – 'a strange almost inhuman concept,' he thought. Prime Minister Baldwin promised to ask the eleven Dominions their view. He was not hopeful.

Meanwhile, Edward was being counselled by, among others, Churchill, Beaverbrook, Monckton and Duff Cooper to be patient, to go through with the coronation, introduce Wallis to the world gradually, and then marry whom he pleased when he was firmly established as sovereign. It was only the king's impatience that had created a constitutional crisis in the first place. Whether he stayed or abdicated, he would still have to wait six months, until 27 April, before Wallis was officially divorced and could remarry. During that time he had ample opportunity to save the throne and his bride. Propelled by furious angels, he had turned a moral issue into an unnecessary constitutional and political tug-of-war between himself and the prime minister, a battle he was bound to lose. As Wallis's friend Elsa Maxwell noted: 'She might have been Queen of England had they been better intriguers, had they kept very quiet and she out of England. When he had been crowned he could have married her and asked no one's permission.'

Churchill and Beaverbrook felt it imperative that Cutie, their nickname for Wallis, leave the country. The king disagreed. The impish Beaverbrook took it upon himself to encourage a journalist from his newspaper, the *Daily Express*, to throw stones at her rented house in Regent's Park. The tactic worked, a flurried Wallis hurrying to the Fort for safety, Aunt Bessie in tow. She was not there for long.

On Thursday, 3 December 1936, the long-predicted storm broke, every British newspaper being filled with stories about the royal friendship or, as H. L. Mencken, the sardonic sage of Wallis's Baltimore, put it: 'The greatest news story since the Resurrection.' Under the banner headline GRAVE CRISIS, *The Times* laid out the Establishment case. In a leader it noted that an American wife for the king would be a not-unwelcome innovation for the House of Windsor. Then came the 'but'. 'The one objection, and it is an overwhelming objection . . . is that the lady in question has already two former husbands living from whom in succession she has obtained a divorce.' This was the settled consensus, so much so that American ambassador Robert Bingham was impressed enough by a 'beautifully conceived and expressed' article in the liberal *Observer* by editor J. L. Garvin to write a warm letter of congratulation. While Garvin's opinion piece, penned in December 1936, praised the 'goodwill and good judgement of the Empire' during the abdication crisis, the king and Wallis were minded to ignore the message, believing that it was the result of an Establishment plot to drive him off the throne.

As he leafed through the morning's newspapers, Wallis's picture on every front page, the king gallantly but reluctantly agreed for Wallis to head overseas so that she did not have to see or hear what was being said about her. Though he was primarily concerned about her health – she had been confined to bed for a week's rest – it was a catastrophic mistake, one Wallis regretted for the rest of her life. At a critical time when every decision led to an inevitable and irreversible conclusion, Wallis needed to be on hand as a trusted sounding board to discuss grave matters regarding her future and that of the monarchy. She may not have known much about the British constitution but she had practical common sense – and knew how to change the obstinate king's mind.

On that fateful day she had one idea in mind – to get out of Dodge and save her own skin. There was no thought of standing by her man in his hour of peril. 'I was hurt deeply and I was desperate. I said I had to leave as my position had become impossible,' she later recalled.

She contacted Herman Rogers, the one man in the world she could rely on, and took him up on his offer to stay with them. After a fluster of packing, she made a hurried late-night exit from the Fort, heading for the place she considered her second home, Lou Viei, in the South of France, where she had spent so many weeks on holiday. Here at least she would be among trusted, loving friends.

The decision may have soothed Wallis's jangled nerves, but it did little to advance her cause to become queen. As Beaverbrook noted of the king and his desire to protect Wallis: 'His anxiety was intense, but he was anxious about the wrong things. All his energies should have been devoted to the main issue, which was the struggle to remain on the throne and to marry in due time.'

It was a doleful parting for the couple on that dank evening of 3 December 1936. As they kissed goodbye, neither knew when or where they would meet again. Wallis left him her dog, Slipper, the first significant present he ever bought her, for company. 'I don't know how it's all going to end,' he told her. 'It will be some time before we can be together again. You must wait for me no matter how long it takes. I shall never give you up.'

Besides a Scotland Yard detective, her companion for the journey was Lord Perry Brownlow, the king's trusted friend and lord-in-waiting. Unknown to his master, Brownlow was involved in a benign conspiracy among the king's supporters to encourage Wallis to renounce the marriage outright and thus avoid the king's abdication.

Essentially, it was a further variation on Beaverbrook and Churchill's playing-for-time argument. They had barely left the

Fort when Brownlow ordered the car to stop and strongly suggested that she stay at his country estate in Lincolnshire, arguing that from there she could more easily influence the king and prevent him from making drastic decisions in the heat of the moment. She was tempted but decided to stick to the plan. She did not want to be blamed if the strategy went wrong, and she wanted to get as far away from this cursed isle as she could. 'Today I am in the pillory, tomorrow I will be in the Tower of London,' she said, somewhat histrionically. It was a fatal mistake. From the moment they reached Dieppe they were playing catch-up, never once at the pitch of discussions in London.

Within minutes of landing in France they were spotted and the hunt was on. For the next two days Wallis endured a nightmare journey of fog, snow, ice, route changes, car chases, near collisions, and escapes from the clutches of the press by climbing through bathroom windows. At roadside inns she made desperate attempts to call the king on crackling phone lines where her words were barely intelligible if heard at all. It was, she later recalled, 'like a nightmare in which one dreamt that one's living soul was suddenly confronted by the corpse from which it had taken leave'.

In the early hours of 5 December, Wallis, crouching in the back of the car with a blanket over her like a fugitive from justice, was driven through the iron gates of Lou Viei. Her new home, high on the hills above Cannes, was a former monastery that had been ransacked by Saracens during the eighth century. It was named Lou Viei or 'Old One' after the ghost of one of the murdered monks who still roamed the house. That night, even Herman, who claimed to see the ghost four or five times a week, was shocked by the apparition before him.

Wallis looked like a wraith, drip-white, exhausted and crumpled, a world away from the figure of neat perfection she normally presented to the world. Katherine gave her a hug of welcome and ushered her inside, where a log fire was blazing.

She awoke late, not to the sound of birdsong but to chatter from the vicinity of the garden gates where the world's media, described by Wallis as a 'ravenous besieging army', were camped. Her first mistake was to open the bedroom windows to admire the view over the seaside resort. The next day, the picture of her in her pink nightgown appeared on front pages around the world.

She would not make that mistake again. It was a salutary reminder that she was a prisoner as surely as if she had been convicted and sent to Alcatraz. Wallis could not go out into the garden to admire Herman's planting, or enjoy the sublime view over the Mediterranean, without being photographed. Katherine told her to keep her curtains closed, as several cameramen had climbed nearby trees and had their long lenses focused on her bedroom. Restful it wasn't, the confines of the modest villa further compressing jangling nerves. After lunch she sat down and wrote a somewhat incoherent fifteen-page letter to the king, which she sent by airmail in the hope it would reach him before he had taken any irrevocable step. As ever, she urged him not to abdicate, and to delay any decision until late the following year – as Beaverbrook and others consistently advised. By the time the letter reached the king, the die was cast.

Meanwhile, Wallis was under siege from without and betrayed from within. Her Scotland Yard detail were more of a nuisance than a help. Herman had one detective sent home after discovering he was leaking information to eager newsmen. Then the remaining officers telegrammed a report to London suggesting that Wallis was about to flee to Germany because she was 'frit', vernacular for 'frightened'. This merely added to the hysterical opinion that she was in the pay of the Nazi high command, ambassador von Ribbentrop being both her controller and her lover.

Local telephone operators were bribed to listen in to phone calls, Herman's butler was offered ten thousand French francs (£120 then but £2,000 today) to allow a newsman to dress as one of the workmen who were installing a new bathroom, and even Herman himself was offered nearly one million francs (£12,000 then or £200,000 today) for his home movies of Wallis's visit to Balmoral and the *Nahlin* cruise.

While Herman turned the offer down out of hand, he did agree to parley with the waiting press, giving daily briefings of a purely factual nature about events in the villa. His straight-talking and truthful manner earned the respect of the hard-boiled news corps. After the crisis was over, the gentleman of the press all signed a letter of thanks for his efforts on their behalf.

Media were one thing, madmen quite another. Wallis had given Herman the task of weeding out the hate mail from the growing pile of letters she received daily. Among the letters in the crackpot file was a worrying series of threatening missives written by a seemingly well-educated Australian who had posted his threats from several London postal districts. He made it clear that he was travelling to France to find Wallis and put a bullet in her. Herman said nothing to Wallis, who was already in a state of high anxiety, but he quietly alerted Inspector Evans, in charge of the Scotland Yard detail, who passed the warning on to London. For the next few months Herman slept in a bedroom adjoining Wallis's, a loaded pistol by his bedside.

Amid this sinister cacophony, Wallis tried to speak to the king. It was a losing battle. What with dropped connections, intense static and echo, Wallis felt like she was speaking from another planet, let alone another country. What Herman remembered from that fevered period was the sound of Wallis shouting down the telephone: 'Do not abdicate. Do nothing reckless. Listen to your friends.'

It was an increasingly hopeless plea. Though she was the cause and possible resolution of the drama, Wallis was now relegated to the role of onlooker as events in London moved to their inevitable climax. The king was resolutely sailing his ship of state alone, implacable in his solitary resolve. He was past counsel, past argument, past pleading. For Wallis it was like talking to a stranger. The king was 'remote and unreachable'. She had pleaded with him. Abdication would be 'disastrous for you and destroy me'. He was deaf to all entreaties.

Terrified of becoming, as she described, 'the blackest woman in history', she decided to take the initiative herself. After discussions with Herman and Perry Brownlow, she settled on a strategy to prevent the abdication. First she would release a statement saying that she would give him up, then she would head for either Genoa or Brindisi in Italy and catch a liner bound for China.

Her detective, Evans, was sent to reconnoitre. She needed to make the king understand that the price of marriage was not only damage to the Crown but, as she said, 'the destruction of my peace of mind, my reputation, and my self-respect'.

However, her announcement, which the king greeted at first with shock and then with reluctant agreement, fell short of a public disavowal, which by now was the only trick left in the game. Her statement proclaimed her innocence but failed to say that she would withdraw from his life forever. It read:

Mrs Simpson, throughout the last few weeks, has invariably wished to avoid any action or proposal which would hurt or damage His Majesty or the Throne. Today her attitude is unchanged, and she is willing, if such action would solve the problem, to withdraw forthwith from a situation that has been rendered both unhappy and untenable.

Brownlow and Herman drove to the Majestic Hotel in Cannes, where Brownlow read it to the assembled throng. Much as Wallis wanted the statement to dilute the animosity towards her, the London newspapers saw it as a sign that the crisis was passed and Edward would remain on the throne.

As Churchill, Beaverbrook and others mulled over the mood music, a most extraordinary twist in this drama came from Cannes. Out of the blue, Wallis's divorce lawyer, Theodore Goddard, arrived in the South of France in the company of the well-known gynaecologist Dr William Kirkwood. Unsurprisingly, the media circus went wild, assuming that Wallis was pregnant by the king – or even by Ernest Simpson.

In her memoir Wallis recalled: 'I was shocked to the core of my being' at this bizarre turn of events. It seemed that Prime Minister Baldwin had asked Goddard to see Wallis with an unknown plan to resolve the crisis. When he learned of Goddard's arrival, the king warned her not to even speak to him.

The addition of Dr Kirkwood was an unexpected plot twist. Eventually it emerged that as Goddard had a weak heart, he wanted his medical friend to accompany him on the hazardous plane journey from London. He didn't realize that the fact that the doctor was a gynaecologist would create such high drama. After a dressing-down from Brownlow for his guileless behaviour, it was a chastened lawyer who explained the reason for his visit: to urge Wallis to withdraw her divorce action against Ernest Simpson and remain married to the shipping agent.

If she went down this road it would prevent any possibility of the king marrying her, and thus the crisis would be resolved. After some reflection she agreed to this last reckless throw of the dice. It was too late. When she finally telephoned the king, she was told by his lawyer George Allen that the formal procedure for the king's immediate abdication was now under way.

What is fascinating is that in her first version of this momentous event, told to her ghost writer Cleveland Amory, it was *she*, not Prime Minister Baldwin, who was the author of this melodrama. 'Mr Goddard came to Cannes at my personal request,' she firmly recalled. She had learned, through Perry Brownlow, that the king had decided to abdicate. Faced with this 'shattering revelation', she wanted to stop him at all costs.

Wallis takes up the story:

> *There is one thing I can do. My plan, which had long been revolving in the back of my mind, was to withdraw my petition from the British courts. By such an action I would in effect admit error in my original application. There could be no marriage, because I would not be free to marry. The king would be confronted with an abyss if he abdicated. I arrived at this conclusion only after a soul-wracking debate within myself.*

Once she had consulted Goddard and he had advised that the plan was practical, she spoke to the king. Though she was 'less than frank' about Goddard's arrival in Cannes, her quixotic scheme was doomed to failure. The king passed the telephone to his lawyer George Allen, who informed her that the machinery of abdication was now in motion.

While this episode vividly illustrates how difficult it is to accept Wallis's memories at face value – her second ghost writer, Charles Murphy, wearily observed: 'Her recollections of the course of events were seldom the same' – it also exposes a deeper fault line in the relationship between the king and Mrs Simpson.

At this critical moment in their lives, when they should have been acting in concert, they were deceiving one another, the king about his decision to abdicate, Wallis about her own intentions for the future. She was busily trying to save herself and her reputation, he was marching obstinately into oblivion. Both were taking life-changing actions that affected the life of the one they ostensibly loved without discussion or debate. As she would later remark: 'He never even asked me to marry him, it was just assumed.' They made their bed of lies, now they must lie in them for the rest of their lives.

Wallis's exasperation was summed up in the telephone call from the king informing her that abdication was now inevitable. Her response, as recorded by the French police, the *Sûreté*, was curt: 'You god-damned fool.' From what the French could gather from their conversations, she was not happy about becoming his morganatic wife. She wanted the top job, to be crowned queen.

Wallis had been firmly led up the garden path, convinced by the king that, if they played their cards right, she could be his queen. The reality was that their love affair was built on the shifting sands of lies and deception, leading, ultimately, as far as Wallis was concerned, to profound and lasting disappointment.

Many, including the king's nanny, believed Edward's underlying motive was to get out of being king and pass on this high responsibility to his brother, the Duke of York. For years he had expressed his dread of becoming king, even as a child, as well as his loathing of day-to-day Court ceremony and the immutable royal round. As passionately as Wallis nursed an ambition to be queen, so Edward held a long-standing view that he never wanted to be king. As a result their future life together was constructed on faulty foundations, the couple doomed to an interior life of disappointment and reproach.

As his biographer Frances Donaldson argues: 'That's why he misled her into believing that they might reach safe ground. The great attraction was that she enabled him to give up the monarchy.' It seems that his great attraction to her was precisely that he was king. Their ambitions ran counter from the start.

Certainly that was the conclusion Cleveland Amory came to after six months of conversations with Wallis. He believed that her ambition was to be queen and that her failure to achieve that goal haunted her for the rest of her life.

As Amory's stepdaughter, Dr Gaea Leinhardt, a professor at the University of Pittsburgh, recalled:

She absolutely wanted to be queen. Absolutely and intensely. It was her ultimate ambition and she wanted it very badly. The abdication was clearly a miscalculation, because Edward believed he could pull it off.

Edward lived his whole life in a bubble, and with the abdication that bubble burst. Wallis assumed that he would stay king and it was based on an understandable misconception of the power of the throne, conflating the symbolic authority with political power.

Typically, Wallis never whispered a word about her true ambition. After the abdication she stuck steadfastly to the party line, always vigorously denying any such thoughts. She told Charles Murphy: 'I never dreamed I could be queen. Let me be positive about that. The idea didn't rhyme with anything. It would have been preposterous – the king as Defender of the Faith, the queen a divorced woman. There were ways around the queen problem. Morganatic marriage was one.'

It is as well she kept her ambition quiet. Few others, apart from Lady Cunard, genuinely believed that she would reign. As John Colville, the private secretary to Winston Churchill, wrote: 'I do know for a fact, because they both told me so, that neither Queen Mary nor Winston Churchill ever contemplated the possibility of Mrs Simpson being Queen of England.' Indeed, Churchill admitted the prospect was 'too horrible to contemplate'.

Even in republican America, there was little appetite for one of their own ascending the throne – as her cousin, writer Upton Sinclair, found to his cost when he wrote *Wally for Queen!* 'I thought it was hilariously funny,' he said. No one else did. First he sent the play to his friend, Broadway producer Arch Selwyn, who wrote back: 'Upton, are you crazy or do you think I am?' His editor wired, 'Swell but unpublishable', while his literary agent cabled: DESOLATED BUT COMPELLED TO AGREE SKIT UNPRINTABLE VERY CHARMING. When his normal printer refused to print the work, he did the job himself, selling copies for twenty-five cents a time. There were few takers.

Beneath the jokes that did the rounds at the Harvard and Yale clubs – Wallis's new title was 'Lady FitzEdward' and the proposed new royal motto was *Honi soit qui Wally pense* (a play on the original, *Honi soit qui mal y pense*: 'May he be shamed who thinks badly of it') – most of the American elite shuddered at the possible damage to the institution of monarchy and the authority of the British Empire. One diplomat's wife noted: 'During one week the British Empire trembled for fear of its very existence.' As for Wallis, former under-secretary of state and ambassador to Japan William R. Castle was not alone in thinking that if Wallis had engineered this crisis in order to become queen, she should be 'shot at dawn'.

VILLAIN OR VICTIM, almost to the last Wallis remained a figment of the collective imagination. Quite simply, nobody knew what she looked like. Newspapers were reduced to using muddy, out-of-date photographs or shots from foreign cameramen who had taken pictures during her various cruises. With the king about to make his historic radio broadcast, she agreed to show the world that she did not have horns growing out of her head and cleft feet. Wallis, together with Perry Brownlow and Herman and Katherine

Rogers, posed for a rather self-conscious picture at the entrance to Lou Viei. At last the public could see for themselves what all the fuss was about. When a photographer asked her to smile, she responded: 'Why smile?'

Her mood had not altered when she was introduced to Hearst Syndicate colour writer and author Stanton B. Leeds, who was chosen from the media pack to give a pen portrait of the most talked-about woman on the planet. She was depleted and downcast, clearly consumed by the events unfolding in London. He wrote:

> She came into the room quietly, like a shadow, looking even a little somber, in a severely cut blue dress, with a slight opening that showed that firm, white throat of hers. There was a wide costume bracelet on her wrist, silvery, studded with large stones. 'How do you do?' she said in a lifeless voice and sat down.
>
> For a brief moment she stroked her hair, then sat very still, folding her hands in her lap. Capable hands, it occurred to me, very white. It seemed fantastic to think of that, for I had looked into her eyes and now I too sat very still. It struck me that I did not want to move, that I should not want to move for quite a long while. I could think of nothing to say. I had never seen such a look in anyone's eyes.
>
> The light in them seemed set far back, beyond memories, beyond tragedies. It may seem far-fetched to say so, but I had the impression that here was a little girl – a little girl who had grown up and grown wise – a little girl from whom they had taken a doll. They were breaking it to pieces before her eyes and throwing it places.

On Friday, 11 December 1936, as King Edward VIII gave his historic address from Windsor Castle and explained he had found it 'impossible to carry the heavy burden of responsibility and to discharge my duties as king as I would wish to do without the help and support of the woman I love', the woman in question lay on the sofa of the Rogers' living room. She and the Lou Viei staff heard the king emphasize that the decision had been 'mine and mine alone'. After he finished, the others quietly left Wallis alone, her eyes closed to stem the tears, as she contemplated her doom. She is supposed to have wisecracked: 'You can't abdicate – and eat it.' Not that fateful night, though. Not that night.

The abdication united foes and friends alike. For once, President Roosevelt, Josef Stalin, Adolf Hitler and Benito Mussolini were all on the same page – baffled and contemptuous of the king's decision. FDR was 'disgusted' by the abdication and thought that Edward 'could have forced this situation. He could have been crowned and then announced that Mrs Simpson was now "the Duchess of Cornwall".'

Wallis's misfortune, though, was Mary Raffray's gain. In a letter to her sister, Ann, she was jubilant.

> *What an excitement we have been living through here. It seems incredible that the king could have actually abdicated – the whole country is shocked and grieved but also there is much bitterness against him and the feeling against Wallis is terrific.*
>
> *Lots of people who used to lick her boots are now saying they hardly knew her – Lady Cunard particularly, I am told. Of course, I did not see her – she has been hateful towards me and I can't pretend that I am sorry she has gone. It will be much easier for me to make my way in London with her gone.*

For the most part, women, especially those who knew the parties, sympathized with Wallis's predicament, none more so than

Constance Coolidge, Comtesse de Jumilhac, who after listening to the historic address in her Paris apartment, asked Helen Worden: 'Can you imagine a more terrible fate than to have to live up publicly to the legend of a love you don't feel? To have to face, morning, noon, and night, a middle-aged boy with no other purpose in life than a possessive passion for you?'

In London the king's former lover Lady Thelma Furness listened to the broadcast with growing horror before putting on a gramophone record by the Ink Spots and playing it at full volume. Her response was remarkably similar to that of Constance Coolidge. 'If I had to wake up every morning and look down at him in bed and realize it was for me he had given up his people and his country and his life . . .' Her voice trailed off and she shook her head. 'He loved his people and he was a good Prince of Wales.'

American journalist Lorena Hickok, the lesbian lover of First Lady Eleanor Roosevelt, caught the mood in Washington. 'I'm sorry for Mrs Simpson. She will have an awful job on her hands. What will he do with himself all these years that are left? He's only in his early forties. They can't go sailing around on yachts forever. I wonder if he won't be very bored and restless and unhappy . . . and if she can keep him happy. He probably doesn't know it now – but I am afraid he is in for some very bad times.'

It was a view shared by Wallis's love rival Courtney Espil: 'They will have no country and he no job. Can any love exist or be nourished on this slender fare? Will it grow stale? For Edward is no longer king. In her eyes he can only be a poor weak man who depends on her now, who has given away his all. Can they dance every night at a different cabaret to keep life gay?'

There was one unintentional winner – if winner is the correct term – from the abdication crisis: Wallis's first husband, Lieutenant Commander Win Spencer. In November 1936, he faced a general court-martial after being found drunk on duty on board his ship,

USS *Ranger*. However, his commanding officer, Sinclair Gannon, decided to sweep the matter quietly under the red carpet, arguing that the publicity surrounding Spencer's ex-wife might lead people to infer that the Navy's punishment of Commander Spencer was disproportionate to the offence and in turn would garner unfavourable headlines for the Navy. Fellow officers were not impressed by the lenient treatment meted out to Spencer, having expected him to be sentenced severely for his behaviour.

FOR THE KING, once a Navy midshipman himself, there was nothing shipshape and Bristol fashion about his own departure. His leaving, like the abdication crisis itself, was a shambles of haste and poor planning. Initially, he was supposed to sail for the Continent on board the HMS *Enchantress*, a Royal Navy sloop that would have been a headline writer's dream.

Once disembarked, he was due to take a train to Zurich, where rooms were booked in a small hotel. Then wiser counsel prevailed, Perry Brownlow contacting Kitty Rothschild and asking if his 'brother', their agreed code for the king, could stay at their home of Schloss Enzesfeld in Austria. She willingly agreed.

Even with these new arrangements, calamity struck. His chauffeur got lost in the sprawling Portsmouth docks as he searched for the new ship taking the ex-king, who was now Duke of Windsor, into exile. Certainly his new transport, HMS *Fury*, had a more fitting title to indicate how his family, some friends and many of his former subjects felt about him.

He let it all wash over him. A few hours later he was ensconced in his new residence, feeling buoyed after a long conversation with Wallis. Conscience clean and clear, he was reported to be 'singing in his bathtub'.

CHAPTER TWELVE

I Want Your Baby

THE GLITTERING PRIZE had slipped and slithered from Wallis's grasp. Another woman, one whom she loathed, would now wear the precious crown she coveted. All that now remained was the abyss, a long headlong fall into social exile, irrelevance and eternal damnation. Albert Pierrepoint, the official hangman, could not have executed a more swift and sudden drop.

In a move choreographed by the new Court, High Society turned its collective back on her. While the purge was not quite up to Stalin's standards, it was a very British affair, quick and quietly effective; nothing showy about these trials. The new king, George VI, ordered all those who swore allegiance to the Crown to stay away from the smart American set of Lady Cunard, Chips Channon, Laura Corrigan, Lady Mendl and others, including Perry Brownlow, the man who accompanied Wallis on her exile to France. They suffered death by a thousand snubs, Brownlow ostentatiously ignored when he went to his exclusive members' club.

Overnight, Emerald Cunard disowned the woman she had groomed for the throne, telling friends she had never even met Wallis. It was no use. She was now reduced to hanging around outside major social events waiting for the royal party to depart. Only then did she and the others tarred with the Simpson brush gain reluctant admission.

Others were equally guilty of studied betrayal. At a dinner a few weeks after the abdication, the Churchills, Chips Channon and Lord and Lady Granard were among the party. When the peer tactlessly attacked the former king and Mrs Simpson, Clemmie Churchill turned on him and said: 'If you feel that way, why did you invite Mrs Simpson to your house and put her on your right?' A long and embarrassed silence followed. Osbert Sitwell wrote a poem he called 'Rat Week' about those who scuttled away from the toxic Mrs Simpson. The new queen – or as Wallis called her, 'The fat Scottish cook' – read it at a sitting, savouring every delicious *mot* and morsel.

After the fall came the deluge, as the woman in question faced a daily torrent of vitriol and anonymous hatred in the morning postbag at Lou Viei. Herman weeded out the death threats and the promises to hurt and maim, but Wallis insisted on reading the rest, even those dipped in poison. She discovered that the Canadians were the most censorious, followed by British expats living in America. 'The world is against me – and me alone,' she complained to Herman, with some justification. Of course, there were sympathetic letters, notably from her ex-husband Ernest, who wrote several times expressing his belief that she did everything she could to prevent what he called 'the final catastrophe', and strangers such as Lord Willoughby telling her through mutual friends that the duke had given Britain great service and that he was still 'the most popular man in the country'.

These, though, were slim pickings. She could not continue this daily diet of venom for long, becoming so sick and depressed that Herman, seeing the effect on her, took charge. One morning he sat her down, held her hands, and had a long heart-to-heart conversation, sympathetically outlining the home truths she was deliberately avoiding.

He told her: 'Whether you like it or not, the world is discovering you.'

'Discovering me?' she exclaimed. 'You mean destroying me.'

Herman went on: 'Wallis, you had better learn to live with these things, because from here on you must expect more rather than less. It's not just that you've become a celebrity; through the action of a king you've become a historical figure and a controversial one.

'You are in for a miserable and unhappy life unless you learn to ignore the lies and inventions, and to say to yourself over and over again, "I won't let it get me down."'

Wallis replied: 'But it *is* getting me down. It makes me feel cheap. It makes me feel disreputable. It makes me want to run away and hide. It hurts.'

Herman continued. 'You can't run away. And there's no place left where you can hide. You've got to learn to rise above all this. Put it out of your mind. Much of what is being said concerns a woman who does not exist and never did exist. Perhaps it would be just as well if you stopped reading about her.'

Sensible advice from her 'rock', but it took Wallis many months to wean herself off this unhealthy addiction, either in the media or in her postbag. Wallis admitted that she was 'repelled but at the same time fascinated' by what people were saying about her.

She was not the only one. It is a curious phenomenon, the urge to read about oneself, knowing beforehand that it is going to hurt or depress. Like a moth to a flame, the late Diana, Princess of Wales, was drawn to reading newspaper stories about her, however unpleasant. She disregarded all advice to ignore them, and as a result was left feeling worthless and impotent.

Wallis had gone from a face in the crowd to *Time* magazine's Woman of the Year. It was hardly a flattering profile, the magazine presenting her as a 24-carat gold-digger. 'Her life up to her meeting with King Edward VIII was inconsequential to a degree . . .

'She resolved early to make men her career, and in forty years reached the top – or almost.' As a helpmate to the infatuated monarch, she had helped him spend most 'royally, imperially, wildly', on expensive yachts, furs and gems from Cartier and other purveyors of conspicuous consumption.

While readers of *Time* complained in their droves about the choice of Wallis, there was no denying the universal fascination with the mystery woman who had caused a king to abdicate his throne. Within weeks there were Simpson and Wallis bars, while her former home at 212 East Biddle Street in Baltimore was turned into a museum where, for an extra charge, the curious could sit in the same bath used by Wallis and have their picture taken. The organizers brazenly contacted Herman Rogers and Lady Furness for artefacts to decorate the tawdry display. They were not forthcoming. That arbiter of public taste, Madame Tussauds wax museum, hastily arranged a new order for the royal family, placing the Duke of Windsor behind his younger brother, the Duke of Gloucester. Facing this formidable group was a vague likeness of Mrs Simpson. The woman who had created the biggest royal crisis since Anne Boleyn, the wife of Henry VIII, was clad in a simple evening gown. She confronted the House of Windsor with a half-smile and questioning eyes.

As for 'the most popular man in the country', the duke behaved as if he had been born again. He was jauntiness personified, facing each new day with a spring in his step and whistling a merry tune. A huge weight had been removed from his shoulders, a burden the new king was now manfully struggling to carry. While Schloss Enzesfeld was hardly heaven on earth, to the former king it was a piece of paradise. He had escaped a date with destiny and his affection for Wallis was unbounded, not just because he worshipped the ground she walked on but because her status as a divorcee had given him, consciously or unconsciously, the reasons he needed to abdicate the throne with a degree of dignity and plausibility. For years he had talked about renouncing his succession, and now he had done the deed, justifying his behaviour to himself on the grounds that the political class would not allow him to marry his choice of wife.

When his former private secretary Godfrey Thomas visited his one-time employer, he saw a man who had 'no regrets about the past and no qualms about the future. In his mind he was booked for a life of perpetual married bliss.'

The first few days, though, were difficult. The Rothschild house and grounds were under siege from a small army of newspapermen, mainly from America. His hostess, Baroness Kitty Rothschild, was startled when she opened her bedroom curtains one morning to discover a Hearst Newspapers reporter clinging to the ivy beneath her window. She promptly went to see the American ambassador, George Messersmith, to lodge a formal complaint, a move that eventually resulted in peace for the besieged occupants.

It was a hollow victory, the duke being resentful of the role the press had played in composing what he saw as a false narrative regarding his relationship with Wallis. 'It is because of the American newspapers that I am here today,' he told Messersmith bitterly.

All that was left was for the former king to sit it out until Wallis's divorce became legally permanent on 27 April 1937. Unlike Wallis, he had plenty of options to kill time, going skiing, hillwalking, and even cataloguing the castle's extensive wine collection. He liked to ask well-wishers what they thought of his abdication speech, always keen to point out that it was mainly his work rather than Churchill's. 'I wrote most of it and Winnie wrote the rest,' he preened.

The most frustrating part of the day was the seven-o'clock phone call to Wallis. As English divorce law prevented the couple from living in the same country, let alone seeing each other, they were reduced to living hundreds of miles apart and speaking on the telephone at a set time every day. It was nerve-jangling, Wallis shouting at her paramour on the crackly, echoing, fizzing service that passed for an international telephone line. Wallis's inability to speak the most basic French to the operator eventually irritated even the placid Katherine Rogers.

'This is ridiculous,' she told her sternly and wrote down in large capitals the phrase *'Je n'entends pas'* – 'I can't hear' – to alert the operator to problems on the line. As he had done when Wallis stayed with them in China, Herman encouraged her to take language lessons. He was no more successful this time around, Wallis proving to be a most unwilling pupil.

The tensions surrounding the seven-o'clock phone call symbolized the changing personal dynamic between Herman, Katherine, the duke and Wallis. From the moment Wallis arrived, Herman moved into the adjoining bedroom in his self-imposed role as her protector. Meanwhile, Katherine was left on her own downstairs. It was an arrangement that became permanent, with disastrous consequences for the couple's intimate life.

As Constance Coolidge later wrote: 'He sleeps outside in his new bedroom and kisses Katherine goodnight and goes to his bed outside. They definitely do not make love any more. It is hard on her and he has always been his own worst enemy.'

It was not just the night-time arrangements that were troubling. As a concerned wife, Katherine was worried about Herman, afraid that he would wear himself out dealing with the many Simpson matters – the media, her correspondence, wedding plans, possible homes, her title and her public. It was an all-consuming occupation, Herman's diligent application to the quotidian details of Wallis's life becoming a full-time job.

It was Herman, not the duke, who was now dealing with matters that, strictly speaking, were the purview of the future man and wife. The wedding venue was a case in point. While the duke was reduced to a tremulous, distant voice, it was Herman who occupied the role of husband.

Wallis hinted at the growing intimacy between herself and Herman, now the only true male friend in her life. As she recalled: 'I knew he was not sleeping well. Often during the night I heard him stirring restlessly or pacing the floor.'

What she didn't say was whether she tried to comfort him during his late-night vigils or if she asked him to comfort her. There had always been an affection and understanding between them that was missing from Katherine's friendship with Wallis. Wallis told Herman everything, even her sexual desires and preferences. Even in today's more liberated times it is unusual for a single woman to discuss these matters with a married man, however close their friendship.

Did Wallis ever try to seduce Herman on those long lonely nights in the South of France? Possibly – but Herman headed her off at the pass. In a cryptic and confidential conversation with her ghost writer Cleveland Amory, he said he told her: 'You can't go beyond that wall' – meaning into his bedroom.

Whether or not she tried to seduce her surrogate husband, Wallis was a study in frustration and disappointment. Her hostess became the immediate target for her quiet wrath, Wallis telling her confidantes, notably her aunt and the duke, about Katherine's shortcomings. Her catalogue of complaints included the fact that the drains smelled, the villa was dirty, the kitchen unhygienic, the Rogers' dogs were always sick, the food was terrible and the public rooms were dungeon-dark.

'The food here is the end – the dirt grows worse,' she wrote to Edward, later grumbling: 'It really has been uncomfortable to a degree – also boring, and then there is Katherine – hard as nails.'

That, coming from a woman universally described as 'hard', suggested an irritation with Katherine that went beyond the difficulties of sharing a small villa. It was Katherine, not she, who was Herman's wife – a bubbling well of resentment and jealousy.

At least with the retreat of the media army Wallis was able to sit out in the garden, take the dogs for walks in the hills behind Cannes, visit her aunt, who stayed for a time at the Carlton Hotel, and make the occasional foray to see novelist Somerset Maugham, Lady Colefax, Singer sewing machine heiress and Society beauty Daisy Fellowes, and others who had remained friends. As Riviera society had decided to shun her, she kept her distance. Popular novelist and beau-about-town Michael Arlen was typical. He made it clear that he would never be present at any party attended by Mrs Simpson.

Shopping was another ordeal, Wallis often attracting curious crowds when she dared to brave the streets. One of her favourite occupations was just no fun any more. When she left the security of the villa, she was living on her nerves, fearful of being physically attacked. Her mood was not helped when political lobbyist Kenneth de Courcy, a supporter of the former king, described to her aunt, in bloodcurdling detail, the possible existence of an anti-Simpson society that was out to do her harm.

Meanwhile, the man who had placed her in jeopardy, turned her into a figure of fun and contempt, and ensured that her life would never be the same again, was nowhere to be seen. For all his protestations of love and devotion – and they were an endless river – the newly minted Duke of Windsor had signally failed to support, comfort or nourish her in her hour of need.

Of course, the English divorce laws saw to that, but Wallis could not help blaming him for putting her in the firing line. She was a woman cocooned in disappointment, her disillusion soon bleeding into bitterness, regret and anger, much of it eventually directed at the man who had placed this noose around her neck.

He had misled her into thinking they might reach safe ground; now he had a lifetime to experience in full measure the dark side of Wallis – her sharp tongue, wild temper, wounding criticism and utter self-absorption. As Ernest's friend Bernard Rickatson-Hatt remarked, her outbursts of anger and cruelty were commonplace, matched only by her later attempts at kindness to heal the emotional wounds.

Wallis's cruel streak, born from her deep-seated insecurity, was not long in bubbling to the surface. After a few weeks in exile, she accused Edward of having an affair with his hostess, Kitty Rothschild. Nothing could have been further from the truth. Not only was Kitty worried about the cost of entertaining a man who had no conception of money, she was counting the days until he left her home. She was even casting around, asking other friends if they would shoulder the burden of looking after the ex-king.

Their insecurity was mutual, the duke being wildly jealous of any man who took Wallis's attention away from him. The mere mention of her former lover Felipe Espil would send the duke into a red-faced fluster.

'Don't dance with her when you next see her,' Kitty told Espil light-heartedly when she visited Washington to escape from her royal guest. 'Edward is horribly jealous. He hates it when any man dances with her – and I know that he knows all about you.'

Indeed he did. Wallis had already exploited his concern ruthlessly. When he was a guest at the Fort, Espil's friend Jose Dodero, the son-in-law of the president of the Central Bank of Argentina, Ernesto Bosch, saw how Wallis used his name as a weapon: 'I have seen her two or three times get so annoyed with him and each time she commences to talk about Espil as the only man she has ever really loved.' Dodero went on to describe how the king would 'stiffen in his chair and rearrange his necktie and turn away nervously. Each time, with this remark, she could win her point.'

The long period of waiting exposed other fault lines in both her character and their relationship. The language she used in their private correspondence, normally affectionate and respectful, became positively contemptuous. In one letter she was worried about reports claiming that he was about to be stripped of his Order of the Garter, the highest rank of chivalry in the land. Wallis addressed him as 'Dearest Lightning Brain' and chided him for never knowing what was going on. Her growing scorn for the duke was balanced only by her contempt for his brother. Both Wallis and Edward referred to King George VI as 'that stuttering idiot'.

For his part, Edward was consumed by guilt at having led the woman he loved obsessively into this position. 'The drawbridges are going up behind me. I have taken you into a void,' he told her. What with the commotion about the Order of the Garter and his gradual removal as honorary colonel in chief from an army of British regiments, he felt that he was being expunged from royal history.

He felt impotent and helpless. Not only had he failed to make Wallis his queen, now even her more modest ambition for the same royal title as her husband seemed in jeopardy. Though she gave the impression that the appellation 'Her Royal Highness' was a mere bauble barely worthy of discussion, her private letters to the duke told a very different story.

The king may have given up his place in the royal succession, accepted exile from his country and contumely from his family, friends and subjects, but from the day he abdicated, as far as Wallis was concerned it was all about her. 'I suppose we will have difficulty about a name for poor me, as York [her contemptuous reference to the new king, George VI], I don't suppose, will make me HRH.' Again, in December 1936, she was singing the same tune. 'It is plain that York guided by her [the queen] would not give us the extra chic of creating me HRH – the only thing to bring me back in the eyes of the world.'

Her fears proved well founded. Shortly before Wallis and Edward married, George VI announced that she would not be given the same title as her husband, a move that many saw as confounding settled case law and natural justice. This unwelcome wedding present soured the duke's relationship with his family until his death.

It was not only her ambitions to have a title that were dashed. As the months to their reunion ticked by, her dreams of a grand wedding attended by high clergy, the royal family and friends came to naught. The king sent out an edict banning anyone linked to the royal family from attending the wedding, planned for June 1937. Even Mary Raffray, now Wallis's sworn enemy, felt sorry for her. She told her sister Buckie: 'As much as I loathe Wallis, I can't help feeling half pleased half sorry for the slap in the face she's had not being Royal Highness and to me much worse – none of their friends or sycophants going to the wedding.'

Before the couple were reunited in April, Wallis had come to realize that she couldn't rely on or trust anyone outside her immediate close circle.

She had to accept that they were quite alone, that in the eyes of the royal family they did not even exist. From now on Wallis drew on her inner toughness to face the world. Whether or not she felt it, Wallis was determined to be the happiest bride in history, her pride in her husband and her smiling face a mute rebuke to her detractors. She would never let them have the satisfaction of seeing her beaten and bowed.

If she had to arrange the wedding without any concessions from the royal family, so be it. She discussed the practicalities of the ceremony with Herman Rogers, while her husband-to-be left the choice of venue to her, saying: 'Any place will do. So long as it's unforgettable.'

Their first thought was Lou Viei. While it was convenient, the place was too small, easily overseen by the press, and anyway Herman was eager to remodel the villa. Next up was the Duke of Westminster's estate in Normandy, but that idea came to nothing. Then Wallis set her heart on a white villa named Château de la Croë at Cap d'Antibes, which was owned by the retired newspaper magnate Sir Pomeroy Burton. When the word came from Buckingham Palace that the new king had decided that anywhere on the Riviera would give the wrong impression, as it was seen as a playground for the rich and infamous, Wallis had to think again.

Waiting in the wings was industrialist Charles Bedaux, who had, from the day of the abdication, offered the duke open house at his Château de Candé in the Loire valley. Herman Rogers had met Bedaux several times, he and Katherine once staying at his château. The colourful millionaire, whose claim to fame was the invention of a time-and-motion system loathed by labour and loved by bosses, made clear his motives were purely romantic, namely to give the royal lovebirds a suitably regal setting for their union.

He told Herman that he had no skeletons in his cupboard – though at the time he was assiduously wooing the Nazi hierarchy – and once Buckingham Palace gave their seal of approval, Herman cabled his acceptance of Bedaux's seemingly generous offer. With its rolling parkland, dense woods and impressive architecture, the Château de Candé was suitably remote, romantic and certainly fit for a former king. Their thoughtful hostess, the beautiful and willowy Fern Bedaux, was waiting for Wallis, Herman and Katherine when they arrived at the end of March following a two-day drive to the Loire valley. Their host, Charles Bedaux, a man Wallis described as 'energetic, quick and alert in conversation and almost too eager to impress with his sympathy', arrived much later.

Once more, the sleeping arrangements bear scrutiny. As Fern Bedaux would not be in residence, she suggested that Wallis use her bedroom as her own and that the duke, when he arrived from Austria in April, take a small guest apartment downstairs. Adjoining Fern's bedroom was a sitting room with a day bed normally used by Charles Bedaux. Herman decided to take these quarters for himself in order to keep a watchful eye on Wallis. Katherine was relegated to one of the upstairs bedrooms.

As the château was well patrolled and guarded – a nightwatchman had been specially hired for the duration of the royal visit – there was no real need for Herman's continued vigilance. With regard to sleeping arrangements, it appeared that Herman and Wallis were the man and wife of the château.

The move to Candé gave Wallis a new lease of life, whiling away the days until she was reunited with the duke with games of golf, long walks, or excursions to nearby châteaux and other places of interest. Her former husband would have been amused by her new-found interest in ancient buildings. It was a marked contrast from her days with Ernest.

There were other compensations. The proximity of the château to Paris ensured that there was a steady stream of well-wishers. On 29 March, Lady Mendl and *Vogue*'s John McMullin visited. Both had suffered socially since the abdication but, unlike some fair-weather friends, they remained true to Wallis. Neither had imagined that Edward would ever abdicate; Lady Mendl had been poised to redecorate some of the important rooms at Buckingham Palace, while McMullin was expecting the king for cocktails at his Knightsbridge apartment the night he renounced the throne. Their visit was not only to show support for the beleaguered Mrs Simpson but also to discuss her choice of Mainbocher for her trousseau and Cecil Beaton as the official photographer. Shortly after they left, Wallis suffered a devastating tragedy. Slipper, who had been sent from Austria by the duke, was bitten by a poisonous viper and died in her arms. She grieved as if she had lost a child, and Elsie and

McMullin immediately returned to comfort a heartbroken Wallis. She, like the duke, saw the death of their beloved pet as an ill omen.

As ever, it was Herman who did the necessary, carefully burying Slipper in the grounds of the château, watched by a tearful Wallis. It was Herman who, as at Cannes, shouldered the duties of press liaison, announcing the news of Slipper's death to the dozen or so correspondents and cameramen camped out at the boundary of the property. Their presence, while not intrusive, did have the effect of curtailing Wallis's shopping trips to Paris. Instead she asked Katherine or Constance Coolidge to purchase the vital essentials for every well-groomed woman. Constance was, for example, despatched to buy her suitable stockings. Even when Katherine was away, Herman never left her side. As Wallis recalled: 'He continued to manage the correspondence. He listened to my problems. His calmness consoled and steadied me. He pulled me back from the abyss of despair.'

Finally, on 3 May 1937, Wallis obtained her divorce and within hours of receiving the happy news, the duke boarded the *Orient Express* for France. As he bounded up the stone steps looking thin and drawn, his first words were: 'That last afternoon at the Fort – I've come just as quickly as I could.'

Later he took her for a walk, where he made clear that even though they were now together, they faced a difficult future. He spoke of them being quite alone, a fact Wallis had realized some weeks before. 'My friends have all disappeared. They have been snuffed out as by a holocaust. I no longer have a family; in its place is a national monument to cover the spot where I fell. I have been cut off from everything that I have always taken for granted. Your life with me will be difficult.'

They were now able to stand as one against the vicissitudes that assailed them. Her first 'frightful ordeal' was in May, when she listened to the new king's coronation on the radio in the sitting room. The king's hesitant speech was heard around the world, Courtney Espil vividly describing the moment: 'He had a pathetic, truly heartbreaking difficulty in getting started. The first word would not come. He swallowed once or twice. We heard it clearly. I pinched myself and tore at a nail on my right hand. Then out came the first painful word.'

For his part, the former king stood by the fireplace, silently listening to the sonorous ceremony. When they had gathered their breath – and their thoughts – the duke told Wallis: 'You must have no regrets. I have none.'

They focused on themselves – their honeymoon, their home and their future together. For their honeymoon the duke had rented Castle Wasserleonburg, which belonged to the Austrian nobleman Count Paul Munster. He also suggested that they make their home in France, a country which, for all its republican sentiment, displayed a certain kind of civility towards fallen royalty.

They even found an English clergyman to marry them. Like the Windsors, he was an outsider, a man of the people who roamed the slums of northeast England. After an interview with the duke's solicitor, the Reverend Robert Anderson Jardine was deemed of suitable cloth. The duke gave him a pair of cufflinks inscribed with 'ER' as a thank you for officiating. He repaid their trust by immediately embarking on a whirlwind tour of America, tittling the tattle from the wedding ceremony.

For all their inner turmoil, private misgivings and dread of what the future might hold, the duke and his bride-to-be put on a brave, jaunty face in public. Their friend Constance Coolidge, who was one of the guests at a party at Candé shortly before their 3 June wedding, wrote a telling pen portrait of the most talked-about couple in the world. 'I have never seen anyone as happy as the duke,' she observed. 'Like a boy let out of school. He is gay, carefree, laughing and terribly in love.'

She noted that at dinner the duke, dressed in a Scottish plaid of the Black Watch, was attentive to a fault, springing up when Wallis left her drink on the table. He was, she thought, 'a little shy of her and adoring'.

After the 'magnificent' dinner, Constance and Wallis were chatting by the fire in the living room. 'Suddenly the duke noticed that Wallis's slipper was undone, and he went down on both knees and tied it up. I caught Randolph Churchill's eye at this moment and his expression was amusing to say the least. Then they all played poker, the duke cautiously. When he passed on one hand, Wallis, who was next to him, said: "What, Sir, with all those aces, really."'

At one-thirty they all retired, but Constance had no sooner crawled into bed when there was a bang on the door and in bustled Wallis and the duke. Constance later wrote of that late night encounter:

'We thought we'd come to see if you were all right,' said Wallis, and they both sat on the edge of the bed and chatted away. Then the duke said: 'I don't think that lamp is right for you. I'll fix it.' And he got down on the floor and crawled about and arranged something so the lamp was nearer to me. I tell you all this so that you can get some idea about them – how simple they are, and attractive. He spoke well about Baldwin, said he made a fine speech. He said he did hope I understood about the wedding. 'None of my family are coming either,' he said.

When I left I was really touched and amazed that the two people who caused such great excitement in the world could still be so simple and unspoiled and so perfectly natural.

They remained, though, creatures of international curiosity. Outside the château grounds the media were gathering for the wedding. The duke was incredulous when he learned that Cornelius Vanderbilt, a scion of one of America's wealthiest families, was a member of the journalist pack camping outside. Unlike the others, Vanderbilt had a large trailer for his comfort. 'It's a good thing my father is not alive,' commented the duke in amazement. 'He would be convinced the world had gone to the dogs.'

His own world would have collapsed around him had he ever learned of the extraordinary conversation between Wallis and the man he trusted implicitly, Herman Rogers, just before their wedding. A few days before the big day, both Katherine and the duke went to Paris, for shopping and on business respectively, leaving Wallis and Herman on their own at the château. In their absence, Herman was seemingly involved in a late-night encounter with the soon-to-be Duchess of Windsor. Wallis blurted out that she loved him and that with the wedding day so close, if she became pregnant by him, it would be considered the duke's child. It was an extraordinary admission, Wallis revealing for once the true feelings behind the mask she routinely hid behind. That fateful night she went further, much further, for the first time expressing her genuine feelings towards Herman. Herman's astonished response can only be imagined.

Given their intense and intimate relationship, Herman and Wallis thrown together by circumstances beyond their control, it would have been surprising had the couple not developed a closeness that went beyond the purely platonic. For months they had been sleeping feet from one another, Herman more a husband to Wallis than to his own wife.

As unexpected as this proposition seems, it comes as no surprise to the Rogers family. Years later Wallis confessed to Herman's second wife, Lucy, on *her* wedding day that Herman was the only man she had ever truly loved.

As Herman's step-granddaughter and family historian Barbara Mason observed: 'I am not at all surprised. I can't help but feel that Wallis barely tolerated the duke. Even before their marriage it was a mother-and-son relationship. He was pathetically reliant on her. So it is logical that she wanted to try a different type of gene pool for the father of her child. Herman was the man she loved, and when you read her autobiography carefully these sentiments are expressed in plain sight.'

Herman's revelation came in a series of interviews in the summer of 1955 when he spent five days discussing the woman he knew so well with Wallis's official ghost writer Cleveland Amory. He recalled the remarkably intimate conversations he enjoyed with Wallis – sexual confessions that he may have hesitated to report back to his wife. His relationship with Wallis was complex: ostensibly close friends but teetering on the brink of greater intimacy. Were Wallis's admissions about her own sex life and her tantalizing offer to have his child a kind of seduction just to prove to herself that Herman was her property? After all, at almost forty-three, she was past the traditional age for child bearing. Amory's cryptic handwritten notes, held in the archive at Boston Public Library, leave many questions unresolved. They read: 'Two days before she married, Kat gone away, also HRH . . . so in middle of night – love – now in two days she would be married and it would be his child.'

Though Wallis's love for Herman is part of Rogers family lore, not everyone in the family believes that they were lovers. Herman's stepdaughter-in-law, Kitty Blair, commented: 'Throughout her life, at the most telling and important times, Wallis depended on Herman, as a wife depends on her husband. Wallis had long been in love with Herman, but I don't think she was ever intimate with him.' She made this assessment based on her own conversations with her mother-in-law, Herman's second wife, Lucy Wann.

There is a sly, evasive quality about this first studio shoot of Wallis and the king. Neither meets the other's gaze. It symbolizes their deceitful behaviour during the abdication crisis, the couple taking life-changing decisions about the other without consultation or seeming concern. It laid the foundation for a shaky marital union, particularly from Wallis's perspective. Reproach and disappointment were never far from the surface.

Wallis posed for this picture with Lord Brownlow and Herman and Katherine Rogers outside their Riviera villa of Lou Viei, where she was staying. Now the world had a chance to see what the woman for whom Edward VIII gave up his throne actually looked like.

Herman Rogers, who reluctantly acted as Wallis's mouthpiece, briefed the waiting media most days about any developments in the crisis. When the emergency ended, the gentlemen of the press signed a round robin letter thanking him for his integrity and honesty.

Due to strict English divorce laws, the newly minted Duke of Windsor was not able to see his bride-to-be until six months after her first court appearance. During this time, Wallis was guest of Fern Bedaux, wife of the industrialist and Nazi sympathizer Charles, at their home, Château de Candé in the Loire valley. Even when the duke arrived, fellow guest Herman never left Wallis's side, sleeping in an adjoining room, a loaded pistol by his bedside.

A pensive-looking Wallis reflects on her future. She had been seduced by the duke and his regal image. Stripped of his title and forced into exile, she pondered if their union would survive the vicissitudes that inevitably assailed them.

After an ecstasy of waiting, finally the royal couple married on June 3, 1937. Appropriately Herman Rogers gave Wallis away and Society photographer Cecil Beaton (left) shot the historic moments.

War or no war, in 1941 Wallis found herself topping the list as the world's best-dressed woman. Her one-time love rival Courtney Espil managed only seventh place. As the wife of the governor of the Bahamas, Wallis had to use surrogates to shop for her in New York, lest she be accused of extravagance.

During their wartime stay in Nassau, Wallis was the power behind the throne. The duke would not make a decision without her say-so. She proved to be a one-woman dynamo, chairing charities that supported the war effort.

1947

DON'T FORGET

Mr. Ladew.

DINNER
at PALM BEACH CASINO - Cannes - A.M.
Saturday August 30th at
9:30 o'clock

Harvey S. Ladew

The decision by King George VI not to confer the appellation 'Her Royal Highness' upon the Duchess of Windsor left a family wound that never healed. Those who entertained them ensured that this surly omission was always corrected. Maryland *bon viveur* Harvey Ladew was their suitably considerate host at a dinner in Cannes in August 1947.

After the war, the Windsors put their heart and soul into redecorating Château de la Croë, their rented villa at Cap d'Antibes. At any one time there were thirty servants, including a fulltime telephone operator, to attend to their needs. Though they entertained lavishly, there remained some in the 'Riviera Set' who refused to accept their hospitality.

Archie and Lucy Wann

Herman Rogers and Lucy

Wallis and Edward

At the end of the Second World War, former Spitfire pilot and war hero Archie Wann and his German-born wife, Lucy, moved to the South of France, where they became friends of the Rogers and the Windsors. Tragically within a year of each other, Katherine Rogers and Archie Wann died. Just months later, on August 3, 1950, Lucy Wann and Herman Rogers married. On their wedding day Wallis told Lucy that Herman was the only man she had ever loved, and did her best to spoil the big day, arriving very late for the reception in a show-stealing white tulle gown, and giving the couple a silver tray engraved only to Herman.

The wedding of Herman and Lucy Rogers marked the end of the closeness between the Rogers and the Windsors. Instead, Wallis, like a woman scorned, transferred her affections to the wholly unsuitable Jimmy Donahue, an outrageous homosexual notorious for his drunken behaviour. The union came close to wrecking the royal marriage. Here, Jimmy looks on as his mother, Jessie, a family friend, and the Windsors enjoy the entertainment at a Paris nightclub in 1952.

The duchess's ghostwriter Cleveland 'Clip' Amory and his actress wife, Martha, in France, where they stayed during his interviews for Wallis's autobiography. He quit after six months claiming that Wallis had difficulty telling the truth about her life.

Though living in exile in France, for years after the war the Windsors were seen as the leaders of the international *demi-monde*. Here they are at a dinner held in the summer of 1948 studded with Hollywood stars and hosted by their friend Elsa Maxwell. From the duke's right is Dolly Dorelis, Clark Gable, Virginia Fox, the Marquess of Milford Haven, the Duchess of Windsor, Darryl Zanuck, Jack Warner, Linda Christian, Tyrone Power, and Elsa Maxwell.

The Windsors decided that if Wallis wrote a book about her life it would help their public image. In August 1955 she wrote a plaintive letter to Herman Rogers asking for help. Even though the resulting biography, titled *The Heart Has Its Reasons*, was an international best seller it did not heal the rift between them.

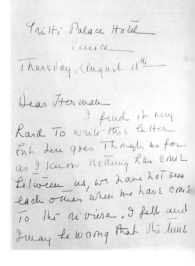

All the balls, big bands, and *bonhomie* could not disguise the fact that the duke eventually became bored with his caviar and champagne lifestyle. While the duchess danced until dawn, he often went home early. It didn't help his dining companions that he became increasingly deaf.

The duchess exchanges a few tart words with the duke at the 1959 'April in Paris' ball at the Waldorf-Astoria in New York. Wallis discovered that living out a great romance in public was a continual strain, often taking out her resentment on her royal husband. 'Will I be going to bed in tears?' was his refrain. He always came back for more, though.

The Duke and Duchess of Windsor exerted a fascination upon the public imagination that spanned the decades, their faces appearing on the covers of magazines and newspapers until they were well past pensionable age.

Artist Trafford Klots has inadvertently captured the emptiness at the heart of the much-vaunted 'royal romance of the century' in this unique, joint portrait painted in 1964. The backdrop may be lush but the interaction between the duke and duchess is arid, the couple inhabiting their own worlds. They gaze away from each other, looking bored, killing time.

In a quiet graveyard in Cannes in the South of France lie Herman, Katherine, and Lucy Rogers. The lives of all three were profoundly affected by their association with the Duchess of Windsor, who, but for an accident of timing, could have been laid to rest here, with her beloved Herman Rogers. Instead, she is next to the duke at Frogmore, the royal graveyard in the grounds of Windsor Castle. She lies next to a man she came to despise, buried in land owned by a family she hated and in a country she loathed.

There is another feature of this extraordinary episode worth exploring. Given her intensely competitive nature, it would not have been out of character for Wallis to want a child in order to have one over on her former best friend Mary Raffray. She knew that Mary and Ernest Simpson planned to marry, and she would know about their desire to have children. When Mary indeed became pregnant, Wallis sent mutual friends to see her in order to question her about the state of her confinement. Shortly after Mary – then forty-one – gave birth to Ernest Junior on 27 September 1939, Wallis was asked why she and the duke did not follow suit. 'Because,' said Wallis witheringly, 'the duke is not heir conditioned.'

This complex and largely unspoken triangular relationship between the duke, Wallis and Herman came to a symbolic point on 3 June 1937, when the two men stood at either side of her, one the groom, the other giving her away. For all the hoopla surrounding the royal romance of the century, their wedding was a strangely muted affair. The guest list was modest to the point of being perfunctory, populated with French functionaries or acquaintances like Randolph Churchill and Charles and Fern Bedaux. Much to the duke's disappointment and contrary to last-minute assurances from his friend Lord Mountbatten, no member of the royal family attended. A brief telephone call from his mother, Queen Mary, telling him 'Congratulations. We are glad because you are happy', didn't really cut it.

The counterpoint to the threadbare guest list was Wallis's blue-silk, floor-length wedding dress by her favourite designer, Mainbocher. No detail was left to chance, her kid gloves specially designed to accommodate the wedding ring. As soon as the photographs of Mainbocher's creation appeared in the popular prints, Wallis's dress was copied by fashion houses around the world. If only Wallis had been allowed to create the wedding of her dreams. That would have been a day to remember.

Instead they had cups of tea on the terrace of the château and a brief photo session with the world's media. 'Keep your head up for the photographers,' he told his bride, his admonition clear to lip readers watching the silent movie reel more than half a century after their union. He also could have told her to keep her spirits up. For failure and disappointment lay at the heart of their union, framing and shaping their future together. It would forever corrode their marriage.

As she watched the unfolding drama from afar, Courtney Espil told her husband that Wallis had a 'terrific responsibility' to make his sacrifice worth it.

Her former lover snorted his derision. 'Responsibility, what does she care? She's the sort of woman if she gets bored to death with him and when the novelty of being "Your Grace" wears off, she will leave him one good day, take the millions he gave her, and come to live in America where she can have a good time.' He further predicted: 'She will be fighting with him – all the time. She will keep him constantly upset. He is finished so long as he is so completely under her influence. She liked it when he had the glory and glamour of being king. Now alone with him in some quiet place, as an exile . . . No, she'll never stay unless things get better.'

The first test was their honeymoon, where the newlyweds were reminded of the titular space between them. When they arrived at the entrance to Castle Wasserleonburg, their hostess, the Countess of Munster, the former Peggy Ward, was there to greet them. She was all smiles, sweeping a deep curtsey to the duke and walking up to Wallis with her hand out: 'Wallis, congratulations, how well you are looking.'

The duke immediately interjected: 'The duchess, you mean.' For the next hour, as Countess Munster recalled, the duke sulked and pouted, his face screwed up 'like a naughty little boy'. Finally he apologized and offered his car to take the countess to the local hotel, where she was staying for the night. It was the first of a lifetime of such performances, the endless small humiliations of their lives to come.

CHAPTER THIRTEEN

'Only One Woman Exists for Him'

INEVITABLY, MARRIAGE BROUGHT about a dilution in the daily intimacy between Herman and Wallis. She turned her attentions to her husband, while the duke, perhaps having sensed their closeness, began to keep Herman at arm's length. The royal couple now had their own secrets and plans from which Herman was firmly excluded.

He first sensed the way the wind was blowing when the newlyweds arrived at the five-star Hôtel Le Meurice in Paris after a lengthy honeymoon, during which they had visited Vienna, Salzburg and Venice as well as the hunting lodge in Hungary of the duke's latest boon companion, Charles Bedaux. Herman watched quietly as the rough-spoken but energetic businessman cast his spell over the former king, mesmerizing him with tales of his early life as a labourer in New York, working for a dollar a day on the Holland Tunnel.

It was not just Bedaux's romantic version of his life that captivated the duke. For the first few weeks of the marriage he and Wallis had bickered and squabbled about the events leading to the abdication. The duke was left in no doubt that Wallis considered she would have been queen had he not played his hand so badly. During one row at a restaurant in the Austrian Tyrol, she angrily moved to the next table, forcing him to follow her.

So when Bedaux suggested an official visit to Germany to tour housing projects, the idea fell on fertile ground. It would give the duke the chance to show his carping wife that while he may have lost his crown he still had the prestige of a king.

Until now, Wallis had experienced only the downside of royalty, harassed and gawped at every time she ventured out in public. Their stay in Paris epitomized her new life. When she and Constance Coolidge visited Elsa Schiaparelli's showroom at 21 place Vendôme, hundreds of curious onlookers gathered outside, mobbing her when she left. It was the same when they went to a movie matinée. The only sanctuary was her suite in the Meurice or Constance's quiet apartment. 'She is nervous and afraid to go out,' Constance told her father. 'It really must be awful.' The strain told on her, Constance noting that the duchess looked 'very thin and tired'.

Socially, too, their lives were awkward. The hostility of the House of Windsor ensured that any potential host was stepping on eggshells by inviting them to dinner. When the duke's former assistant private secretary Lloyd Thomas, now minister at the British Embassy in Paris, hosted a dinner party in their honour, only a handful of French royals accepted the invitation. Others were fearful of social retribution. Inevitably, the English aristocracy were conspicuous by their absence.

Into this void stepped the beguiling Mr Bedaux, using his contacts to organize the contentious visit to Nazi Germany. In late September, Hitler's adjutant Fritz Wiedemann flew to Paris from Berlin for a meeting at the Ritz hotel, where the trio sealed the deal.

Somewhat belatedly Herman, who had joined the Windsors in Paris, realized that Bedaux was a confirmed Nazi sympathizer, speaking of Hitler, his henchmen and the Third Reich in glowing terms. The duke and the time-and-motion maestro were 'as thick as thieves', and Herman and Katherine, who utterly loathed the Nazi regime, were 'horrified' when they heard them talk.

Knowing of the Rogers' opposition to Hitler, the duke and Wallis kept them out of the loop, changing the subject abruptly whenever Herman entered the room. On one occasion, not realizing that Herman was in earshot, the duke, referring to the forthcoming visit, said: 'Well, has Charles got it fixed?' Wallis shot him a look and the duke, as Herman recalled, shut up 'like a clam'.

Shortly before 3 October 1937, when the duke announced his visit, he asked Herman's opinion. Herman replied: 'Sir, my advice is . . .' Before he could finish the sentence, the duke interjected sharply: 'People don't give me advice, they give me suggestions.' Duly put in his place, Herman kept his counsel, aware that the duke and Wallis were determined to go ahead with a visit that would inevitably create concern in London, controversy around the world and a glorious propaganda coup for the Nazi regime.

SO IT PROVED. Squired around a variety of selected housing and labour projects by the bibulous Dr Robert Ley, head of the Labour Front, they were feted by the Nazi leadership, played with Hermann Göring's famous model train set at Carinhall, his palatial country estate, discussed classical music with Albert Speer, and – the highlight of the trip – took tea with Hitler at his mountain lair at Berchtesgaden in Bavaria. For once, Wallis, admired for her penetrating scrutiny of her conversational partner, was outgazed by the German leader; his eyes, she recalled, 'unblinking, magnetic, burning with a peculiar fire'. Even as an accomplished flirt, Wallis found no response with Hitler. 'I decided he did not care for women,' she concluded.

In a visit mired in controversy, the duke's decision to return several Nazi salutes forever sealed his reputation as a Nazi sympathizer. For her part, the duchess disingenuously said they made the trip as 'nothing more than tourists'. She later explained that 'It never for an instant crossed David's mind that his mere appearance in Germany might put him in conflict with British foreign policy.' Tourists indeed. Given the knowing secrecy surrounding the planning and the complicity between the duke, the duchess and the Bedaux, she and the duke were fully aware of the potential for political blowback.

Years later she confessed to Cleveland Amory: 'David and I made a foolish mistake, one that both of us were to regret. We allowed ourselves to be persuaded to visit Adolf Hitler's Germany, and the consequence of that decision, casually arrived at, a fresh barrage of criticism crashed around us.'

The immediate fallout was the last-minute cancellation of a more extensive visit to the United States in November 1937, when the Windsors planned to visit more housing projects across the nation. American labour unions and Jewish organizations mounted angry protests at the prospect of a royal visit so soon after they had toured a country where labour unions were outlawed and Jews persecuted. Once again the trip had been masterminded by Charles Bedaux.

They were in a real quandary. Their suite on the German liner *Bremen* was already booked and paid for, and they had sent seventy-one pieces of luggage to be loaded on board. The mood of uncertainty in Paris was not helped when Bedaux's public relations guru, Lee Olwell, arrived from New York and told the Windsors face to face that their safety could not be guaranteed should they sail for America. Initially the duchess was defiant: 'America is my country and nobody is going to hurt me,' she insisted.

After consultations with the British ambassador in Washington and their friend Bill Bullitt, the American ambassador to France, as well as reviewing the increasingly wild cables from Bedaux, the duke climbed down and cancelled the visit. It was a humiliating debacle, the duchess so angry that she threw herself on the floor of their hotel suite in a hysterical screaming fit as she realized that her dream of being treated like the homecoming queen had disappeared before her eyes. Olwell later spoke to his friend Thelma Furness about it: 'Can you imagine? She had been thrown out of England and the last thing she wanted was to be thrown out of America.'

Everyone, friends and foes, had counselled caution, but the Windsors would not listen. Constance Coolidge observed that the proposed tour was 'a most foolish thing to do', while Herman Rogers described the decision to visit America as 'untimely'; he thought the tour could 'jeopardize his [the duke's] eventual usefulness' on the world stage.

Others were more critical, Courtney Espil observing trenchantly: 'Poor stupid boy with no balance and no judgement. It was his unfortunate choice of friends who threw him in with the group among whom played Mrs Ernest Simpson. Now he adds to the crumbling walls of his life's stronghold another American friend [Charles Bedaux] who causes him almost as great a scandal as the choice of wife.'

If the visit to Nazi Germany and the cancelled tour of America exposed the Windsors' political naivety, another proposed visit was simply foolhardy. He planned to tour the recently independent Republic of Ireland to discover for himself the 'real root of evil' that had provoked widespread anti-British feeling in that country and beyond, especially in the United States. Contrary to the settled policy of the British government, the duke believed in a united Ireland, the rallying cry of the terrorist group the Irish Republican Army to the present day. He told the diplomat and writer Sir Shane Leslie: 'I have always held very strong views in favour of Ireland becoming united and in fact always refused official invitations to visit Ulster for this reason.' Such a trip, however well meaning, would have been incendiary, domestically far more inflammatory than his controversial visit to Nazi Germany.

Now that he was free of his constitutional shackles as monarch, the duke felt no compunction about voicing his opinion on world affairs, publicly or privately. At this time he was a vigorous appeaser, in favour of peace at any price. During a dinner party at Constance Coolidge's Paris home in March 1938 he characteristically dismissed all thought of going to war to save Czechoslovakia, a country which gained independence only after the First World War and was now next on Hitler's shopping list of conquests. 'Czechoslovakia is a ridiculous country. How could anyone go to war for that?' he argued. 'It's not a country at all, just an idea of President Wilson.'

Years later the duke reflected on his folly, bemoaning the lack of advice he had received at this critical juncture of his new, detached royal life. Remembering his own experience in Paris, Herman asked him if he or the duchess would have listened if advice had been at hand. Ruefully the duke admitted that it would have changed nothing.

With his uniquely intimate insight, Herman concluded that they were two strong people who needed even stronger people to counsel them. Wallis needed a stronger man than her husband to guide her, and the duke needed a wiser partner. When she dabbled in politics, as in the proposed visit to her home country, she was a disaster who became, in Herman's view, like a 'wild animal when angry'.

While the ex-king had escaped the cage of Buckingham Palace, it left him prey to an exotic and sinister array of oddballs, misfits and conspiracy theorists. As Prince of Wales, he had been targeted by several stalkers, usually women, whose behaviour brought them to the attention of Scotland Yard. One such obsessive, a kindergarten teacher, became involved at the fringes of a spy plot and was jailed for a time.

In the feverish climate before the outbreak of the Second World War, the Windsors and their allies were natural targets. Perhaps the most extraordinary intrigue involved Wallis's friend Constance Coolidge, several months after the Windsors' visit to Germany.

Unwittingly, she found herself at the heart of a plot to blackmail the duke and the royal family.

In March 1938, Constance was contacted by a certain Madame Maroni, who wanted to see Wallis and the duke urgently about some incriminating photographs, papers and letters. Reluctantly, after much pestering, Constance agreed to take tea in Maroni's Paris apartment. The building was seedy, the third-floor apartment as 'queer' as the woman who lived there. As she talked, Madame Maroni, who Constance concluded was an 'adventuress', revealed that she had followed the duke around Austria before and during his honeymoon as well as to the seaside town of Le Touquet in northern France. Bizarrely, she promised to burn the incriminating papers if she met with the duke in order to see for herself if he was happily married. At this point Constance's butler, Victor, worried that his mistress had come to harm, burst into the room, effectively ending the interview.

Eventually, Constance told Wallis and the police about this curious encounter. Both the French police and Scotland Yard were called in. They discovered that Madame Maroni had worked for a time as a maid for the duke and had sensitive letters relating to the duke's German cousin, the Nazi diplomat Prince Philipp von Hessen.

At this delicate time, with the peace of Europe hanging in the balance, Hessen was used as a go-between, a man linked by blood to the House of Windsor who also had the ear of Hitler. His correspondence, if made public, would have been highly discomforting, especially to the new king and his brothers, who were secretly negotiating with their German cousin.

Constance was interviewed by the police on several occasions, once in front of the duke himself. She was even forced to repeat Maroni's allegation about 'a man who renounced a throne and had a mistress in Austria' – clearly a reference to the duke and his hostess at Schloss Enzesfeld, Kitty Rothschild. 'It was very embarrassing,' Constance noted in her diary.

The unsubstantiated allegations of an affair aside, the possible existence of correspondence between the House of Windsor and Prince Philipp von Hessen was potentially embarrassing for all concerned, as the royal family would have been seen to be meddling in matters of sensitive diplomacy, which went well beyond their constitutional remit. At the time, the incident was promptly hushed up, the ducal couple never speaking of the matter again even with Constance.

In any case, they had other matters on their minds: furnishing their first house. While the royal couple announced through Constance's newspaper contacts that they would one day settle in England, their immediate plans were focused on France, where they had finally decided to rent the palatial Château de la Croë, the Riviera mansion where Wallis had originally wanted to marry. Her talk was now of servants, furnishings and fabrics, place settings rather than politics, spies and stolen letters.

Elsie Mendl and Johnnie McMullin, together with designers Stéphane Boudin and Tony Montgomery, helped to integrate the duke's furniture and personal effects in the Windsors' Cap d'Antibes home. Their goal, according to Mendl's biographer Charlie Scheips, was 'to create a semi-royal ambiance befitting the exiles' continued illusions of grandeur, despite their fall from grace'. They used so many mirrors to emphasize the sense of space that the duchess was nicknamed 'Wallis through the looking glass'.

The duke's priceless collection of royal silverware and other family heirlooms was transported from storage in Windsor Castle. During the entire process of unpacking and redecorating, the duke took great delight in designing his insignias and crests, which decorated everything from the stationery to the liveried footmen's red-and-gold frock-coats.

The duchess, too, was in her element, her relentless eye for detail and near-photographic memory ensuring that her new home ran with clockwork precision. Less kindly visitors, seeing at first hand the duchess's total domination over her husband, described their home as organized like a well-run nursery. It was, though, this home that would seal her status as one of the most celebrated hostesses of her era.

There was a nagging undertow of disappointment, not with her new home but her new neighbours. She and the duke had yet to win over the 'Riviera Set'. It piqued her protective nature to see the English so rude to their former sovereign; she likened a visit to the casino at Monte Carlo to being an exhibit in a zoo. The crowd were 'just awful, standing around and looking' at them.

It angered her even more that the duke didn't even seem to notice what people were saying or doing. 'Do you realize he has never told his side of the story?' Wallis asked Constance. 'He has never said one word. Do people give him credit for that?'

One consolation was that Herman was only a short car journey away, he and his wife being their regular companions, be it for dinner, lunch or holidays. That summer, the two couples hired the yacht *Gulzar* for a leisurely cruise along the Italian coast, visiting Portofino, the Leaning Tower of Pisa and Sorrento. In celebration of their new home, the newlyweds decided to hold their first Christmas party, inviting friends from London and Paris to the grand affair.

Johnnie McMullin decorated the huge Christmas tree in the entrance hall, and Wallis, rising to the challenge, looked 'stunning' in a heavily embroidered evening dress and a sparkling diamond necklace, which the duke gave her as a Christmas present. A gypsy orchestra played until the early hours, and Lady Brownlow tried to teach the guests – who included the Rogers and the Mendls – the Lambeth Walk.

The duke didn't even seem to mind that no one curtsied to his wife when she entered the room. If he did, he affected not to notice. All evening he only had eyes for her. Her friend Constance Coolidge, Comtesse de Jumilhac, who was seated next to the duke, later remarked: 'He is difficult to talk to, for having a single-track mind, only one woman exists for him. All the others are just bores. This is really true yet he likes to talk to me.'

She stayed as a guest of the Rogers, finding the newly remodelled Lou Viei not to her taste. Even the 'house' ghost agreed, Constance noting that it had not been seen since the renovation had been completed. As for Katherine and Herman, not only were they no longer sleeping together, their drinking habits were making them tiresome. 'Neither Herman nor K [Katherine] can drink as well as before. They don't get a bit tight. Katherine becomes more intense and positive, and H can't enunciate words properly. Herman has lost his pep.' And he was lost in his own world. On Christmas Day, he came into the living room, took his presents, and returned to his bedroom, where he opened them on his own.

If she noticed, Wallis never mentioned it, nor did it impair her intimacy with him. When she and the duke were considering renting a home in Paris, it was Herman she asked to give 24 boulevard Suchet the once-over. After he approved her choice, she called in Elsie Mendl to help with the interior design. Elsie used her unique contact book to help Wallis in her search for antiques and other *objets* for their townhouse. On the way, she introduced Wallis to the rich Americans and well-heeled Parisiennes who would populate her dining table. Much to Herman's astonishment, Wallis even started taking French lessons and read four French newspapers a day to get a sense of the country she was living in.

The Windsors now entertained at home twice a week, usually one or two tables of ten. By then the routine was more settled. The butler announced the arrival of 'Her Royal Highness' the Duchess of Windsor after guests gathered for cocktails.

'It was,' observed the Countess Munster, 'quite a performance.' When Wallis arrived, fashionably late, she expected the various groups of guests to break up to await her greeting. 'I wouldn't have expected such a behaviour from the queen herself,' recalled Countess Munster. 'It was as if in two years she had learned that people weren't going to accept her and learned to face them down herself.'

The one place where the duke and duchess were assured a deferential welcome was the German Embassy. It was here, on 22 June 1939, just weeks before war was declared, where they were guests of honour, Wallis sparkling in a white gown decorated with rubies and diamonds, which the duke had given her for her forty-third birthday. The following night, the duke's forty-fifth birthday saw the couple at a charity ball to celebrate the fiftieth anniversary of the opening of the Eiffel Tower.

The declaration of war on 3 September 1939, which was provoked by Hitler's invasion of Poland, changed everything – and nothing. The Windsors briefly returned from exile, the duke visiting his brother the king at Buckingham Palace to discuss a suitable job. At this time of national peril there was no thaw in royal relations. Though the duke did see his mother, Queen Mary, the royal family gave Wallis the complete cold shoulder.

With such a frigid atmosphere at home, the duke, who was seconded as a liaison officer between the British and French forces in Vincennes, northern France, was glad to return to their adopted country. He spent weeks visiting French troop positions and writing several reports about the lack of preparedness of French antitank batteries. Like the duke himself, his findings were studiously ignored. As a result he spent more time on his golf than his gunnery, staying at their home in Paris for much of the so-called Phoney War.

When Wallis's friend Clare Boothe Luce suggested he lobby for more time at the front, the duchess cried: 'What! And get himself killed in this silly war?' It was a sentiment that pithily summarized their thinking. Sidelined and treated with suspicion by the top brass, the duke found himself acting as a cheerleader for his bride, who for once found herself the busier of the two. As honorary president of the Colis de Trianon-Versailles, a charity set up by Elsie Mendl to send care packages to French front-line troops, she found herself hard at work organizing volunteers. She also delivered plasma, bandages and other supplies to front-line units, the duke eager for the world to recognize her pluck. She was, he said proudly, often 'billeted near the sound of gunfire'. Even though as an American she was neutral, Wallis admitted that she 'was busier and perhaps more useful than I had ever been in my life'.

All that changed on 10 May 1940, when German divisions advanced through Belgium, threatening French and British lines and creating panic in Paris. Elsie Mendl abandoned her war work and together with her husband, Charles and John McMullin, headed south, Gertrude Stein and her lover Alice B. Toklas not far behind. The duke gravely gave Wallis two hours to pack before they shut up their rented house and joined the general retreat.

She was not so easily convinced, nor, after the farrago of the abdication, did she have much faith in his judgement. Before she agreed to his demand, she decided to seek the advice of her friend, American ambassador Bill Bullitt, before making up her own mind.

Bullitt, multilingual, whip smart and shrewd, was the Paris version of Herman, a sensible backstop by which to measure her husband's often half-baked decisions. Suggestions advanced by her biographer Charles Higham that Bullitt and Wallis were lovers are wide of the mark. While their private correspondence was friendly, it consisted mainly of thank-you notes.

Though superficially affable, Bullitt had little respect for the couple. 'He left me realizing more fully what a pathetic, ineffectual but charming little fellow Edward really is,' recalled Courtney Espil after a confidential conversation with the diplomat. Yet Bullitt, a regular diner at the boulevard Suchet table, had to acknowledge that their uneven relationship worked. 'I have never seen any man in all of my life who is so blindly in love with a woman as the poor little duke. When she enters the room he seems to immediately forget all else.'

On that day, his advice to Wallis was to forget anything other than leaving that very afternoon. She and the duke did as he bid, the couple driving off without a word to the duke's loyal equerry and boon companion, Fruity Metcalfe, who had hosted them at his country home during their brief stay in England. The Irishman, who had to make his own way back to England without transport, told his wife furiously: 'He deserted his job in 1936, well he's deserted his country now, at a time when every office boy and cripple is trying to do what he can. It is the end.' It was an early example of a pattern, the duke and duchess discarding those who had served them loyally without a backward glance.

It has since been argued that the duke left his military post without permission. Others have suggested that the Army hierarchy breathed a collective sigh of relief when he headed south. After stopping the night at Blois, he and Wallis headed for Biarritz, watering hole of the rich and famous. While they were eating luncheon of fruit and cheese under the shade of a tree, they were overtaken by the Mendl convoy. Wallis told Elsie that she had slept in a sleeping bag the night before because their room was so dirty. As the duke slept, she heard him whispering 'England', muttering that he must go to England.

Once they arrived in Biarritz the scene that greeted them was simply extraordinary. As John McMullin wrote: 'I have never seen so many Rolls-Royces, maids, valets, and dogs gathered together under so few roofs. It is the last stand of elegance. All the rich people of Europe are here.'

When German radio correctly stated the hotel room number where Wallis was staying, the duke having returned to his military mission in Vincennes, she was treated like a bad smell by fellow guests, who believed that the hotel would now be the Nazis' number-one bombing target. The duke returned a few days later with orders to join the forces assembled on the Italian border, where Mussolini's troops were massing.

He gave Herman Rogers another, less savoury, reason why they left. In a letter to his sister Anne, dated 4 June 1940, Herman wrote: 'First they battled their way through refugees to Biarritz, which they found so revoltingly overflowing with all the Jews of Europe that they couldn't stand it and came on to Croë.'

During that journey the duke heard on his portable radio that his friend King Leopold of the Belgians had surrendered to the Germans. Wallis saw his face set in the same grim mould as during the abdication crisis. The bleak news triggered something deep inside the duke, as Wallis observed: 'All his pent-up emotion came out over the empty role forced on him.' It was all too much. 'God, I wish there was something I could do,' said the duke. 'I feel so useless. As an Englishman I hate running.'

Once back in their Riviera retreat, Wallis suggested that she stay with Herman and Katherine while he returned to England. He dismissed the idea out of hand. Until the situation became clearer, they decided to follow the advice of US ambassador Anthony Biddle, who had just made a perilous escape from Warsaw, Poland's capital. He told them that a slit trench and a steel helmet were the best defence against air raids. The duke had a trench dug out in the La Croë garden, complete with food hamper, magazines, thermos flask and a padded garden chair for the duchess.

When Herman came to inspect the royal fortifications, he pronounced them acceptable but preferred the thick walls of Lou Viei. Under the circumstances, he found the couple 'cool and collected', even though that very morning an air-raid siren had sounded and the subsequent raid by Italian bombers had killed a three-year-old girl.

The sojourn in the Riviera sunshine was brief. With the news that Nazi panzer tank brigades were heading to Bordeaux, royal packing 'went forward in the utmost frenzy'. As they couldn't take the duke's priceless family silverware, he decided to leave his precious collection in trustworthy French hands, a friend recommending a village in the mountains behind Cannes where it could be stored for the duration of the conflict. The duke rented a truck and despatched the valuable cargo. Later, Wallis told her friend Eleanor Miles that it cost the scarcely believable sum of £2,400 (£40,000 at today's prices) to hide the silver and a further £2,400 (£40,000 today) to recover it after the war.

As for Wallis's extensive jewellery collection, they held that close, packed away in their personal luggage. They still joshed one another about the time on their honeymoon when Wallis's gems were left on the running-board of their car during a trip to Salzburg. Fortunately, the jewels were recovered safe and sound. As they pondered their uncertain future, they weren't about to make the same mistake again.

CHAPTER FOURTEEN

'A Whole Nation Against One Woman'

ROYAL PRIDE COMING before the fall of France threatened to place the Windsors in danger. Even as they packed their precious belongings, the duke hesitated about leaving his newly adopted country. The dramatic arrival in mid-June 1940 of the dishevelled, ravenous figure of their comptroller Gray Phillips changed all that. He had hitchhiked his way from Paris, loyally bringing with him several of the duke's treasured George II silver bibelots. His exhausted presence now embodied their increasingly perilous situation.

Yet when the local part-time British consul offered them a berth on one of two cargo ships that were due to sail from Cannes the following day, the duke considered it an insult that they were restricted to only two suitcases. He thought a destroyer should be sent to collect them. Stubborn and wilful, the duke decided to sit it out, much against the advice of Phillips, who had seen for himself the utter capitulation of France.

Their neighbours Captain George and Rosa Wood added to the chorus urging retreat. Their daughter, Marie-Thérèse, who was married to Prince Ernst of Hohenberg, had been arrested when the Nazis invaded Vienna and had not been seen since. (The couple were incarcerated in Dachau concentration camp but both survived the war.) With the duke's habitual obstinacy stopping him from seeing sense, in desperation Wallis contacted the one man she could always rely upon – Herman Rogers.

He agreed with the others, reminding them of an uncomfortable home truth, namely the widespread suspicion concerning the couple's pro-German behaviour. 'Remember if you stay and the Germans take you, many people will say that you gave yourselves up deliberately,' he told them. 'The Germans will see to it that such an impression gets abroad.'

As a clinching point he added: 'You have seen enough of the Nazis to know that they are extremely nasty people. I wouldn't anticipate a comfortable internment in their hands.'

His argument tipped the balance. The Windsors decided to leave for Spain on Wallis's birthday, 19 June, their precious linens, porcelains and family heirlooms left behind.

Curiously, in a letter to his sister Anne, Herman gave an entirely different version. He told her that he thought the Windsors should have remained in France rather than join the general retreat. 'I think the Duke should have stayed – better still the Duke should never have left his military mission – though he was ordered out of Paris by the British ambassador. Nearly everyone lost his head during the last days and it is hard to blame them. The panic amongst the English Colony was indescribable – pitiful but somehow revolting.'

He and Katherine remained in Cannes until September 1941, Herman becoming a Red Cross organizer, delivering wheat and other basic supplies to remote mountain villages. From time to time he sent letters to Under-Secretary of State Sumner Welles, a fellow Groton alumnus, describing bombing raids and the sense of fear and panic that now gripped the civilian population. Welles forwarded his missives to President Roosevelt to give him a first-hand flavour of the war in France. The president was so impressed by his communiqués that, once Herman had returned to New York, he received an invitation for lunch at the White

House to give the president a trusted first-hand account of life in Vichy France.

As for the Windsors, their vacillation about staying or going continued long after they finally reached Madrid in Fascist but still nominally neutral Spain. Their prevarication was to have sinister consequences. The initial plan was for the Windsors to drive west from the Spanish capital to Lisbon in Portugal and fly back to London on two Sunderland seaplanes, which had been despatched on Prime Minister Churchill's orders.

The duke, pig-headed to the last, chose this moment of national peril to negotiate an improved position for himself and his wife. He refused to return to Britain unless he was given a significant post and Wallis was granted equal status to himself and received by his family at Buckingham Palace, this meeting to be acknowledged in the Court Circular. Without this agreement, he proposed to remain on mainland Europe.

During this back-and-forth between Madrid and London, the Windsors considered returning to La Croë, feeling that the immediate threat from the Nazis and Mussolini had passed. Wallis telegrammed Herman on 9 July hinting at this possibility and asking if all was still safe in the South of France. 'Perhaps they are going to try to come back,' he mused.

In behaviour that could be described as foolhardy or treacherous or both, on two separate occasions, while in Madrid and later in Lisbon, the duke used a Spanish intermediary to secretly contact the Germans to ask them to guard their homes. The German High Command willingly agreed to these requests. Unbeknown to the Windsors, the Nazis had already hatched a plot, codenamed Operation Willi, to kidnap the royal couple and use them as pawns in the coming invasion of Britain. They employed similar tactics when they overran other European monarchies, notably Norway and the Netherlands. They wanted to use the royal heads of state as puppets to order the military and civilian population to accept Nazi rule. Fortunately, these royal families had escaped Nazi clutches.

As the plot to kidnap the Windsors unfolded, Hitler and von Ribbentrop were encouraged by reports, sent by their ambassadors in Madrid and Lisbon, of the Windsors' contempt for George VI and their defeatist talk, suggesting that heavy German bombing would soon bring Britain to its knees.

While the duke and duchess were unaware of the Nazi plot, their behaviour dovetailed neatly with German ambitions. Their utter self-absorption caused them to teeter on the brink of a Nazi trap. As the duke's younger brother Prince George noted sadly: 'They are extraordinary people and never bother about anyone except themselves.'

It was only when Churchill used the carrot-and-stick approach that the crisis was resolved. First he reminded the duke that he was a serving Army officer and should obey orders. Failure to do so could result in a court-martial. Then he offered him the governorship of the Bahamas, which he reluctantly accepted. It was, as Wallis sourly observed, their Elba, a reference to Napoleon's exile on a small Mediterranean island.

Significant questions about the behaviour of the royal couple remain. As they had already squirrelled away their silverware and other valuables in the mountains, why would the duke, a serving major-general, even feel the need to contact the Nazis to safeguard their rented homes?

The American consul had already agreed to seal their Cannes property, thus technically safeguarding it from all access. Furthermore, at the duchess's request the consul had visited La Croë and sent her favourite swimsuit to Lisbon, where she and the duke were then staying. As a further fail-safe, Herman Rogers was acting as the duke's unpaid agent, overseeing payments to staff as well as undertaking other administrative work. The duke sent him £1,000 initially to pay 'hungry and faithful' servants as well as outstanding bills. Further amounts were sent during the first years of the war.

More by luck than design, the plot to kidnap the ducal couple came to naught. On 1 August, watched by the bitterly disappointed German spymaster Major Walter Schellenberg, the couple sailed for Bermuda on board the *Excalibur* in the company of several senior American diplomats, including William Phillips, ambassador to Italy, George Gordon, the minister to The Hague, and Anthony Biddle, ambassador to Poland.

During the voyage the Windsors regularly entertained them to tea, regaling them with their indiscreet views on Hitler, Churchill and the progress of the war.

The duke painted himself as a pro-German appeaser who thought the fighting 'stupid' and openly claimed that their tenure in the Bahamas was not going to be long. They thought they were going to return to England in a 'high capacity' once the warring parties had come to terms.

Given his diplomatic audience, his pessimistic view soon reached the ears of officials in the State Department and the White House. As for Wallis, 'She was even more stupidly outspoken against the British government than he,' recalled Alice Gordon, the wife of Minister George Gordon.

She had been a friend of Wallis's during her days in Washington when Wallis was the down-at-heel estranged wife of Navy flier Win Spencer. Alice had given her clothes and let her stay in her apartment when she had nowhere else to go. During that fateful Atlantic crossing, Wallis brazenly chose to ignore Alice, not even acknowledging her when they passed in the corridor. It was as if she did not want to recognize her past or allow her husband a glimpse into the world she once occupied.

This new Wallis now ruled a domain of some twenty-nine islands and seventy thousand people, mainly poor blacks and people of mixed race. It was a Ruritanian world seemingly designed to keep her in a state of exasperation, irritation and humiliation. To her mind, it was as if she had been shipwrecked on an inhospitable desert island, forced to endure the stifling heat and humidity, which she abhorred, and subject to the endless stings and bites of the cloud of two-bit socialites who surrounded her.

From the moment she set foot in Nassau to the day she left, she occupied a secondary status to her husband. The standing Foreign Office instruction was that islanders should bow and curtsey to the governor, but not to the governor's wife. She was 'Her Grace', he was 'His Royal Highness'. Every day, in every way, she was reminded that Buckingham Palace rules held sway.

It gnawed away at her soul, blaming 'that woman', the new queen, as the unseen hand behind her continued 'persecution'. At the official welcome, she sat on a chair lower than the duke's but above the rest of the official audience. The duke, as he did for the rest of his life, insisted that their staff at Government House refer to Wallis as 'Your Royal Highness'. It was too much for an English maid called Firth, who walked out in protest. 'I couldn't do it, I would have choked,' she explained.

The homemaker in Wallis was horrified by the state of their ersatz palace, Government House, the official home of every governor since 1801. After carefully and lovingly redecorating La Croë and boulevard Suchet, she could hardly bear to stay a night in the crumbling, careworn official residence. She had spent half a lifetime in dingy, threadbare lodgings, with either her mother or her first husband.

Now the woman who came within an ace of being crowned queen was reduced once again to the shabby and the utilitarian. Government House was not, in her opinion, fit for an ex-king, and it was certainly not fit for Wallis, who wanted to bury her past, not embrace it.

When she first toured the seven-bedroom, six-bathroom wooden house, complete with termites, she sniffed: 'But how primitive.' The last straw was when a chunk of ceiling came crashing down in their sitting room.

Wallis demanded that the duke do something, insisting that the residence be remodelled. The new governor managed to snag a grant from the island's executive council to restore the building to his wife's liking. In the meantime the itinerant royals lodged elsewhere, for a time staying in Westbourne, the mansion of the island's wealthiest man, Sir Harry Oakes, where, three years later, he would be murdered.

They stayed there reluctantly, the Colonial Office having turned down the duke's request to sojourn at his ranch in Alberta, Canada, for the duration of the renovations. This set the pattern which lasted throughout their five-year tenure, the duke and duchess the royal version of Robinson Crusoe and his Girl Friday. They looked for any excuse, any life raft, to allow them to escape from the islands they both 'hated'.

Madison Avenue not Bay Street, Nassau, was Wallis's natural hunting ground. Long-established families quickly sensed her resentment at being posted to this benighted territory, feeling that she always had one hand on the door, one foot on the floor, eager to leave. 'We were provincials to her. She didn't warm to us and we didn't warm to her,' recalled one Nassau socialite. No one was on first-name terms with her.

As far as she was able, Wallis lived, if not physically then vicariously, through her home country. 'Be sure to say hello to New York for me,' she would tell departing American visitors. She sent her dry-cleaning to New York and quietly flew in her Manhattan hairdresser, Forest of Antoine, putting him up in a local hotel. She liked his recipe for keeping her hair shiny and nourished: an egg shampoo with two jiggers of rum. During the renovations and beyond, she used Elsie Mendl and John McMullin, now living on the Upper East Side, to shop discreetly for her. Otherwise she relied on the services of Mary Bourke, her former secretary, who had left her to work for Kitty Rothschild.

What with currency restrictions, import duty, and of course Wallis's image as a spendthrift, she had to be careful in her purchases, which ranged from candlesticks, cocktail glasses, furs and gloves, to silver picture frames and fancy Christmas gifts chosen by Mr Cartier himself. More prosaic items included Frances Fox hair ointment and Ogilvie Sisters dandruff tonic.

She was highly sensitive to accusations that she was splashing out on fripperies when Britain was suffering bombing and rationing. In spite of her best efforts, one newspaper report suggested that she had bought thirty-four hats during a brief shopping trip. Wallis was quick to contradict it, saying that the number was five, which she felt was not outrageous. Many others did.

This hostility perhaps explains why she sent a tart note to Mary Bourke reminding her that her silence was vital in this undercover shopping enterprise, emphasizing that certain arrangements were 'of the most confidential and private nature'. Of course, Wallis would have preferred to visit luxury stores herself so that she could replace what she called her 'refugee rags' with a more modish wardrobe.

It was, though, their own folly that kept them imprisoned on the islands longer than was strictly necessary. Prime Minister Churchill feared, with good reason, that their defeatist talk would only give succour to isolationists who saw the duke as their poster boy in keeping America out of the war. It was why the ducal couple were prevented from sailing to the Bahamas via New York, lest the loose-lipped duke commit some diplomatic *faux pas*.

Their unpatriotic chatter with American diplomats on board the *Excalibur* simply continued once they arrived in Nassau. Nor did their choice of friends assuage suspicion regarding their loyalties.

The duke's close association with Swedish businessman and suspected Nazi collaborator Axel Wenner-Gren was an immediate red flag. The Swede, a confidant of Hermann Göring, was in the crosshairs of the governments of both Britain and the United States, intelligence experts believing he was an enemy agent. It was yet another example of the duke's lack of judgement and discretion.

Such was his attachment to Wenner-Gren, described by Roosevelt's advisor Harry Hopkins as 'violently pro-Nazi', that Churchill took it upon himself to send a top-secret cable in March 1941 warning him to steer clear of the dubious Swede. His caution coincided with the publication of an interview the duke gave to *Liberty* magazine, which the prime minister deemed 'defeatist' and 'pro-Nazi'. The Windsors paid the price. Churchill decided that it would not be prudent to allow them to visit America until their views more closely chimed with those of the British government.

If anything, Wallis was more trenchant than the duke in her criticism of the British, asserting that the suffering of the man and woman in the street was karmic payback for the way the royal family had treated her. At dinner one evening, Wallis told Captain Wood, who was now working for them as an unpaid aide, that she wished Germany had 'licked' England, observing that but for Roosevelt's decision to lend and lease warships to Britain, the country would surely have been defeated. On another occasion, during a discussion about a new American loan to Britain, she blurted out: 'Wouldn't you think that now they are asking for this money the least they could do would be to recognize me?'

Much as she tried to make light of it, the absence of an HRH appellation was a permanent scar. Her self-absorption even shocked her friends. During the early days of the war, she was with Clare

Boothe Luce, who expressed her sympathy for innocent civilians living on the south coast of England who had been strafed by Luftwaffe fighters. 'After what they did for me I can't say I feel sorry for them – a whole nation against one woman.' It became a staple of her wartime conversation.

Apart from a brief visit to Miami, where Wallis had a painful molar tooth extracted, the couple remained on their steamy open prison for more than a year before Churchill relented. In September 1941, he gave them licence to travel to the 4,000-acre ducal ranch in Alberta, Canada, and to visit her family in Baltimore, with stopovers in New York and Washington.

While President Roosevelt signalled his approval, inviting them for lunch at the White House, he privately remained leery, instructing FBI chief J. Edgar Hoover to have his agents monitor the Windsors during their stay. Indeed, such was the suspicion surrounding Wallis that her mail was formally censored long after America joined the war. If anything, mistrust of the couple only intensified after the arrest in November 1942 of their friend Charles Bedaux on charges of collaboration. He committed suicide in 1944 while in a Miami prison awaiting trial. When asked for comment, the duke nervously remained silent.

Though the Washington Establishment were chary, Wallis was thrilled at the opportunity at last to show her husband her home town. Baltimore did not let them down, more than 200,000 flag-waving people lining the streets as the royal homecoming queen waved and posed, Mayor Howard W. Jackson insisting that they call Baltimore their second home. This was more like it. They stayed at the farm home of her uncle, General Henry Warfield, the duchess making sure that the local delicacies of crab cakes and fried chicken were on the menu.

During her stay, her one-time friend Mary Kirk, now married to Ernest Simpson, died in London of cancer. She was just forty-five and had only recently given birth to a baby son, Ernest Jr. Mary had found genuine and true love with Wallis's second husband, the couple living up to the description of 'soul mates'. After her death Wallis wrote to Ernest telling him: 'God is difficult to understand at times, for you deserved a well-earned happiness. . . . I know the depth of your sufferings – your son will be a stronghold for the future.' Unlike Wallis, Mary truly loved England, electing to be buried in Somerset in the West Country.

As one link to her past was broken, another was gratefully renewed. Wallis's extended visit gave her the chance to see her oldest male friend, Herman Rogers, after a parting of nearly two years. She quietly slipped into the Carlton House in Washington for a reunion. The couple were later joined by the duke, who had to attend an official function. During their get-together Wallis insisted, nay pleaded, that he and Katherine join them in Nassau at any time of their choosing. The castaways were desperate for company.

Just four weeks after they returned to Nassau, Wallis's holiday plans for Herman and his wife were truncated following the bombing of Pearl Harbor in December 1941. Herman was put in charge of the French section of the new Voice of America radio station, which transmitted short-wave broadcasts into enemy territory.

The entrance of America into the war at least gave Wallis a purpose and a focus. As chair of the local Red Cross, she organized food, blankets and medical assistance for the survivors of ships sunk by German U-boats, which were operating in the vicinity. At the same time, the Allies decided to use the islands as a training base for RAF and American air force officers and men. While the duke, as governor, watched over the building of a new runway, the duchess helped to feed the thousands of young men swarming around the new base. Wallis was a familiar face at the canteen, serving up breakfast for the hungry squaddies. By war's end she estimated that she had doled out forty thousand plates of bacon and egg.

Even her sternest critics acknowledged her selfless endeavours. Her friend Rosa Wood wrote to Edith Lindsay in New York saying: 'I really admire the way Wallis has thrown herself into all her various jobs, she really is wonderful and does work hard. I do hope people everywhere are realizing all the good she is doing. I think she has such charm and is always amusing to be with. I really don't know what I would do without her.'

Brisk, businesslike and decisive, Wallis was the power behind the throne, the duke asking her advice on everything, big and small. It became a standing joke in the ruling executive council that he would never make a decision of any consequence without reference to her. During discussions at Government House he would often excuse himself and race upstairs, an agenda in hand, looking for his wife.

'I have rarely seen an ascendancy established over one partner in a marriage by the other to so remarkable a degree,' remarked British Embassy press attaché René MacColl. 'He deferred to her constantly and consistently, always remarking, "I'll see what the duchess has to say about that."'

Those in his circle knew exactly how to play him. On one occasion when his aide, Captain Wood, asked the duke to wear a dress uniform for a parade, he petulantly refused, saying that it was too hot. Wood replied that it was a significant occasion and emphasized that it was important to obey the social niceties. He made the same case to Wallis, who told him: 'Leave it with me.' A few minutes later the duke appeared in full dress uniform and said, somewhat sheepishly: 'I've changed my mind.'

In spite of his dithering, the duke's term as governor of the Bahamas was assessed as a success, especially given the inherent difficulty of working with an insular, bigoted cabal of local businessmen known as the Bay Street Boys, who effectively controlled the islands' economy. Though he liked to give the impression of being a fervent believer in democracy, it was an attitude, recalled Wood, that held good only if everyone agreed with him. He was no reformer, continuing the traditions of segregation as practised by the indigenous ruling white population. When a black resident entered Government House, he came in through the back door. Wallis's military canteen was also segregated. Indeed, at one charity event, after she found herself shaking hands with a multitude of well-wishers including Arthur, their black chauffeur, Wallis, who had black servants during her childhood, remarked to local historian Mary Moseley: 'It's the first time in my life I have ever shaken the hand of a coloured person.'

In spite of her charity efforts, Wallis found that time hung heavily, life in Nassau being an endless horizon of tedium. 'It really is so intensely <u>DULL</u> here,' she wrote. 'I long for news of the big world no matter how trivial.'

Her letters to friends were peppered with complaints about seeing the same old faces on an endless loop. 'There is very little news here – same people – behaving the same way and the RAF not producing any Don Juans.'

So when US Republican congressman Joe Martin and a fellow politician arrived in Nassau for a vacation, Wallis wasted no time in inviting them to lunch at Government House. Martin, a lifelong bachelor, was cornered by Wallis and got the full flirty treatment. As he was leaving, she said coquettishly: 'Mr Martin, I think I should like you for my next husband.' Martin blanched – and hurried away.

This was a jolly luncheon in a sea of monotony. One worrying development was her husband's pronounced drinking, insisting on 'No Buckingham Palace measures here' as he shakily poured his evening livener. Amid the litany of complaint, what is striking about her private correspondence is her enthusiasm to see Herman and Katherine Rogers. She sent a confetti of letters to their apartment in New York and then, in desperation, took to writing to mutual friends, asking them to encourage the Rogers to make the journey south. In a note to one friend, Edith Lindsay, she admitted she was 'heartbroken' that they were not coming and complained that she hadn't heard a word from them. It seems Herman was busy with his war work for Voice of America.

Wallis explained their absence by citing the 'Nassau disease': everyone looking for excuses to avoid the islands. 'If I was in the same boat I would do the same,' she confessed. On 17 October 1942, she wrote plaintively: 'How I long for the sight and sound of human beings my mentality is getting dim after over two years here and only two months leave.' How bright would she have shone if 'the only man she had ever loved' had visited. Certainly she made clear who she really wanted to see, confiding in Rosa Wood that she considered Katherine to be 'a dull, stupid, boring woman'. Or in other words, that Katherine had snagged Herman before Wallis had a chance.

From time to time the outside world intruded, invariably in the form of bad news. On 25 August 1942, the duke was informed of the death of his younger brother, the Duke of Kent, in a flying accident. They had once been boon companions and the closest of friends, but the abdication changed that forever. The duke's reaction said much about the distance that now existed between himself and the rest of his family.

While the duchess dutifully replied to the messages of sympathy, writing of the 'terrible shock' and the 'irreparable loss' of Prince George, neither ever wrote a note to the grieving widow, Princess Marina, since they knew that she and Queen Elizabeth were the most vocal members of the royal family in opposing Wallis and any possible title.

In the days before the memorial service, to be held in Nassau's Christ Church Cathedral, the duke fretted that the Nazis, knowing that he and the duchess were to be present, would find a way to bomb the church. As a result, information about the church service was summarily withdrawn, lest it get into enemy hands.

It worked both ways. An olive branch sent by Wallis to Queen Mary, suggesting that she might wish to meet the retiring Bishop of Nassau, who was sailing to England and could fully describe her son's positive contribution to the islands, remained unanswered. When the bishop did indeed meet with Queen Mary, he spoke warmly of the duchess. The queen's response was icy indifference. Wallis remained a non-person.

Eventually it all became too much. The heat, humidity, workload, and the strain of entertaining her husband, took a medical toll, and the duchess was taken ill with stomach ulcers. It was a condition that affected her for much of her life. She was paying the price of keeping everything 'tightly wrapped'. A nasty fall down stairs in 1943, which left her badly bruised, immobile and depressed, merely added to her medical woes. Though the duke was anxious that she go to the mainland to recover, she declined, shuddering at the thought of being criticized for once again leaving her post. The couple were highly sensitive to the merest hint of criticism; the duke, for instance, threatened journalist Helen Worden with a criminal libel suit following an astringent portrait in the *American Mercury* magazine.

By the end of 1944, the heat and her hard work had shaved Wallis down from a slender 110 pounds to a gaunt 100 pounds. While she liked to remark that a woman can never be too rich or too thin, there were limits. Her noticeable weight loss coincided with another visit to New York – this time to have her appendix removed. These bouts of ill health, as well as visits to see another invalid, Aunt Bessie, who had broken her hip in a fall, meant long periods of recuperation and relaxation away from the dreaded islands. In total the couple were absent for four months in 1943 and a further eighteen weeks the following year.

By then, they were desperate to escape for good and were deeply envious of others who did not have to secure the agreement of the Colonial Office before moving on. When their friends and aides, George Wood and his Austrian wife, Rosa, informed them in December 1944 that they were sailing for Lisbon, the Windsors reacted with fury. They saw the decision as a personal betrayal, a slight to the duke and a snub to the duchess. The Woods became yet another entry in the lengthening roster of loyal supporters who were once cherished and then discarded by the ducal couple. An anguished Rosa Wood expressed her shock in a letter to their mutual friend Edith Lindsay.

We were in Nassau for a fortnight to pack up and say goodbye. Our goodbye unfortunately was a very unpleasant one. The moment the Windsors knew we were leaving they both suddenly became very nasty – made out that we were letting them down and only used them while it suited us. Almost funny when George worked for the Duke for four years without one penny pay, and I certainly did <u>ALL</u> to help Wallis. A very unpleasant ending and undeserved . . . it has somehow left us with a bitter and disillusioned feeling.

Yet no sooner had Captain and Rosa Wood departed than the Windsors followed suit. They spent Christmas with a fully recovered Aunt Bessie and, after some discussion, decided to curtail the duke's tour of duty. The couple left for New York in March rather than August 1945, the official date his tour of duty was over. While they were showered with engraved silver trays, boxes and parchments of appreciation from the grateful Bahamians, there was no official recognition of their service from the Colonial or Foreign Office. No letter of thanks, let alone a campaign medal.

As for Buckingham Palace, the silence was deafening. Though the war in Europe was nearing its conclusion, a new royal Cold War was about to begin.

CHAPTER FIFTEEN

'The Only Man I've Ever Loved'

Flight Lieutenant Archibald Wann was a pioneer: brave, coolheaded and lucky. He needed to be. In the experimental world of dirigibles and military balloons, Wann was something of a human guinea pig, testing these newfangled flying machines to the limit – and beyond.

He began his military career in the Royal Navy, in the same term at the Royal Naval College, Osborne, as Prince Bertie, but transferred to naval airships in 1915. Their paths crossed again, however, Prince Albert becoming the first member of the royal family to learn how to fly, followed shortly afterwards by his elder brother. On 23 August 1921, when Wann was commanding the airship R38 on a test flight over Hull in the north of England, his luck ran out.

Flying at sixty-two miles an hour at a height of 2,500 feet, the bulky airship, as long as the *Lusitania*, broke in two and burst into flames, thousands of onlookers watching in horror as the burning structure plunged into the Humber estuary. Of the forty-nine crew, only five men survived. Wann, who was plucked from the grey waters, was burned so badly that he was never expected to fly again. He proved the doubters wrong, qualifying as a Spitfire and flying-boat pilot, commended time and again by senior officers for his total dedication, talent and leadership.

With his film-star looks (he had something of both Gary Cooper and Alan Ladd about him), his colourful background – and of course his status as a senior RAF officer – Archie was quite the catch. When he was commanding officer of the RAF base at Boscombe Down in Wiltshire, he met Marie Lucy Fury, the couple marrying in London on 6 January 1938. The daughter of Alsatian farmers, Lucy, then thirty-two, had been married twice before, first to a farmer named Richfeur with whom she had a son, Danny; then to a Parisian artist and businessman who killed himself.

Socially ambitious, forceful and very attractive, she had the hint of naughtiness in her coquettish glance that men found irresistible. She was, though, much more than a pretty face: she was a strong character with the ability to hold her own in a group – and in a catfight. She fitted in well as a hostess at military functions. Archie was duly smitten. On their third anniversary in January 1941, when he was in command of the RAF in Northern Ireland, he sent her a tender love note reflecting on their future together.

My darling,
This is just to say that the past three years have been the
happiest of my life and that I feel quite sure that they are but
the prelude of the many happy years in front of us. Together
there is nothing we cannot do but apart we are lost. Je t'aime.

A year after the war's end, during which time he was promoted to air commodore in Malta in charge of 212 (Fighter) Group, Archie retired, the couple moving to the sunny climes of the South of France. He was fifty, Lucy was just forty.

A social mountaineer *par excellence*, Lucy was thrilled when Archie renewed his acquaintance with the Duke of Windsor, whom, it seems, he met through flying, the prince touring various airfields during and after the war before learning to fly himself. She could have been Wallis's prettier younger sister, for both women were cut from the same cloth: tough, conniving, strong-willed and socially ambitious with tart tongues and tempers touched by the furies. Like Wallis she skilfully presented a front to the world, hiding or disguising that which was socially unpalatable. For example, she always gave the impression that Danny was Archie's son by birth rather than adoption.

Though Lucy recognized herself in Wallis, she was smart enough to disguise her motives, always deferring to the older and more famous woman. Their raw rivalry would come to the surface later. After all, Wallis was royalty of sorts and Lucy was enthralled by those of noble birth and breeding.

Excited but daunted at the same time, Lucy was in seventh heaven when she and Archie were invited for dinner at La Croë, where the Windsors were once again established in regal splendour – cotton sheets, silverware and all. The German mines in the garden, the concrete pillboxes and the radar aerial on the roof had all been cleared away. Installed in their place were twenty-six staff, including a switchboard operator, concierge and three gardeners, this miniature kingdom ruled by Wallis with a gimlet eye for dust and dirty linen.

It was at Wallis's groaning table that the Wanns first met Herman and Katherine Rogers, the old quartet becoming a sextet as Lucy inveigled her way into the charmed circle. They played golf, backgammon and bridge together, went shopping, and of course dined regularly, either at home or in one of the many famous local restaurants. While Lucy did not have the grooming of Wallis, not only did she have youth and beauty on her side, but the duke was delighted to have a regular dinner-table guest who spoke German, his favourite language.

The proximity of the Wanns, the Windsors and the Rogers confounded the Riviera gossips. After the war the talk was that the Rogers were no longer welcome at the top table, their places having been taken by Lucy and Archie. Not so, asserted Eleanor Miles, a long-time friend and correspondent of Wallis's who came to stay with the ducal couple for ten days in August 1947. 'The Herman Rogers come over from Cannes to swim and lunch. I told Wallis that so many people had said they were all on the "outs". This is, however, not true, as you will see we saw a great deal of them.' Then, with a hint at Wallis's fascination with Herman, she added: 'He is extremely attractive, I found.'

The duchess presided over a peripatetic court, travelling to Paris, then sailing to New York before heading to Palm Beach and thence back to the South of France. Consistently denied an official position by an assortment of ministers and governments, the Windsors were leaders of society in other ways, the Pied Pipers of the international demi-monde, slaves to a modern-day version of the golden triangle, the notorious trade in human flesh. As society hostess Elsa Maxwell observed: 'Wherever the duke and duchess go the world goes, the world of the Beautiful People.'

Their life revolved around entertaining, the duchess a perfectionist impresario of the nightly theatre, their salon a small court in exile where guests were expected to observe the same formalities as if the duke were still king and Wallis his consort. As fashion guru Eleanor Lambert noted: 'They were both formal and informal; this meant curtsying to them both on arrival and leaving and allowing them to start any conversation or amusement. In short, you always deferred to their leadership.'

Yet clouds invariably hovered over this scene of sunny perfection. It was a rare evening where the duchess failed to take a dig at the royal family, particularly 'Cookie', Queen Elizabeth. The Windsors felt their position as royal outsiders keenly. It soured their public behaviour and stained their marriage. The duke was kept abreast of upcoming family events by his mother, Queen Mary, such as with the wedding of Princess Elizabeth and Prince Philip in November 1947. However, they remained studiously uninvited. Around the time of the royal wedding, with the king's health precarious, the duke was drawn into a half-baked plot to replace George VI as regent. It proved a non-starter, one of many hare-brained schemes initiated by controversial political insider Kenneth de Courcy, who fed off the red meat of rancour at the duke's table.

De Courcy, who later adopted the grandiose title the Duc de Grantmesnil, recalled: 'I never stayed or dined without hearing a bitter sarcasm directed at the royal family. George VI (a stupid man) could never have successfully competed with the Duchess of Windsor's tongue, and the duke could not control it.' As a result, the official Court would never give an inch to the royal outcasts:

The Court's attitude was directed by the Queen. She felt that however loyal the duke might be to his brother, Wallis would egg him on into activities which were harmful to the king, while her witty, sarcastic attitude to the royal family would become the talk of London as it had of Paris.

The duke's party piece was to mock his acquisitive mother, Queen Mary, an after-dinner skit that amused but also shocked. The queen had the reputation of acquiring *objets* from the homes of those she visited. She would admire the object in question and then the hostess would say: 'We would love to give it to Your Majesty. We will send it.' In the voice of Queen Mary, the duke replied: 'Oh no, I will take it right along with me in my car.' The Windsors' American house guest Harvey Ladew, who watched the duke's performance at Somerset Maugham's home, remarked: 'His audience laughed – but I thought it was in very bad taste to do such an imitation of his wonderful mother.'

During this postwar period Wallis's one-time lover Felipe Espil and his wife, Courtney, who had so feared Wallis's influence, quite fortuitously enjoyed privileged ringside seats at these rival royal courts. In 1946, Felipe was briefly transferred from Washington to become the ambassador to the Court of St James's in London, before being summarily summoned home by the new junta in Buenos Aires. During that time the couple had the chance to cast a critical eye over the four protagonists – and to explore their own past connections with the ducal couple.

They first broke the ice when the Windsors invited them to their Paris home on boulevard Suchet. Courtney noted in her diary: 'The table was a dream and the food and wines perfect. The duke was very cordial and gay, speaking amazingly good Spanish to Felipe. Wallis was smart as always in a low-necked green satin gown but is too thin and ate practically nothing at dinner.'

Then Felipe travelled to Buckingham Palace for an audience with the king. He found him similar in temperament to his brother but slower: 'Just a nice boy with not much intelligence.' As for the Queen, they were both enchanted by George VI's consort. Courtney described her as 'graciousness itself'.

Her smile is radiant. It lights up her bright grey eyes. She gives one the feeling of warmth and womanly friendliness. Certainly not pretty or handsome and rather too roundish of face she nevertheless has a deeper quality which captivates one and holds you quite spellbound.

While with her I thought of her who could have been queen of England and who also has a quality of holding one spellbound. How utterly different these two women are. It would be difficult to find a greater contrast.

Yet for all her previous animosity and contempt, Courtney found herself forging an unlikely friendship with Wallis Windsor. The Windsors accepted an invitation by the departing Argentinian ambassador to be guests of honour at the Espils' last official dinner at the embassy in London in October 1946.

It was a move that sealed their friendship, Courtney noting: 'At any rate the old ghost of the old affairs is now laid away forever. The four of us, including the duke, who was considerably bothered undoubtedly by the silly and persistent references to Espil, have become friends. Perhaps one might even say friends in adversity.'

Just as the Espils had been treated badly by their government, so the Windsors were leaving for New York empty-handed, without an official job and without most of the duchess's jewels, which had been stolen during their visit. Not that anyone would have known. That night Wallis was 'slim and straight as a pencil, beautifully gowned in the last word from Balenciaga in Paris'. She showed no sign of the shock of most of her jewels being stolen from the home of Eric Dudley near Windsor Great Park, where the couple were staying. A popular theory was that the royal family had ordered the heist to reclaim some of the gems they had 'lost' when the duke abdicated.

'Most unfortunate,' Wallis confided. 'The whole unhappy incident has cast an unpleasant shadow on our visit to England.' She was more direct with her husband, conflating the jewel heist with the official treatment of the duke. 'I hate this place,' she said, looking out over the misty English countryside. 'I shall hate it to my grave.'

Later, the duke's financial advisor Sir Edward Peacock told Courtney that the duke was very depressed and disappointed not to be offered an official job. The king, he claimed, had tried to get him something but the socialist Labour government had said no to the idea of him becoming governor of any of the Dominions, including Canada. The duke told Eleanor Miles that he had in fact been offered the governor-generalship of Australia but had turned it down.

After arriving in New York, they ruled over a rather smaller kingdom, suite 28A of the Waldorf-Astoria. Within hours, though, Wallis had transformed the anonymous hotel rooms into a tiny piece of ducal territory, tricked out with family portraits and photographs as well as silver and bejewelled trinkets. One wall was dominated by a three-quarter-length portrait of Wallis painted at the time of the abdication. 'It hasn't got your expression at all,' said one guest. 'I don't know,' replied Wallis, with a half-smile. 'It has that puzzled look.'

As ever, the tables and the food were impeccable, though the guests left something to be desired. 'All the Palm Beach crowd, the café society, the rich, the idle. We listened to a poor piano player and drank champagne,' commented Courtney Espil after attending one dinner party.

For all the perfectly placed photo frames, considered cushions and important knick-knacks, there was an emptiness at the heart of the duchess's restless existence. 'She is the most unhappy of women, always trying to get away from life, rushing on feverishly to keep from thinking,' confided her close friend Betty Lawson-Johnston. It was a condition sensed by those sensitive souls who found themselves in her company. While New York socialite Betsey Barton found her 'witty, bright and charming', she also thought her garrulous, mistaking mindless chatter for conversation.

She talks very rapidly, scarcely giving anyone time to say anything and after trying to act intelligent. I finally found myself nodding at her and exclaiming with little 'No reallys' and 'You don't says.' She spoke of her figure and keeping thin

and said she had been accused of never taking any exercise.
'But I say, my problems exercise me.'

Barton, who was wheelchair-bound, reflected: 'I wondered what problems she might have and visualized the ordinary shopgirl who thinks of the duchess as having everything in the world. I would say that she has nothing. She and her husband are exiles. They must wander everywhere but in their home country, which is where they long to be. They receive adulation and awed acclaim from people whom they do not care to get it from; they must meet the people who they do not really care to meet. Looking at the duke, he is a sorry specimen of a man. Small, nervous, rather unformed and not awfully bright.'

In the immediate postwar years this became a frequent observation of those, particularly the English, who had not seen Edward since the abdication. 'One is almost unpleasantly shocked to see how old, wrinkled, and worried his face is and how pathetic his expression,' commented Lady Cynthia Gladwyn, wife of a senior British diplomat, who saw him on Mount Street in Mayfair during one of his sporadic visits to London in May 1947. When Washington *grande dame* Susan Mary Alsop saw him in Paris she was scathing. 'He is so pitiful. I never saw a man so bored. The highlight of his day was watching his wife buy a hat.'

Increasingly eccentric, too, as Robert D. Levitt, the former husband of musical-comedy star Ethel Merman, attested when he was asked why the duke hummed to himself all the time. 'I'm not sure but I think he's on AC and you know the Waldorf is on DC,' he quipped. Back in the South of France, the duke was similarly out of tune when concert pianist Barbara Reid, Katherine Rogers' niece, played for him at Lou Viei. As she recalled: 'He wandered around and hummed off-key to himself, clearly not interested in listening to classical music. Most distracting but an experience.'

This was something of a polite understatement, the duke being a musical philistine to his fingertips. Once, after fidgeting through a private concert organized by Lady Cunard, he asked pleasantly: 'Did that Mozart chap write anything else?'

He was happiest on a sunny day with a 3-iron in hand and companionable playing partners to share the afternoon four-ball.

A regular at the tee-off was his friend from his flying days, Archie Wann. The retired pilot was sadly missed when he contracted stomach cancer. His was a particularly lingering death. As Lucy Wann was a convert to Christian Science, which practises prayer rather than using pills to relieve pain, Archie's last days were played out in excruciating agony. Lucy's mother, who came to nurse her son-in-law, was often so distressed by his screams and whimpering that she had to leave the house. He died on 11 October 1948.

Archie's ill health coincided with growing concern about Katherine Rogers. Just two weeks before Archie died, she was in a hospital in Montpellier undergoing extensive tests as well as an exploratory operation on her throat. Wallis, for all the unkind things she had said and written about one of her oldest friends, took the trouble to be with her – and Herman.

During her visit she wrote to Constance Coolidge, urging her to write Katherine a 'newsy' note. It was a letter of concern, hoping for the best but fearing the worst. 'I was with Katherine Friday up until seven. She was wonderful – the operation was done with a local and really was a preparation for some new kind of X-ray treatment just over from America.' After describing the treatment, she finished: 'I know how you feel about Katherine and as I said today I do feel worried about her condition.'

She was right to be concerned. Herman's wife of nearly thirty years was suffering from inoperable throat cancer and her health deteriorated quickly. On 24 March 1949, two months before she died, she wrote to Constance apologizing for failing to respond to her earlier letters. 'You are a lamb to write and it means a lot to me. I just did not feel like answering – knew you would understand as I have no energy at all and tire so very easily, only weigh 50 kilos [110 pounds].' She went on to explain that two major operations in six months had left her listless and feeling like 'hell most of the time'. She reported that she had been seen by three specialists who had mistakenly given her a clean bill of health.

Katherine died on 31 May 1949 and was buried in June at the Grand Jas cemetery in Cannes, the final resting place for many in the English and American expat community.

In a heartfelt letter to Constance Coolidge, her grieving widower wrote:

> *Thank God she went when she did, in her sleep, her heart just stopped. Further terrible suffering lay just ahead of her, I know it, and the knowledge broke my heart. Everything was done for her that could possibly be done. I am sure she could not have had better care or treatment even in America.*

Within a few short months the sextet had become a quartet, Herman, whom Wallis had always considered her 'property', now being a widower and Lucy a widow. Herman was, though, completely unprepared for Wallis's greedy response to Katherine's death. At first she asked him to stay with her and the duke in Paris but he declined, feeling that he had too much to do in Lou Viei.

When the Windsors eventually came to their Riviera home, Herman asked Wallis to choose a keepsake of Katherine's to remember her by. He expected her to pick a framed picture of his late wife or some other personal item. So he was taken aback when she asked for the two gold bracelets she had heard him say that he had paid 10,000 francs [£317,000 at today's prices] for.

As Herman absorbed this latest grotesque and hurtful example of Wallis's acquisitive nature, he was having to come to terms with the sad fact that his own well-ordered life was over. While his marriage to Katherine had long lost its excitement and sexual tension, she had been a faithful and stimulating companion for nearly thirty years, travelling the world by his side. Now he was alone. Wealthy, well educated, well connected, he was a catch, a catch that Lucy Wann was determined to snare. 'What Lucy wanted, Lucy got,' recalls her daughter-in-law, Kitty Blair. 'She was a piece of work.'

Almost before Katherine's body was cold, Lucy was on the scene. She knew she had to act quickly. Instinctively Lucy realized that she would have competition for Herman's hand from Wallis. Though Lucy did not know then about Wallis's offer to have a child by Herman or their sexually intimate conversations, her feminine instincts were on high alert. She suspected that they may have been lovers from years before – and that that flame could quickly be reignited.

Moreover, Herman had been Wallis's de facto husband for all the critical moments in her life. It had been Herman, not the duke, who had given her shelter and comfort when she most needed it. Both now had their eyes on the prize, Herman Livingston Rogers.

'There is no question that these women were rivals in love,' recalls Lucy's daughter-in-law, who spent many hours alone with her discussing Herman and Wallis. 'Both wanted Herman. Wallis would have grabbed him and told the duke to go. Lucy knew that.'

Such was her fear of Wallis winning out that within months of Katherine's death she was putting pressure on Herman to marry. It became a nagging theme in their budding relationship, to the point where he wrote reassuring her that he would marry but wanted more time to grieve his late wife. Even if Wallis did not throw her garter into the romantic ring and decided to stay with the duke, Lucy was concerned that she would try and convince Herman that this farmer's daughter was well beneath the station of a Groton and Yale man. He could do better, much better.

During this critical time, Lucy had one clear advantage – the duchess was in America. She planned to return to France in mid-May 1950, sailing on the *Queen Mary*. The clock was ticking. She had to work fast.

Herman, gentleman to the last, was as good as his word. He asked Lucy to marry him in June 1950. It was not a moment too soon. When Herman wrote to Wallis, probably the first person he contacted with the news, all Lucy's worst fears were realized. The sound of the duchess's jaw dropping could be heard all the way from Manhattan to Cannes. It was a profound shock, all the more so coming weeks after the death on 29 May of her first husband, Win Spencer, in a hotel room in Coronado.

Herman explained that the wedding was arranged for 6 August, and he expressed the hope that she and the duke would be their witnesses at the civil ceremony, which was due to take place in Cannes Town Hall. Wallis responded that they were booked for 6 August, but if Herman and Lucy could change the date they would naturally be present. Herman duly obliged, altering their wedding day to 3 August to accommodate the Windsors. Wallis's telegram ended with the battle cry: DON'T DO ANYTHING UNTIL I GET THERE. YOUR GUARDIAN ANGEL. That phrase hid a multitude of emotions, none of them feelings of affection towards Lucy. Battle was now joined.

'Wallis had come to look on Herman as a form of reserve capital, which Katherine's death now promised to make available for the first time,' a family friend told her biographer Charles Murphy. 'For the prize to fall so swiftly and easily to a comparative stranger wounded Wallis deeply, and the wound was plain to see. Her boredom in her own marriage had become acute, and she was no longer as discreet as before when it came to hiding her feelings.'

During the run-up to the big day, Wallis did her best to unsettle Herman, reminding him that when he married Katherine, the daughter of a doctor from Colorado Springs, his own family were cool about the match, believing he was marrying beneath himself. What, she cooed, would they think of him marrying a farmer's daughter – and a German to boot.

For a time Lucy Wann bit her tongue. Since she had come into the royal circle she had been careful not to antagonize the duchess, seeing in her a reflection of herself, one social climber recognizing another. As the 3 August wedding day approached, neither woman took the trouble to hide their mutual animosity – at least in private. 'They despised one another,' recalled Kitty Blair. 'They were cut from the same cloth, socially ambitious vipers who would do anything, walk over anyone, to get what they wanted.'

Not that Wallis publicly gave any hint of her true feelings. On 1 August 1950, shortly before the wedding day, she penned an affectionate and friendly letter to her love rival, writing:

Dear Lucy

Just a little thought for you on your wedding day. May it bring with it all my wishes for happiness with my dear friend Herman – may you both have many long years together. I hope very much that you and I will become friends as the Rogers house has always been like my second house and I would miss that feeling very much. The Duke and myself are so glad that we are able to be with you on this very important day.

With all good wishes to my dear Lucy
I am yours very sincerely
Wallis Windsor

However, Wallis revealed the true state of her heart in the wedding gifts she and the duke chose for the couple. They gave Lucy a little straw bag, which, the bride-to-be contemptuously remarked, was the kind of present they would give a maid. In addition they gave the Rogers an antique silver salver, bearing their monogram and an inscription that made Lucy's blood boil. Not only was the date wrong – they married on 3 August 1950 – but, to add insult to injury, the dedication was to Herman alone. It read:

To

Herman Livingston Rogers
On the occasion of his marriage
August 9th 1950
From
Edward and Wallis

Lucy Fury Wann was well named. On the day she opened their gift she threw an 'absolute tantrum'. 'She had a temper on her and it came out then,' recalls her daughter-in-law.

As her wedding day dawned, Lucy vowed to herself that she was not going to allow 'that woman' to spoil her moment in the sun. It was a close-run thing, the temperature rising the moment Wallis arrived at Lou Viei. She had chosen to wear a beautiful white dress, a clear breach of wedding etiquette. It was an obvious attempt to upstage the bride, as if it was Wallis who was marrying Herman, not Lucy. To compound matters, just before the bridal party set off for the town hall – or *mairie* – in Cannes, Wallis started adjusting Lucy's wedding dress, saying that it didn't fit properly. She tugged at the satin collar, pulling it this way and that, until it was quite out of shape. 'There,' she said. 'That's better.' Lucy simmered but bit her tongue. In the wedding pictures, it seems that any damage done by the duchess had been rectified.

After the short ceremony, which was also witnessed by Lucy's son, Danny, the party went for a wedding breakfast at La Bonne Auberge in Antibes. Then the party separated to rest before the main reception, which was due to be held at Lou Viei between six and eight o'clock. By eight o'clock the guests of honour, the duke and duchess, had not arrived, and many guests started to drift away, clutching their pieces of wedding cake, provided by the absent Windsors. By the time they arrived at eight forty-five, all but two guests had gone. Wallis apologized, saying that they'd had an urgent appointment with their architect which could not be delayed. 'But Wallis, he was at our reception,' said Lucy sweetly. Their behaviour was, in Herman's words, 'purposeful selfishness'.

Lucy, though, had the final word. When they were alone together, Wallis seized Lucy by the hands and told her: 'I'll hold you responsible if anything ever happens to Herman. He's the only man I've ever loved.'

Lucy let those final seven words linger long enough for the enormity of what Wallis had said to sink in.

Then she replied: 'How nice for the duke,' looking hard into Wallis's eyes.

Wallis blushed and said quickly: 'There was never anything between Herman and me.'

Lucy replied, triumphantly: 'Of course not, Wallis.'

Then she spat: 'You got your king, but I got *your* Herman.' And she turned away in triumph. 'It was like she had conquered the world,' recalled Kitty Blair.

That night the foursome were joined by a number of friends, including the oil tycoon and art benefactors Charles and Jayne Wrightsman, for dinner at a restaurant in Cannes. Wallis spent the whole evening 'trying to eat Herman up' and ignoring her dining partner, Charles Wrightsman. A Spanish guest, who was seated next to Lucy, asked her quizzically: 'Aren't you jealous?'

Lucy replied: 'My husband doesn't notice it.'

At one point during the evening, Wallis recalled the years they had spent together, remembering 'dear China'. 'Let's talk Chinese,' she said brightly as a transparent attempt to show her continued ownership of Herman while excluding Lucy from the conversation.

Herman, knowing full well that she spoke only three words of Chinese, was not going to be a party to her games. So he said that he had forgotten all his Chinese, even though he was still fluent. As they drove home, Herman told his bride: 'She will *never* be satisfied. Never.'

For their honeymoon Herman had hired a yacht – his own yacht the *Angélique* had been commandeered by the Italian navy during the war – and had already asked the Windsors to join them. On the first night, they docked in Monte Carlo and joined friends at the Hôtel de Paris restaurant. During dinner Lucy showed Wallis the enormous gold-and-diamond wedding ring Herman had given her.

Lucy thought Herman had been way too extravagant and pondered sending it back. Wallis whisked her to the ladies' room, where she told her: 'Don't be a fool. When a man gives you something, take it – it means money.' Lucy was struck not only by her predatory instincts but by how she never referred to a husband but always a man, as if she were talking about a bank.

Her walking, talking 'bank' arrived the next day when the Rogers' yacht docked alongside a boat hired by Woolworth heir Jimmy Donahue. Wallis insisted the party join him for lunch on board. Herman, never having met the man but aware of his reputation as an outrageous homosexual, demurred. 'You two go if you wish. Lucy and I will stay here.'

From that moment, Wallis pulled down the flag on the not-so-jolly Rogers, for the next four years going overboard for the much younger man. It marked a sea change in her life, Wallis now spending all her time with Jimmy Donahue rather than her Riviera friends. She was enchanted by his lavish attention and his generosity. Though she wanted for nothing, the scars of her sense of childhood deprivation, real or imagined, cut deep. As with the expensive mementos she had chosen to remember Katherine Rogers by, Wallis was seduced by the costly and lavish. Over the years, Donahue showered her with jewels, including a magnificent sapphire ring, furs, flowers, chartered yachts, billets-doux, but above all else uncomplicated devotion. It was a very public relationship that shocked and surprised even the most sophisticated. Many thought Wallis had gone quite mad; others could see that Jimmy was 'the rebound guy' now that Herman Rogers was once again tantalizingly out of reach.

The observant Lady Gladwyn reflected on Wallis at this time: 'She became rude, odious and strange. One had the impression she was either drugged or drunk. She spent all her time with effeminate young men staying in nightclubs until dawn and sending the Duke home early: "Buzz off, mosquito." What a way to address the once king of England.'

The beginning of her dalliance with Donahue marked not only a new coolness between Wallis and Herman but also a step change in her treatment of her poor whimpering husband. She had always been sarcastic and sharp tongued – 'I wasn't castle born like you' was a frequent retort – now she became increasingly cruel and careless of his feelings. 'Will I be going to bed in tears tonight?' was his pathetic refrain when she was particularly unpleasant. Yet he seems to have taken a lifelong delight in this degradation. As veteran courtier Ulick Alexander observed, the former king was possessed by the 'sexual perversion of self-abasement'. The duke always came back for more.

The 'affair Donahue' began harmlessly enough, Wallis being a long-time friend of Jimmy's mother Jessie, one of three wealthy daughters of Frank W. Woolworth, the founder of the Woolworth stores. Bankrolled by his indulgent mother, Jimmy came along for the ride, a jester in search of a court, as biographer Joe Bryan put it. Jessie Woolworth Donahue, who first met the Windsors in April 1941 at Palm Beach, was the principal guest when the duke threw a birthday party for his wife at La Croë after the war. And why not? After all, it was Jessie who funded much of their extravagant lifestyle, her investment in the Windsors giving her social status and cachet. It was an unspoken exchange and naturally Jimmy was part of the Donahue ticket. That night Wallis was in a gay, affectionate and self-deprecating mood. At the appropriate moment, the duke signalled the butler to bring in the magnificent five-tier birthday cake. As the cake, adorned with a solitary candle, made its stately entrance, the duchess quipped: 'Darling, you've been messing in my kitchen.' Then she stood poised with a knife ready to cut into the elaborate creation. 'I don't know where to begin. I guess I will just have to start at the bottom and work my way up.'

Everyone hooted and Jessie stood ready to give a toast to her royal friend. Before she could begin, Wallis butted in and said: 'Once my ambition was to be Queen of England. Now it's to get Jessie Donahue drunk.'

While Jessie soberly bankrolled the Windsors, it was her son who gradually insinuated himself into their lives. Jimmy was an ever-present, joining them at dinner, late-night cabarets and parties. Much to the delight of the duke, who was blessed with a thick streak of parsimony, he always picked up the cheque. The inclusion of a gay man in their inner circle was nothing unusual, even though the duke had a well-known disdain for homosexuality. On one occasion when they were having an argument about their gay friends, Wallis spat: 'You should listen to them, they are much brighter than you.'

The reality was that his attitude towards the gay community was at the very least ambivalent. The duke had been raised at Buckingham Palace, where the entire edifice was dependent on the unstinting service of confirmed bachelors. His favourite brother, Prince George, was said to be bisexual. During their secret romance in 1936, King Edward met Wallis at the Belgravia apartment of *Vogue*'s John McMullin, himself a lifelong bachelor. He was their go-between, and together with Elsie Mendl he decorated the Windsors' home and became a dinner-table regular – one of those known by society hostesses as 'the Little Brothers of the Rich'.

During the mid-1940s his place was taken by the wealthy American equestrian Harvey Ladew, who regularly hosted raucous stag parties at his Maryland hunting estate, Pleasant Valley Farm. He became a frequent companion to both the duke and duchess, on one occasion accompanying the duke when he reviewed a Royal Navy ship docked at Cannes. Primarily, though, Ladew was the duchess's walker, attending events the duke would not or could not be bothered with. When Ladew was staying at the Ritz in Paris, he was thrilled when the duchess accepted his invitation to lunch. As she liked to say: 'I married David for better or worse – but not for lunch.' That honour went to Ladew. 'We lunched *alone* at Maxim's,' he wrote. 'Can you imagine how everyone stared! Wallis had never gone out to lunch without the Duke before. Wouldn't Cholly Knickerbocker [the gossip columnist] like this bit of information.'

Shortly afterwards, on 13 November 1946, he told his sister: 'Wallis W has asked me to take her to Noel Coward's opening [of *Present Laughter*]. The Duke disapproves of Noel's morals and won't go.' This was an odd decision, as Noël Coward, along with

Somerset Maugham, dined regularly with the Windsors, to the point where Coward complained he saw too much of them.

Enter into this milieu Jimmy Donahue. Unlike other gay men in the Windsor circle, discretion was not his strong point. He loved to shock – a regular party trick was to strip naked during dinner. When sober he was witty, charismatic and charming, always ready with a well-honed anecdote, a pithy remark, or a song on his lips when he played the piano. In drink it was a different story, Donahue being reckless and aggressive, a wealthy young man who had had a number of costly brushes with the law, one involving a naked salesman, a razor blade and a partly severed ear. Weekends were too complicated, too drunken and much too dangerous, Donahue hosting wild parties at his Long Island home.

Usually several Carey cars brought his guests, boys and young men, who would drink until insensible. Then they would be taken to his basement rooms, which were decorated in all black or all red, to await the master of the house. 'All I want to be able to see is their teeth and their eyeballs,' he instructed his interior designer friend Billy Baldwin.

The Windsors regularly attended much more decorous affairs at Jimmy's home, his formal parties usually being replete with a full dance orchestra and a more traditional guest list – though not from the very top drawer, as many of the so-called Astor 400, society's crème, did not approve of Donahue. On one occasion Jimmy insisted on showing the duke and duchess his basement rooms, explaining that they were for visiting servants. The couple politely and innocently admired the opulent Moorish design of these quarters, which were in reality used for late-night orgies. It was Jimmy's sly, knowing joke at their expense.

However, as one professional to another, Wallis appreciated the fact that Donahue ran a faultless household. Everything ran like clockwork. As Billy Baldwin recalled: 'Nobody ever served better food, had nicer servants, nor treated his guests with such kindness and generosity.'

Such was Wallis's respect that Donahue, together with Princess Ghislaine de Polignac, were the first outsiders invited to the Moulin de la Tuilerie, the eighteenth-century mill house situated twenty miles southwest of Paris, which they bought in 1952 and spent years converting. She shared, too, his love of porcelain, Jimmy having quietly acquired one of the finest collections of Meissen in America. Such was their eventual intimacy that there was a period when Donahue, an active Catholic, tried to convert Wallis to his faith.

From these companionable beginnings, the friendship between Jimmy and Wallis intensified to the point where tongues began to wag. In the autumn of 1950, while the duke was in France working on his biography, *A King's Story*, with Colonel Charles Murphy, the duchess sailed for New York, licking her wounds following the emotional fallout from the Rogers wedding.

Jimmy was her consolation prize, a daring diversion during the daily social round. Twenty years her junior, he made her feel young and lively again. Above all he made her laugh. He was gay, in all senses of the word, a fizzy antidote to her suffocating husband and a jolly companion to help share the onerous burden of perpetually entertaining the duke. 'You have no idea how hard it is to live out a great romance,' she once said.

The two became inseparable, giggling and whispering in restaurants and nightclubs, their intimacy plain for all to see. One lunchtime, Billy Baldwin was dining at his favourite restaurant just off Park Avenue on 59th Street when he heard an 'absolute roar of laughter and into the room, like two children, rushed the duchess and Jimmy'. They didn't see Billy and headed for the back of the restaurant, where there was very little light. Afterwards, they quietly went to Jimmy's apartment.

Baldwin viewed their relationship as a heady flirtation, a chance for the duchess to lose herself a little. In short, Jimmy got beneath the duchess's rigid façade.

> *I know that during that time in her life she had more fun than ever before. In a strange sense Wallis had never had a beau, and Jimmy became her beau and treated her like a young girl.*
>
> *Jimmy said to me one evening before dinner, 'I just want to tell you something about your little duchess. She's the best I've ever known. She's always considerate and adorable and never hurts me as almost all the others do.'*

Some have suggested that Jimmy and Wallis were the most unlikely of lovers. Others refused to believe that their relationship was anything other than platonic, especially as Jimmy had a long-time partner. Donahue begged to differ. After their eventual fallout he boasted of performing oral sex on the duchess, a sexual favour eagerly reciprocated. Those who knew him as a man instinctively sexually repelled by women see this as typically Jimmy – just boastful spite. As interior designer Nicholas Haslam, who was part of that wider circle, recalled: 'Having known Jimmy I can't think he could have touched any woman, let alone one as rigidly un-undressable as Wallis.'

Moreover, Donahue had a self-inflicted infirmity that made any kind of meaningful sexual congress painful and difficult. One night in a state of drunkenness he had circumcised himself with a penknife. Never in his life had he suffered such pain and agony. As a result, as Billy Baldwin delicately put it, 'He was grotesquely scarred and painfully sensitive.'

The duke, too, was sensitive to the stories now regularly appearing in the New York press about his wife's antics. His

American lawyer, Henry G. Walter Jr, even telephoned Charles Murphy to see if the duke knew what was being written about him and to enquire if indeed their marriage was over. To Murphy's enduring frustration, the duke scuttled work on his autobiography, claiming he had to be with the duchess in New York, as it seemed likely that the Soviet Union was about to launch an attack on Europe. This was so much baloney, the duke, rather, being distraught that his wife was studiously ignoring his increasingly frantic phone calls. When Walter Winchell, the dean of the gossips, wrote in the New York *Daily Mirror* that 'The Duke and Duchess of Windsor are *phfft*', the duke was sailing to meet his wife for a well-publicized dockside reunion, where they embraced several times for the benefit of the cameras.

It was but a brief respite before Jimmy and Wallis resumed their whispering and giggling, passing notes to one another at dinner if perchance they were separated. The duke was left in the cold, his presence barely tolerated by his wife.

There was now a callousness and calculated cruelty about her scolding, the duchess being easily exasperated by her husband's slightest transgression. One evening she ranted at him for leaving the dinner table littered with his papers, knowing that she had guests arriving for dinner.

Their relationship, which always had a dominatrix-and-submissive element, was now shorn of the bond of trust and affection that tethers such an intimate and complex human transaction. In short, she no longer loved him or was even particularly fond of him. With every passing day, she found him more boring, mean and limited. What once charmed now irritated, what once captivated now bored, and what once delighted now exasperated. Winchell was on the money when he wrote: 'The Duke is a very sad person these days.' Nothing he could do would satisfy her. When she was hospitalized in February 1951 for a hysterectomy after it was discovered she had ovarian cancer, he visited her every day, always bringing red roses and beluga caviar to tempt her taste buds. The lady was not for tempting, complaining that it was 'too salty' and shooing him away.

When she had recovered, she was soon back in the late-night routine. The duke would tag along to nightclubs and restaurants with his wife and Jimmy, but was sent home earlier and earlier, Wallis continuing the party with Donahue and his friends. When Edward returned to London for his mother's funeral in March 1953, on the day of the burial Wallis dined in New York with Jimmy at the Colony before going on to the El Morocco nightclub, where at some point Jimmy played the banjo. So much for Court mourning; Wallis's behaviour was disrespectful not just of the late queen and the royal family but of her husband, too.

She was clearly beyond caring. 'Why, they [Jimmy and Wallis] are in love,' exclaimed the Marquesa de Portago to Charles Murphy in tones of disbelief. Theirs was a love affair replete with lovers' tiffs. During one row between the duchess and her unlikely paramour she yelled: 'And to think I gave up a king for a queen.'

For such a self-controlled woman to be so publicly reckless dismayed her friends, she and gossip writer Elsa Maxwell falling out badly over Wallis's attachment to the Woolworth heir. The final straw was a series of phone calls the tipsy duchess made very late one night demanding that Elsa tell her where Jimmy had gone. Elsa said she wasn't his keeper and presumed he had gone home. The duchess was insistent that he should be located. Eventually Elsa said: 'I have no idea where he went. I could care less and you ought to be ashamed of yourself.'

Of course, this public humiliation of the once king and emperor could not continue indefinitely. The duke's secretary, Anne Seagrim, recalled the duchess's demeanour after one late-night confrontation with her husband. He had been informed earlier that, in his own interests, he should be aware that his wife was going out every night with the same single young man.

She heard him say, 'It's not because you are the Duchess of Windsor, it's because you are my wife. Any man would mind his wife doing this.' As Seagrim noted: 'She was very quiet and submissive for a long time afterwards.' Even though she cancelled that night's engagement with Donahue, as Seagrim saw it, the duchess was, within reason, able to do as she liked. It was a 'shoddy little success' reflected the duke's secretary.

Though a divorce was unthinkable, Wallis gave little thought to the impression her liaison gave to the outside world – not to mention the humiliation for her husband. This was a woman of iron self-discipline and control who gave nothing away even to her close friends. Yet since Herman Rogers had made his fateful decision to marry Lucy Wann in the summer of 1950, her mask had slipped, Wallis being unmanned by the loss of her closest companion and as a result throwing herself heedlessly into a wild and improbable romance.

The crowning moment came on New Year's Eve 1953 when Donahue, ever the practical joker, organized a mock coronation for the duke and duchess at El Morocco. Watched by a rowdy cocktail-drinking crowd, Donahue placed two elaborate paper party hats in the form of crowns reverently on the heads of the man who was once king and the woman whose greatest desire was to be his queen. It was the closest they got to the real thing. The clicking cameras captured the self-conscious embarrassment of the moment, a joke tinged with tragedy.

Later they went to a party where the duchess went along the receiving line wearing her crown, the duke resolutely holding his. Partygoer Bill Nichols, one of the few Englishmen to witness the affair, recalled: 'One didn't know whether to be more surprised at the awesome insensitivity of the duchess or the awful weakness of the duke.'

Gradually, though, the joke began to wear thin, even for the duchess. As with most love affairs, it was the little things that irritated at first. Always a stickler for punctuality, Wallis was infuriated that Jimmy turned up late for meals, particularly during a three-week Mediterranean cruise where Greta Garbo and English actor Rex Harrison were among the guests. There was a carelessness about his behaviour that no amount of 'I'm sorry' flowers could disguise. He offended the housekeeper in her. As theatrical as he was, for his part too Jimmy was becoming weary of the *faux* formality of life with the Windsors. He was all play-acted out.

The end was messy, bloody and unpleasant. Jimmy had taken to kicking the duchess under the table when she was regaling the company with a tale he thought boring. While the three of them were eating at a spa in Baden-Baden in August 1954, Jimmy lashed out when Wallis chided him over his garlic breath.

He kicked Wallis so hard that she cried out. The duke helped her to a sofa and stopped the bleeding on her shin. This was a lese-majesty too far. Red faced and coldly furious, the duke turned to Donahue. 'We've had enough of you,' he told him. 'Get out.'

They never saw each other again. Typically, Jimmy had the last word.

When asked about the rift between him and the Windsors, Jimmy quipped: 'I've abdicated.' Or as Walter Winchell would have written, Wallis and Jimmy were *phfft*.

As for Wallis, the shutters came back down with a clank. From that moment her mask was fixed. A few weeks after the end of her grotesque dalliance, she was back to her hard-boiled, wise-cracking best. She was having lunch with Constance Coolidge in a starred Parisian restaurant. Over a perfectly prepared salad, Constance told her that the author Iles Brody, an ex-Hungarian cavalry officer who penned the tawdry bestseller *Gone with the Windsors*, which depicted the duke and duchess as monsters of egotism and self-indulgence, had dropped dead of a heart attack in a San Francisco street.

Wallis paused mid-fork and said: 'At last I can believe in God.'

CHAPTER SIXTEEN

'Ice Runs Through Their Veins'

THE LETTER WAS very un-Wallislike. It was hesitant, apologetic and nervous, with the tremulous tone of an errant lover asking for forgiveness.

She was lost and she needed help. As ever, she turned to the man to whom she had always reached out in times of trouble and doubt – Herman Rogers.

Since the farrago of their wedding and honeymoon, he and his new bride, Lucy, had kept a deliberate distance from the duke and duchess. She acknowledged as much in her letter of 18 August 1955, sent from the Gritti Palace hotel in Venice.

I find it very hard to write this letter, but here goes. Though as far as I know nothing has come between us, we have not seen each other when we have come to the Riviera. I felt, and I may be wrong, that the time you and Lucy dined with us at the Bonne Auberge you had completely withdrawn your friendship from us, something I need not tell you that I have prized very highly, and it has caused me great distress, and if you can think me capable of this emotion – shyness – therefore I have not communicated with you on recent visits.

Then she went on to explain why she was now in touch after so long.

> *However, I am on the advice of George Allen [her lawyer] writing my memoirs. I personally detest this task as again the flare of publicity will be mine. George's idea is that if I write my own memoirs the books so inaccurately written about us will after my death not be used as reference in whatever way the future may depict me.*

She added that the duke's ghost writer, Charles Murphy, who had originally assisted Wallis, had been replaced by Boston-born humourist Cleveland Amory, whose touch she felt was much lighter and more in tune with her own thinking and style.

> *I am telling a simple story – no bitterness or reproach etc. I have no diaries, nothing in fact but my memory to fall back on, and that is why I am writing to ask you if you could spare a few hours for Amory. It would be to check a few dates of the China days – a short picture of the life there – Peking as it was then – I seem so stupid about conveying the real atmosphere to him.*

As Herman had learned long before, nothing was as it seemed in Wallis's world. While she genuinely wanted to set the record straight for posterity, it was only one part of the puzzle. For some years the Windsors had been concerned about two issues: their image and their bank balance.

At an earlier brainstorming session about improving their public profile, their friend Clare Boothe Luce suggested they adopt a British war orphan and call him David. This, she argued, would help soften their image as leaders of café society and make them seem more sympathetic and compassionate. Even the Windsors realized that this was a non-starter. Not only would it be inconvenient for their own lifestyle, it would doom the boy's life. He would be forever compared to Prince Charles, the young heir to the throne. Their action would be dismissed as cynical opportunism. Instead the duke suggested inaugurating the Windsor awards, which would sponsor travel for young artists. Not that they took much interest in the art world – on one occasion the duke, who preferred traditional to modern art, deliberately hung an abstract bought by Wallis upside down in their sitting room. She never noticed. Unsurprisingly, the awards lasted for only a couple of years before they were abandoned.

The duke and duchess had a more pressing concern. For the clock was ticking on the release of official German Foreign Office telegrams and other correspondence which, while not depicting the duke as a traitor to his country, revealed the embarrassing rift between him and his family, his empathy towards Hitler, and his defeatist wartime attitude. Without careful public relations handling, the documents could be a damning indictment of his wartime record. The duke was duly agitated, concerned about the possible effect on his reputation.

If Wallis were to publish her own story before the documents' scheduled release in 1957, this would help them defuse and deflect any judgement about their links to the Nazis. Of course, there were financial considerations, too.

The Windsors, like many rich people, constantly complained that they were living in virtual penury, even though their coffers at the Morgan Bank in New York were regularly replenished with inside stock tips from top businessmen like Robert Young, as well as the Mellons, the Dillons and the Paleys. Their belief that the wolf was howling at their door conditioned their behaviour. With avenues for official work consistently blocked by the royal family and the British government, they cast around in the private sector.

During a visit to Los Angeles the duchess approached Hollywood mogul Sam Goldwyn for some kind of job for her husband. She came away empty-handed, Goldwyn remarking, somewhat gnomically: 'I liked the duchess's frankness. But frankness and honesty aren't the same thing.'

Such was the duke and duchess's reputation that it was said they asked for appearance fees when they honoured an event with their presence. The 1951 Kentucky Derby was the most notorious example, rumours swirling that they had been paid for their attendance, a story that the duke's biographer Charles Murphy always heartily denied. Yet at the time, this widespread belief informed the behaviour of Louisville high society who were scheduled to entertain the ducal couple. Well-to-do Louisville matriarch Standiford Danforth Gorin wrote to her son, Standiford, also known as Tank, informing him of the local gossip.

> We do not know if they are paid a set sum to make their appearance at the Derby and if their hosts have to pay them so much for the privilege of entertaining them. The story goes that [the wife of] the President of Churchill Downs, Mrs Corum, called up Mrs Benning Chambers and asked her if she would like to give a cocktail party for the Windsors. She said: 'H*** NO!!!' Even though she was to be reimbursed for their outlay.

In the end the couple returned to the tried and tested, and decided that the duchess should follow in her husband's footsteps and write her own book. The duke had done very well out of his ghosted autobiography, *A King's Story*, making more than £6 million in today's currency in book sales and serialization. Could lightning strike twice? Even though *Life* magazine and the *Express* newspaper group had seen record rises in circulation as a result of their serialization of the duke's story, *Life* chairman Daniel Longwell did not think the duchess's story was worth publishing. He noted that the duchess wanted 'quite a lot of money' and he did not think the book was worth the risk. THERE'S NO ENTHUSIASM HERE FOR THE PROJECT, he cabled Charles Murphy. Murphy, along with feminist writer and critic Dame Rebecca West and, somewhat improbably, Ernest Hemingway, who had met Wallis in Cuba in 1950 when he created a local sensation after meeting them in his trademark shorts, were the names in the frame to ghost-write the tome.

When *Life* dropped out, in America, *McCall's* magazine stepped in, the British rights staying with the *Express* group. As a first advance Wallis was handed a $500,000 cheque by Kennett Rawson of the David McKay publishing house in New York. In Britain, *Express* publisher Max Aitken wanted the same winning formula that had propelled the duke's memoirs to bestselling status. Murphy, somewhat reluctantly, was once more dragooned into service. He struggled with the project, the duchess, like the duke, proving difficult to pin down for the rigorous timetable needed for literary reminiscence. Moreover he discovered that the duchess had only a passing acquaintance with the truth, adapting or removing inconvenient facts from her story and, in tape-recorded interviews, changing her story at whim.

The duchess described it differently, telling Herman: 'I felt Charlie, though excellent for the Duke, was *not* for me – his writing combined with mine was not a natural melange, therefore I changed writers in mid-stream, I switched to Cleveland Amory.'

During the 1950s, Boston-born Cleveland 'Clip' Amory was one of America's best-known humorous writers, his two bestsellers, *The Proper Bostonians* and *The Last Resorts*, gently poking fun at the pretensions of American high society. When he was first approached by the Windsors he was sympathetic and enthusiastic, feeling that the Duchess of Windsor had been traduced by the British Establishment. As an unapologetic Francophile, he was also eager to spend a few weeks working in Paris with his actress wife, Martha, along for company. The £8,000 advance was not to be sneezed at, either. The duke was equally impressed, telling a friend: 'That's a very self-assured young man. If I had his assurance when I was King of England my life might have been very different.'

As Amory's stepdaughter, Dr Gaea Leinhardt, recalls of Clip and Martha: 'They entered the project thinking that the snooty British were disdainful of the duchess because of her sexual activity and numerous marriages. They initially believed that she had been misrepresented but soon came to realize that that wasn't so.'

The six months Amory spent talking to the duke and duchess – and their friends and family – gave him a unique window into Wallis's world and her fractious relationship with her husband. His wife, Martha, watching from the wings, found herself 'appalled' by their personal interaction, her meanness, his cowardice.

Though sophisticated and worldly, Clip showed his naivety in all matters royal family with his first suggestion of a title for the proposed autobiography. He called it *Untitled*, a clever play on the book title and the duchess's own lack of the appellation Her Royal Highness. It was a proposal met with 'dead silence' by the duke and Wallis. Clip, not for a moment aware how deep a wound that lack had caused in their lives, soldiered on, keen to amuse them with his cleverness and wry humour. So he was further bemused when Wallis, with her reputation as a wit, never once laughed at one of his *mots*. In desperation he asked Noël Coward how she had earned such a standing. 'In those circles, old boy, it was not that difficult,' Coward deadpanned.

The scales were rapidly falling from Clip's eyes. On their first day of working together he had a clear sense of who ruled the roost. He never forgot it. Clip and the duchess were having tea and talking about the book when the duke wandered in, teacup in hand. He started to talk about how he and Colonel Murphy had worked on *his* book. Wallis snapped: 'We're not talking about *your* book, we're talking about *my* book. Take your tea in the other room.'

He duly went, leaving Clip wondering that if she treated him like that in the presence of a relative stranger, how did she talk to him when they were alone? Soon he and Martha began to appreciate how gratuitously vicious she was towards the duke, exhibiting a consistent cruelty that left him, if not crying openly, certainly in tears. She would, for example, allow her pug dogs into the sitting room, but keep his out, much to his distress. 'My mother was appalled by Wallis's behaviour towards a man who, after all, had been the king,' recalls Dr Leinhardt.

She was like the Joan Crawford character in the movie *Mommie Dearest*, switching from siren to saint to sadist. Martha described their fights as ducal 'duelling', this domestic description being endorsed by a former private secretary who recalled that in the evening, when drink had been taken, 'the sound of their drunken bickering was unbearable'.

As the duke's biographer Philip Ziegler succinctly observed: 'She was harsh, dominating, often abominably rude. She treated the Prince at the best like a child who needed keeping in order, at the worst with contempt. But he invited it and begged for more.'

As with so many fading marriages, it was the little things about the duke that would send her into a frenzy of irritation. She hated his incessant singing of jingles from adverts he had seen on television and his use of Americanisms such as 'I guess' or 'making a buck'. As Wallis admitted: 'It made me simply furious.'

'The duchess was a complicated person – cold, mean-spirited, a bully and a sadist,' observed Dr Leinhardt. 'My parents found the duke not very bright, a wimp, and basically a very sad man. He had made an appalling choice and knew that he had taken the wrong path and now had to live with the consequences. They found him pathetic.'

Every day he would appear in the duchess's quarters at precisely 11:30 to receive his daily marching orders. When the duchess called, he came running, on one occasion leaving his barber mid-haircut to attend to his wife. Yet however mean she was to him, he was always considerate of her. He refused, for example, to allow her to handle old francs, so each day he gave her a wad of freshly minted notes.

'He was like a child in her hands,' Lady Alexandra Metcalfe told Clip. 'Poor little man, he was given hell; it was a stranglehold she had over him.'

Their empathy towards him was, though, tempered by his anti-Semitism and continued sympathy for Hitler. Clip, a Second World War vet, had little time for his views, especially as he began to see that the duke's support for Hitler was much more comprehensive than he had ever imagined. 'My parents were horrified by their dinner table talk, where they made it perfectly clear that the world would have been a better place if Jews were exterminated,' recalls Dr Leinhardt. Clip recounted two stories to illustrate the duke's views. On one occasion he 'amazed' an English friend when the subject of Hitler came up. 'I have never thought Hitler was such a bad chap,' said the duke.

At another dinner party, admittedly after the duke had been drinking heavily, he took hold of the hands of a lady guest, intertwining his fingers in hers to illustrate the point that before the war the Jews had their tentacles around German society. 'All Hitler tried to do was free the tentacles,' he told her as the other guests looked on in horrified silence. Finally, New York advertising executive Milton Biow interjected. 'Sir,' he said. 'With all due respect, I never believed I would ever hear, at a civilized dinner table, a defence of Adolf Hitler.' Even the duke had the grace to blush.

The Amorys were given a window not only into the beliefs of the duke and duchess but also into their extravagant, if vacuous, lifestyle. As sophisticated as they were, even the Amorys were impressed. In an excited letter she sent to Clip's parents in July 1955, Martha recalled a 'fabulous' weekend at the newly renovated mill near the village of Gif-sur-Yvette:

It has to be seen to be believed. I think she has done a brilliant job of combining bold colours and various styles, which result oddly enough in a comfortable conservative effect. The Fort Belvedere furniture looks lofty and relaxed in its new setting. The grounds around are like a Corot painting come to life. The duke spends every waking hour in his garden and the results are breathtaking. . . . There was monumental excitement when we arrived, as the duke had cut his finger weeding.

Cocktails on the terrace, the duchess wore a periwinkle and large collar necklace of sapphires and aquamarines, the duke wore a kilt, which suited him. It doesn't make him so old and shrivelled. I was terribly amused as Princess Dimitri turned to me as we were all wallowing in caviar and helping ourselves and said: 'I do love pretentious picnics, don't you?'

As for the interior, Martha described chandeliers like mushrooms, exquisite Louis XV furniture, fabulous porcelains and crystal. There was a caveat. 'Although she is warm and informal to be with, the atmosphere of formality and protocol around here is nerve jangling.' Not that everyone was impressed; interior designer Billy

Baldwin described the duchess's handiwork as 'awfully tacky'. 'But that's what Wallis had, tacky Southern taste, much too overdone, much too elaborate and no real charm,' he observed.

Amory could be forgiven for thinking the same about his subject. As Murphy discovered earlier, she was as tricky as mercury to pin down on facts and, like her husband, she routinely cancelled scheduled interviews. Or as Amory put it: 'Here today, gone to Italy for ten days tomorrow.' When she was ready for a tape-recorded interview, she rarely allowed a chink of daylight behind her mask. Martha reported: 'Clip sees duchess every other day depending on how much material we get. She loosens up a bit but no sooner does she start to give things than she clams up again.' He complained to his publisher, Kennett Rawson, about her 'repetition, vagueness, and insatiable desire for change'.

Eventually, he suggested to the duchess that if she was going to write a book it might be helpful if she had ever read one. Not that her husband was any better. His nervy character never allowed him to settle with a book or a magazine. 'Who is the "Bront" woman?' he once asked Freda Dudley Ward when she handed him a copy of *Wuthering Heights*. When Winston Churchill dutifully sent him the latest signed volume in his multi-volume work, *A History of the English-Speaking Peoples*, the duke wrote back: 'Thank you so much for sending me a copy of your latest book. I have put it on the shelf with all the others.'

Though Wallis had, as her second husband, Ernest Simpson, testified, a near-photographic memory, she was forced to admit there were large chunks of her life that were absent from her recollections. As a result Amory was sent off to London and elsewhere to interview Ernest Simpson, Fruity Metcalfe, Lord Brownlow – the hero of the flight to Cannes during the abdication – and others to help flesh out her story. It meant Amory was learning the true story rather than Wallis's version of events.

The interviews were arranged by Wallis's lawyer, now Sir George Allen, Martha and Clip sensing that he was eager for them to understand the real Wallis rather than the fake public image. Martha wrote: 'He was wonderful to us in London, but we felt he didn't think much of either of them and had done his best to give us the TRUE story through others.' They went right to the top of the tree, spending several hours with the queen and her young children, Prince Charles and Princess Anne, at Windsor Castle. Sadly, Clip's notes from that historic encounter have not survived. Ironically, Martha remembered that the informality of dealing with the sovereign was a refreshing change from the stiffness of the exiles' Court in Paris.

As they insinuated themselves into Wallis's inner circle, the Amorys discovered that there was little enthusiasm among her family and friends for an autobiography, nor any feeling that it would be a truthful account of her life. Her ever-faithful Aunt Bessie simply didn't think she was worthy. 'If she had done anything important in her life – art, literature, philanthropy – by the time she became a duchess, then all right. But these little stories of childhood don't amount to much. If I said this to her she would take my head off, but I don't think she holds the position in life she should – but don't tell her any of this.'

Herman and Lucy Rogers, in the middle of building a new villa, which they named Crumwold after his family home, entertained Clip and Martha for five days, the foursome becoming fast friends. As Martha told her in-laws: 'We loved them and learned so much from them. So much that we can't use, but it was exhausting and fascinating.' Herman cast his eye over Clip's early drafts and thought he had done a 'great job'.

There were caveats, though – not about the writer but the subject herself. The Rogers felt that Wallis should never have embarked on a project that involved a close relationship with the truth.

In the coming weeks Clip found himself unable to reconcile Wallis's version of events when measured against the testimony of those – including the queen – he had spoken with during his research. He discovered, for instance, that almost everything the duchess had told him about Ernest Simpson, his first wife, and their divorce was simply not true. Furthermore, he found the duchess's meddling with his prose exasperating, writing to his editor, Kennett Rawson: 'My worst problem aside from her desire to change ideas is that never in my experience have I seen anyone who knows so little what a paragraph is, what a chapter is, and what a book is. She has absolutely no conception of unity.'

In mid-September Amory severed all connections with the duchess and his publisher, deciding that he was no longer able to be associated with such a 'dishonest book'. Explaining why he had given up the ghost, he told the media: 'I couldn't turn the duchess into *Rebecca of Sunnybrook Farm*' – that is to say, a plucky and endearing innocent at large. (Ever the journalist, it was his wife's phrase, which he used as his own.) Even though he had thrown in the literary towel, he and Martha were invited to dine with the Windsors before they departed.

'It is all coolly amicable,' wrote Martha to her in-laws in September 1955. 'The casual way they can be dishonest makes you know that ice runs through their veins. Sir George Allen looked at Clip this morning as though he'd wished he had the guts to do what Clip was doing twenty years ago.'

Wallis, who re-engaged Charles Murphy to finish the tome, told quite a different story. In a letter to Herman in December, she thanked her long-time confidante for his 'time and trouble' but then went on to describe Amory as a 'vicious character' whose work had been rejected by the various publishers underwriting the project. 'I never had a cross word with him and felt very badly about the whole affair. However, he turned upon me in the press like a viper.'

She was especially irked by what Herman had apparently said to him about her. 'He is particularly delighted with your having, so he says, told him that I never stuck at anything that appeared in banner headlines.' As her marriage to the Duke of Windsor had made headlines around the world, it was a clear reference to her disillusion with her third husband.

Herman subsequently took issue with Clip. 'Did I really say this to you? If so I don't remember having said it and I don't think the remark would be fair – until just recently.'

He and Lucy, though, were very much behind the Amorys, believing that Clip had made the correct move to walk away from the project. In a letter to them in January 1956, Lucy reported that Wallis had sent them a copy of Murphy's final manuscript and asked Herman to comment on the contents. Lucy wrote:

> *There will be no comments on the Truth, she can't take it so it is no good telling her and to make a hypocritical analysis Herman would never do it – it would not be him.*
>
> *We think it would have been much wiser <u>not</u> to publish the book – qui s'excuse, s'accuse and there are at least three phrases in the chapters we are reading which are enough to make her unlikable to every decent human being; as much as one would like just for Christian brotherly spirit's sake to point it out to her – one can't do it. Herman says what's the use she would not understand anyhow.*

In spite of their misgivings, the serialization of the book, named *The Heart Has Its Reasons*, a phrase taken from the writings of the Enlightenment thinker Blaise Pascal, was launched with a lavish fanfare at the Waldorf-Astoria in New York on 20 February 1956.

While specially invited guests feasted on 'six pounds of the finest caviar, 300 clams casino, oysters Rockefeller, and tiny Roquefort cheese feuilletés passed in small heaters', Wallis held court, the royal author confiding to Phyllis Battelle of the *Baltimore News-Post*: 'To tell your heart to the world is a terribly difficult thing to do. Like sitting looking in a mirror all day long. You must be truthful, correct, and not too dull.' While it was an assured international bestseller, the critical pickings were slim, especially in England. In the *Spectator* Gerald Fay wrote that 'the opening events of the book are commonplace and would not detain the busy reader for more than a few minutes'.

Wallis saw only the positives. Several days after the launch she wrote to Herman saying that 'the press has been kind and I think it has been well received – I am glad this launch is over. I hope you'll think the style is dignified.'

All through her correspondence about the book, Wallis extended an enthusiastic invitation for Herman and Lucy to join them at the mill. Lucy graciously declined on the clearly spurious grounds that they were too old to travel such a distance from the South of France to Paris.

It was perfectly plain that Lucy, though still beguiled by royalty, had no wish to repeat the competitive confrontation that marred her wedding and honeymoon. If Herman's second marriage was the last sentence in his long love affair with Wallis, the publication of her autobiography was the full stop.

Wallis and the man she called the 'love of my life' would never see each other again. At some point during the year, Herman developed Parkinson's disease. He travelled to the Presbyterian Hospital in New York in a desperate attempt to find a cure. In vain. In October 1957, Lucy wrote to the duke and duchess informing them of the gravity of Herman's illness. The duchess sent a heartfelt letter on Saturday, 19 October, that expressed their affection for their ailing friend.

Dear Lucy,

We have just returned from a shooting expedition and found your note with the sad news about Herman. You can well imagine how deeply the Duke and I feel about his illness. Though we have seen little of Herman these last few years – our love and gratitude to him for his staunch friendship to me for many years and to the Duke at the most difficult time of his life [remains].

I hesitate to telephone to hear his voice once more – in case my unexpected call would make him suspicious.

I hope, Lucy, that if there is anything that we can do for you that you will feel free to call upon us in any capacity you would need us.

This has been a sad year for me, I have lost several good friends but no one could leave the gap that Herman will should his illness prove fatal.

Dear Lucy, my heart goes out to you at this distressing time – let me hear how things go – my love and understanding,
Wallis.

Two days later, on 21 October 1957, Herman died in Lucy's arms. Grieving, bewildered and heartbroken, Lucy focused her anger on the Windsors. She was furious that they didn't make the effort to attend his funeral or even send flowers, despite that, before Herman died, Wallis had written to say how much she loved him. Of course it was all about Wallis. According to Lucy, when she finally sent a telegram of sympathy it read in part: ALL MY LOVE AND SYMPATHY OVER YOUR AND MY LOSS. Lucy wrote back saying that Herman had already been buried along with Katherine and described his 'beautiful, serene, dignified' service.

Lucy vented her true feelings in a furious letter she sent to the Amorys.

What do you think of it – she did not even send a flower – not that we cared but I think in such a circumstance the Duke should have flown down from Paris and pay a last homage to their only real friend – I am afraid you can't teach little people to be grand and grandeur comes from the heart. Herman should have left them a bit of it in his will – he had so much. He was really the most outstanding person I ever met. He had all qualities and no faults. I adored him and always will continue to do so.

For all Lucy's anger, she had a bizarrely contradictory attitude to the Windsors. She had enjoyed her previous proximity to the ducal couple, basking in the social cachet it had given her. In her heart and mind she wanted to be recognized by future generations as the Mrs Rogers who was closest to the royal couple.

Shortly after Herman's death she busily began to put that warped plan into effect. When Katherine died, Herman had the phrase 'Strength and honour were her clothing' engraved on her tombstone. After his death Lucy had the words chiselled off in a frankly unhinged attempt to expunge the public record of her influence on his life.

As a further bizarre twist, Lucy changed her name to Lucie and also took the name Catherine for herself. When she died, on 4 January 2000, she was buried in the same plot as Katherine and Herman.

Moreover, she left instructions that she was to be interred wearing a dress once worn by Katherine. She felt that if she, Katherine and Herman were ever exhumed from the plot they now shared, people would identify her body as that of Katherine, who was much closer to the duchess than she had ever been.

Her astonishing behaviour, this weird royal obsession, helps explain why, for all her vitriol towards the Windsors, a few weeks after Herman's death Lucy immediately accepted an affectionate open invitation from the duchess to visit them in Paris in December. After all, when Herman was alive she and her husband regularly turned down invitations to the mill.

On her weekend stay in December the only other guest was to be Queen Mary's official biographer, James Pope-Hennessy, who, Wallis reassured her, was 'charming'. He planned to interview the duke about his late mother. During their conversation, the duke complained to Pope-Hennessy: 'I played fair in 1936, but I was bloody shabbily treated.'

It must have given Lucy a satisfying sense of control to know that she was now the font of all knowledge about 'dear Herman'. She could now hold court over Wallis, tantalizing her about the 'only man I have ever loved'. The ultimate triumph was hers – two social climbers but only one reached the summit of Mount Herman.

As Wallis admitted: 'I want so much to hear *all* about Herman these last years. I have never had such a sad year – so many friends gone and tragedies to others.'

Sadly, her losses would continue. A year later, on 30 November 1958, her second husband, Ernest Simpson, died. He was sixty-one.

And then there was one.

CHAPTER SEVENTEEN

'Wallis, Wallis, Wallis, Wallis'

TUCKED AWAY IN a concrete storage facility at the rear of the Maryland Historical Society in Baltimore is a painting that gives an unexpected insight into the interior life of the Duke and Duchess of Windsor.

While they had been photographed together endlessly, this work was the first commissioned painting of the two of them since their marriage. The commission, undertaken by local artist Trafford Klots, in part to commemorate their twenty-fifth year of married life, is unique.

Klots, a society artist who had also painted the Queen Mother, the widow of King George VI, set the couple in the lush Palm Beach garden of Arthur Gardner, the former American ambassador to Cuba. The duke was seated on a padded garden chair looking out into the middle distance, the spiritual home, as they like to say, of the English intellectual. The duchess, in a canary-yellow day dress, was perched, somewhat uncomfortably, on the arm of a garden sofa. Significantly, she occupied a position higher than that of the former king.

While she is looking in his direction, she is not looking at him. Her whole demeanour is blank, expressionless, her bored gaze reflecting perhaps the tedium she felt at the whole artistic exercise. Or her marriage. For what Klots depicts, either deliberately or unconsciously, is a married couple without an ounce of personal interaction. The two people at the centre of the royal romance of the century inhabit two separate universes, lost in their own thoughts. Neither gives the other a hint of acknowledgement or recognition. As Mark Letzer, president of the Maryland Historical Society, observes: 'As a couple that epitomized the love story of the century they seem somewhat disengaged and posed. Interesting, too, is that they look into space and not at one another nor at the viewer. The palette is fresh and verdant but it belies the bored countenance of the sitters.'

If Klots was trying to make a shrewd statement about the state of their union, he never admitted as much. His private correspondence about his 1961 work focused on his interesting conversations with the duke about the First World War and the difficulty of getting the duke's pug dog, Mr Chou, to sit still. Yet Klots, perhaps in spite of himself, succeeded in capturing the sense of emptiness, estrangement and distance that existed between them, a state of affairs familiar to those who knew them at that time.

It is as if the ghost of Gertrude Stein was hovering over the portrait; there is no there there. Appropriate, too, as, by a curious quirk of geography, the duchess had artistically come full circle. During the war, Stein, her one-time neighbour on Biddle Street, had written a book, *Ida*, about a woman, modelled on Wallis Simpson, who was famous for being famous. Twenty years later Klots put the finishing touches on his portrait of the ducal couple at his studio in Branch Alley Mount Vernon, just four blocks away from Wallis's former Baltimore home.

Neither work, though, found favour with the duchess. She sent Stein a somewhat baffled note of thanks when she received a copy of *Ida*, while she and the duke smiled politely at Klots's efforts – and moved on, gracefully distancing themselves from a portrait that was a touch too close to home.

During the time Klots was working with them, the Windsors were generally viewed as a couple killing time, their lives one of entertainment, dancing from one party to another. The duke had become such a bore that guests would inwardly shudder if they were seated next to him at dinner. His increasing deafness did not help. 'Morning glory' was how Churchill dismissively described the man he became, his extraordinary promise bleeding into emptiness. 'It was a really empty life but it was what they enjoyed,' noted a former private secretary. 'She loved anything to do with a party. They were wretched personalities, completely egocentric.'

Their rigid daily routine was effectively the third wheel in their marriage; their 11:30 morning meeting, her lunch with friends, his afternoon golf, his 7:00 p.m. date with a bottle of twenty-five-year-old malt, her 7:30 hairdresser appointment, their dinner party at 9:00.

They were always aware that they were under scrutiny, whether in public or private, and acted accordingly. If they went to a restaurant and their conversation faltered, the duchess insisted that they recite the alphabet to one another so that other diners would see their animation. On one occasion, they were in the same restaurant as Hollywood actor Clark Gable and his new wife, Kay Williams. They noticed that the couple were looking silently at one another, and they started to discuss the state of the Gables' marriage based on their lack of conversation. Then they burst into laughter, realizing they were guilty of doing to the Gables what so many others had done to them. If anything, that incident made them more determined to keep up the happy façade. At home, as Martha Amory observed: 'Even if there was an audience of one around, you could guarantee a lovey-dovey scene to silence any doubters. I have seen it scores of times.' At the same time, as Clip experienced during one of his first meetings with the duchess, she was capable of casual cruelty towards her whimpering but ever grateful husband.

AS THE DECADES ticked by, however, no one really cared any more. With the 1960s in full swing, the Windsors were left behind, international society turning to new darlings like Elizabeth Taylor, Richard Burton, and Aristotle and Jacqueline Onassis. When President Nixon invited the pair to the White House in 1970, they were no longer as socially active as they once had been. 'We're just too old,' said the duchess. 'We even spent Easter in bed.'

When their ghost writer Charles Murphy visited them at their Paris home in April 1972 shortly before the duke's death, he was shocked and dismayed by their lifestyle. In a letter to his collaborator Joe Bryan, he wrote: 'How pitiable it all is. Now at the end, except for the black Sidney, [their butler] a late imperial acquisition from the Bahamas, they are quite alone among comparative strangers. The lady made it so. Whatever Court there was, she was determined to rule. And now it is made up mostly of shadows – and the worst of the collaborationists and the robber barons.'

Age brought the ailing couple some compensations. By then there had been a slight thaw in relations with Buckingham Palace, the duke's receipt of a telegram from the queen congratulating him on his seventieth birthday proving to be a prelude to visits to their Paris home by various junior members of the royal family, including Prince William of Gloucester and the Duke and Duchess of Kent. It was all rather too little too late – after all, Emperor Hirohito of Japan had paid a courtesy call some years before. Nonetheless this modest rapprochement was crowned by a visit – just before the duke's seventy-eighth birthday in May 1972 – from his niece, Queen Elizabeth, and Prince Philip.

The ailing duke, who was suffering from cancer of the throat, insisted on getting out of bed and disconnecting what he called the 'damned rigging' – his various tubes delivering morphine and other palliative care – before dressing in a suit and tie to meet his sovereign. Even though this was a courtesy call during the queen's official visit to France, the duke could not help raising, for what proved to be the last time, the possibility of his wife being given the appellation 'Her Royal Highness'. Once again he was denied, the queen leaving open the family wound.

At this critical time in his life, the duke made the acquaintance of another girl from Baltimore, Julie Chatard Alexander, a feisty twenty-six-year-old feminist who was earning money to pay for a trip of a lifetime to India with her fiancé. During the day she ran an art gallery, at night she worked a twelve-hour shift as the night nurse on call for the Duke of Windsor at their final residence in Paris, 4 route du Champ d'Entraînement in the Bois de Boulogne.

By now there was no pretence that he was anything other than a patient under constant medical monitoring; it was a question of ensuring that he was made comfortable for his last remaining days and hours. The duke had sacked several nurses but seemed to like Julie, as she hailed from his wife's hometown.

For her part, she was not altogether sure how to talk to him. 'As a women's lib American I was determined not to be intimidated by his title and position,' she recalls, speaking for the first time about her experience. So she called him 'Duke', as in 'Hey, Duke, how you doing tonight?' As his favourite film that year was a John Wayne Western, *The Cowboys*, he seemed to like that. They chatted about her upcoming visit to India, the duke recommending a book in his library on that subject by the journalist and adventurer Lowell Thomas.

There was one moment of excitement during her stay. The quiet of the evening was rudely shattered when the duke's second-floor bedroom window was shoved open and a man peered in. 'Don't be alarmed,' he said. 'I am a policeman. Someone has pushed the panic button.' Julie ran down the hall to alert the sleeping duchess. 'Don't worry, darling,' she said. 'I've pushed the button before when I'm bored.'

Apart from his night nurse, the duke had no other company in the evening apart from his pug dog, Black Diamond. During the two weeks Julie was with the ex-king, he was never once visited by his wife, whose quarters were on the same floor of their home but separated by what Wallis liked to call 'the boudoir'. At the time, she had an American female guest and spent the evenings with her. Julie recalled: 'She never came to see him or kiss him good night or see how he was. Not once. Poor fellow. He would call her name over and over: "Wallis, Wallis, Wallis, Wallis." Or "darling, darling, darling". It was pitiful and pathetic. Just so sad, like a lamb calling for its mother.'

On the night he died, Julie sensed that his life was drawing peacefully to a close. What the French call *les corbeaux* (black ravens) had chosen that evening to roost in the trees outside his bedroom window. These birds, traditionally seen as harbingers of death, had come for him. They were not to be denied.

His breathing became more agitated, Julie holding his hand to calm him. As he became increasingly restless she cradled him in her arms, holding and soothing him. At 2:20 in the morning of Sunday, 28 May 1972, the once king and emperor died in the arms of a woman from Baltimore. 'Right city, wrong woman,' recalled Julie. So ended the royal romance of the century.

The doctor, Jean Thin, was summoned and pronounced him dead, after which the duchess was woken and she sat with him, holding his hand and whispering sweet nothings. No tears, no cries of anguish, just a gentle goodbye. Her own memory was, typically, rather different. She told her friend Aline, Countess of Romanones, that shortly after two in the morning she was awakened by doctors and summoned to the duke's bedside. As he breathed his last she took him in her arms, his blue eyes gazing tenderly into hers. He uttered one word, 'Darling', and then he was gone. Her butler, Sydney Johnson, suggested that he actually said 'Mama, mama, mama, mama.'

Given that all are agreed that the duke died in the early hours of the morning when night nurse Julie Chatard Alexander was on duty, her recollection, especially given the duchess's waning faculties and her lifelong habit of altering the *actualité*, seems the most authentic.

When the news was announced in the media, one of the first to send a note of condolence was her old rival Lucy Rogers. Since her visit to the mill in December 1957, she had seen little, if anything, of the Windsors. As she knew all too well, Wallis had been interested in Herman and not her, and the only reason she had been invited to stay with them since his death was so that Wallis could soak up news of the only man she had ever loved. Lucy's note, which attempted to put aside decades of rivalry, ended with the words 'I shall always remain your friend, in memory of Herman and the Duke.' To her dismay, Lucy, who now lived in an apartment in Monte Carlo, received merely a regulation engraved card of acknowledgement.

In fairness, the duchess was somewhat overwhelmed by the outpouring of affection for the lost king. When the duchess arrived in London for the duke's funeral, she was gratified to learn that more than sixty thousand mourners had filed past the bier inside Windsor Castle. No longer the forgotten man, he was buried in Frogmore in the castle grounds, the duchess telling her remaining friends that she hoped that one day in the not-too-distant future she would be by his side, the first commoner allowed into the royal burial ground.

That day was a very long time coming, the duchess lingering on and on, becoming progressively more and more physically and mentally debilitated. Her home in the Bois de Boulogne became something of a 'living tomb', Wallis's circle shrinking to an ever-changing parade of hired nurses.

In the first months after the duke's death she was simply forgetful. That quickly changed. Her descent into dementia was rapid, Wallis displaying alarming mood swings, one moment charming, the next aggressive and rude. During her slide, her indomitable lawyer Maître Suzanne Blum, who had represented Charlie Chaplin, Walt Disney and Darryl Zanuck, hovered over her, an avenging angel towards those who attempted to get too close. She crossed swords with Mountbatten, who was eager to reclaim the duke's correspondence and historical artefacts for the Royal Collection at Windsor Castle. Blum complained that he was persistently on the telephone to her. 'There are,' she said pointedly, 'nothing but vultures crowding around the garbage cans.'

When photographers flagrantly intruded upon the duchess in 1976, taking pictures of nurses placing her limp form onto a sunbed, Blum, under strict French privacy laws, took legal action, winning the duchess heavy damages.

Not that the duchess knew about the efforts on her behalf. Now beyond looking after herself, she had withdrawn into her own world, her mind wandering further and further back in time. Her friend the Countess de Romanones described the gradual decline of the duchess, the woman who had dreamed of becoming queen now living in a dream world of her own making. She recalled: 'Visiting was no longer like paying respects to a dying friend. It was like watching someone who had gradually, slowly reached a new life, where memories could keep her alive forever.'

Once, her memory wandered all the way back to February 1935, and she began humming a sentimental waltz that had meant so much to her and the duke. As she danced and glided in her mind, perhaps she remembered the shadowy figures who had spun her around the dance floor; the diplomats, the businessmen, salesmen and others who had tried to win her heart. Here comes the ardent Carter Osburn, the jovial Win Spencer and the urbane Felipe Espil. Then there is Gerry Greene, Ernest Simpson, Guy Trundle and of course 'dear Herman, dear, dear Herman', eager to fill up the rest of her dance card only for the Duke of Windsor to cut in.

When she finally died on 24 April 1986, aged eighty-nine, the royal family stuck to their side of the bargain and allowed her to rest next to her late husband at Frogmore. At the funeral service, held at St George's Chapel, Windsor Castle, and attended by the royal family, the duke would have been pleased to see that her coffin was carried by eight soldiers from one of his former regiments, the Welsh Guards.

There was, though, a bitter and immutable irony in her send-off. For in this final act of damnation she found herself lying next to a man she barely tolerated, in the private cemetery of a family she loathed, covered by the earth of a country she hated. Even in death she would never be in peace. As her mother so often predicted.

But for the decisions and revisions made in a moment, the girl from Baltimore could have been lying with Herman Rogers, the man she loved, in the quiet corner of a graveyard in the South of France that is forever America.

Acknowledgements

In Pursuit of Wallis

Perhaps inevitably the long journey of discovery into the life of the oh-so-stylish Duchess of Windsor began with a ride in a vintage white Rolls-Royce.

At the wheel was Philip Baty, duchess fanatic, royal collector and part-time drag queen, who has a museum, some would say shrine, to the wife of the former king Edward VIII in the basement of his home known as Adele Corner. It is just a few doors down from where plain Wallis Warfield was raised at 212 East Biddle Street in the historic Mount Vernon district of Baltimore.

While Philip proudly showed his extensive collection of memorabilia – including imitation jewellery, gloves, souvenir teacups and plates as well as a trove of rare magazines, newspaper clippings, and even the FBI file on the errant Windsors – next door, his bedridden father listened to a noisy born-again preacher on the radio. It was an unusual, somewhat rococo beginning to the pursuit of one of the most discussed yet elusive women of the last century.

Phil kindly let me browse his collection – and even posed for a couple of snapshots – before ferrying me back to the quiet simplicity of the Holiday Inn.

It is as well that Phil, who holds a duchess charity ball every year, is keeping the memory of Wallis alive. There are few other signs in the Mount Vernon district to indicate the presence of the woman who upturned a dynasty. The local guidebook has her house incorrectly numbered – as the current owner, Maria High, patiently explained. Her former home at 212 East Biddle Street is now an assisted-living facility, every piece of coving, balustrade and plasterwork having been ripped out, as if exorcizing a ghost. Even the Emmanuel Episcopal church on Cathedral Street, where she was baptized Bessie Wallis Warfield on 19 October 1896, boasts, incorrectly, that she was christened there in 1928.

At the private, women-only Mount Vernon Club, in the shadow of the 178-foot column of George Washington, the first public monument to the first president of the republic, they have more of a sense of these things. After all, the duke and duchess, who visited Baltimore frequently, stayed here in 1959, the duchess pointing out her old haunts to the former king.

Over a lunch of pumpkin soup and famed Maryland crab cakes – a Wallis speciality – Gail Ostergaard, Bill Fritz and Sally Miller, who sadly died in 2016, regaled me with the cloud of local gossip and opinion that envelops the memory of Wallis. I learned that the more established Baltimore families, who still regard the city as the spinning centre of the known universe, are apt to dismiss one of her best-known daughters thus: 'Oh, she married a foreigner and then moved away.'

It is just a short stroll to the men-only Maryland Club, where amid the mahogany panelling and silent herd of animal heads, Mark Letzer, executive director of the Maryland Historical Society, recalled the time a youthful Wallis dressed as a man to enter this hallowed male bastion. He is the insightful custodian of a cornucopia of Wallis material, including the famous Givenchy monkey dress, which has only ever been worn by Wallis, as well as the intriguing portrait of the Windsors by local artist Trafford Klots which now hangs in the museum.

Local interior designer Stiles Colwill opened his commodious little black book and sketched in more details of Wallis's local reputation. His suggestion of a visit to the Ladew Topiary Gardens, where horseman and *bon viveur* Harvey Ladew once held the reins, paid dividends. Thanks to Emily Emerick, executive director of the gardens, and archivist Fran Scully I was able to dig out letters and other documents relating to Ladew's friendship with the Windsors. Equally hospitable was Dr Parnell Hagerman, then the headmistress of Wallis's alma mater, Oldfields. On a bitterly cold January day we stomped around the dorm where Wallis once slept and identified the fire escape which she probably used in order to meet the various *beaux* who secretly picked her up in their fathers' cars and took her for jaunts in the countryside. My thanks, too, to the Oldfields team, including the new interim head Ansley Smithwick, Anne Finney and Karen Miller for answering endless follow-up queries.

I often find that fate plays an important but inexplicable role in my biographies. So it was with *Wallis in Love*. By the purest fluke, the woman who nursed the Duke of Windsor in his Paris home during his final hours lived just a few miles south of the school. Julie Chatard Alexander had never spoken before about the last poignant moments of a king.

It helped that we had a friend in common, Irish nurse Oonagh Toffolo, who not only cared for the duke herself but later became a friend and confidante of the late Diana, Princess of Wales, assisting me with my subsequent biography. Julie's memories painted a vivid and affecting portrait of the duke's final days and his interaction, or rather lack of, with Wallis.

Another woman who had maintained a discreet silence about the Windsors was Courtney Letts de Espil, the wife of the Argentinian ambassador Felipe Espil who conducted a torrid affair with Wallis in Washington during the 1920s. Courtney, a society beauty, writer and traveller, kept a diary about those tumultuous days. Fearing that her occasionally acerbic comments could land her in trouble with the far-right junta of Argentinian president Juan Perón, she hid her secret handwritten volumes in a vault of First National City Bank in Buenos Aires.

Now they are kept in the manuscript room of the Library of Congress in Washington, DC – and what an extraordinary story they have to tell about Wallis, men, love, jealousy, regret . . . the whole nine yards. I was grateful that her granddaughter, Courtney S. Hagner, was able to fill in some of the gaps.

My next stop was Boston. I had previously visited the august chambers of the Massachusetts Historical Society where, accompanied by the ticking of a grandfather clock, I had delved into the steamy sexually charged correspondence of Constance Coolidge, Comtesse de Jumilhac, a friend of Wallis's since her days in China. This time I was on the trail of Cleveland Amory, a Boston-born writer who had spent a short but intense time as the Duchess of Windsor's ghost writer. His name had cropped up briefly in the various Wallis biographies. I was interested to see if he was more than a footnote in her story.

It didn't look promising. His stepdaughter, Dr Gaea Leinhardt, vividly remembered some of his withering insights into the lives of the duke and duchess but also recalled him unsuccessfully searching for papers about this period in his writing career. After his death in 1998, his personal assistant Marian Probst, had collected all his books, trophies and other memorabilia and donated them to the Boston Public Library.

In later life the socialite historian had turned animal rights activist, so most of the material dealt with topics such as bear-baiting in Wyoming, pit bull fighting dogs, as well as the plight of goats, bison and other creatures.

The trove included cowboy hats, chess sets, reindeer candle holders, shaving brushes and framed certificates. It amounted to a staggering 166 boxes or so stacked away somewhere in municipal storage. Earlier I was bleakly informed by senior BPL librarian Beth Prindle that the material was off-site and, due to reorganization, would not be available for many months.

Fate once more played a hand. By some miracle, Amory's material was discovered and thanks to Beth Prindle's good offices, in early January I found myself in the cavernous archival storage facility in West Roxbury, a thirty-minute cab ride from the city centre. With the indefatigable assistance of librarian Mary Bender, we manhandled a selection of boxes onto a table for inspection. It seemed, though, like a wasted trip, yielding only animal rights material.

Then an entry on the catalogue reading 'Picture: Man, woman and child' caught my eye. I looked in the relevant folder and there was a picture of King George VI, Queen Elizabeth and Princess Elizabeth, now the queen. It soon became clear that the Amory collection had been catalogued by an animal rights activist with no understanding of the other material buried within.

After a few minutes digging among the mountain of boxes, we found pictures of a bare-chested King Edward, Wallis in a swimming costume, and other shots showing her relaxing with friends. Here was the biographical equivalent of an Aladdin's cave comprising taped interviews with the duchess, letters, notes, interviews with her circle, and even a postcard about Amory's meeting with Queen Elizabeth II and her children, Prince Charles and Princess Anne, at Windsor Castle. The haul gave a fresh and intimate perspective on the woman who enraged a royal dynasty and divided a nation.

It became clear, too, that Cleveland, known as Clip, and his actress wife, Martha, had struck up quite a friendship with one of the central figures in Wallis's life, Herman Livingston Rogers. Herman's descendants have looked hard and long for material to help paint a clearer picture of the relationship between Wallis and Herman as well as the two wives, Katherine and Lucy. I am particularly indebted to Michael Reid who spent several days hunting through his barn in Belfast, Maine, for correspondence and diaries relating to his grandmother Constance Moore, the sister of Herman's first wife, Katherine. Sadly the barn was bare, though family historian Christopher Rogers Browne produced a number of fascinating wartime letters from Herman to his sister Anne Webb.

In helping to trace the Rogers' family ancestry and the connections to Wallis and the royal family I am indebted to DeDe Biles, the late Kitty Blair, John Feitig, Claudia S. Fortunato, Debbie Hobler, Irvin Muritz, Heather Nash, Carney Rhinevault, Eddie Rogers, Cissie Schley, David Tavernier and Gilly Vurpillot.

I am especially grateful to Barbara Mason who has been most generous in allowing me access not only to the home movies made by Herman Rogers and his extensive photographic collection but also to correspondence between the duchess, Herman, and latterly Lucy Rogers, her grandmother. Her enthusiasm for the project has never dimmed.

I am very appreciative, too, of the guidance and insights of Marilyn Greenwald, Charles Stuart Kennedy, director of the Foreign Affairs Oral History Program, Adam Lewis, Andrea Lynn, associate professor Craig Robertson of Northeastern University and Charlie Scheips, as well as the endeavours of researchers Philip Armstrong-Dampier, Jewell Fenzi, Anne Trevor and Louis Wallen. A special thanks to archivist Gina Petrone of the Hotel del Coronado in San Diego who succeeded in sniffing out never-before-seen pictures of Wallis. The librarians at the numerous universities and historical societies I have consulted have been consistently patient and helpful but I would like to specially thank Eric Stoykovich of the University of Maryland Libraries and Jennie Cole at the Filson

Historical Society for going above and beyond. My thanks, too, to lip-readers Janine McQuillan and Lee Fullwood from the Blanche Nevile School for deaf children in north London, who valiantly tried to make sense of Wallis's mouthings to camera on Herman Rogers' silent home movies.

As ever, the vision and perseverance of my agent, Steve Troha, helped get the show on the road, while the keen insights, encouragement and enthusiasm of my editor, Gretchen Young, helped bring *Wallis in Love* alive. Thanks, too, to assistant editor Katherine Stopa for keeping everything shipshape. Writing and researching a biography is a long journey and I would like to thank my darling wife, Carolyn, for keeping me company on the road. Rolls-Royce not included!

Andrew Morton

Source Notes

Abbreviations

AB: Aunt Bessie
CA: Cleveland Amory
CAP: Cleveland Amory Papers, Boston Public Library
CC: Constance Coolidge, the Comtesse de Jumilhac
CLE: Papers of Courtney Letts de Espil, Manuscript Division, Library of
     Congress, Washington, DC
DoW: Duke of Windsor
FDW: Freda Dudley Ward
HHR: Duchess of Windsor, *The Heart Has Its Reasons*
HLR: Herman Livingston Rogers letters
HWE: Helen Worden Erskine Papers, Rare Book and Manuscript
     Library, Columbia University, New York, NY
LLR: Lucy Livingston Rogers
LTF: Lady Thelma Furness
MB: Michael Bloch, ed., *Wallis and Edward: Letters 1931–1937*
MdHS: Maryland Historical Society, Baltimore, MD
MKR: Mary Kirk Raffray, Buckner Hollingsworth Papers, 1911–1964,
     Schlesinger Library, Radcliffe Institute, Harvard University,
     Cambridge, MA
TOMS: Anne Kirk Cooke and Elizabeth Lightfoot, *The Other Mrs Simpson*
W: Wallis

Chapter One: 'All is Love'

Unless stated otherwise, Duchess of Windsor quoted from interviews
with Cleveland Amory, Cleveland Amory Papers, Boston Public Library.

5   **'I want to come home'**: MKR, 15 May 1912, box 1, file 1–7.

6   **'I had a huge crush'**: Cleveland Amory interview with Duchess of Windsor, May 1955, CAP, reel 11.

6   **'earliest spring flowers'**: Mary King McPherson, *Oldfields School, 1867–1989: A Feeling of Family* (Glencoe, MD: Oldfields School, 1989), 42.

6   **'came in contact with her'**: CA interview W, May 1955.

6   **'terrifically wild with excitement'**: MKR, undated, 1913.

7   **'Wallis all the time'**: MKR, 1912.

10   **'Slavery as I knew it'**: Box 7, folder 15, Warfield Family Papers, Special Collections, University of Maryland Libraries.

11   **it involved cousin Edwin**: *Chicago Tribune*, 27 July 1906.

11   **'they will tell you so themselves'**: CAP, box 84.

12   **'Never marry a Yankee'**: Duchess of Windsor, *The Heart Has Its Reasons* (London: Michael Joseph, 1956), 9.

13   **It helped pay the bills**: CAP, box 84.

14   **'any child I ever saw'**: CA interview AB, CAP, box 84.

15   **'spoilt child, terribly spoilt'**: CA interview W, May 1955.

16   **'what he had tipped you'**: Ibid.

16   **'inevitably thrown much together'**: *HHR*, 12.

18   **'room to room'**: CA interview AB, CAP, box 84.

19   **'He called her 'Minnehaha'**: Dr Charles F. Bove, *A Paris Surgeon's Story* (Boston: Little, Brown, 1956).

19   **'very hard time making the grade'**: Billy Baldwin with Michael Gardine, *Billy Baldwin, an Autobiography* (Boston: Little, Brown, 1985), 294.

21   **'spinach and fresh air'**: CA interview W, May 1955.

21   **'knew what she wanted'**: CA interview AB, box 84.

22   **'come back after Christmas'**: MKR, 31 October 1912.

23   **'British stiff upper lip'**: CA interview W, May 1955.

23   **'every occasion imaginable'**: MKR, 30 July 1911.

24   **'gloomy and awful' day**: MKR, 4 November 1912.

24   **'everyone else was so envious'**: MKR, spring 1914.

24 **'a good person to be in school with'**: Maxine Sandberg biography, MS 2901, MdHS.

25 **'go for a drive'**: *Baltimore News-Post*, 1 October 1936.

26 **too extravagant**: MKR, 20 May 1912.

27 **'quite a show'**: Maxine Sandberg, MS 2901, MdHS.

27 **'nice girl'**: Anne Sebba, *That Woman: The Life of Wallis Simpson, Duchess of Windsor* (New York: St Martin's Press, 2012), 18.

28 **'no chance at all in our town'**: Upton Sinclair, *Wally for Queen! The Private Life of Royalty* (Pasadena, CA: Station A, 1936).

28 **'it was very sophisticated'**: Author interview, January 2016.

31 **'it was a crushing blow'**: CA interview W, May 1955.

Chapter Two: I Married a Sadist

Unless otherwise stated, Duchess of Windsor interviews from box 9, *'Mother I Met a Man'* and *'A Navy Wife'*, Cleveland Amory Papers, Boston Public Library.

34 **$25 a month**: Letters to Corinne Mustin, Henry C. Mustin Papers, MSS52860, Manuscript Division, Library of Congress, Washington, DC.

35 **'very moral'**: CA interview W.

35 **'most fascinating aviator'**: *HHR*, 46.

35 **'adventurous realm'**: *HHR*, 49.

36 **'mine were fliers'**: CA interview W.

36 **'a better shipmate'**: *The Lucky Bag*, vol. 17 (Annapolis, MD: US Naval Academy, 1910), https://archive.org/details/luckybag1910unse.

36 **'strong, assured, sophisticated'**: *HHR*, 48.

36 **'totally and helplessly'**: *HHR*, 49.

37 **'Florida and flying'**: CA interview AB, CAP, box 84.

37 **'married him out of curiosity'**: *HHR*, 51.

37 **'hand at every opportunity'**: CA interview W.

39 **'rest is up to you'**: CA interview AB, CAP, box 84.

39 **'Here comes Carrie Nation'**: CA interview W.

40 'you couldn't for life': CA interview AB, CAP, box 84.

41 'nothing would come between us': CA interview W.

42 'opportunity to fight': Lieutenant Spencer to Commander Kirkpatrick, 13 August 1918, NavAir 3944, National Archives.

42 'hard work': Captain Irwin to Lieutenant Spencer, undated, NavAir 3944, National Archives.

42 central role in Wallis's life: *HHR*, 72.

43 'enjoying informal parties': *San Diego Union*, 20 March 1977.

43 'focus was on her': Ibid.

44 'and ordered it': CA interview W.

44 'avoid the truth': CA interview notes, CAP, box 9.

45 'received by the prince': 'The Duchess of Windsor and the Coronado Legend, Part II', *San Diego Historical Society Quarterly* 34, no. 1 (Winter 1988).

45 'dressed to kill': J. Bryan III and Charles J. V. Murphy, *The Windsor Story* (London: Granada, 1979), 67.

46 'topic of conversation': Benjamin Sacks, 'The Duchess of Windsor and the Coronado Legend', *Journal of San Diego History*, 34, no. 1 (Winter 1988).

46 'one can be at a party': *HHR*, 71.

47 'pleasure at all times': Rear Admiral W. F. Fullam to Secretary of the Navy (Operations), 9 November 1921, 26521-477, National Archives.

49 'not a woman at all': Sebba, *That Woman*, 27–28.

50 'she loved it': CA interview Herman Livingston Rogers, CAP, box 85.

50 'she would throw things': Ralph G. Martin, *The Woman He Loved* (New York: Simon & Schuster, 1974), 63.

51 'could not live with': CA interview AB, CAP, box 85.

52 face of their mothers: *New York Times*, 14 February 2016.

52 'I will still be around': *HHR*, 80.

53 'little to be said or done': CAP, box 85.

53 'at sea with the fleet': *News-Herald* (Franklin, PA), 11 November 1936.

Chapter Three: 'He was Simply Irresistible'

54   'terrific success': *Washington in the Time of FDR*. Courtney Letts de Espil Papers (hereafter cited as CLE), box 8, Manuscript Division, Library of Congress, Washington, DC.

55   'casualness of chorus girls': F. Scott Fitzgerald, 'The Crack-Up', *Esquire*, February 1936.

56   'disguise it': Author interview, October 2015.

57   'slapstick wit which always amuses': CLE, box 9, folder 1.

58   'as if I was a child': CA interview W, *Reveille in Washington*, CAP, box 9.

59   the thinking of the British government: Donald A. Ritchie, *Reporting from Washington: The History of the Washington Press Corps* (New York: Oxford University Press, 2005), 95–96.

59   'make a lady of me': *HHR*, 83.

60   'women on their own': CA interview W, CAP, box 9.

60   'a special paradise': *HHR*, 83.

61   'scholarship and wide experience': CA interview W, CAP, box 9.

62   'girls he dated': Author interview, October 2015.

62   'good established family': Ibid.

62   'resistance was at a dangerous low': CA interview W, CAP, box 9.

63   'a woman so in love': Ralph G. Martin, *The Woman He Loved*, 71.

63   'Vindictive, too': Author interview, October 2015.

63   'Edward the Eighth had': J. Bryan III and Charles Murphy, *The Windsor Story*, 20.

63   '*Ça ne se fait pas*': Ibid., 19.

64   'I will never forget you': CLE, box 9, folder 2.

65   'I was tired of it': Ibid., folder 1.

67   'We became a foursome': *HHR*, 89.

67   'a past without a future': CA interview W, CAP.

69   'He went off, I thought sadly': CLE, box 9, folder 2.

71   'the press had treated him': CLE, box 8, folder 2.

71   what remained of the night: *Chicago Tribune*, 3 May 1959.

Chapter Four: 'The World's Biggest Tease'

Unless otherwise stated, Duchess of Windsor interviews from box 9, *The Lotus Years*, Cleveland Amory Papers, Boston Public library.

74 **'it was no use'**: CA interview W.

74 **'utterly satisfying second honeymoon'**: *HHR*, 94.

74 **'fuss over the girls'**: *HHR*, 95.

76 **'lose what we began with'**: Ibid.

76 **courtesan houses and 401 courtesans**: Gail Hershatter, *Dangerous Pleasures: Prostitution and Modernity in Twentieth-Century Shanghai* (Berkeley: University of California Press, 1997), 508.

77 **'something of a curiosity'**: Author interview, January 2016.

77 **'such favorable odds'**: CA interview W.

77 **'intentions were not so attractive'**: Ibid.

78 **safety of these trains**: *US Department of State: Papers Relating to the Foreign Relations of the United States, 1925*, vol. 1 (Washington, DC: US Government Printing Office, 1940). See University of Wisconsin digital collection, http://digital.library.wisc.edu/1711. dl/FRUS.FRUS1925v01.

79 **member of a delegation**: Author interview, January 2016.

81 **'jumping out of the window'**: Lewis Clark, US Foreign Service Officer, 1926–1958, 'Diplomacy as a Career: Hard Work, Hardship, and Happy Times', Foreign Affairs Oral History Collection, Association for Diplomatic Studies and Training, Arlington, VA. At www.adst.org/wp-content/uploads/2013/12/Clark-Lewis-memoir. pdf.

81 **'touched by a divine fire'**: Crowninshield-Magnus Papers, box 6, Massachusetts Historical Society.

81 **her ardour cooled**: Andrea Lynn, *Shadow Lovers: The Last Affairs of H. G. Wells* (Boulder, CO: Westview Press, 2001), 238.

82 **'I had a marvellous time'**: CA interview W.

83 **'She kept everyone laughing'**: Interview Butler Brayne Thornton Robinson Franklin, Foreign Affairs Oral History Project, Foreign

Service Spouse Series, www.adst.org/OH%20TOCs/Franklin,%20 Butler.toc.pdf.

84 **'a lasting friendship'**: Charles Higham, *The Duchess of Windsor: The Secret Life*, rev. edn (Hoboken, NJ: John Wiley, 2005), 34–35.

84 **never able to have children**: Anne Sebba, *That Woman*, 56.

84 **this tale seems unlikely**: *Deseret Morning News* (Salt Lake City, UT), 5 January 2007.

85 **'look of an athlete'**: *HHR*, 100.

86 **'if I survive the war'**: *HHR*, 101.

87 **'very good looking and attractive'**: Andrea Lynn, *Shadow Lovers*, 240.

88 **'whatever milieu chance placed him'**: J. Bryan III and Charles Murphy, *The Windsor Story*, 25.

88 **'lyric interval of my youth'**: *HHR*, 103.

88 **'complete uselessness'**: CA interview W.

88 **'never does with anything'**: CA interview Herman Livingston Rogers, CAP, box 85.

89 **'the world's biggest tease'**: Ibid.

89 **'you go too far'**: Ibid.

91 **'human drives and foibles'**: *HHR*, 106.

91 **'in love with him'**: J. Bryan III and Charles Murphy, *The Windsor Story*, 25.

92 **'always remain friends'**: CA interview W.

92 **'why I stopped off'**: Ibid.

Chapter Five: Wallis Stole My Man

Unless otherwise stated, Duchess of Windsor interview from box 9, *Warrenton*, Cleveland Amory Papers, Boston Public library.

94 **'Yours, Win'**: Ralph G. Martin, *The Woman He Loved*, 87.

95 **'into the wilderness to reflect'**: CA interview W.

95 **'inferior decorating'**: *HHR*, 110.

95 **'buried alive for two years'**: CA interview W.

96 **'I vegetated with equal satisfaction'**: *HHR*, 112.

96 **'we both need money'**: J. Bryan III and Charles Murphy, *The Windsor Story*, 27.

96 **'the *Daily Racing Form'***: John Toler, 'Romance, Abdication and Exile: Wallis Warfield in Warrenton, and Beyond', *News and Notes from the Fauquier Historical Society*, 22, no. 2 (Spring and Summer 2000).

97 **'marry the rich Jew'**: Michael Bloch, ed., *Wallis and Edward: Letters, 1931–1937* (New York: Summit, 1986), (hereafter cited as MB), 123.

98 **'made any party something special'**: *Washington Herald*, 9 December 1936.

99 **'clawing the air in ecstasy'**: Anne Kirk Cooke and Elizabeth Lightfoot, *The Other Mrs Simpson: Postscript to the Love Story of the Century* (New York: Vantage, 1977), (hereafter cited as *TOMS*), 18.

102 **'you may be falling in love again'**: *HHR*, 123.

102 **black sheep of the family**: CA interview W.

103 **jaws of victory**: Anne Sebba, *That Woman*, 60; J. Bryan III and Charles Murphy, *The Windsor Story*, 30.

104 **'departed friends'**: Ralph G. Martin, *The Woman He Loved*, 87.

104 **'she helped herself to my husband'**: Cleveland Amory, *The Best Cat Ever* (New York: Little, Brown, 1993), 136.

105 **'ways of his father's people'**: *HHR*, 118.

106 **'wear them with an air'**: Helen Worden Erskine Papers, box 80, Rare Book and Manuscript Library, Columbia University, New York (hereafter cited as HWE).

107 **'go ahead with the wedding'**: Author interview, February 2016.

108 **bursting her eardrum**: Andrea Lynn, *Shadow Lovers*, 247–250.

108 **'love into a man's life'**: CA interview W.

109 **'I was happy'**: Ibid.

109 **'snowy white hair'**: Ibid.

109 MARRYING ERNEST TOMORROW MUCH LOVE: J. Bryan III and Charles Murphy, *The Windsor Story*, 35.

110 **'cold little job'**: *HHR*, 127.

Chapter Six: This Weird Royal Obsession

Unless otherwise stated, Duchess of Windsor interviews from *The Good Life on a Small Weekly Budget* and *British Goods are Best*, box 9, Cleveland Amory Papers, Boston Public library.

111 **'see something young'**: CA interview W.

112 **'manage Ernest's life'**: Ibid.

112 **'alien to the human spirit'**: *HHR*, 134.

113 **'British goods were best'**: CA interview W.

113 **'aggressively American'**: Anne Sebba, *That Woman*, 67.

113 **'like a parrot's'**: Christopher Wilson, *Dancing with the Devil: The Windsors and Jimmy Donahue* (London: HarperCollins, 2000), 56.

113 **'when in Rome'**: CA interview Ernest Simpson, CAP, box 85.

114 **'what would become of me'**: CA interview W.

114 **'seemed to me incomprehensible'**: Ibid.

115 **'that was the Prince of Wales'**: *HHR*, 134.

116 **'he had a wistful face'**: CA interview W.

117 **'frugally but well'**: *HHR*, 136.

118 **'a twenty-four-hour memory'**: CA interview W.

118 **'such an unbecoming colour'**: *HHR*, 143.

119 **'not enough head'**: Ibid.

120 **'one in joy'**: *Daily Mail*, 16 April 2005.

120 **'a really happy person'**: CA interview Ernest Simpson, CAP, box 85.

121 **'good things of the present'**: *HHR*, 145.

123 **'as quickly as possible'**: CA interview W.

Chapter Seven: 'Mission Accomplished'

Unless otherwise stated, Duchess of Windsor interviews from *The Fuss and the Feathers*, box 9, Cleveland Amory Papers, Boston Public Library.

124 **'old maids'**: HWE, series 11, subseries B, box 74, Lady Thelma Furness and Gloria Vanderbilt, 'We Took the High Road' (unpublished manuscript), 2.

125 **'never tell even your pillow'**: HWE, box 74, 'We Took the High Road', 9.

126 **'the world was theirs'**: HWE, box 74, Sonia Rosenberg interview, 22.

126 **'I kicked her out'**: HWE, box 74, Rosenberg, 4.

127 **'Little Disraeli'**: Ibid.

127 **'Gloria Vanderbilt's twin sister'**: Ibid.

127 **join him for the journey**: Ralph G. Martin, *The Woman He Loved*, 133.

127 **'rich and important men'**: HWE, box 74, Rosenberg, 23.

129 **'I was his wife in all but name'**: HWE, box 74, 'We Took the High Road', 110.

129 **'no sense of wit or repartee'**: Ralph G. Martin, *The Woman He Loved*, 132.

129 **'men not their husbands'**: HWE, box 74, 'We Took the High Road', 137.

130 **'where the voyage would end'**: Gloria Vanderbilt and Thelma Lady Furness, *Double Exposure: A Twin Autobiography* (New York: David McKay, 1958), 279.

130 **for the rest of his life**: *The Independent*, 11 May 1995.

131 **'height of bad manners'**: HWE, box 74, 'We Took the High Road', 160a.

131 **'I did like her'**: Ibid., 160.

132 **'Consuelo brought her'**: Ibid.

132 **'I was fascinated by this'**: CA interview W.

132 **'Mission accomplished'**: Ibid.

132 **'lunch with me tomorrow'**: HWE, box 74, 'We Took the High Road', 202.

134 **'his father little'**: Ibid., 133.

135 **'what she did to Prince George'**: Ibid., 15.

136 **Lord Birkenhead looked like a child**: Christopher Sykes Papers,

box 3, folder 18, Booth Family Center for Special Collections, Georgetown University Library, Washington, DC.

136 **'and don't fit in'**: *New York Times*, 8 June 2003.

137 **'I wouldn't be a good one'**: *American Weekly*, 11 December 1955.

137 **'good propaganda'**: *Daily Mail*, 18 March 2015.

138 **'doesn't do much for the women'**: *HHR*, 163.

138 **'matter of life or death'**: HWE, box 74, interview LTF.

139 **'climbing into that car'**: CA interview W.

139 **'of course through Thelma'**: MB, 53.

139 **'I love the look of it'**: Mary Kirk Raffray to Mrs H. C. Kirk, 2 June 1931, *TOMS*, 4.

140 **'no one wants to leave'**: Mary Kirk Raffray to her mother, 7 June 1931, *TOMS*, 15.

141 **'a great fascination on lesbians'**: MB, 56.

142 **'Not to the manor born'**: HWE, box 75, Erskine interview LTF.

Chapter Eight: A Shortlist of One

143 **'I can't stand her voice'**: HWE, box 74, Erskine interview LTF.

144 **'Those damn weekends, I suppose'**: Michael Bloch, *The Secret File of the Duke of Windsor* (London: Corgi, 1989), 217.

146 **'trying to please'**: HWE, box 34, Erskine interview LTF.

146 **'like a lap dog'**: CA interview, CAP, box 9.

146 **'He must always be doing something'**: HWE, box 74, 'We Took the High Road', 202.

147 **'very, very sad for a long time'**: Ibid., 265.

147 **'suitable marriage to please his family'**: Andrew Morton, *17 Carnations: The Royals, the Nazis, and the Biggest Cover-Up in History* (New York: Grand Central Publishing, 2015), 22.

148 **'interfered and stopped it'**: Neil Balfour and Sally Mackay, *Paul of Yugoslavia: Britain's Maligned Friend* (London: Hamish Hamilton, 1980), 93.

148 **bore the rumours with good humour**: *Daily Telegraph*, 26 November 2013.

149 'I was wrong': HWE, box 74, 'We Took the High Road', 208.

151 'I enjoyed every minute of it': *HHR*, 179.

152 'I was unaware of his interest': *HHR*, 178.

153 'laughed and went downstairs': CLE, box 9, folder 1.

154 'an engagement immediately after': Ibid.

155 deluge of gems to come: MB, 97.

156 'I am going to miss Thelma terribly': MB, 104.

156 'won't you look after him?': *HHR*, 182.

156 'the little man': HWE, box 74, 'We Took the High Road', 228.

157 'making a play for the prince': Ralph G. Martin, *The Woman He Loved*, 143.

158 'the prince leads nowhere': HWE, box 74, 'We Took the High Road', 234.

158 'that was very nice of him': HWE, box 74, 'We Took the High Road', Erskine interview LTF, 7.

159 'the answer is definitely no': *HHR*, 184.

160 'let him know she is doing it': Upton Sinclair, *Wally for Queen!*

161 'we like to dance together': MB, 116.

161 'eat with your fingers': HWE, box 74, 'We Took the High Road', 238–242.

161 'gone to for advice': Ibid.

161 'Don't be silly': Ibid.

162 'dog in a manger': Ibid.

162 'She went to the well too often': HWE, box 74, Rosenberg, 24.

163 'not a figure of fun': HWE, box 74, Erskine interview LTF, 20.

Chapter Nine: A Bounder, a Libertine and a Spy

Unless otherwise stated, Duchess of Windsor interviews from *A Heart's Story*, box 9, Cleveland Amory Papers, Boston Public Library.

165 'I was still married and that was that': CA interview W.

166 'more thoughtful of others': Herman Rogers to sister Anne, August 1934, author archive.

166 'everything you have known before': *HHR*, 119.

167 'no happy outcome': MB, 126.

167 'to be picked out': CA interview AB, CAP, box 85.

167 'king would abdicate over her': CA interview W.

167 'they were forgotten': Ibid.

168 'her husband knowing about it': HWE, box 74.

168 'Royalty could do no wrong': Ibid.

169 'move all the time': MB, 129.

169 'cannot bear being away from you': *New York Times*, 8 June 2003.

169 'he was much too abject': *New York Times*, 18 March 1979.

170 'cold jealous English eyes': MB, 134.

171 'one long horror': CA interview W.

172 promptly put the phone down: Ibid.

172 'show you the ropes': HWE, box 74, 'We Took the High Road', 129.

173 'and reads Balzac': Brian Masters, *Great Hostesses* (London: Constable, 1982), 140.

173 'I don't drink': CA interview W.

175 'should be attracted to me': Ibid.

176 'shake hands with the king's mistress': CA notes, CAP, box 84.

176 'disintegrating influence': Ibid.

176 'he never forgave her': Christopher Sykes Papers, box 24, folder 6, Booth Family Center for Special Collections, Georgetown University Library, Washington, DC.

177 'don't bother me with that now': CA interview W.

177 'I never call men': Ibid.

179 'every woman falls for him': Susan Williams, *The People's King: The True Story of the Abdication* (New York: Palgrave Macmillan, 2004), 74–76.

179 'she was selling champagne', Helen Worden Erskine interview LTF, HWE, box 74.

180 an intimate of von Ribbentrop: CLE, box 10, folder 2.

180 'she wouldn't tell her pillow': HWE, box 74, interview LTF.

181 'icy menace for such as me': *HHR*, 207.

181 **'sorry for the deserted host, Ernest'**: *San Diego Union*, 20 March 1977.

182 **'God bless WE'**: MB, 158.

182 **'man's love is capable of'**: MB, 149.

183 **'with a flourish'**: MB, 167.

183 **'man of my dreams'**: MB, 160.

183 **'prevent our ultimate happiness'**: MB, 170.

184 **'become a royal duchess'**: J. Bryan III and Charles Murphy, *The Windsor Story*, 115.

185 **'profited from his friendship'**: J. Bryan III and Charles Murphy, *The Windsor Story*, 112.

186 **'a façade to show the outer world'**: *HHR*, 209.

186 **'make us *one* this year'**: MB, 178.

Chapter Ten: *Wally for Queen!*

Unless otherwise stated, Duchess of Windsor interviews from *A Heart's Story*, box 9, Cleveland Amory Papers, Boston Public Library.

187 **'It's over'**: CA interview W.

188 **'live as he pleased'**: J. Bryan III and Charles Murphy, *The Windsor Story*, 130.

189 **'have any real friends'**: Ronald Tree to Nancy Tree, 1937, Langhorne Papers, MSS 1L2653 B281-362, Virginia Historical Society, Richmond, VA.

189 **'soon pull down the throne'**: Robert Self, *Neville Chamberlain: A Biography* (Aldershot, UK: Ashgate Publishing, 2006), 40.

189 **'stay the course'**: J. Bryan III and Charles Murphy, *The Windsor Story*, 127.

190 **'mad'**: Susan Williams, *The People's King*, 62.

190 **'Wallis at my side'**: Andrew Morton, *17 Carnations*, 86.

191 **'prolonged agony for me'**: J. Bryan III and Charles Murphy, *The Windsor Story*, 125.

192 **'mangy foreign princesses left'**: MB, 192.

192 **'good influence'**: MB, 190.

193 **together in privacy**: J. Bryan III and Charles Murphy, *The Windsor Story*, 106.

193 **'jewels of the crown of England'**: CLE, box 9, folder 3.

193 **'going to do about it'**: CA notes, CAP, box 3.

194 **'It was not the other way around'**: HWE, box 74.

194 **'think you do things well'**: MB, 162–163.

195 **'very genial, very witty'**: Elizabeth W. Weddell, MSS IW4126cFA2, Weddell, A. W., Weddell Collection, box 4, Virginia Historical Society, Richmond, VA.

195 **'brittle and hard'**: Robert Worth Bingham Papers, box 1, diaries, Manuscript Division, Library of Congress, Washington, DC.

195 **'steal silently away'**: MB, 213.

196 **'I think is the case with her'**: Andrea Lynn, *Shadow Lovers*, 323.

196 **'venom, venom, venom'**: CA notes, CAP, box 9.

197 **'from the time his father died'**: CLE, box 9, folder 2.

197 **'free from impropriety or grossness'**: Susan Williams, *The People's King*, 21.

197 **'spiritual companionship'**: Ibid.

198 **'values of life were the same'**: CA notes, box 9.

199 **'It would also draw criticism on lady'**: Cable, 20 April 1951, Daniel Longwell Papers, box 23, Rare Book and Manuscript Library, Columbia University, New York, NY.

199 **'put detectives on us'**: J. Bryan III and Charles Murphy, *The Windsor Story*, 140.

199 **'A boy loves a girl more and more and more'**: MB, 208.

199 **'amusing kings in mourning isn't easy'**: MB, 209.

200 **'I see, very convenient'**: Andrew Morton, *17 Carnations*, 89–90.

201 **'whole divorce wasn't agreed on together'**: Constance Coolidge, Comtesse de Jumilhac, to her father, 28 October 1936, Crowninshield-Magnus Papers, reel 5, Massachusetts Historical Society (hereafter cited as MHS).

201 **'prove the truth of this'**: HLR to Sara Delano Roosevelt, January 1937, estate of the late Mrs Herman Livingston Rogers.

201 'it's only fair for me to do it': MB, 205.

202 'my future wife': J. Bryan III and Charles Murphy, *The Windsor Story*, 168.

202 'pressing, pleading, conspiring, cajoling': MB, 216.

202 'WE really are one': MB, 217.

202 'in royal circles any more': J. Bryan III and Charles Murphy, *The Windsor Story*, 141.

203 'most wonderful person in the world': Robert Worth Bingham Papers, box 1, diaries, Library of Congress, Washington, DC.

204 'they believe a king is in love with you': *HHR*, 221.

205 'I'm perfectly sure they did': *New York Times*, 18 March 1979.

206 'don't think you can me': MB, 235.

206 'admiration and such confidence': MB, 236.

207 'Down with the American whore': Ralph G. Martin, *The Woman He Loved*, 178.

208 'her eyebrows look attractively surprised': Ibid., 181.

208 'In fact he told me so': Ibid., 268.

210 'call us if you want to': MB, 249.

Chapter Eleven: 'You God-damned Fool'

Unless otherwise stated, Duchess of Windsor interviews from *The Abdication*, box 9, Cleveland Amory Papers, Boston Public Library.

211 'Can you believe it?': CA notes, CAP, box 84.

212 'the marriage will be purely morganatic': Ralph G. Martin, *The Woman He Loved*, 208.

212 the monarchy 'in danger': Robert Worth Bingham Papers, diary, December 1936.

212 'Church's influence and teaching': Ralph G. Martin, *The Woman He Loved*, 196.

213 'In August or September': *Sunday News*, 7 October 1956.

214 'refused a lesser sacrifice': Ralph G. Martin, *The Woman He Loved*, 217.

215 'a strange almost inhuman concept': Ibid., 222.

215 'asked no one's permission': CLE, box 9, folder 1.

216 'beautifully conceived and expressed': Robert Worth Bingham Papers, diary, December 1936.

217 'my position had become impossible': J. Bryan III and Charles Murphy, *The Windsor Story*, 266.

217 'to marry in due time': Ralph G. Martin, *The Woman He Loved*, 225.

217 'I shall never give you up': *HHR*, 247.

218 'in the Tower of London': CA, *The Abdication*.

218 'it had taken leave': Ibid.

220 'Listen to your friends': CA interview Herman Rogers, CAP, box 84.

221 'my self-respect': CA, *The Abdication*.

222 'to the core of my being': *HHR*, 265.

223 'debate within myself': CA, *The Abdication*.

224 'it was just assumed': CA notes, CAP, box 84.

224 'You god-damned fool': Lewis Clark, US Foreign Service Officer, 1926–1958, 'Diplomacy as a Career: Hard Work, Hardship, and Happy Times', Foreign Affairs Oral History Collection, Association for Diplomatic Studies and Training, Arlington, VA. At www.adst.org/wp-content/uploads/2013/12/Clark-Lewis-memoir.pdf.

224 Their ambitions ran counter from the start: *New York Times*, 18 March 1979.

225 'symbolic authority with political power': Author interview, November 2015 .

225 'Morganatic marriage was one': J. Bryan III and Charles Murphy, *The Windsor Story*, 266.

225 'Mrs Simpson being Queen of England': John Colville to Kenneth de Courcy, 4 January 1979, Kenneth Hugh de Courcy Papers, Hoover Institution Archives, Stanford University, Stanford, CA.

226 'Swell but unpublishable': Upton Sinclair, *Wally for Queen!*

226 'shot at dawn': William R. Castle diaries, 1918–1960, vol. 32, MsAm2021, Houghton Library, Harvard University.

227 **'throwing it places'**: Stanton B. Leeds, *Cards the Windsors Hold* (Philadelphia: J. B. Lippincott, 1937), 177.

228 **'You can't abdicate – and eat it'**: Miles Jebb, ed., *The Diaries of Cynthia Gladwyn* (London: Constable, 1995), 56.

228 **'with her gone'**: 14 December 1936, *TOMS*.

229 **'possessive passion for you'**: Helen Worden Erskine interview CC, HWE, box 74.

229 **'a good Prince of Wales'**: Helen Worden Erskine interview LTF, HWE, box 74.

229 **'in for some very bad times'**: Blanche Wiesen Cook, *Eleanor Roosevelt, Volume 2: 1933–1938* (New York: Viking, 1999), 403.

229 **'cabaret to keep life gay'**: CLE, box 9, folder 1.

230 **'singing in his bathtub'**: Ralph G. Martin, *The Woman He Loved*, 304.

Chapter Twelve: I Want Your Baby

Unless otherwise stated, Duchess of Windsor interviews from *Abdication* and *Reflections at Candé*, box 9, Cleveland Amory Papers, Boston Public Library.

232 **'put her on your right'**: Mary Soames, *Clementine Churchill: The Biography of a Marriage* (New York: Houghton Mifflin, 1979), 274.

232 **'and me alone'**: CA, *The Abdication*, CAP, box 9.

232 **'the final catastrophe'**: HHR, 273.

232 **'the most popular man in the country'**: HWE papers, letter from June Jeannette James, undated 1937.

233 **'if you stopped reading about her'**: HHR, 272.

234 **'royally, imperially, wildly'**: *Time*, 4 January 1937.

235 **'a life of perpetual married bliss'**: Neil Balfour and Sally Mackay, *Prince Paul of Yugoslavia: Britain's Maligned Friend*, 138

235 **'I am here today'**: George S. Messersmith Papers, MSS 109 2017–00, Special Collections, University of Delaware Library, Newark, DE.

235 **'Winnie wrote the rest'**: Ibid.

236 **'his own worst enemy'**: CC, Crowninshield-Magnus Papers, reel 5, MHS.

237 **'pacing the floor'**: CA notes, CAP, box 84.

237 **'beyond that wall'**: CA interview Herman Rogers, CAP, box 84.

237 **'Katherine – hard as nails'**: MB, 310.

239 **'he knows all about you'**: CLE, box 9, folder 3.

239 **'she could win her point'**: Ibid.

240 **'that stuttering idiot'**: Cleveland Amory, *The Best Cat Ever*, 140.

240 **'I have taken you into a void'**: *HHR*, 281.

240 **'in the eyes of the world'**: MB, 276.

241 **'sycophants going to the wedding'**: MKR to Buckie Kirk, 30 May 1937, Schlesinger Library, Radcliffe Institute, Harvard University.

241 **'So long as it's unforgettable'**: CA, *Reflections at Candé*.

242 **'impress with his sympathy'**: Ibid.

244 **'I've come just as quickly as I could'**: Ibid.

244 **'Your life with me will be difficult'**: Ibid.

245 **'the first painful word'**: CLE, box 9, folder 1.

245 **'I have none'**: *HHR*, 289.

245 **'What, Sir, with all those aces, really'**: Ibid.

245 **'anyone as happy as the duke'**: CC to 'Crownie,' May 28, 1937, MS 1772, Windsor Collection, MdHS.

246 **'a little shy of her and adoring'**: Ibid.

246 **'so perfectly natural'**: CC to 'Crownie', 28 May 1937, MS 1772, Windsor Collection, MdHS.

247 **'world had gone to the dogs'**: CA interview W.

248 **'expressed in plain sight'**: Author interview.

248 **'ever intimate with him'**: Author interview.

249 **'the duke is not heir conditioned'**: CA notes, CAP, box 84.

250 **'she'll never stay unless things get better'**: CLE, box 9, folder 2.

250 **'like a naughty little boy'**: CA interview Countess Munster, CAP, box 85.

Chapter Thirteen: 'Only One Woman Exists for Him'

Unless otherwise stated, Duchess of Windsor interviews from *We Visit Hitler's Germany* and *The Aftermath*, box 9, Cleveland Amory Papers, Boston Public Library.

253 **'very thin and tired'**: CC to her father, 1937, Crowninshield-Magnus Papers, reel 5, MHS.

254 **'like a clam'**: CA interview Herman Rogers, CAP, box 84.

254 **'they give me suggestions'**: Ibid.

254 **'burning with a peculiar fire'**: *HHR*, 300.

255 **'conflict with British foreign policy'**: CA interview W, *We Visit Hitler's Germany*.

255 **'criticism crashed around us'**: Ibid.

255 **'nobody is going to hurt me'**: HWE interview LTF, box 74.

256 **'thrown out of America'**: Ibid.

256 **'untimely'**: HLR to his former headmaster Dr Peabody, 1937, estate of Mrs H. L. Rogers.

256 **'choice of wife'**: CLE, box 9, folder 2.

256 **'visit Ulster for this reason'**: Sir Shane Leslie Papers, box 31, folder 21, Booth Family Center for Special Collections, Georgetown University.

257 **'an idea of President Wilson'**: CC diary, 22 March 1938, private collection.

257 **'wild animal when angry'**: CA interview Herman Rogers, CAP, box 3.

257 **'It was very embarrassing'**: CC diary, 5 April 1938, private collection.

259 **'their fall from grace'**: Charlie Scheips, *Elsie de Wolfe's Paris: Frivolity Before the Storm* (New York: Abrams, 2014), 41.

260 **'standing around and looking'**: CC diary, 24 December 1938, private collection.

260 **'Do people give him credit for that?'**: CC diary, 10 March 1938, private collection.

261 **'he likes to talk to me'**: Ibid., 29 December 1938.

261 **'Herman has lost his pep'**: Ibid., 22 December 1938.

262 **'face them down herself'**: CA interview Countess Munster, CAP, box 84.

263 **'killed in this silly war'**: J. Bryan III and Charles Murphy, *The Windsor Story*, 416.

263 **'more useful than I had ever been in my life'**: *HHR*, 320.

264 **'immediately forget all else'**: CLE, box 10, folder 2.

264 **'It is the end'**: Anne Sebba, *That Woman*, 230.

264 **'England'**: CA interview W, *My Second Retreat Through France*, CAP, box 9.

265 **'the rich people of Europe are here'**: Charlie Scheips, *Elsie de Wolfe's Paris*, 140.

265 **'came on to Croë'**: HLR to sister Anne, 4 June 1940, author collection.

265 **'As an Englishman I hate running'**: CA interview W, *My Second Retreat Through France*, CAP, box 9.

266 **'cool and collected'**: HLR to sister Anne, 15 June 1940, author collection.

Chapter Fourteen: 'A Whole Nation Against One Woman'

Unless otherwise stated, Duchess of Windsor interviews from *Je Suis le Prince de Galles*, box 9, Cleveland Amory Papers, Boston Public Library.

268 **'comfortable internment in their hands'**: CA interview W, *Je Suis Le Prince de Galles*.

268 **'pitiful but somehow revolting'**: HLR to sister Anne, 4 July 1940, author collection.

269 **'try to come back'**: Ibid., 9 July 1940.

270 **'anyone except themselves'**: Neil Balfour and Sally Mackay, *Paul of Yugoslavia: Britain's Maligned Friend*, 137.

271 **'hungry and faithful' servants**: DoW to Herman Rogers, 5 December 1940, estate of Mrs H. L. Rogers.

271 **'British government than he'**: CLE, box 10, folder 2.

272 **'I would have choked'**: CA notes, CAP, box 84.

273 **No one was on first name terms with her**: Ralph G. Martin, *The Woman He Loved*, 409.

274 **'confidential and private nature'**: W letters to Mary Bourke, 1940–41, box 85, Cleveland Amory Papers.

275 **'would be to recognize me'**: CA interview George Wood, CAP, box 85.

276 **'a whole nation against one woman'**: J. Bryan III and Charles Murphy, *The Windsor Story*, 418.

277 **'stronghold for the future'**: Anne Sebba, *That Woman*, 243.

278 **'what I would do without her'**: Rosa Wood to Edith Lindsay, 25 October 1942, MS 1772, Windsor Collection, MdHS.

278 **'the duchess has to say about that'**: René MacColl, *Deadline and Dateline* (London: Oldbourne Press, 1956), 124–125.

278 **'I've changed my mind'**: CA interview George Wood, CAP, box 85.

279 **'hand of a coloured person'**: CA notes, CAP, box 85.

279 **'not producing any Don Juans'**: Ms 1772, Windsor Collection, MdHS.

279 **'I should like you for my next husband'**: CA notes, CAP, box 85.

280 **'only two months leave'**: MS 1772, Windsor Collection, MdHS.

282 **'a bitter and disillusioned feeling'**: CA notes, Rosa Wood letter to Edith Lindsay, 1944, CAP, box 85.

Chapter Fifteen: 'The Only Man I've Ever Loved'

284 **his luck ran out**: C. Michael Hiam, *Dirigible Dreams: The Age of the Airship* (Lebanon, NH: ForeEdge, 2014), 118

285 **'we are lost. *Je t'aime*'**: Archie Wann to Lucy Wann, January 1941, estate of Mrs H. L. Rogers.

287 **'He is extremely attractive, I found'**: Eleanor Miles letter, 5 August 1947, MS 1772, Windsor Collection, MdHS.

287 **'the world of the Beautiful People'**: J. Bryan III and Charles Murphy, *The Windsor Story*, 459.

287 **'you always deferred to their leadership'**: Eleanor Lambert to Maxine Sandberg, MS 2901, Windsor Collection, MdHS.

288 **'as it had of Paris'**: Kenneth de Courcy letter to unidentified recipient, 10 November 1984, Kenneth Hugh de Courcy Papers, Hoover Institution Archives, Stanford University.

289 **'imitation of his wonderful mother'**: Christopher Weeks, *'Perfectly Delightful': The Life and Gardens of Harvey Ladew*. Baltimore, MD: Johns Hopkins University Press, 1999), 206–207.

289 **'ate practically nothing at dinner'**: CLE, box 6, folder 10.

289 **'difficult to find a greater contrast'**: Ibid.

290 **'from Balenciaga in Paris'**: Ibid.

290 **'our visit to England'**: Ibid.

290 **'I shall hate it to my grave'**: J. Bryan III and Charles Murphy, *The Windsor Story*, 459.

291 **'It has that puzzled look'**: CLE, box 6, folder 10.

291 **'poor piano player and drank champagne'**: Ibid.

291 **'to keep from thinking'**: CA notes, CAP, box 85.

292 **'not awfully bright'**: Betsey Barton sketch, CAP, box 9.

292 **'how pathetic his expression'**: Miles Jebb, ed., *The Diaries of Cynthia Gladwyn* (London: Constable, 1995), 163.

292 **'watching his wife buy a hat'**: J. Bryan III and Charles Murphy, *The Windsor Story*, 456.

292 **'the Waldorf is on DC'**: CA notes, CAP, box 85.

292 **'Most distracting but an experience'**: Obituary, Barbara Reid, *Republican Journal* (Belfast, ME), 21 March 2016.

293 **'Did that Mozart chap write anything else'**: CA notes, CAP, box 85.

293 **'worried about her condition'**: W to CC, 7 October 1948, Crowninshield-Magnus Papers, reel 5, MHS.

294 **'hell most of the time'**: Katherine Rogers to CC, 24 March 1949, Crowninshield-Magnus Papers, reel 5, MHS.

294 **'treatment even in America'**: HLR to CC, 5 June 1949, Crowninshield-Magnus Papers, reel 5, MHS.

295 **'She was a piece of work'**: Author interview, February 2016.

295 **'Lucy knew that'**: Ibid.

296 YOUR GUARDIAN ANGEL: J. Bryan III and Charles Murphy, *The Windsor Story*, 522.

297 **'hiding her feelings'**: Ibid., 523.

297 **'get what they wanted'**: Author interview, February 2016.

297 **'good wishes to my dear Lucy'**: W to LLR, 1 August 1950, estate of Mrs H. L. Rogers.

298 **'it came out then'**: Author interview, February 2016.

299 **'purposeful selfishness'**: CA interview Herman Rogers, CAP, box 85.

299 **'only man I've ever loved'**: Author interview, February 2016.

299 **'she had conquered the world'**: Author interview, February 2016.

300 **'Let's talk Chinese'**: CA interview HLR, box 85.

300 **'She will *never* be satisfied. Never'**: Ibid.

300 **'it means money'**: CA interview LLR, CAP, box 85.

300 **'Lucy and I will stay here'**: J. Bryan III and Charles Murphy, *The Windsor Story*, 524.

301 **'the once king of England'**: Miles Jebb, ed., *The Diaries of Cynthia Gladwyn*, 179.

301 **'bed in tears tonight'** J. Bryan III and Charles Murphy, *The Windsor Story*, 478.

301 **'sexual perversion of self-abasement'**: Quoted in Christopher Wilson, *Dancing with the Devil*, 175.

302 **'work my way up'**: CA notes, CAP, box 85.

302 **'get Jessie Donahue drunk'**: Ibid.

303 **'they are much brighter than you'**: J. Bryan III and Charles Murphy, *The Windsor Story*, 469.

303 **'like this bit of information'**: Harvey Ladew to sister Eliza Grace, 13 November 1948, Harvey S. Ladew Papers, Ladew Topiary Gardens, Monkton, MD.

303 **'morals and won't go'**: Letter to sister Eliza Grace, 3 November 1948, Harvey S. Ladew Papers.

304 **'their teeth and their eyeballs'**: Billy Baldwin with Michael Gardine, *Billy Baldwin, an Autobiography*, 291.

305 **'such kindness and generosity'**: Ibid., 287.

305 **'live out a great romance'**: Christopher Wilson, *Dancing with the Devil*, 179.

306 **'almost all the others do'**: Billy Baldwin with Michael Gardine, *Billy Baldwin, an Autobiography*, 295.

306 **'as rigidly un-undressable as Wallis'**: Anne Sebba, *That Woman*, 269.

306 **'painfully sensitive'**: Billy Baldwin with Michael Gardine, *Billy Baldwin, an Autobiography*, 289.

307 **'The Duke and Duchess of Windsor are *phfft*'**: Quoted in Christopher Wilson, *Dancing with the Devil*, 163.

307 **'a very sad person these days'**: Ibid., 165.

308 **'Why, they are in love'**: J. Bryan III and Charles Murphy, *The Windsor Story*, 470.

308 **'gave up a king for a queen'**: Christopher Wilson, *Dancing with the Devil*, 159.

308 **'ashamed of yourself'**: CA interview Elsa Maxwell, CAP, box 85.

309 **'this shoddy little success'**: *Mail on Sunday*, 21 September 2014.

310 **'awful weakness of the duke'**: CA notes, CAP, box 85.

310 **'Get out'**: Christopher Wilson, *Dancing with the Devil*, 218.

310 **'I've abdicated'**: Ibid., 219.

311 **'At last I can believe in God'**: Andrea Lynn, *Shadow Lovers*, 322.

Chapter Sixteen: 'Ice Runs Through Their Veins'

313 **'the future may depict me'**: W to Herman Rogers, August 1955, estate of Mrs H. L. Rogers.

313 **'real atmosphere to him'**: Ibid.

315 **'honesty aren't the same thing'**: CAP, box 85.

315 **'reimbursed for their outlay'**: Mss A G 669 10, Gorin Family Papers, Filson Historical Society, Louisville, Kentucky.

316 NO ENTHUSIASM HERE FOR THE PROJECT: Daniel Longwell to Charles Murphy, 31 July 1952, Daniel Longwell Papers, Columbia University.

316 'I switched to Cleveland Amory': W to Herman Rogers, 18 August 1955, estate of Mrs H. L. Rogers.

317 'that wasn't so': Author interview, November 2015.

317 'not that difficult': CA interview Noël Coward, CAP, box 85.

318 'Take your tea in the other room': Cleveland Amory, *The Best Cat Ever*, 142.

318 'had been the king': Author interview, November 2015.

318 'drunken bickering was unbearable': *New York Times*, 18 March 1979.

318 'begged for more': Philip Ziegler, *King Edward VIII* (New York: Alfred A. Knopf, 1991), 237.

318 'It made me simply furious': CA notes, CAP, box 85.

319 'They found him pathetic': Author interview, November 2015.

319 freshly minted notes: J. Bryan III and Charles Murphy, *The Windsor Story*, 464.

319 'stranglehold she had over him': *New York Times*, 18 March 1979.

319 'Jews were exterminated': Author interview, November 2015.

319 'Hitler was such a bad chap': Cleveland Amory, *The Best Cat Ever*, 141.

320 'a defence of Adolf Hitler': Ibid.

320 'protocol around here is nerve jangling': Martha Amory to Mr and Mrs Amory, CAP, box 138.

321 'no real charm': Billy Baldwin and Michael Gardine, *Billy Baldwin, an Autobiography*, 292.

321 'ten days tomorrow': CA notes, CAP, box 85.

321 'she clams up again': Martha Amory to Mr and Mrs Amory, CAP, box 138.

321 'insatiable desire for change': CAP, box 85.

321 'on the shelf with all the others': Anthony Montague Browne, *Long Sunset: Memoirs of Winston Churchill's Last Private Secretary* (Ashford, Kent: Podkin Press, 2009), 225.

322 'TRUE story through others': Martha Amory to Mr and Mrs Amory, CAP, box 138.

322 'don't tell her any of this': CA interview AB, CAP, box 85.

323 **'no conception of unity'**: CA to Kennett Rawson, CAP, box 85.

323 **'*Rebecca of Sunnybrook Farm*'**: *Houston Post*, 6 October 1955.

323 **'twenty years ago'**: Martha Amory to Mr and Mrs Amory, September 1955, CAP, box 138.

323 **'like a viper'**: W to Herman Rogers, 28 December 1955, estate of Mrs H. L. Rogers.

324 **'until just recently'**: Herman Rogers postscript to CA letter, 3 January 1956, CAP, box 138.

324 **'would not understand anyhow'**: LLR to Cleveland and Martha Amory, 31 October 1957, CAP, box 138.

324–325 **'passed in small heaters'**: *McCall's* press release, 20 February 1956.

325 **'not too dull'**: *Baltimore News-Post*, 21 February 1956.

325 **'more than a few minutes'**: Frances Donaldson, *Edward VIII* (Philadelphia: Lippincott, 1975), 426.

325 **'style is dignified'**: W to Herman Rogers, 26 February 1956, estate of Mrs H. L. Rogers.

326 **'my love and understanding, Wallis'**: W to LLR, estate of Mrs H. L. Rogers.

326 **YOUR AND MY LOSS**: Ibid.

327 **'will continue to do so'**: LLR to Cleveland and Martha Amory, CAP, box 85.

328 **'bloody shabbily treated'**: Frances Donaldson, *Edward VIII*, 423.

328 **'tragedies to others'**: W to LLR, 6 December 1957, estate of Mrs H. L. Rogers.

Chapter Seventeen: 'Wallis, Wallis, Wallis, Wallis'

330 **'bored countenance of the sitters'**: Author interview, April 2017.

330 **pug dog, Mr Chou, to sit still**: Trafford Klots Papers, MS 3019, MdHS.

331 **'Morning glory'**: Anthony Montague Browne, *Long Sunset*, 225.

331 **'wretched personalities, completely egocentric'**: *New York Times*, 18 March 1979.

331 'I have seen it scores of times': Rex North interview Martha Amory, *Sunday Pictorial*, October 1955.

332 'We even spent Easter in bed': *New York Times*, 18 March 1979.

332 'the robber barons': Charles Murphy to Joe Bryan, 3 April 1972. Charles Murphy papers. (File: Mss 5.9 B 8405:97-160), Virginia Historical Society, Richmond, VA.

333 'how you doing tonight': Author interview, February 2016.

334 'lamb calling for its mother': Ibid.

334 'Right city, wrong woman': Ibid.

335 'in memory of Herman and the Duke': J. Bryan III and Charles Murphy, *The Windsor Story*, 565.

336 'crowding around the garbage cans': *New York Times*, 18 March 1979.

336 'could keep her alive forever': *Vanity Fair*, June 1986.

Select Bibliography

Airlie, Mabell, Countess of. *Thatched with Gold*. Edited by Jennifer Ellis. London: Hutchinson, 1962.

Amory, Cleveland. *The Best Cat Ever*. New York: Little, Brown, 1993.

Baldwin, Billy, with Michael Gardine. *Billy Baldwin, an Autobiography*. Boston: Little, Brown, 1985.

Balfour, Neil and Sally Mackay. *Paul of Yugoslavia: Britain's Maligned Friend*. London: Hamish Hamilton, 1980.

Bloch, Michael. *The Duke of Windsor's War*. London: Weidenfeld & Nicolson, 1982.

——. *The Duchess of Windsor*. London: Weidenfeld & Nicolson, 1996.

——, ed. *Wallis and Edward: Letters, 1931–1937*. New York: Summit, 1986.

Boyd, William. *Any Human Heart*. London, Hamish Hamilton, 2002.

Bryan, J., III and Charles J. V. Murphy. *The Windsor Story*. London: Granada, 1979.

Colville, John. *The Fringes of Power: Downing Street Diaries 1939–1955*. London: Weidenfeld & Nicolson, 2004.

Cook, Blanche Wiesen. *Eleanor Roosevelt, Volume 2: The Defining Years, 1933–1938*. New York: Viking, 1999.

Cooke, Anne Kirk and Elizabeth Lightfoot. *The Other Mrs. Simpson: Postscript to the Love Story of the Century*. New York: Vantage, 1977.

Corrigan, Maureen. *So We Read On: How The Great Gatsby Came to Be and Why It Endures*. New York: Little, Brown, 2014.

Donaldson, Frances. *Edward VIII*. London: Weidenfeld & Nicolson, 1974.

Greenwald, Marilyn. *Cleveland Amory: Media Curmudgeon and Animal Rights Crusader*. London: University Press of New England, 2009.

Hiam, Michael C. *Dirigible Dreams: The Age of the Airship*. Lebanon, NH: ForeEdge, 2014.

Higham, Charles. *The Duchess of Windsor: The Secret Life*, rev. edn. Hoboken, NJ: John Wiley and Sons, 2004.

Jackson, Robert H. *That Man: An Insider's Portrait of Franklin D. Roosevelt*. New York: Oxford University Press, 2003.

Jebb, Miles, ed. *The Diaries of Cynthia Gladwyn*. London: Constable, 1995.

King, Greg. *The Duchess of Windsor: The Uncommon Life of Wallis Simpson*. London: Aurum, 1999.

Leeds, Stanton B. *Cards the Windsors Hold*. Philadelphia: J. B. Lippincott, 1937.

Lovell, Mary S. *The Riviera Set*. London: Little, Brown, 2016.

Lynn, Andrea. *Shadow Lovers: The Last Affairs of H. G. Wells*. Boulder, CO: Westview Press, 2001.

Martin, Ralph G. *The Woman He Loved*. New York: Simon & Schuster, 1973.

MacColl, René, *Deadline and Dateline*. London: Oldbourne Press, 1956.

Masters, Brian. *Great Hostesses*. London: Constable, 1982.

McPherson, Mary King. *Oldfields School 1867–1989: A Feeling of Family*. Glencoe, MD: Oldfields School, 1989.

Mitford, Diana. *The Duchess of Windsor: A Memoir*. London: Gibson Square, 2011.

Montague Browne, Anthony. *Long Sunset: Memoirs of Winston Churchill's Last Private Secretary*. Ashford, UK: Podkin Press, 2009.

Morton, Andrew. *17 Carnations: The Royals, the Nazis, and the Biggest Cover-Up in History*. New York: Grand Central Publishing, 2015.

Pope-Hennessy, James. *Queen Mary 1867–1953*. London: George Allen & Unwin, 1959.

Rhinevault, Carney. *Colonel Archibald Rogers and the Crumwold Estate*. Hyde Park, NY: Town of Hyde Park Historical Society, 2003.

Ritchie, Donald A. *Reporting from Washington: The History of the Washington Press Corps*. New York: Oxford University Press, 2005.

Scheips, Charlie. *Elsie de Wolfe's Paris: Frivolity Before the Storm*. New York: Abrams, 2014.

Sebba, Anne. *That Woman: The Life of Wallis Simpson, Duchess of Windsor*. New York: St Martin's Press, 2012.

Sinclair, Upton. *Wally for Queen! The Private Life of Royalty*. Pasadena, CA: Station A, 1936.

Stein, Gertrude. *Ida: A Novel*. Edited by Logan Esdale. New Haven, CT: Yale University Press, 2012.

Vanderbilt, Gloria and Thelma Lady Furness. *Double Exposure: A Twin Autobiography*. New York: David McKay, 1958.

Vickers, Hugo. *The Private World of the Duke and Duchess of Windsor*. London: Harrods Publishing, 1995.

Weeks, Christopher. *'Perfectly Delightful': The Life and Gardens of Harvey Ladew*. Baltimore, MD: Johns Hopkins University Press, 1999.

Williams, Susan. *The People's King: The True Story of the Abdication*. New York: Palgrave Macmillan, 2004.

Wilson, Christopher. *Dancing with the Devil: The Windsors and Jimmy Donahue*, London: HarperCollins, 2000.

Windsor, Duke of. *A King's Story: The Memoirs of H.R.H. the Duke of Windsor, K.G.* London: Cassell, 1951.

Windsor, Wallis, Duchess of. *The Heart has Its Reasons: The Memoirs of the Duchess of Windsor*. London: Michael Joseph, 1956.

Ziegler, Philip. *King Edward VIII*. New York: Alfred A. Knopf, 1991.

Archival Collections

Amory, Cleveland. Papers. Boston Public Library.

Bingham, Robert Worth. Papers. Manuscript Division, Library of Congress, Washington, DC.

Bismarck, Mona. Papers. (File: MsB621), Filson Historical Society, Louisville, KY.

Bullitt, William C. Papers. Manuscripts and Archives, Sterling Memorial Library, Yale University, New Haven, CT.

Castle, William R. 1918–1960. Papers. (File: MsAm2021), Houghton Library, Harvard University, Cambridge, MA.

de Courcy, Kenneth Hugh. Papers. Hoover Institution Archives, Stanford University, CA.

de Espil, Courtney Letts. Papers. Manuscript Division, Library of Congress, Washington, DC.

de Jumilhac, Constance Coolidge, Comtesse. Papers. Crowninshield-Magnus Papers 1834–1965, Massachusetts Historical Society, Boston, MA.

Erskine, Helen Worden, 1896–1984. Papers. Rare Book and Manuscript Library, Columbia University, New York, NY.

Gorin family. Papers. Filson Historical Society, Louisville, KY.

Howard, Jean. Papers. (Collection 10714), American Heritage Center, University of Wyoming, Laramie, WY.

Kinross, Patrick. Papers. Huntington Library, San Marino, CA.

Kirk family. Papers. Buckner Hollingsworth Papers 1911–1964, Schlesinger Library, Radcliffe Institute, Harvard University, Cambridge, MA.

Klots, Trafford. Papers. (File: MS 3019), Maryland Historical Society, Baltimore, MD.

Ladew, Harvey S. Papers. Ladew Topiary Gardens, Monkton, MD.

Leslie, Sir Shane. Papers. Booth Family Center for Special Collections, Lauinger Library, Georgetown University, Washington, DC.

Longwell, Daniel. Papers. Rare Book and Manuscript Library, Columbia University, New York, NY.

Messersmith, George S. Papers. Special Collections, University of Delaware Library, Newark, DE.

Murphy, Charles. Papers. (File: Mss 5.9 B 8405:97-160), Virginia Historical Society, Richmond, VA.

Mustin, Henry. Papers. (File: MS 52860), Manuscript Division, Library of Congress, Washington, DC.

Sandberg, Maxine. Papers. (File: MS 2901), Maryland Historical Society, Baltimore, MD.

Sinclair, Upton. Papers. Huntington Library, San Marino, CA.

Sykes, Christopher. Papers. Booth Family Center for Special Collections, Lauinger Library, Georgetown University, Washington, DC.

Tree, Ronald. Papers. (File: Mss1L2653 B281-362), Langhorne collection, Virginia Historical Society, Richmond, VA.

Warfield family, 1801–1960. Papers. Special Collections, University of Maryland Libraries, Hornbake Library, College Park, MD.

Weddell, Alexander. Papers. (Mss1W4126 CFA2 Box 4), Virginia Historical Society, Richmond, VA.

Windsor, Duchess of. Papers. (File: MS 1772), Duke and Duchess of Windsor Scrapbooks, 1936–1938, Maryland Historical Society, Baltimore, MD.

Picture Acknowledgements

Page 1. All images: Baltimore News American collection, Special Collections; University of Maryland Libraries.

Page 2. (1) Baltimore News American collections, Special Collections, University of Maryland Libraries; (2) Courtesy of Oldfields School; (3) Courtesy of Dr Gaea Leinhardt; (4 & 5) Courtesy of Oldfields School.

Page 3. (1) Special Collections, University of Marylands Libraries; (2) US Naval and Heritage Command; (3 & 4) Collection of the Coronado Historical Association.

Page 4. (1) Courtesy of Hotel Coronado; (2) Collection of the Coronado Historical Association; (3 & 4) Courtesy of Hotel Coronado.

Page 5. (1) Library of Congress; (2) Elbridge Gerry Greene, 1911: HUD 31.870 (folder 8), Harvard University Archives (3) Library of Congress.

Page 6. (1 & 2) National Archives and Records Administration. (3) Courtesy of the Estate of the late Mrs Herman Livingston Rogers.

Page 7. (1) Granger; (2 & 3) Mary Evans.

Page 8. (1 & 2) Boston Public Library, Cleveland Amory Collection; (3) Courtesy of Michael Tenzer; (4) Rogers collection.

Page 9. (1) Granger; (2) Mary Evans; (3) Rogers collection.

Page 10. (1 & 2) Rogers collection; (3) © Cecil Beaton/Victoria and Albert Museum, London.

Page 11. (1) Courtesy of author; (2) Mary Evans; (3) Courtesy of author; (4) © Schall collection.

Page 12. (1) Rogers collection.

Page 13. (1) David Seymour/Magnum Photos; (2) Dr Gaea Leinhardt.

Page 14. (1) Jean Howard Papers, American Heritage Center, University of Wyoming; (2 & 3) Rogers collection.

Page 15. (1) Elliot Erwitt/Magnum Photos; (2) Courtesy of author. (3) Courtesy of Maryland Historical Society, Item 196586.

Page 16. (1) Courtesy of author.

Index